TOWARDS A COMPARATIVE INSTITUTIONALISM: FORMS, DYNAMICS AND LOGICS ACROSS THE ORGANIZATIONAL FIELDS OF HEALTH CARE AND HIGHER EDUCATION

RESEARCH IN THE SOCIOLOGY OF ORGANIZATIONS

Series Editor: Michael Lounsbury

Recent Volumes:

Volume 31:	Categories in Markets: Origins and Evolution
Volume 32:	Philosophy and Organization Theory
Volume 33:	Communities and Organizations
Volume 34:	Rethinking Power in Organizations, Institutions, and Markets
Volume 35:	Reinventing Hierarchy and Bureaucracy – From the Bureau to Network Organizations
Volume 36:	The Garbage Can Model of Organizational Choice – Looking Forward at Forty
Volume 37:	Managing 'Human Resources' by Exploiting and Exploring People's Potentials
Volume 38:	Configurational Theory and Methods in Organizational Research
Volume 39A:	Institutional Logics in Action, Part A
Volume 39B:	Institutional Logics in Action, Part B
Volume 40:	Contemporary Perspectives on Organizational Social Networks
Volume 41:	Religion and Organization Theory
Volume 42:	Organizational Transformation and Scientific Change: The Impact of Institutional Restructuring on Universities and Intellectual Innovation
Volume 43:	Elites on Trial
Volume 44:	Institutions and Ideals: Philip Selznick's Legacy for Organizational Studies

RESEARCH IN THE SOCIOLOGY OF ORGANIZATIONS
VOLUME 45

TOWARDS A COMPARATIVE INSTITUTIONALISM: FORMS, DYNAMICS AND LOGICS ACROSS THE ORGANIZATIONAL FIELDS OF HEALTH CARE AND HIGHER EDUCATION

EDITED BY

RÓMULO PINHEIRO
University of Agder, Norway

LARS GESCHWIND
KTH Royal Institute of Technology, Sweden

FRANCISCO O. RAMIREZ
Stanford University, USA

KARSTEN VRANGBÆK
University of Copenhagen, Denmark

Emerald

United Kingdom – North America – Japan
India – Malaysia – China

Emerald Group Publishing Limited
Howard House, Wagon Lane, Bingley BD16 1WA, UK

First edition 2016

British Library Cataloguing in Publication Data
A catalogue record for this book is available from the British Library

ISBN: 978-1-78560-275-7
ISSN: 0733-558X (Series)

CONTENTS

PART IV
RESISTANCE AND TRANSFORMATION

LIST OF CONTRIBUTORS

John Appleby	The King's Fund, London, UK
Laila Nordstrand Berg	Department of Political Science and Management, University of Agder, Kristiansand, Norway
Johan Bernardini-Perinciolo	Institute of Public Management and Territorial Governance, Aix-Marseille University, Marseille, France
Haldor Byrkjeflot	Department of Sociology and Human Geography, University of Oslo, Oslo, Norway
S. Kubra Canhilal	Centre for Organisational Research – Management and Performance of Research and Higher Education Institutions, University of Lugano, Lugano, Switzerland
Teresa Carvalho	Department of Social, Political and Territorial Sciences and Centre for Research in Higher Education Policies (CIPES), University of Aveiro, Aveiro, Portugal
Jürgen Deeg	University of Hagen, Hagen, Germany
Lars Geschwind	Department of Learning, KTH Royal Institute of Technology, Stockholm, Sweden
Sarah Gregory	The King's Fund, London, UK
Corinne Grenier	KEDGE Business School and Aix-Marseille University, Marseille, France
Kutay Güneştepe	Faculty of Management, Istanbul Technical University, Istanbul, Turkey

Charlotte Kiland Department of Public Health, Sport and Nutrition, University of Agder, Kristiansand, Norway

Tanja Klenk Department of Social Work and Social Welfare, University of Kassel, Kassel, Germany

Gro Kvåle Department of Political Science and Management, University of Agder, Agder, Norway

Benedetto Lepori Centre for Organisational Research – Management and Performance of Research and Higher Education Institutions, University of Lugano, Lugano, Switzerland

Diórgenes Falcão Mamédio Business School, Pontifical Catholic University of Paraná, Paraná, Brazil

John W. Meyer Department of Sociology, Stanford University, Stanford, CA, USA

Victor Meyer Jr. Business School, Pontifical Catholic University of Paraná, Paraná, Brazil

Lucilaine Pascuci Department of Administration, Federal University of Espírito Santo, Espírito Santo, Brazil

Rómulo Pinheiro Department of Political Science and Management, University of Agder, Kristiansand, Norway

Francisco O. Ramirez Graduate School of Education, Stanford University, Stanford, CA, USA

Rui Santiago Department of Social, Political and Territorial Sciences and Centre for Research in Higher Education Policies (CIPES), University of Aveiro, Aveiro, Portugal

Marco Seeber	Centre for Higher Education Governance Ghent, Department of Sociology, Ghent University, Ghent, Belgium
Markus Seyfried	Chair for Political Science, Administration and Organisation, University of Potsdam, Potsdam, Germany
Dag Olaf Torjesen	Department of Political Science and Management, University of Agder, Kristiansand, Norway
Deniz Tunçalp	Faculty of Management, Istanbul Technical University, Istanbul, Turkey
Karsten Vrangbæk	Department of Public Health, University of Copenhagen, Copenhagen, Denmark

EDITORIAL ADVISORY BOARD

PART I
SETTING THE STAGE

FOREWORD☆

John W. Meyer

Worldwide forces have changed the nature of social organization everywhere, in an epidemic of cultural rationalization. The direction of the change is always toward more formal organization, with more rules and roles, more formalization, and more articulated rationalization. The change occurs in all sorts of countries: even the most unlikely places now experience rapid organizational expansion. It occurs in all the fields or sectors of social life: governmental structures shift from bureaucratic forms to modern managerial organizations, and so do traditional firms. Most strikingly, a whole array of more traditional social structures come to take the forms of modern organization in now called the "non-profit sector." So schools, charities, recreational associations, churches, religious orders, and many social movements now become organizations, with all the trappings. So do universities and health care institutions – the focus of the studies here.

Managers appear, and take the lead in building the new world. They plan and create strategies. They erect elaborate information and control systems. They track and record resources: human and material. They

☆Some themes here are taken from Bromley, P., & Meyer, J. W. (2015). *Hyper-organization: Global organizational expansion*. Oxford: Oxford University Press. This work was supported by aid from the National Research Foundation (Korea).

Towards a Comparative Institutionalism: Forms, Dynamics and Logics Across the Organizational Fields of Health Care and Higher Education
Research in the Sociology of Organizations, Volume 45, 3–7

ISSN: 0733-558X/doi:10.1108/S0733-558X20150000045027

engage in the rituals of formalized and explicit "decision-making," including explicit structures for participation.

In one way or another, whole new structures appear, relating what was once a simpler enterprise to an expanding array of "stakeholders." A large human resources department is created, with programs for supporting human rights and participation. Relations with the physical and social environment are codified. Some of these take legalized forms: much social control that was once neglected or left to informal arrangements is now conducted under explicit hard- or soft-law controls from local or national or even supra-national public or professional authorities. Similarly, organization arises to meet the new demands for transparency and accountability: monetary accounting, but also other sorts of statistical information, expand. In the for-profit world, corporate social responsibility becomes an important institution and ideology, and the newly expanding multinationals take on many expanded structures to come to terms with it.

Understanding why all this happens in so many social arenas and so many places in the world is an important task. It is aided by our awareness that the whole social movement toward more formalized organization takes its upward trajectory principally in a very specific time period: it occurs rapidly through most of the post-World-War-II time period, and explodes in the neoliberal decades since the 1980s. Further, it is clearly aided by the broadly liberal forces of the whole period, and the dramatic neoliberal crusade more recently. The old authoritative nation-state, often linked to a corporatist social structure, did not look good in 1945, and looked even worse in the Cold War. The decline in its authority (though not its scale), combined with an enormous rise in awareness of supra-national interdependence, led to bursts of liberal ideology celebrating the value and capability of the sub-units of society rather than the central state structures – rights-bearing individuals and the organizations they create.

In many social sectors – industry, for example – the new ideology could play out in fairly straightforward ways. Production and exchange could in fact be organized in great multi-national firms, operating on a worldwide scale. In the same way, activities formerly directly managed by the state could be spun out to for-profit and non-profit organizations. Whether or not the new world was more efficient or effective than the old one is a legitimate question, but the new order does in fact operate.

The problem arises when the attempt to organize reaches out into social sectors producing activities difficult to standardize, measure, and control. These include the domains of the traditional professionals – corporate bodies with roots in the medieval university: the Church and its theologians and priests; the legal order; and most importantly, the doctor, and the professors in the core knowledge system. Here, the new system of rationalized organization runs up against two related realities. First, there is great uncertainty and invisibility in the core work of the domain: what do salvation, education, and health mean, and how can they be produced, and if produced, measured? Second, these domains are already managed by the professions and thus carry much autonomous authority. This authority is embodied in professional occupations with their own corporate status and their own charisma (reflected in medieval saints and modern Nobel laureates).

In this book, Rómulo Pinheiro and his colleagues have assembled a valuable set of studies of what happens when the era of managerialist organizations, infused with the powers and responsibilities of organizational actorhood, confronts the recalcitrance both of the professionals and of the realities with which they deal. The researchers focus on the health system with its hospitals and doctors, and on the system of higher education with its professors and researchers. The cases come mainly from Europe, though the issues are clearly worldwide.

The studies show the wide variety of outcomes that result from the collision between rationalizing and standardizing schemes and the realities faced in hospitals and universities. Higher education and the health system differ. This is partly because in much of the medical care system there is a fairly clear bottom line in terms of health, efforts to organizationally control and standardize can reach further down: there is high agreement on whether a patient is dead or not, and mortality can thus be counted. Further, there are in many cases fairly clear technologies that can be employed and managed. The definitions involved may be socially constructed and maintained, but they are often visible, clear, and measurable. There is much less consensus on whether or not a graduate in history is well educated, or on how to produce a well-educated one. The social constructions involved vary within universities and across them.

National contexts matter too, perhaps even more. Organizational and professional life function rather well together in Scandinavia, with long histories of cooperation. And ideas about markets and competition have long histories in the United Kingdom (and even stronger ones in the United States), so that organizational expansion is facilitated. In France or Germany, the history of resistance to organizational control and raw competition is stronger.

So the studies here quite successfully explore the many variations that they find: there is variation in the control efforts put forward in the wider environment, in the older structures come under these controls, and thus in the organizational patterns that result. But some core observations are very general, and describe the whole array of observations.

First, the contemporary binge of rationalization is to be found everywhere in the modern social environment. It seems that all health systems face it, as do all higher educational systems. The notions of the correct world-class university, or the medical system rooted in scientific best practices, are strong and worldwide. Local settings in all the cases under review in this book are under continuing inspection from expanding and rationalized standards of an essentially global character. The days when a local doctor can imagine conforming to the best standards of Danish medicine as set in a traditional medical community are gone. And every higher educational institution comes under pressure to conform to the imagined model of the "American research university."

Second, as a result, everywhere the researchers look, they find increases in the elaboration of local organizational systems. Managers appear, and organizational staffs expand. Every university is pressed to become more of an organization, with more accountability, more decision-making, and more responsiveness to more environments. And every hospital comes under pressure to manage its business in light of standard measures and criteria: management becomes more and more important, and the traditions of autonomous medical authority decline. The old professionalism declines, and a new more managerial form rises.

Third, decoupling of one sort or another is endemic in the social fields under investigation here. The realities of the treatment of the patient, or the schooling of the students, or the difficulties and uncertainties of the research project, are everywhere in part buffered from the sweeping regulatory regimes of the organization and its environment. The old professionals, princes of their establishments, lose out to the managers; but the work of the new professionals adapted to the new world goes on with only limited scrutiny from the expanded organizational structures of the evolving environment. The researchers here evaluate the decoupling they observe in differing ways, but they all observe it.

As a result, fourth, the researchers here – reflecting the organizations they study – can (and need) give very little attention to what happens to the actual patients in these new health care systems, or what happens to the students in the reformed universities. In fact, neither the researchers nor the organizations they study are all that well informed on the matter. The social science of higher education, it turns out, studies the ever-expanding organizational and career systems involved, not the substance of teaching and research. And the social science of health care is a subfield of political science more than of medicine.

But to qualify this point, fifth, it is clear that health and health care, and education and research in the university, are incorporated in the growing organizational systems of education and health. They are incorporated, not in the traditional case-by-case way, but as statistics. The expanding organizational systems work, not with students and patients, but with data, and data are rapidly expanding throughout the world. One can criticize this as governmentality, or control "at a distance," or one can defend it as ensuring the spread of equality and proper standards, but it is certainly a dominating trend.

Carvalho and Santiago capture the decoupled rationalization involved with a quote from a doctor:

> To me what is more painful and takes more time is the huge number of documents we need to have to respond to management and administration. Sometimes things are a bit repetitive ... it gives me the idea that managers who are in health still do not know much about health. Often ... a document requested is the repetition of another and they end up not realizing where is the problem of the patient in the middle of those squares where there are only numbers ....

As a sixth and final generalization, it is important to understand, in reading the studies in this book, that the systems they analyze have undergone very rapid expansion over recent decades. We see expanding organization and (often decoupled) regulation, and expanded management of abstract and statistical sorts, but this goes on in association with massively expanded higher education and health care arrangements. In most of the countries here, higher education now captures a substantial majority of people in a cohort: this would have been unthinkable a few decades ago. Similarly, expanded medical systems touch the lives of many more people than would have been the case in earlier periods.

The editors and authors here have done the field a real service with detailed and empirically grounded analyses of what happens around the world when widespread standardizing rules impact inevitably messy local situations. They track a wide variety of outcomes – all of which seem to involve some sort of organizational expansion in local settings. And they provide ample evidence that these outcomes involve a great deal of decoupling. The researchers rarely find the straightforward implementation of sweeping rules and programs reflecting global ideas about virtuously standardized arrangements for education and health.

THE VALUE IN COMPARING ORGANIZATIONAL FIELDS AND FORMS

Rómulo Pinheiro, Lars Geschwind, Francisco O. Ramirez and Karsten Vrangbæk

ABSTRACT

Following the spirit of an earlier volume in the series focusing on 'Comparative Approaches to Organizational Research', the mandate of the current volume is to provide a comparative account of dynamics across two organizational fields – health care and higher education – and, subsequently, two specific types of organizational forms – hospitals and universities. In so doing, we take a broader perspective encompassing various conceptual and theoretical points of departure emanating from, mostly, the institutional literature in the social sciences (and its various perspectives), but also from public policy and administration literatures – of relevance to scholars and the communities of practice working within either field. In this introductory paper to the volume, we provide a brief overview of developments across the two organizational fields and illuminate on the most important scholarly traditions underpinning the study of both system dynamics as a whole as well as universities and hospitals as

Towards a Comparative Institutionalism: Forms, Dynamics and Logics Across the Organizational Fields of Health Care and Higher Education
Research in the Sociology of Organizations, Volume 45, 9–32

ISSN: 0733-558X/doi:10.1108/S0733-558X20150000045011

organizations and institutions. We conclude by reflecting on the implication of the volume's key findings in regards to comparative research within organizational studies.

Keywords: Comparative research; health care; higher education; organizational field; hospitals and universities as organizations; institutional environment

INTRODUCTION

Organizational scholars have, for long, been occupied with the interaction between environments and ways of organizing internal activities (March & Simon, 1993; Selznick, 1948; Thompson, 1967). Proponents of the new institutional perspective in the social sciences have been particularly keen to highlight the similarity between forms resulting from exposure to environmental forces at the (collective) level of a given *organizational field* – defined as 'sets of organizations that, in the aggregate, constitute a recognized area of institutional life; key suppliers, resource and product consumers, regulatory agencies, and other organizations that produce similar services or products' (DiMaggio & Powell, 1983, pp. 148–149), that is, it refers to the domain where an organization's actions are structured by the network of relationships in which they are embedded (Wooten & Hoffman, 2008, p. 131). Among other things, this has meant that substantial scholarly attention has been put on comparisons among organizational forms and macro (field-level) dynamics *within* rather than *across* organizational fields (Powell & DiMaggio, 1991; Thornton & Ocasio, 1999).

Earlier suggestions that organizational fields are, by and large, characterized by increasing homogeneity – as a result of *isomorphic* pressures (DiMaggio & Powell, 1983) – have been complemented by more nuanced accounts as regards the considerable variations when it comes to forms, logics, strategic postures (agency), social positioning, etc. (Battilana, 2006; Wooten & Hoffman, 2008). This seeming heterogeneity, in turn, has been explained along two main perspectives. There are those – belonging to the so-called 'Scandinavian school of institutionalism' – that suggest (and empirically account for) that within field variations are part and parcel of localization processes associated with the translation of global scripts, archetypes and/or hegemonic ideas in light of specific historical circumstances (path dependencies), actors' intentionality, institutionalized norms, values and traditions, and, lastly, the endogenous features – strengths and weaknesses – of organizations (Sahlin & Wedlin, 2008). Alternative accounts suggest, instead, that within specific, collective domains of social life (fields), the heterogeneity of forms and postures is largely the result of the ways in which specific organizations handle or balance seemingly contradictory demands – internal and environmental alike – exercised in the form of institutional logics (Greenwood, Díaz, Li, & Lorente, 2010; Thornton, Ocasio, & Lounsbury, 2012). Either perspective has been paramount in advancing the notion that organizations (and the actors composing them) are not simply at the mercy of their environments (deterministic view) but that, instead, they engage into sophisticated mechanisms (strategic agency) to not only adapt, but also, equally important, shape environmental circumstances.

As of today, we know a great deal about the intricacies associated with macro-level dynamics and meso- and micro-level responses within a considerable number of distinct organizational fields – from social enterprises (Pache & Santos, 2013) to publishing (Thornton, 2004) to creative industries (Pinheiro & Hauge, 2014) to modern cuisine (Byrkjeflot, Pedersen, & Svejenova, 2013) to fine wine (Voronov, De Clercq, & Hinings, 2013) to finance (Lounsbury, 2002), including how they first emerge and become institutionalized (DiMaggio, 1991; Fligstein & McAdam, 2012; Padgett & Powell, 2012). Less attention, however, has been given to comparisons *across* organizational fields on the one hand and organizational forms on the other. This is understandable since scholars have prioritized *in-field* comparisons as a means of realizing how similar types of organizations respond to, and are affected by, the same environmental dynamics. That being said, the problem, in our view, is that we end up with stylized accounts as regards what makes fields and the organizational actors composing them unique – rather than attempting to draw broader lessons – similarities and differences – on the ways in which different fields and distinct organizational types first arise and co-evolve over time.

Following the spirit of an earlier volume in the series, focusing on 'Comparative Approaches to Organizational Research' (King, Felin, & Whetten, 2009), the mandate of the current volume is to provide a comparative account of dynamics across two organizational fields – health care and higher education – and, subsequently, two specific types of organizational forms – hospitals and universities. In doing so, we take a broader perspective encompassing various conceptual and theoretical points of departure emanating from, mostly, the institutional literature in the social sciences (and its various perspectives), but also from public policy and administration literatures – of relevance to scholars and the communities of practice working within either field. We subscribe to the view that comparative analysis 'is situated between inductive and deductive reasoning [although most contributions in this volume are of the latter type], theoretical abstraction and empirical description' on the one hand, and 'the organization and its context' on the other (King et al., 2009, p. 4). We also agree with the notion that 'comparative research should consider the interaction between levels of analysis' (p. 16), and, in this volume, contributors pay attention to the interface between macro-, meso- and micro-level factors of significance for underpinning the evolution of fields and organizational forms (Wooten & Hoffman, 2008, p. 141) across health care and higher education. Yet, before we move on sketching out the individual contributions in this volume, and its key findings and implications, it is worth reflecting, briefly, on the specificities and similarities inherent to the health care and higher education fields – and their respective organizational forms – as social arenas for undertaking social science studies.

HEALTH CARE AND HIGHER EDUCATION AS STUDY FIELDS

Both health care and higher education can be considered applied fields of study, that is, the knowledge produced by social science scholars in either field aims to address issues of practical importance to policymakers and/or practitioners. In so doing, studies use a wide variety of disciplinary perspectives – political science, public policy and administration, economics, sociology, anthropology, history, etc.

Several research disciplines have investigated the dynamics facing public health care sectors across the world. Some of the most influential approaches have been developed within the field of health economics and health services research. They tend to take a functionalistic approach to comparing and assessing system features. Examples include the many reports from the European Observatory on Health Systems, OECD and the Commonwealth Fund. Within the political science tradition, there has been an interest in analyzing policy processes in health care, and more generally in understanding how health care systems are embedded in broader state structures and how the state attempts to regulate and steer health sector organizations (Blank & Burau, 2004; Grand, 2007; Moran, 1994; Tuohy, 1999). Other political scientists have emphasized decision processes, for example, in regards to the introduction of New Public Management (NPM) instruments (Magnussen, Vrangbaek, & Saltman, 2009; Vrangbaek, Robertson, Winblad, Van De Bovenkamp, & Dixon, 2012), or choice in the European Union (Martinsen & Vrangbaek, 2008).

Within sociology, there has been a keen interest in the development of the health care professions and their importance for organizing and steering the health care sector. It is argued that professional power is rather pervasive within this field, although, as many political scientists have pointed out, the steering pressure from the state and the introduction of transparency regimes combined with economic incentives and market mechanisms has challenged this position over the past decades (Starr, 1982).

Organizational theory has often followed the sociologists in emphasizing the power of professions in this sector (Mintzberg, 2000). Other contributions have analyzed dynamics in health care fields in particular settings. A seminal example is the study of the bay area by Scott and colleagues (Scott, Ruef, Mendel, & Caronna, 2000). Other examples include Scandinavian studies of the introduction of new steering mechanisms and organizational ideas (Brunson & Sahlin-Anderson, 2000; Magnussen et al., 2009). Other organization theory scholars have developed prescriptive models for reorganizing health care, for example, based on outcome value assessments (Porter & Lee, 2013). The results are parallel to ideas in health services research about bundling services and organizing care delivery around patient pathways rather than in specialized departments and units.

All in all, the field of organization studies in health care is characterized by a multitude of different disciplines, theories and methodological approaches. This is probably a reflection of the high political and economic salience of this sector and the high level of complexity, which has intrigued scholars from many different directions. Looking across the different contributions, it is striking that there is an oscillation between contributions emphasizing convergence of steering mechanisms, organizational forms, etc., over time, and contributions that highlight continued divergence across countries, system types and organizational contexts. Furthermore, there is significant variation in the contributions in terms of their ontological and epistemological vantage points. Similarly, we see several different aims represented with a constant tension between prescriptive, evaluative and explorative study types. Overall, this provides for a very dynamic field of study, which is not easily summarized into a single typology.

Scholarly interest in higher education dynamics first emerged in North America following the exponential growth in enrolments (1950s and early 1960s) triggered, firstly, by the GI Bill of Rights, allowing extended access (financial support) to War veterans and their families, and, secondly (late 1960s and mid-1970s), by rising demand associated with pressures for upward social mobility resulting from the emergence of middle class America, which was itself a side effect of the unprecedented economic growth in the post-WWII period (Gumport, Iannozzi, Shaman, & Zemsky, 1997). Enrolment expansion – from 3 million students in 1955 to 11 million in the 1975 (p. 3) – resulted in substantial growth in the size and number of providers, leading to what is known as the phenomenon of *massification* (Trow, 1972; Trow & Burrage, 2010) – which has also occurred in other parts of the world from the 1970s onwards (Meyer, Ramirez, Frank, & Schofer, 2007; Schwartzman, Pinheiro, & Pillay, 2015).

Massification brought to the fore two main problems. The first pertains to the ways in which the various national higher education systems were governed by the state. The increase in complexity led, gradually, to a move from tight state control towards that of steering at a distance (Neave & Van Vught, 1991). The latter meant, first and foremost, that universities and other types of higher education institutions were provided with relatively high levels of autonomy when it comes to internal organization – decisions on enrolments, the internal reallocation of funding, course development, institutional profiling, organizational design and structure, geographic reach, etc. This, in turn, led to the second dilemma resulting from massification, namely how best to organize teaching, research and service-related activities in ways that were both *equitable* (providing access to a wide variety of studies and diverse student publics) and *efficient* (good use of financial and human resources largely emanating from the public purse).

A number of seminal studies, from both sides of the Atlantic, set the pace for what would become an ambitious research agenda amongst scholars interested in the dynamics of higher education systems and their respective providers – enabling, amongst other aspects, a comparative agenda to emerge. Trow's (1970) seminal work on massification led to global attention as regards the complexities associated with enrolment expansion, providing a suitable categorization on system evolution – *elite*, *mass* and *universal* levels – that is still in use today. Earlier, on the basis of experiences from California, Kerr (2001) advanced a rather controversial term to categorize meso-level dynamics in the early 1960s, substantiated around the notion of the *multiversity*. The latter shed light on the emergence of the mass university, focusing on its multiplicity of purposes or functions and the links with, and direct contributions towards, surrounding society. An influential figure in the comparative studies of higher education systems and institutions was Burton Clark, a follower of Philip Selznick, the grandfather of institutional theory within organizational sociology. In the early 1970s, and following the lines of 'old' institutionalism, Clark published a number of insightful sociological accounts on how, over time, higher education institutions have a tendency for developing a sense of distinct character and identity (Clark, 1972, 1995). Earlier, in his doctoral dissertation (mid-50s) and following Selznick's seminal works on the 'foundations of the theory of organizations' and on 'the sociology of organization' (Selznick, 1948), Clark shed light on the importance of organizational values and leadership in preventing *co-optation* to occur (Clark, 1956). In the late 1970s, Clark's contributions provided the original foundation for comparing national higher education systems.

> Higher education is a social structure for the control and distribution of advanced thought and technique. Its basic organizational forms are locations for discovering, conserving, refining, transmitting, and applying advanced ideas and skills [...] Compared to other social institutions and to education at lower levels, the configuration of tasks is uniquely knowledge intensive and knowledge extensive [...] Around the multitude of knowledge tasks, each national system of higher education has a historically derived arrangement. (Clark, 1978, p. 242)

The above work was then followed by his 1983 treatise on academic organization from a cross-national perspective where, amongst other aspects, Clark illuminates on the so-called 'triangle of coordination' composed of the *state*, the *market* and the *academic oligarchy* (Clark, 1983). Over the years, this simple heuristic would become the foundation for enabling comparisons – allocation of power/authority and the role of stakeholders – across a multiplicity of countries and world regions (cf. Jongbloed, 2003; Pinheiro & Antonowicz, 2015). The field of higher education studies attracts social scientists from all the major disciplines. Sociologists are largely concerned with issues of access and also the evolving nature of the academic profession. Political scientists prefer to focus on the changing role of the state in the governance of higher education affairs, as well as the rise of (external) stakeholders. Economists put an emphasis on the contribution of higher education to the local and national economy, and the rise of quasi-markets. Historians tend to focus on system evolution (path-dependencies), pinpointing important turning points. And finally, anthropologists have shed light on the tribal nature of academic work, and their effects on structural and cultural fragmentation (a topic of interest to sociologists as well).

HOSPITALS AND UNIVERSITIES AS ORGANIZATIONS AND INSTITUTIONS

As indicated in the various contributions in this volume, hospitals and universities share a number of important structural characteristics which makes it possible for us to compare them. They, like many other organizations, operate in highly institutionalized environments (Meyer & Rowan, 1977; Scott & Christensen, 1995), laden with explicit rules and regulations and implicit norms, values and professional identities. These environments, to a large degree, provide the building blocks for the ways in which their formal structures are arranged and the means by which the internal coordination of tasks is attained (Scott, 2014; Scott & Meyer, 1994). Both are *professional bureaucracies* (Mintzberg, 2000), that is, their professionals – nurses, medical doctors, academics, etc. – are highly trained/competent and, thus, rather autonomous in the daily execution of core tasks. Due to the inherent complexity associated with their core technologies – care in the case of hospitals and teaching and research in the case of universities – there is a considerable degree of *specialization*, which also results into structural decoupling – or *loose coupling* (Orton & Weick, 1990; Weick, 1976) – both *within* as well as *across* internal subunits; faculties, clinics, departments, research units, etc. What is more, and as described in detail in some of this volume's individual contributions, both types of organizations have been the target of 'modernization efforts' – primarily aimed at making them more *complete organizations*, that is, internally coherent (e.g. clear lines of authority), more efficient and responsive to environmental dictates and stakeholders demands (cf. Ramirez, 2010), including becoming more entrepreneurial in nature (Busse, Van Der Grinten & Svensson, 2002).

That being said, it is worth acknowledging key differences as well. Universities and hospitals differ in their societal functions, as indicated earlier. But, whereas there is a general understanding on what the purpose of hospitals is – that is, to provide cure and care to citizens – the situation as regards universities is much more contested, largely as a result of the multiplicity of disciplinary values and identities inside universities (Becher & Trowler, 2001), but also due to its different roles and functions, sometimes at odds with one another (Castells, 2001). For example, there is a lack of a consensus on what a 'proper education' and/or 'useful knowledge' ought to entail, with academics from 'softer fields' (humanities and social science) having different takes from those held by their counterparts from the 'harder fields' of the natural sciences, maths and technology (STEM) (cf. Benneworth & Jongbloed, 2010). Furthermore, there is a clash between *popular functions* that (most but not all) universities are pressured to undertake from the outside – such as providing mass education or engaging with external partners like industry – and those (*autonomous functions*) that academics are willing/keen to do since they are an integral component of their professional socialization and directly contribute to their carrier progression and peer recognition (Trow, 1970). Finally, historically, universities – as *archetypes* (Greenwood & Hinings, 1993) or *ideal forms* (Weber & Parsons, 1997) – go back more than 800 years (Janin, 2008), implying that institutionalized features (e.g. 'autonomy' and 'knowledge for the sake of knowledge') are rather prominent, particularly so in the case of older institutions. Stated differently, their formal and informal structures are laden with history (Krücken, 2003; Suddaby, Foster, & Mills, 2013). Finally, another distinctive feature of universities, when compared to hospitals, lies on the fact that external attempts at modernizing their internal structures and activities not only are much more recent (last decade or so) but have been met with considerable resistance at the local level. A number of studies on (European) universities – of various sizes, types and from various countries – suggests that a considerable degree of *symbolic compliance* and *structural decoupling* exists insofar the accommodation (adaptation) of core tasks – teaching and research – to external demands driven by governmental reforms and other external stakeholders (Arbo & Eskelinen, 2003; Huisman, Norgård, Rasmussen, & Stensaker, 2002; Pinheiro, 2012). This is not to say that change is not happening, but that, traditionally, change in higher education has been a rather opaque and incremental process laden with pulls and pushes in various directions (Clark, 1983) and that the observed outcomes are not necessarily a result of rational design per se (Pinheiro, Benneworth, & Jones, 2012). In recent years, scholars like Clark (1998, 2004) have helped in popularizing the notion of the 'entrepreneurial university' (for a similar account on hospitals, see Busse et al., 2002), as a means of describing the degree of adaptation and internal transformation in light of changing environmental circumstances, most notably rising competition for students, funding and status (see also Pinheiro & Stensaker, 2014; Shattock, 2009).

> [...] enterprising universities are places that actively seek to move away from close governmental regulation and sector standardization. They search for special organizational identities; they risk being different; they take chances in the 'market'. They adhere to the belief that the risks of experimental change in the character of universities should be chosen over the risks of simply maintaining traditional forms and practices. (Clark, 1998, p. xiii)

Although there is more consensus on the basic role of hospitals as providing cure and care, it is also evident from the brief literature review above that there are extensive pressures and significant ongoing changes in both the internal organization of hospitals and in the configuration of hospitals' interaction with external partners, stakeholders and users. There are several drivers behind these pressures: firstly, the significant increases in the costs of health care; secondly, the rapidly evolving medical technologies (which also contribute to cost increases); thirdly, the rise of the quality management culture combined with increasing expectations among health care users; fourthly, the inherent logic of specialization within the medical profession; and fifthly, the potential for applying ICT for digitalization of communication and reorganization of care processes. Combined, these pressures have led to strong change dynamics within this field. There has been an import of many organizational and management ideas from the private sector or based on the broad movement of NPM. Hospital structures have been centralized and reconfigured from in-patient to more efficient ambulatory services. Meanwhile, there has been extensive experimentation with the application of rationalization and quality management ideas with inspiration from service and manufacturing industries, and a significant turn towards digitalization of patient records, imaging and communication.

Hospitals have also been subjected to significant changes in their interaction with their external organizational context. This is evident in their dealings with purchaser organizations, insurers and public authorities, that tend to tighten their steering, and expand the requirements of financial and quality reporting over time. It is also clear in the interaction with primary and community care services, where much more emphasis is placed on prevention, collaborative practices and coordination of services. In some countries, this has led to the creation of integrated health maintenance organizations with their particular organizational set-up, and in National Health Service (NHS)-type countries, the parallel tendency has been to reinforce the bureaucratic linkages and to establish economic incentives for collaborative practices.

A concurrent and somewhat contradictory trend has been the introduction of market-based practices and competition in health care. This has been introduced as extended patient choice (the Nordic countries and within the European Union) and as competitive contracting with competition among insurers (Switzerland and the United States) or sickness funds (the Netherlands and Germany). This has created a new logic in many countries in terms of publication of quality data, marketing and reputation management.

ABOUT THIS VOLUME

The current volume is born out of a conference panel entitled 'Public Sector Reforms and Organizational Responses: Comparing Universities and Hospitals', hosted by Rómulo Pinheiro, Francisco Ramirez and Karsten Vrangbæk at the 30th EGOS – European Group for Organizational Studies – annual event in Rotterdam, on July 3–5, 2014. A total of 21 papers were presented at the panel, and selected authors were invited to develop their original papers in the light of the volume's focus and ambition. Some of the papers are comparative in nature (both fields/types of organizations), and others go in-depth into a specific critical domain of significance to either health care or higher education. Authors were given autonomy to select the theoretical and conceptual perspectives that they thought useful in making sense of their case/empirical descriptions, with the volume editors providing constructive advice and suggestions throughout the entire writing process (fall 2014 to summer 2015). Two rounds of editorial reviews were undertaken, in some exceptional cases three. Needless to say, as is often the case, the individual contributions differ somewhat both in their use of theory as well as the attention paid to the comparative dimensions highlighted in the volume. Each contribution stands on its own right, but they also add significant value to the common project executed in here. We are grateful to both Professor Michael Lounsbury and Emerald for the invitation to be part of the *Research in the Sociology of Organizations Series*, and for the unconditional support and wise guidance provided throughout the entire publication and production process. Finally, the current volume has benefited widely from parallel discussions undertaken by scholars directly involved with, and with a keen interest in, higher education- and health care fields throughout the Nordic countries – in the context of a research project (2015–2016) entitled *'The global financial crisis and the public sector in the Nordic countries'* funded by the Nordic Joint Council for the Humanities and the Social Sciences.

The volume is organized around *four* distinct parts. Following the preface by renowned Stanford-based sociologist John Meyer, one of the leading figures behind the new institutional tradition in the social sciences, the introduction – by the editors – sets the stage for the comparative analysis undertaken in parts II–IV, in addition to reflecting on the major empirical findings and implications for both theory development and future studies.

Part II – three papers – sheds light on field-level dynamics and is composed of three separate contributions, one of which is truly comparative in nature (both fields simultaneously).

Ramirez, Byrkjeflot and Pinheiro resort to macro institutionalism or world society (the seminal work of John Meyer) and the concept of *actorhood* to illuminate on the impact of two hegemonic ideas: 'world class' and 'best practices' in higher education and health care. Their underlying assumption is that change has been aided by the porousness of national borders associated with the phenomenon of globalization, and that this, in turn, has led to a considerably degree of historical decontextualization: '…"world class" aspirations and "best practices" imaginaries give rise to the sense that universities and hospitals are progress-seeking organizational actors that can learn from their more successful peers around the world'. Their findings suggest that, despite commonalities at the field level, there are significant differences across the two types of organizations. For example, when compared to hospitals, universities are much less contained within the sphere of the nation state, partly because students are much more mobile when compared to patients.

Deeg provides a description of the sweeping changes linked to the unending renewal of the public university and links ongoing reform processes – led by the state – to both unintended outcomes and unforeseen challenges. In so doing, the paper explores new analytical bridges between the university as an institution and its context (field). The paper provides a contribution to evolving theories of institutional development and change – for example, around the notion of 'recursive contingency' and 'shifting versus blending frames' – across the field of higher education: '… change takes place both between co-existing ideas and the creation of novel, radically different ideas'. The author critically challenges widespread assumptions as regards the salience of coherent, unitary forces driving recent university reforms that are thought to result into greater uniformity. Instead, it is argued, 'many and manifold forms (and faces) of reform (co-) exist'. This, in turn, implies that the public university as we came to know it, will, in the near future, 'become less foreseeable in its further evolution and much less stable in its composition'.

The paper by Vrangbæk, Appleby, Klenk and Gregory provides a cross-country comparison – Denmark, Germany and England – of the institutionalization of performance management schemes – an element of NPM – throughout the hospital sector. Building on the Scandinavian version of institutionalism – and the concept of 'transparency templates' – the authors first investigate how such schemes were translated locally, and second shed light on the extent though which the schemes represent a paradigm shift in the ways in which the three national health care systems have traditionally been governed. The data show many similarities, but also significant cross-national differences. Broadly speaking, there is a tendency of increasing ambitions as regards performance management. Detected differences encompassed country-specific variations with respect to the general *logic* of the performance measurement (control and sanctioning vs. organizational learning) and the *governance* of performance measurement (centralized vs. decentralized). Overall, the paper found a strong emphasis on 'transparency templates' within the field, in tandem with support for the notion that local 'editing' of a global script (like performance management) leads to rather different solutions at the national level. Finally, in contrast to the bulk of the neo-institutional literature, which tends to downplay or even ignore the role of political decision makers and their power to impose organizational templates at the field level, policy decisions were found to be paramount in the introduction of new templates.

Part III – four papers – sheds light on the interplay between 'old' and 'new' institutional logics across the health care and higher education fields. The first two papers are comparative in nature, whereas the remaining ones look more specifically at the rise, institutionalization and coexistence of institutional logics within each of the chosen sectors.

The contribution by Grenier and Bernardini-Perinciolo questions and compares competing logics hybridization within French hospitals and universities against the backdrop of major NPM-inspired reforms. Linking meso- and micro-level dynamics, their core argumentation lies on the premise that the ways in which professionals hybridize their prevailing logic is contingent upon an overarching mode of hybridization that results from the way their organization deals with (responds to) government-mandated reform efforts. The authors adopt an agentic perspective on logics hybridization. Their data identify two contrasting manners in which the case organizations deal with such change, which they term *overarching strategic logic hybridization* and *overarching enforced logics hybridization.* In the first case, university professionals are offered enough supportive arguments and resources either to hybridize their prevailing logic with the new (economic) logic or to resist hybridization. In contrast, hospital professionals, despite evidence of some agentic behaviour (e.g. resistance to the newly introduced logic via decoupling) were, by and large, found to be unable to escape the changes required by the law. Overall, the authors contend, overarching 'hybridization sustains ways actors make sense of the new regulations, helping how they interact to collectively reduce the ambiguity of a situation'. What is more, this study sheds light on the fact that, as a dynamic process, hybridization is sustained by the specific (dual) role of key agents located at the boundaries between the lower and the higher organizational levels; acting both as 'translator-actor' – facilitating appropriation of the reforms – and as 'closure-actor', protecting professionals against the growing dominance of the newly introduced logic.

The paper by Berg and Pinheiro builds on the concept of *hybrid organizing* to investigate how professionals across Norway's health care and higher education sectors are responding to the new (managerial) institutional logic that was infused as part of recent NPM-inspired reforms. Amongst other aspects, the authors draw attention towards a set of dilemmas facing professional communities and, in turn, the ways in which so-called 'clash of logics' are mediated locally. The empirical findings suggest the rise of a *hybrid leadership* form as a means of coping with the (often contradictory) demands of three relatively distinct logics – professional, managerial and neo-bureaucratic. This, in itself, suggests that, as organizations, universities and hospitals are evolving in ways – *logic coexistence* – that do not necessarily converge towards the goals of reformers aimed at substituting traditional professional logics centred on strong autonomy, shared identity and trust by purer managerial forms emphasizing shared purposes, accountability and control.

Canhilal, Lepori and Seeber's contribution focuses on strategic responses to reform processes in European higher education by illuminating – on the basis of a quantitative inquiry – the adoption of practices associated with two distinct institutional logics: managerial and academic. NPM-inspired reforms were found to be associated with the introduction of both *hierarchy* and *rationality* within universities. That being said, the data suggest that compliance to the new practices is contingent upon, and strongly influenced by, key aspects pertaining to the academic logic. Compartmentalization effects were identified, that is, universities develop differentiated responses according to the types of institutional – managerial and academic – pressures they currently face.

In the last contribution of Part III, Torjesen, Kiland and Kvåle investigate how and to what extent the logic of *integrated health care* manifests itself in the Scandinavian health care field. Conceptually, the authors build their analysis on the classic coordinative mechanisms of *hierarchy*, *market* and *network* – and their respective institutional logics. Their findings reveal that the mix of coordinating mechanisms in both Denmark and Norway lean heavily towards a hybrid composed of hierarchy and network elements, supported by market-inspired incentives. In contrast, in Sweden the integration of health services was found to be strongly based on a network mode of organizing and coordination, with a parallel use of market-like models. The authors' central conclusion is that, as of today, it is still too early to contend that the dominant hospital-centred institutional logic (of cure) has been replaced by a new integrative logic substantiated on both cure and care, yet significant change dynamics are underway nonetheless.

Part IV is dedicated to 'resistance and transformation' (organizational and field levels) and is based on four contributions, of which two cut across the chosen organizational fields.

Klenk and Seyfried investigate what happens when universities and hospitals are confronted with a similar reform trend, namely, the urge towards developing internal systems for managing the quality of service provision. The paper's conceptual point of departure is the theory of *isomorphism* and its variant forms – coercive, mimetic and normative. The central assumption being tested in the paper is that particular models of quality management adopted by universities and hospitals – in terms of the instruments applied and the actors involved – result from differences both at the level of the two organizational fields (macro) and at the level of organizations (meso and micro). Their findings suggest that major differences between the organizational structures of quality management at German hospitals and universities exist. Quality management in the health care field was found to be both much more elaborated – in terms of quality instruments – and standardized when compared to higher education – which is more individualistic in nature. What is more, a negative correspondence was identified between the power held by the profession and the level of professional autonomy. The authors conclude that the levels of isomorphism in a given organizational field tend to rise when organizations are faced with centralized regulation and fierce competition on the one hand, and when techniques are clear and professional autonomy is restricted on the other.

Carvalho and Santiago resort to a mixed-method research design to investigate the impact of political initiatives to transform the Portuguese health care and higher education fields and the ways in which professionals both perceive and react to the enacted changes. Their conceptual approach brings together central tenants from new institutional theory and classic public management perspectives on the basic characteristics and transformation of professional bureaucracies in the context of an evolving welfare-state. Three key aspects are investigated, as pertaining to, the legal status, organizational structure (archetypes) and professional regulation. Amongst other aspects, their findings show that structural changes in the governance and management of hospitals were imposed in a much more coercive way when compared to universities. Across the higher education sector, the traditional governance model based on bottom–up collegiality (professionals in charge) was replaced by a new top–down collegial model substantiated on the presence of external stakeholders and stronger authority at the level of the central administration. Professionals' perceptions on change dynamics were found to differ substantially across sectors.

Meyer Jr., Pascucci and Mamédio undertake an analysis of strategic planning practices in complex systems by investigating the experiences of non-profit hospitals in Brazil. Their qualitative analysis builds on the literature on strategic planning/management, combined with insights on hospitals as complex organizational forms. Their findings reveal the following: firstly, the unsuitability of strategic planning for complex, professional organizations like hospitals; secondly, the significant role played by core operating professionals in strategy making; and thirdly, the representation of strategic planning as 'fancy management' in the eyes of internal and external stakeholders, conferring organizational legitimacy and generating trust. Their overall conclusion is that, as a traditional managerialist approach applied in a hospital context, strategic planning was both dysfunctional and failed to produce a significant contribution to organizational performance.

In the last contribution of Part IV, Günestepe and Tunçalp qualitatively explore the role of resistance – by individual and collective actors – in both the maintenance and change of institutions. On the basis of a hybrid ethnographic approach using both online and offline data sources, the authors investigate the framing tactics of two emerging social movements in Turkish higher education. Their findings show that framing tactics of institutional entrepreneurs – aimed at de-institutionalizing enforced employment practices at two case universities – comprise different discourses and rely on different forms of power. A major conclusion of the study is that, 'even if social movements start out with very similar demands and in the same organizational field, their outcomes may diverge according to the differences and changes in their framing strategies during their lifecycle'. The paper contributes with a novel framework for power dynamics and temporality in framing in the context of institutional change and contestation.

TOWARDS EMBRACING A COMPARATIVE INSTITUTIONALISM

The empirical findings emanating from the individual contributions in this volume attest to the multiplicity of conceptual and theoretical approaches for assessing change processes within organizational fields as well as at the meso and micro levels of analysis. Following King et al.'s (2009) appeal for the need to refine our current tools for comparative analysis within organizational studies, we will try here, in broad strokes, to take account of the most significant findings of this comparative volume. In doing so, we first reflect on the key findings and their implications at the macro (field), meso (organization) and micro (professionals) levels, before turning to a discussion on the interplay between these three levels and the effects these may have in future comparative inquiries.

Hinings, Greenwood, Reay, and Suddaby (2004) have proposed a cyclical, process-based model – based on five key phases – for assessing change patterns within organizational fields (Fig. 1). We briefly reflect upon aspects linked to each of the (5) stages in the light of the data presented in the individual papers.

Health care and higher education fields have both been the target of major reform efforts in the last two decades or so. Reforms have largely been informed or inspired by NPM ideologies that first emerged in the

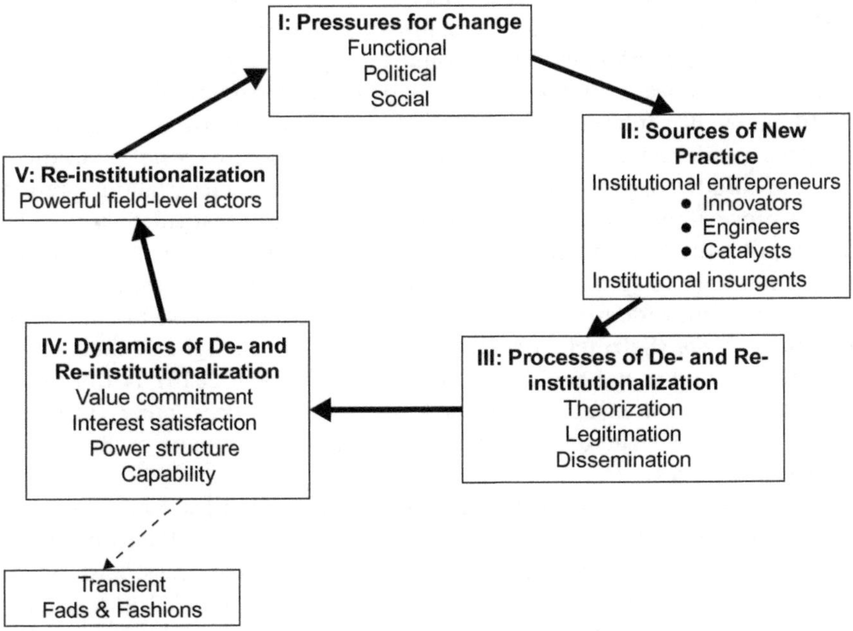

Fig. 1. The Dynamics of Institutional Change. *Source*: Hinings et al. (2004, p. 306).

mid-1980s, emphasizing efficiency and effectiveness, enhanced autonomy, in addition to quality control and accountability to various stakeholder groups (Pollitt & Bouckaert, 2011). Such modernization efforts are intrinsically linked with the evolving nature of the welfare-state in the light of major *economic* (globalization), *technological* (ICT/Internet), *political* (regional blocks/integration, e.g. the European Union) and *demographic* (ageing of population) changes. A major aim of reform efforts was to change the internal fabric of universities and hospitals – from relatively loose coupling professional bureaucracies – towards more *complete organizations* accountable for their own strategic actions and performance (Brunsson & Sahlin-Andersson, 2000). One mechanism for doing this – as referred to in various contributions in this volume – was to replace (*de-institutionalize*) the dominant, professional institutional logic by a stronger top–down orientation in the form of strategic management and/or managerialism. Such attempts, however, have led to mixed results, with managerialism coexisting with other dominant (deeply institutionalized) logics, in the form of *hybrid* approaches and/or through *compartmentalization* or structural *decoupling*.

The evidence provided suggest that within universities and hospitals, as is the case with other types of organizational forms, actors compete for both power and influence, with some taking strategic advantage of the new opportunities at hand (Battilana, Leca, & Boxenbaum, 2009; Leca, Battilana, & Boxenbaum, 2008). Agency was found to occur along different lines and levels. Some actors – close to formal managerial positions – top and middle organizational layers – tend to pursue a change agenda that is more aligned with government objectives and institutional policies. Others, like the bulk of the professional groups at hospitals and universities, tend either to resist reform processes that go against established practices, values and identities (Oliver, 1991), or, alternatively, take strategic action to *co-opt* (Selznick, 1949) such practices in the light of their strategic interests and social positions (Mahoney & Thelen, 2010). A third common alternative was also identified, namely, the *decoupling* (Orton & Weick, 1990) of structures from policies and/or dominant or hegemonic reform discourses.

Social positioning (Battilana, 2006) was also found to be a relevant feature of both universities and hospitals – either in the form of the clashes for power and influence amongst doctors–nurses and academics–administrators on the one hand and between internal and external stakeholders as change agents on the other. As suggested in earlier studies, the dissemination or *institutionalization* of organizational innovations was, to a large degree, dependent on change agents securing adequate *legitimacy* (Deephouse & Suchman, 2008) on the one hand and additional *resources* (Pfeffer & Salancik, 2003) on the other. In a handful of cases, the *re-institutionalization* of new forms and mechanisms (e.g. strategic management, top–down decision-making bodies) were found to be at odds with the structural and cultural complexity inherent to modern universities and hospitals.

Fashion-following and *local translation* or editing (Sahlin & Wedlin, 2008) were found to be central elements underpinning isomorphic tendencies (DiMaggio & Powell, 1983) and/or the need to adapt global scripts to local circumstances, a process largely shaped by path-dependency and institutionalization patterns (Suddaby et al., 2013). *Hybrid* organizational forms (Pache & Santos, 2013) were found to provide a balance – meso and micro levels – between forces geared towards the *de-institutionalization* (Oliver, 1992) of older forms of organization and the *re*-institutionalization of new ones, with power and social positioning playing a key role. More importantly perhaps, the analysis provided in this volume underscores the differences between the fields of health care and higher education on the one hand, and the specificities associated with dominant organizational archetypes (Greenwood & Hinings, 1993) embodied in the form of the typical or 'ideal type' hospital and university on the other.

The empirical data also shed light on the perennial and complex interplay between different levels of analysis. Structural arrangements determine, in part, dynamics at the field and organizational levels, yet these same structures – de- and re-institutionalization processes – are part and parcel of the proactive efforts – co-optation, contestation, strategic actor-hood, etc. – by some of the actors involved. In other words, structure and agency are interlinked at various levels (Hay & Wincott, 1998), defining the nature and evolution (change vs. stability) at both the field and organizational levels.

Finally, when it comes to the robustness of various perspectives on institutionalism, the contributions of this volume attest to the fact that these – either alone or in combination with other conceptual perspectives – offer a tremendous avenue for: (a) comparing change dynamics across a multiplicity of organizational fields; (b) illuminating on the specificities associated with the rise and transformation of specific organizational forms; and (c) shed light on the role played by certain agents in the rise, diffusion and eventual replacement of certain forms of organizing. Going forward, we hope this volume marks the beginning of a new research agenda that attempts to provide new empirical, conceptual and theoretical insights on how the various types of perspectives within the institutional tradition in the social sciences can – alone or combined (also with other perspectives outside the institutional tradition) – be of relevance in the context of comparative studies that move beyond a particular societal/economic sector and/or specific organizational form.

ACKNOWLEDGEMENTS

We would like to thank Professor John W. Meyer, Stanford University, for the kind foreword, and Professor Michael Lounsbury (Editor-in-Chief of the series), University of Alberta, for the invitation to be part of the series and his unconditional support throughout the entire process. Any remaining errors are our own.

REFERENCES

Arbo, P., & Eskelinen, H. (2003). The role of small, comprehensive universities in regional economic development: Experiences from two Nordic cases. Paper presented at the 43rd ERSA Congress, Jyväskylä, Finland, 27–30 August.

Battilana, J. (2006). Agency and institutions: The enabling role of individuals' social position. *Organization*, *13*, 653–676.

Battilana, J., Leca, B., & Boxenbaum, E. (2009). How actors change institutions: Towards a theory of institutional entrepreneurship. *Academy of Management Annals*, *3*, 65–107.

Becher, T., & Trowler, P. (2001). *Academic tribes and territories: Intellectual enquiry and the culture of disciplines*. Buckingham: Society for Research into Higher Education & Open University Press.

Benneworth, P., & Jongbloed, B. (2010). Who matters to universities? A stakeholder perspective on humanities, arts and social sciences valorisation. *Higher Education*, *59*, 567–588.

Blank, R. H., & Burau, V. (2004). *Comparative health policy*. New York, NY: Palgrave Macmillan.

Brunsson, N., & Sahlin-Andersson, K. (2000). Constructing organizations: The example of public sector reform. *Organization Studies*, *21*, 721–746.

Busse, R., Van Der Grinten, T., & Svensson, P.-G. (2002). Regulating entrepreneurial behaviour in hospitals: Theory and practice. In R. B. Saltman, R. Busse, & E. Mossialos (Eds.), *Regulating entrepreneurial behaviour in European health care systems* (pp. 126–145). Buckingham: Open University Press.

Byrkjeflot, H., Pedersen, J. S., & Svejenova, S. (2013). From label to practice: The process of creating new Nordic cuisine. *Journal of Culinary Science & Technology*, *11*, 36–55.

Castells, M. (2001). Universities as dynamic systems of contradictory functions. In J. Muller, N. Cloete, & S. Badat (Eds.), *Challenges of globalisation. South African debates with Manuel Castells*. Cape Town: Maskew Miller Longman.

Clark, B. (1972). The organizational saga in higher education. *Administrative Science Quarterly*, *17*, 178–184.
Clark, B. (1995). *Places of inquiry: Research and advanced education in modern universities*. Oakland, CA: University of California Press.
Clark, B. R. (1956). Organizational adaptation and precarious values: A case study. *American Sociological Review*, *21*, 327–336.
Clark, B. R. (1978). Academic differentiation in national systems of higher education. *Comparative Education Review*, *22*, 242–258.
Clark, B. R. (1983). *The higher education system: Academic organization in cross-national perspective*. Los Angeles, CA: University of California Press.
Clark, B. R. (1998). *Creating entrepreneurial universities: Organizational pathways of transformation*. New York, NY: Pergamon.
Clark, B. R. (2004). *Sustaining change in universities: Continuities in case studies and concepts*. London: Society for Research into Higher Education & Open University Press.
Deephouse, D., & Suchman, M. (2008). Legitimacy in organizational institutionalism. In R. Greenwood, C. Oliver, K. Sahlin, & R. Suddaby (Eds.), *The SAGE handbook of organizational institutionalism* (pp. 49–77). Los Angeles, CA: Sage.
DiMaggio, P. (1991). Constructing an organizational field as a professional project: US art museums, 1920–1940. In W. W. Powell & P. DiMaggio (Eds.), *The new institutionalism in organizational analysis* (pp. 267–292). Chicago, IL: University of Chicago Press.
DiMaggio, P., & Powell, W. (1983). The iron cage revisited: Institutional isomorphism and collective rationality in organizational fields. *American Sociological Review*, *48*, 147–160.
Fligstein, N., & McAdam, D. (2012). *A theory of fields*. New York, NY: Oxford University Press.
Grand, J. L. (2007). *The other invisible hand: Delivering public services through choice and competition*. Princeton, NJ: Princeton University Press.
Greenwood, R., Díaz, A. M., Li, S. X., & Lorente, J. C. (2010). The multiplicity of institutional logics and the heterogeneity of organizational responses. *Organization Science*, *21*, 521–539.
Greenwood, R., & Hinings, C. (1993). Understanding strategic change: The contribution of archetypes. *Academy of Management Journal*, *36*, 1052–1081.
Gumport, P., Iannozzi, M., Shaman, S., & Zemsky, R. (1997). *Trends in United States higher education: From massification to post massification*. Stanford, CA: National Center for Postsecondary Improvement, Stanford University.
Hay, C., & Wincott, D. (1998). Structure, agency and historical institutionalism. *Political Studies*, *46*, 951–957.
Hinings, C. R., Greenwood, R., Reay, T., & Suddaby, R. (2004). Dynamics of change in organizational fields. In M. S. Poole & A. H. Van De Ven (Eds.), *Handbook of Organizational Change and Innovation* (pp. 304–323). Oxford, UK: Oxford University Press.
Huisman, J., Norgård, J. D., Rasmussen, J., & Stensaker, B. (2002). Alternative universities revisited: A study of the distinctiveness of universities established in the spirit of 1968. *Tertiary Education and Management*, *8*, 316–332.
Janin, H. (2008). *The university in medieval life, 1179–1499*. Jefferson, NC: McFarland.
Jongbloed, B. (2003). Marketisation in higher education, Clark's triangle and the essential ingredients of markets. *Higher Education Quarterly*, *57*, 110–135.
Kerr, C. (2001). *The uses of the university*. Cambridge, MA: Harvard University Press.

King, B. G., Felin, T., & Whetten, D. A. (2009). Comparative organizational analysis: An introduction. *Research in the Sociology of Organizations*, *26*, 3–19.

Krücken, G. (2003). Learning the new, new thing: On the role of path dependency in university structures. *Higher Education*, *46*, 315–339.

Leca, B., Battilana, J., & Boxenbaum, E. (2008). *Agency and institutions: A review of institutional entrepreneurship*. Cambridge, MA: Harvard Business School.

Lounsbury, M. (2002). Institutional transformation and status mobility: The professionalization of the field of finance. *Academy of Management Journal*, *45*, 255–266.

Magnussen, J., Vrangbaek, K., & Saltman, R. (2009). *Nordic Health Care Systems: Recent Reforms and Current Policy Challenges*. Maidenhead: Open University Press.

Mahoney, J., & Thelen, K. (2010). *Explaining institutional change: Ambiguity, agency, and power*. Cambridge, UK: Cambridge University Press.

March, J. G., & Simon, H. A. (1993). *Organizations*. London: Blackwell.

Martinsen, D. S., & Vrangbaek, K. (2008). The Europeanization of health care governance: Implementing the market imperatives of Europe. *Public Administration*, *86*, 169–184.

Meyer, J. W., Ramirez, F. O., Frank, D. J., & Schofer, E. (2007). Higher education as an institution. In P. Gumport (Ed.), *Sociology of higher education: Contributions and their context* (pp. 187–220). Baltimore, MD: Johns Hopkins University Press.

Meyer, J. W., & Rowan, B. (1977). Institutionalized organizations: Formal structure as myth and ceremony. *American Journal of Sociology*, *83*, 340–363.

Mintzberg, H. (2000). The professional bureaucracy. In I. Jenniskens (Ed.), *Management and decision-making in higher education institutions*. New York, NY: Lemma Publishers.

Moran, M. (1994). Reshaping the health-care state. *Government and Opposition*, *29*, 48–63.

Neave, G., & Van Vught, F. (Eds.). (1991). *Prometheus bound: The changing relationship between government and higher education in Western Europe*. Oxford, UK: Pergamon.

Oliver, C. (1991). Strategic responses to institutional processes. *Academy of Management Review*, *16*, 145–179.

Oliver, C. (1992). The antecedents of deinstitutionalization. *Organization Studies*, *13*, 563–588.

Orton, J. D., & Weick, K. E. (1990). Loosely coupled systems: A reconceptualization. *Academy of Management Review*, *15*, 203–223.

Pache, A.-C., & Santos, F. (2013). Inside the hybrid organization: Selective coupling as a response to competing institutional logics. *Academy of Management Journal*, *56*, 972–1001.

Padgett, J. F., & Powell, W. W. (2012). *The emergence of organizations and markets*. Princeton, NJ: Princeton University Press.

Pfeffer, J., & Salancik, G. R. (2003). *The external control of organizations: A resource dependence perspective*. Stanford, CA: Stanford Business Books.

Pinheiro, R. (2012). *In the region, for the region? A comparative study of the institutionalisation of the regional mission of universities*. Oslo: University of Oslo.

Pinheiro, R., & Antonowicz, D. (2015). Opening the gates or coping with the flow? Governing access to higher education in Northern and Central Europe. *Higher Education*, *70*(3), 299–313. doi: 10.1007/s10734-014-9830-1

Pinheiro, R., Benneworth, P., & Jones, G. A. (2012). Understanding regions and the institutionalization of universities. In R. Pinheiro, P. Benneworth, & G. A. Jones (Eds.), *Universities and regional development: An assessment of tensions and contradictions* (pp. 11–32). London: Routledge.

Pinheiro, R., & Hauge, E. (2014). Global scripts and local translations: The case of cultural and creative industries (CCIs) in Norway. *City, Culture and Society*, *5*, 87–95.

Pinheiro, R., & Stensaker, B. (2014). Designing the entrepreneurial university: The interpretation of a global idea. *Public Organization Review*, *14*, 497–516.

Pollitt, C., & Bouckaert, G. (2011). *Public management reform: A comparative analysis – New public management, governance, and the Neo-Weberian State*. Oxford, UK: Oxford University Press.

Porter, M. E., & Lee, T. H. (2013). The strategy that will fix health care. *Harvard Business Review*, *91*, 50–70.

Powell, W. W., & DiMaggio, P. (1991). *The new institutionalism in organizational analysis*. Chicago, IL: University of Chicago Press.

Ramirez, F. O. (2010). Accounting for excellence: Transforming universities into organizational actors. In L. Portnoi, V. Rust, & S. Bagely (Eds.), *Higher education, policy, and the global competition phenomenon* (pp. 43–58). Basingstoke: Palgrave Macmillan.

Sahlin, K., & Wedlin, L. (2008). Circulating ideas: Imitation, translation and editing. In R. Greenwood, K. Sahlin-Andersson, & R. Suddaby (Eds.), *The sage handbook of organizational institutionalism* (pp. 218–242). Los Angeles, CA: Sage.

Schwartzman, S., Pinheiro, R., & Pillay, P. (2015). *Higher education in the BRICS countries: Investigating the pact between higher education and society*. Dordrecht: Springer.

Scott, W. R. (2014). *Institutions and organizations: Ideas, interests, and identities*. Thousand Oaks, CA: Sage.

Scott, W. R., & Christensen, S. (1995). *The institutional construction of organizations: International and longitudinal studies*. Los Angeles, CA: Sage.

Scott, W. R., & Meyer, J. W. (1994). *Institutional environments and organizations: Structural complexity and individualism*. Thousand Oaks, CA: Sage.

Scott, W. R., Ruef, M., Mendel, P., & Caronna, C. (2000). *Institutional change and healthcare organizations: From professional dominance to managed care*. Chicago, IL: University of Chicago Press.

Selznick, P. (1948). Foundations of the theory of organization. *American Sociological Review*, *13*, 25–35.

Selznick, P. (1949). *TVA and the grass roots: A study in the sociology of formal organization*. Berkeley, CA: University of California Press.

Shattock, M. (2009). *Entrepreneurialism in universities and the knowledge economy: Diversification and organizational change in European higher education*. London: Society for Research into Higher Education & Open University Press.

Starr, P. (1982). *The social transformation of American medicine*. New York, NY: Basic Books.

Suddaby, R., Foster, W. M., & Mills, A. J. (2013). Historical institutionalism. In M. Bucheli & D. Wadhwani (Eds.), *Organizations in time: History, theory, methods* (pp. 100–123). Oxford, UK: Oxford University Press.

Thompson, J. D. (1967). *Organizations in action: Social science bases of administrative theory*. New York, NY: McGraw-Hill.

Thornton, P., & Ocasio, W. (1999). Institutional logics and the historical contingency of power in organizations: Executive succession in the higher education publishing industry, 1958-1990. *American Journal of Sociology*, *105*, 801–843.

Thornton, P. H. (2004). *Markets from culture: Institutional logics and organizational decisions in higher education publishing*. Redwood City, CA: Stanford University Press.

Thornton, P. H., Ocasio, W., & Lounsbury, M. (2012). *The institutional logics perspective: A new approach to culture, structure, and process.* Oxford, UK: Oxford University Press.

Trow, M. (1970). Reflections on the transition from mass to universal higher education. *Daedalus, 99*, 1–42.

Trow, M. (1972). The expansion and transformation of higher education. *International Review of Education, 18*, 61–84.

Trow, M., & Burrage, M. (2010). *Twentieth-century higher education: Elite to mass to universal.* Baltimore, MD: Johns Hopkins University Press.

Tuohy, C. H. (1999). *Accidental logics: The dynamics of change in the health care arena in the United States, Britain, and Canada: The dynamics of change in the health care arena in the United States, Britain, and Canada.* New York, NY: Oxford University Press.

Voronov, M., De Clercq, D., & Hinings, C. (2013). Institutional complexity and logic engagement: An investigation of Ontario fine wine. *Human Relations, 66*, 1563–1596.

Vrangbaek, K., Robertson, R., Winblad, U., Van De Bovenkamp, H., & Dixon, A. (2012). Choice policies in Northern European health systems. *Health Economics, Policy and Law, 7*, 47–71.

Weber, M., & Parsons, T. (1997). *The theory of social and economic organization.* New York, NY: Free Press.

Weick, K. E. (1976). Educational organizations as loosely coupled systems. *Administrative Science Quarterly, 21*, 1–19.

Wooten, M., & Hoffman, A. J. (2008). Organizational fields: Past, present and future. In *The Sage handbook of organizational institutionalism* (pp. 130–147). Los Angeles, CA: Sage.

PART II
FIELD LEVEL DYNAMICS

HIGHER EDUCATION AND HEALTH ORGANIZATIONAL FIELDS IN THE AGE OF "WORLD CLASS" AND "BEST PRACTICES"

Francisco O. Ramirez, Haldor Byrkjeflot and Rómulo Pinheiro

ABSTRACT

The paper sets forth and examines the assumptions underlying two global ideas – world class and best practices – and their application to (higher) education and health organizations. Our basic (ex-ante) assumption is that both sectors are influenced by organizational fields that embody these ideas. However, we also assume that these sectors differ, and thus, that one should find between sector variations in the influence of such ideas. The findings suggest that both sectors have been affected by hegemonic ideas, yet in rather different ways, and that these ideas, particularly the metrics being used, pose different challenges in the two sectors.

Keywords: World class; best practices; organizational fields; policy discourse; loose coupling

Towards a Comparative Institutionalism: Forms, Dynamics and Logics Across the Organizational Fields of Health Care and Higher Education
Research in the Sociology of Organizations, Volume 45, 35–57

ISSN: 0733-558X/doi:10.1108/S0733-558X20150000045012

INTRODUCTION

Much of the literature on organizations and organizational sectors recognizes that these are deeply embedded in environments that influence their development (Scott, 2008). These environments, in turn, have traditionally been imagined in local or national terms until the recent focus on globalization and its transnational impacts and the ideas circulating across national and organizational boundaries (Drori, Meyer, & Hwang, 2006). In this paper, we reflect on the influence of the ideas "world class" and "best practices" on two different organizational sectors or fields: higher education and health. The paper sets forth and examines the assumptions underlying these global ideas and their application to education and health organizations. Our basic (ex-ante) assumption is that both sectors are influenced by organizational fields that embody these ideas (Czarniawska-Joerges & Sevón, 2005; Musselin, 2000). However, we also assume that these sectors differ, and thus, that one should find between sector variations in the influence of such ideas. Thus, this reflection will stress both commonalities and variations in the influence of "world class" as regards higher education and "best practices" when it comes to health.

The paper is organized as follows. The section "Underlying assumptions" depicts the underlying assumptions surrounding the importance attributed to ideas of "world class" and "best practices" in the (re-)construction of both organizations and organizational fields. The section "The transformation of universities and hospitals into organizations" focuses on the transformation of universities and hospitals into organizations, a transformation often justified by invoking "world class" and "best practices" ideas. Finally, we conclude by briefly summarizing our argument and sketching future research directions that would allow scholarship to critically assess its empirical implications.

UNDERLYING ASSUMPTIONS

Ideas "travel," both across geographic contexts (Christensen & Lægreid, 2001) and across distinct sectors of the economy (Pinheiro & Stensaker, 2014). There are multiple ways of documenting the widespread use of the ideas "world class" and "best practices." Despite its limitations, we have decided to undertake a Google search on these two terms as to give us a sense of their widespread diffusion, both within science and society at large.

A 2015 (April 22) Google search for the terms "world class" and "best practice(s)" delivered 492 million and 230 million hits, respectively.[1] When Google scholar was used instead, the figures were 4 million and 3.5 million hits, respectively. Similarly, an earlier search (April 1, 2014) of publication titles on Thomson's Web of Science found more than 6,768 scientific historical records for the term "best practices" and 1,407 for "world class." In geographical terms, 39% of all records on "best practices" emanated from the United States, followed by England (16%), Canada (7%), and Australia (6%).

As for "world class," the country order was the same, albeit a slightly different distribution: 36% (United States), 8% (England), 4% (Canada), and 3% (Australia). A more detailed analysis of record counts by category shows that "best practices" were particularly salient (by a long margin) within health-related sciences, followed by management, and education research. As for "world class," defined by Merriam-Webster's dictionary as "being of the highest caliber in the world,"[2] the term is particularly popular among historians, as well as scholars associated with the fields of management, sport science, sociology, and educational research. For example, within the influential field of management, the notion of "world class" has been linked to strategic approaches toward managing human as well as technological resources (High, 2009), in addition to embracing prevalent social and economic phenomena like globalization (Marquardt, 1999) in the context of a rapidly changing (and increasingly volatile) external environment (Gerschel & Polsky, 2013). A thorough review (mid-1990s) by the United States Army, in the context of "World-Class Research and Development," concluded that:

> The phrase world-class is widely used to describe products and services. However, world-class can reasonably mean different things to different people. To athletes, it means being competitive with the best athletes in the world. To General Motors, it means a balanced approach to excellence. To others, it means having and implementing a winning strategy, being able to anticipate customer needs, and meet those needs faster and with higher quality products than competitors can … world class organizations generally have a balanced approach in that they perform very well in the areas of operation they choose to focus on, and exceptionally well in some of these areas … [and that] the concept of world class [is used] as a method of internal focusing to achieve excellence rather than an external mechanism to advertise organizational virtues. Excellence is advertising enough. (US Army, 1996, p. 16)

Turning to the idea of "best practices," the latter is defined by the Oxford dictionary as: "Commercial or professional procedures that are accepted or prescribed as being correct or most effective."[3] A more precise definition pertains to a set of interrelated work activities that are repeatedly utilized by individuals and/or groups and that, in turn, are associated with a specific body of knowledge that is thought to yield an optimal result (Tucker et al., 2007, p. 894 in Wellstein & Kieser, 2011). The term comes from industry but is now widely used also in health care and education. A quick review of the existing literature shows that "best practices" have been connected to various organizational (and organizing-related) aspects such as *benchmarking* (van Lent, de Beer, & van Harten, 2010), *customer-focused solutions* (Andersen, Heibeler, Kelly, & Ketteman, 2000), *accounting practices* (Bragg, 2010), *strategic global sourcing* (Sollish & Semanik, 2011), and *project-* as well as *human resources management* (Secord, 2003). In a recent review of how the term is used in health care, it is noted that there are dozens of definitions in use, but in general some scholars contend that the best practices idea implies that there is an ultimate benchmark against which all other practices may be judged (Goes, Savage, & Friedman, 2015). Furthermore, the same authors argue that, if used as a gold standard, best practices work against innovation and that there is a danger that all are regressing to the mean. Others have also pointed to the paradoxical relationship between excellence and best practices: through benchmarking, organizational processes become increasingly similar, which may mean less excellent; if by excellence one means outstanding and distinctive in one way or the other (Walgenbach & Hegele, 2001).

Undoubtedly, there are more complex content analyses and refined strategies that can be undertaken, but in the context of this inquiry it suffices to say that more and more organizations live with such paradoxical imperatives. They are expected to aspire to become "world class" and are, accordingly, confronted with the need to become more attuned to "best practices," which may mean becoming more similar to others. To be sure, there is much skepticism about the sensibility of these abstract ideas as blueprints to organizational reforms (cf. Pinheiro & Stensaker, 2014). But even the skeptics know that they cannot simply ignore these ideas and often invoke them to achieve pragmatic ends; for example, while establishing or maintaining a positive organizational identity in order to secure resources and/or external support toward organizational goals (cf. Fumasoli, Pinheiro, & Stensaker, 2015; Stensaker & Norgård, 2001). Both educational and health organizations recognize that, in order to be taken seriously and enhance their legitimacy, they are expected to make diffuse commitments to world class and best practices emanating from elsewhere (Claxton, Sculpher, & Drummond, 2002; Hazelkorn, 2009), and that standards to gauge-related dimensions, such as excellence, are increasingly transnational ones (Aksnes et al., 2012; Heidemann, 2000). In short, local virtue is not in vogue in this day and age, at least not at the level of articulated policies (cf. Deem, 2001).

Moreover, as these ideas sweep across national and local borders much translation or embedding work occurs. Translation leads to variations in policy adaptations to the pressures to aspire to (or at least pretend to care about aspiring to) "world class" status via "best practice" commitments. Regional and national rankings emerge. Our point is not that all has changed but that there have in fact been changes and that these changes have been facilitated by the porousness of national borders. This is especially evident at the level of policy and even within this domain one should perhaps find more variation when observing universities and hospitals rather than educational and health ministries. The latter may be more directly linked to transnational organizations that foster similar policy talk. That being said, these changes are more pronounced as regards policy than practice. Loose coupling and translation work go hand in hand.

In the late 19th century, universities were hailed as "laboratories of nationalism" (Reisner, 1927). On the other hand, hospitals, particularly in the United States and in the United Kingdom prior to 1948, were not that profoundly associated with the nation-state, perhaps because they were earlier linked to transnational science and its universalistic claims. Nevertheless, the field of medicine has been organized in national medical associations and health education systems, and these have put strong restrictions on international mobility of both patients as well as medical personnel (Evleth, 1995; Llewellyn & Northcott, 2005). Particularly in the period after 1945, there was a drive toward taking pride in the development of national health care systems, such as the United Kingdom's National Health Service. This is largely still the case, but such identifications have been challenged recently by the development of cross-national associations and statistics as well as the deregulation of mobility restrictions for health personnel. As in the case of the educational sector, there is now a much more active media and consulting industry eager to discover problems and provide advice and solutions to them, which may have undermined some of the trust that has historically existed among citizens and employees in relation to the hospital system.

Let us now identify and consider some of the underlying assumptions regarding "world class" and "best practices." These assumptions constitute influential models or blueprints and these motivate consultants and the advice they proffer to educational and health organizations throughout the world. First, there is a general assumption that ongoing practices are no longer best justified by references solely attuned to historical legacies or established practices (for the case of higher education, consult Clark, 1970 and Krücken, 2003 and Starr, 1982 and Timmermans & Berg, 2003 for hospitals). Second, more organization-specific storytelling in order to make sense of the practices of this or that other university/hospital may have become less relevant as both types of organizations are increasingly merging with their respective counterparts and thus losing some of their local embeddedness. Third, earlier national culture or character may have been used to explain and develop support for organizational policies or practices (cf. Clark, 1978). As systems become increasingly fragmented and accountability is delegated to regional and local quasi-corporations, the grand narratives of the development of national higher education and hospital systems may lose some of their appeal. Fourth, as these organizations are expected to pursue goals that can be attained through rational strategies, their internal structures become more formalized, that is, more "rule oriented" and more "role differentiated" (Hetherington, 1991; Ramirez & Christensen, 2013). The mechanisms through which the organization is supposed to attain its goals need to be identifiable, and progress toward goal attainment needs to be measurable (Deem, 1998; Voelker, Rakich, & French, 2001).

These assumptions involve a considerable degree of historical de-contextualization. Nationally grounded institutions with specific sagas become formal organizations with both identifiable goals and goal attainment strategies and standards for gauging progress. At the extreme, one can imagine lining up a range of very different organizations and rating these on an organizational or management quality scale. For example, the global benchmarking network promotes a set of standards that cut across sectors of the economy and types of organizations.[4] International consulting firms such as McKinsey also play an important role in developing common metrics (Kipping & Wright, 2012; Wright, Sturdy, & Wylie, 2012) and thus in defining how progress ought to be assessed. However, such pressures for reforming and standardization may not necessarily increase the number of excellent organizations.

Llewellyn and Northcott (2005) argue that best practices methodologies such as benchmarking are leading to "averageness" in the hospital sector in the United Kingdom. "Average hospitals will be cheaper to run and easier to control than highly differentiated ones; they may also score more highly on certain measures of service improvement" (p. 555). However, this may be a short-term effect of benchmarking and best practices methodologies. Certainly it was the aim of the British government to create a privileged sector of hospitals that could set standards for the others as well, and this means that averageness is not a legitimate aim, but rather an unintended temporary outcome of the strive for excellence.

A basic assumption in the (strategic management) literature is that it is clearly better to have well-delineated goals, properly distinguishing between short and long term ones (Foss, 1997). It is even better to have transparent strategies with which these goals are to be attained, step-by-step (Grant, 2003). Thus, in the case of higher education, Burton Clark's earlier interest in distinctive colleges and their organizational sagas (Clark, 1970, 1972) shifted to his later focus on the "entrepreneurial university" as a presumed universal blueprint for successful adaptation to a changing environment, regardless of specific contextual factors (Clark, 1998, 2004). Similarly, across the health sector, new public management (NPM) inspired reforms and their associated recipes (e.g., management by objectives and results) have promoted managerialism as the solution for enhancing organizational performance and for fostering accountability (Byrkjeflot, Christensen, & Lægreid, 2014).

These assumptions add up to the vision of *organizational actors* that has now become a worldwide reality, replacing earlier forms involving looser associations between masters and students or doctors and patients (see Enders, Kehm, & Schimank, 2015; Krücken & Meier, 2006 for universities; and Risse, 1999; McKee & Healy, 2002 for hospitals). Not so long ago, it would have been difficult to imagine mission statements and strategic plans as features of higher education, hospitals, and other health organizations. This level of organizational rationalization is, whether one likes it or not, increasingly the global norm (see Oertel & Soll, 2015 for the spread of mission statements in German universities or Byrkjeflot & Angell, 2007 for Norwegian hospitals).

In principle, organizational actors could continue to *only* rely on national frames of reference, even if the weight of their institution-specific historical legacies has diminished. But the fifth underlying assumption is that organizations can learn from, or imitate, other organizations, regardless of where the latter are situated. Increasing mobility of people and ideas, coupled with new generation information and communication technologies like social media, facilitate learning across national borders (Redecker, Ala-Mutka, & Punie, 2010). More importantly, national differences are no longer seen as insurmountable obstacles. No culture is perceived as inhibiting learning or dooming an organization to less than "world class" aspirations, as long as the right standards are adopted and performance is continuously assessed (Oakland, 2001). This rather optimistic assumption is interwoven with a sixth and final assumption, namely, the rise of the transnational expert or professional that can foster the required organizational learning (Sahlin-Andersson & Engwall, 2002). The former need not have much by way of local knowledge; all that is needed is just intense familiarity with the right goals and the right strategies with which to realize these ends. Both of these assumptions undermine national frames of reference and are rooted in cultural globalization that has intensified in recent decades (Drori et al., 2006). Transnational experts facilitate the development of mission statements and strategic plans that often appear to be scripted and tend to have a transnational flavor (Bartlett & Gosha, 1999). That being said, some scholars argue that there is a difference between "best practice" and "world class" ideas. The former are taken seriously as guidelines or standards, at least in health care, though they are less well defined in higher education. The latter is much easier to disregard, as lofty aspirations and dinner speeches, thus functioning as a rhetorical gimmick rather than a solid performance measurement per se.[5]

To summarize, our chief argument is that "world class" aspirations and "best practices" imaginaries give rise to the sense that universities and hospitals are progress-seeking organizational actors that can learn from their more successful peers around the world. Idea diffusion, legitimation, and consequent adoption are aided by major supranational organizations like the Organization for Economic Co-operation and Development (OECD), the World Bank, and/or the European Union, as well as a cadre of professional experts without borders, whose support these organizational actors seek in order to upgrade themselves or at least to look more like rationalized actors. This upgrading goal in turn is seen as a crucial means to secure both *resources* – human and financial – and *legitimacy* (Drori & Honig, 2013; Pfeffer & Salancik, 2003).

Taken as a whole, these assumptions add up to models of the university and hospital in which the dominant *institutional logic* (Thornton, Ocasio, & Lounsbury, 2012) favors imagining these social institutions as formal organizations. Like other formal organizations, universities and hospitals are increasingly subjected to external pressures to display and communicate their excellence (and relevance) to an ever-growing number of stakeholder groups. In the European context, the change is from a more state-oriented institution to a more market-influenced organization (see Pinheiro, 2015 for higher education and Martinsen & Vrangbæk, 2008). In the United States, the earlier triumph of the logic of the market is intensified (see Ramirez, 2010 for higher education and Swayne, Duncan, & Ginter, 2012 for health care).

We now turn to examining the impact of "world class" and "best practices" ideas on the development of universities and of hospitals as organizations. By "impact" we mean both that these ideas are influential sources of change but also that all sorts of changes are theorized and justified by invoking "world class" and "best practices" ideas.

THE TRANSFORMATION OF UNIVERSITIES AND HOSPITALS INTO ORGANIZATIONS

Universities

Universities have evolved over time, gradually transforming from medieval assemblies of masters and scholars to national elite producing institutions to formal organizations that are expected to be both more inclusive and more useful (Pinheiro, 2012; Scott, 2006). Universities have also shifted from a more political and cultural orientation to one more linked to the economy (Slaughter & Rhoades, 2004). They are expected to be an engine of progress a source of technical innovations that meet the needs of the "knowledge society" (Temple, 2011). Universities increasingly constitute a higher education organizational field (Dimaggio, 1991) that is not limited to the national territory (for the case of Europe, see Maassen & Olsen, 2007). Core teaching and research activities are increasingly assessed through formal mechanisms influenced by standards grounded in these developments, for example, the identification of "A" journals (overwhelmingly English language dominated) as the preferred publication outlets. What is more, these mechanisms also include soliciting a greater number of external reviewers and these reviewers are expected to use transnational standards of excellence in evaluating local scholars. The latter increasingly imagine that they operate in a broader environment facing transnational standards applied to their scholarship. To reiterate, local virtue as a yardstick of excellence fades away.

Each of these transformations is well known. Access to higher education has greatly expanded in the post-World War II era (Meyer & Schofer, 2007). While this growth started earlier in the United States, by the end of the 20th century several countries had surpassed the United States in their levels of higher education enrollments and graduates (Trow & Burrage, 2010). Explanations for American distinctiveness collapsed. The more inclusive system of higher education is favored on both equity and efficacy grounds. Human capital and fairness doctrines trump earlier more elitist and more socially buffered visions of the university (Ben-David & Zloczower, 1962). Since universities are now expected to actively engage in society and economy (Stachowiak, Pinheiro, Sedini, & Vaatovaara, 2013), the boundaries between universities and other social institutions inevitably become more permeable (Colyvas & Powell, 2006). Universities are expected to function as engaged "good neighbors" (Benneworth, 2013) but also to maintain their autonomy and authority (Olsen, 2007). But the latter can no longer effectively rely on university sagas or even national culture to do so. Universities increasingly present themselves as formally rationalized organizations or suffer the risk of being dismissed as antiquarian or irrelevant.

As engines of progress, universities are often cast in economic terms (Ramirez & Tiplic, 2014). While one can imagine a "world-class university" measured by the number of dead languages its learned scribes can decipher and translate, this is not the yardstick associated with the term "world class." The latter is increasingly linked to innovations, especially in the domains of science and engineering. This is evident from the Shanghai academic ranking of world universities[6] that privileges publications in these domains. Not surprisingly, both the Massachusetts Institute of Technology and the California Institute of Technology are in the top 10 in this and in other university ranking schemes that also emphasize productivity in science and engineering. These innovations are supposed to, directly or indirectly, lead to solutions to problems: poverty, disease, illiteracy, lack of infrastructure, bad governance, inequality, and so on. These problems and their solutions are framed in trans-local idioms often best articulated by experts without borders that consult with universities.

Universities are thus embedded in a global institutional context (Frank & Gabler, 2006; Meyer, Ramirez, Frank, & Schofer, 2007) and in the case of Europe a strong regional context as well. The models of the good university fostered by experts and consultants within global and regional environments lead to much convergence on standards of excellence (Maassen & Olsen, 2007). When universities enact these standards, universities affirm their identities as formally rationalized organizations pursuing progress (Brunsson & Sahlin-Andersson, 2000), often defined as the "knowledge economy" (Rooney, Hearn, & Ninan, 2008). Furthermore, the explosion of ranking systems dramatizes what constitutes "world class" standards (Hazelkorn, 2009; Kehm & Stensaker, 2009). "World class" university consciousness is on the rise: consider the growing number of conferences, books, and government reports on "world class universities" (cf. Altbach & Salmi, 2011; Wang, Cheng, & Liu, 2013). Even under-resourced universities in less-developed countries embrace this discourse, often advertising their national, regional, and world ranking as universities (Wangenge-Ouma & Langa, 2010). Benchmarking metaphors soar and further dramatize "best practices" that need to be emulated (cf. Charles & Wilson, 2012). To be sure, these transformations generate *loose coupling* between policy talk and actual practice (Bastedo, 2007). That said, universities do undergo changes in organizational practices that make them look more like each other than in the past, setting in motion isomorphic processes (Morphew & Huisman, 2002; Pinheiro, 2013). These changes include, but are not limited to expanded enrollments (Schwartzman, Pinheiro, & Pillay, 2015), greater organizational rules and roles (Ramirez & Christensen, 2013), more connectedness both within sub-units and to other institutions (Beerkens, 2004), and enhanced centrality in societal development (Pinheiro, Benneworth, & Jones, 2012). These aspects are, in one way or another, linked to the "world class" agenda that is driven either externally (by government) or internally (by university leadership), and are thought to enhance legitimacy within the field.

Hospitals

Hospitals have probably experienced even more dramatic transformations than higher education institutions, from charitable, but dangerous guest-houses of care to centers of cure and scientific excellence and more recently a coordinating unit or node in a supposedly "integrated care" system (McKee & Healy, 2002; Risse, 1999). In most countries, hospitals have developed locally and slowly, becoming integrated in regional and national health systems. Developments in medical technologies and health sciences, in combination with new organizational paradigms, have challenged the place-bound structure of hospitals. In any given nation-state, hospitals are targeted by the international medical industry and are also included in governmental and transnational plans for research and development. There is a great deal of emphasis on developing medical innovation clusters or innovation systems that may improve the competitiveness of nation states and regions (Isaksen, 2009). There has also been a movement toward corporatization and integration of public health care institutions (Preker & Harding, 2003; Scott, Martin, Mendel, & Caronna, 2000), international re-regulation of health care systems (Wright, 2009), as well as medical tourism (Cohen, 2013).

To an even greater extent than is the case in the higher education sector, countries have adopted different models to govern access to the consumption of health care by citizens. These are expressed in some of the standard classifications of health care systems: the National Health Service (or *Beveridge*) model is characterized by universal coverage, funding out of general taxation, and public control and ownership of health care delivery (e.g., United Kingdom, New Zealand, and the Scandinavian countries). By contrast, in the social insurance (or *Bismarck*) model, compulsory, universal coverage is part of a system of social security. Health care is financed by employer and employee contributions via non-profit insurance funds, and the providers of health care are either public or private entities (e.g., Germany, Japan, and the Netherlands). Finally, the *market* model is characterized by a predominance of privately owned health care provision financed by private health insurance purchased by the employer/individuals or a combination of the two (primarily the United States but historically also Australia and Switzerland). Hybrid or mixed systems can also be found. Private and public health institutions around the world have adopted systems for accreditation, "best practices," and rankings that have initially been developed to serve North American institutions (Byrkjeflot, 2009, 2011). Indeed, the international movement toward evidence-based medicine (EBM) might be one of the strongest forces for changing organizational practices in health care (Timmermans & Berg, 2003).

EBM is the application of the scientific method in health care decision-making, which means that the health care professions have to follow guidelines for how to make such decisions at all levels based on reviews of existing research. EBM does not primarily provide a motivation or the means for becoming world class or excellent institutions but rather something like "better than average." The high status such guidelines have in the medical world is often attributed to NPM and similar reform movements, but it cannot be understood independently from the strong impetus among doctors to use science as a legitimation for what they do, although most decision-making in medicine is based on clinical judgment, not science (Montgomery, 2005). However, the strong movement toward making hospital treatment more scientific and evidence-based may rather represent a drive toward standardization rather than hospitals becoming world class. The modern hospital, which Llewellyn and Northcott (2005, p. 555) refer to as "the average hospital will be cheaper to run and easier to control than highly differentiated ones; they may also score more highly on certain measures of service improvement."

The higher costs of health care compared to higher education may lead to greater efforts to standardize health care. Furthermore, hospitals are much more "risky" institutions to be held accountable for, since potential failures are about life and death and may therefore have much more severe consequences for local as well as central placed managers and politicians. The tax burden from hospital funding also increases the pressure on the government to use statistics and numbers to show that hospital performances are improving, that the best are rewarded for their efforts, and that waste is reduced. Furthermore, the gap noted by Montgomery (2005) between *medicine as representation* (science) and *medicine as practice* makes for an interesting duality in the legitimation of what goes on in hospitals.

Assessing organizational and individual performance via indicators of "best practices" and ranking lists has become a central device of governance in health care on a worldwide scale (cf. Daniels et al., 2000). Similarly, there has been a steady increase in the number of transnational organizations and agencies involved in the production of such indicators and comparisons. Yet, with the exception of the United States, these are less oriented toward ranking individual institutions and more oriented toward ranking health care systems or particular fields of treatment domains within welfare states. Most European countries now also operate performance measurement systems that allow benchmarking of individual institutions, but the complexity associated with such measurements has still kept them away from producing common ranking systems. Reform of health care systems has become the watchword not only for the OECD and the World Bank, but also for the United Nations Children's Fund and the World Health Organization. Some of the work undertaken by such agencies, not to mention by the many international consultancy agencies, is to introduce and infuse governance models in new settings, often without taking into account the contexts in which such models were initially developed, as well as the specific contexts into which they are to be "translated" (cf. Sahlin & Wedlin, 2008). Policy makers and other influential stakeholders increasingly use international comparisons to figure out what kind of health care organization, system, or policy is most effective in meeting specified criteria (Byrkjeflot, 2009).

SUMMARIZING AND SKETCHING FUTURE RESEARCH DIRECTIONS

Universities and hospitals today are more attuned to transnational standards and practices, including those much removed from their historical legacies and organizational sagas. Higher education as an organizational field is less contained within the nation-state, whereas hospitals are for steering and financial purposes still more seen as units within regional, local, or national systems of health governance. Nevertheless, medical science and standards (e.g., EBM) and increasingly also the medical profession are internationalized and relate to international "best practice" and available evidence. Consultants without borders attend to higher education and hospitals everywhere (Wright et al., 2012). Their professional influence is evident in scripted mission statements and strategic plans. Armed with "world class" and "best practice" imaginaries, educational and health care reformers chip away at the historical distinctiveness of universities and hospitals, making attempts to transform them into formal organizational actors. Hence, a similar universalistic dynamic impinges on the respective fields, yet not necessarily with identical consequences.

A rational, instrumentalist organizational logic permeates both higher education and health sectors, giving rise to many of the common organizational developments discussed in this paper. But, at least in Western Europe, the impact of "best practices" on hospitals does not give rise to an organizational field with the same *competition ethos* that characterizes higher education. The reason for this may be found in the different purposes of the two sectors. The purpose of most hospitals is not to attract international patients, but rather to treat patients within a particular geographical area, for the most part within the nation-state or the region. Patients are not as mobile as students. Students are much easier to attract on an international scale. Garman and Johnson (2015) contend that rather little has been achieved in international benchmarking of hospitals, and that this may be because the metrics are structured for within-country comparisons. Unless hospitals seek to attract international patients, which they seldom do, except in elite hospitals in the United States, they have no interest in developing cross-national comparative data. Furthermore, the international epistemic community related to the health systems tend to give priority to *health* rather than *health care*, which means that the emphasis is on health statistics on a national level and related to population rather than to hospitals' performance. Furthermore, it should be noted that it is a quite different task to measure whether a medical procedure/operation has been a success than assessing whether a graduate from a university has become a more skilled person. So, it would appear that the metrics of best practices in the two sectors pose different challenges. Perhaps that is why the "world class" mantra is more pronounced as regards universities when compared to hospitals, and that the use of the terms "evidence-based practices" or "best practices" are less prevalent in universities (albeit not entirely absent) than in hospitals (van Lent et al., 2010).

Further studies are needed to gauge commonalities and differences in the ways in which educational and health sectors are influenced and transformed by transnational forces for benchmarking, standardization, and discourses of excellence. In what follows we briefly sketch some of these research directions. First, and perhaps most obviously, one can examine the degree to which terms like "world class" and "best practices" appear in university and hospital statements regarding goals, missions, and strategic plans. This calls for longitudinal research to see if these terms appear increasingly over time. One can also undertake the same research but now focusing on the educational and health ministries as the units of analysis. If we, in fact, live in an age of "world class" and "best practices," one should expect a greater number of universities and hospitals as well as educational and health ministries to use this language in order to make sense of changes in organizations and organizational fields. This, in turn, raises a number of pertinent questions for future investigation: What are the templates for the excellent university and how are these similar to or different from templates for the excellent hospital? Who travels where to learn from whom in these fields? How are these global templates locally adopted (by the so-called "rationalizers") and, consequently, how are they diffused or institutionalized throughout the organization and/or (domestic) organizational field? Are the older institutions more likely to resist pressures to become organizational actors? Is age or prestige or level of resources the more crucial predictor of early adoption? Does national context matter? Are some national borders more permeable than others? And if that is the case, what are the characteristics of these countries that either allow them to resist or to embrace the impact of global pressures toward organizational rationalization?

Such research endeavors would allow us to gauge the rate of change as well as cast light on the underlying conditions in which some organizations are more likely to adopt, early on, this type of language and, in turn, infuse it as part and parcel of formal rules and standard operating procedures. Further, such inquiries would also permit us to distinguish between what is taking place in higher education and universities from what occurs in health and hospitals. That is, we could formally ascertain whether "world class" is preferred in educational rather than in health discourse where "best practices" talk may prevail. Is there a clash between the imagery of continuous innovation and the idea of benchmarking or are they combined in creative ways? At risk or event history analyses are now common in social science research (Bucheli & Wadhwani, 2013), including cross-national analyses (Schwartzman et al., 2015). We propose such analyses to tackle the questions we and other scholars have raised regarding the changing character of universities and hospitals as organizations (structures) and institutions (rules). The role of mergers and international alliances in the development and translation of new organizational paradigms (Pinheiro, Aarevaara, Berg, Geschwind, & Torjesen, forthcoming) may also be a useful avenue to approach such critical questions.

This research direction calls for quantitative studies, preferably across national contexts, to see whether similar or different dynamics are at work. That being said, talk or discourse analysis clearly calls for more than examining the appearance of some key words in isolation. A second line of research could examine whether, over time, some words are more likely to be used in tandem with other words. For example, do references to "world class" increasingly co-vary with references to international standards or even to international competitors? How do institutions relate to the paradoxical relation between making use of best practice standards that everyone has access to and becoming world class or excellent? Do "best practices" references co-vary with emphases on accountability and/or transparency? How are the terms "science" and "scientific" used in these discourses? Is evidence-based management and medicine part of the discourse of world class or is it an alternative? The goal here is to see whether a more fleshed out organizational commitment to excellence and benchmarking discourse takes place over time. Here again there may be variations in discourse across both organizational fields and national societies. The terms "world class" and "best practices" may go together more so in the United States than in Western Europe across both organizational fields. If this is indeed the case, it would suggest that sector differences between higher education and health care continue to be more consequential in Western Europe. This would further suggest that institutional distinctiveness was less established in the United States and that organizational rationalization was more prevalent therein. We expect organizational commitment to excellence discourse to emerge and get more established over time. The proposed network or cluster analysis will directly examine this expectation. With data over time one can ascertain the degree to which differences in historical roots continue to manifest themselves in linkages between the uses of "world class" and "best practices" imaginaries. Or, alternatively, whether these historical differences fade.

A third and related line of inquiry might examine what a range of actors think of when they reflect on excellence in universities and hospitals. This research would focus on sense-making activities (Weick, 1995, 2009), paying special attention to the uses of the terms "world class" and "best practices." One should expect to find a greater range of actors making use of these terms but meanings may vary across actors as well as across situations. Here what is called for is qualitative research that engages different kinds of actors in different situations. These actors would include consultants, ministry officials, administrators, professors, and doctors, as well as students and patients. In this inquiry, the issue is not mainly frequency of use, though some actors are more likely to invoke "world class" and "best practices" than others; perhaps university and hospital administrators are more attuned to these terms than professors and doctors. But the fine-grained questions center on what these terms mean to different actors in different situations. In the context of a national research assessment exercise, especially a high stakes one in which "winners" are more rewarded, one would expect more agreement across actors on the need to commit to excellence and to assess movement toward excellence. Under an influential evaluative gun, everyone "performs" excellence. But as the context or situation changes, there is more space for skepticism and some actors may be more prompt to "perform" skepticism. Part of this research endeavor thus involves identifying different situations that are likely to sensitize different actors to the transnational emphasis on world class and best practices. Sense-making may be situation sensitive, be these national, sectoral, or institutional situations.

Finally, one can rather directly ask key actors what these terms mean to them and their organizations or organizational fields. These actors can be individually interviewed, or more interestingly, the use of focus groups can be undertaken to gauge meanings. Does the sense-making vary when doctors or professors talk in a group of others like themselves as opposed to a more heterogeneous group where other kinds of actors are present? The point of this line of research is to ascertain whether there are some core understandings that are stable regardless of the composition of the focus group. If there are such understandings but if there are also some meanings that vary, this inquiry may shed light on which understandings prevail across groups and situations. This finding in turn may open the door to further studies that seek to explain why some meaning constellations are more pervasive than others.

Taken as a whole these research directions address the core ideas advanced in this paper. They will allow us to gauge the rate of change in the adoption of policy talk between sectors and across countries. They will further allow us to ascertain what national and organizational properties favor or hinder discursive adoptions. They will facilitate our understanding of whether the policy talk becomes more coherent over time and whether some meanings are more stable across actors and situations. These studies will leverage both the more quantitative approaches of neo-institutionalists who study diffusion processes and the more qualitative research of those who focus on translation. This two-pronged strategy will shed light on both common trends and variable outcomes in the transformation of universities and hospitals in the age of "world class" and "best practices."

NOTES

1. As a comparative point of reference, the terms "excellence" and "efficiency" – also widely used across both sectors – delivered 298 million and 350 million hits, respectively.
2. Online at: http://www.merriam-webster.com/dictionary/world%20class
3. Online at: http://www.oxforddictionaries.com/definition/english/best-practice
4. Online at: http://www.globalbenchmarking.ipk.fraunhofer.de/benchmarking/
5. We would like to thank Karsten Vrangbæk for drawing our attention for this critical distinction.
6. Online at: http://www.shanghairanking.com/

REFERENCES

Aksnes, D., Benner, M., Brorstad Borlaug, S., Hansen, H., Kallerud, E., Kristiansen, E., … Sivertsen, G. (2012). *Centres of Excellence in the Nordic countries: A comparative study of research excellence policy and excellence centre schemes in Denmark, Finland, Norway and Sweden*. Working Paper 4/2012.

Altbach, P. G., & Salmi, J. (2011). *The road to academic excellence: The making of world-class research universities*. Washington, DC: World Bank Publications.

Andersen, A., Heibeler, R., Kelly, T. B., & Ketteman, C. (2000). *Best practices: Building your business with customer-focused solutions*. New York, NY: Touchstone.

Bartlett, C., & Gosha, S. (1999). Managing across borders: The transnational solution. *American Foreign Policy Interests*, *21*, 20–22.

Bastedo, M. N. (2007). Sociological frameworks for higher education policy research. In P. J. Gumport (Ed.), *Sociology of higher education: Contributions and their contexts*. Baltimore, MD: Johns Hopkins University Press.

Beerkens, E. (2004). *Global opportunities and institutional embeddedness: Higher education consortia in Europe and Southeast Asia*. Unpublished doctoral dissertation, University of Twente.

Ben-David, J., & Zloczower, A. (1962). Universities and academic systems in modern societies. *European Journal of Sociology*, *3*(1), 45–85.

Benneworth, P. (2013). *University engagement with socially excluded communities*. Dordrecht: Springer.

Bragg, S. M. (2010). *Accounting best practices*. Hoboken, NJ: Wiley.

Brunsson, N., & Sahlin-Andersson, K. (2000). Constructing organizations: The example of public sector reform. *Organization Studies*, *21*, 721–746.

Bucheli, M., & Wadhwani, R. D. (2013). *Organizations in time: History, theory, methods.* Oxford: Oxford University Press.
Byrkjeflot, H. (2009). Comparing worlds of welfare and systems of healthcare – Lessons from recent research on hospital reforms and healthcare systems. In *Healthcare systems and medical institutions* (pp. 13–32). Oslo: Novus Forlag.
Byrkjeflot, H. (2011). Healthcare states and medical professions: The challenges from new public management. In T. Christensen & P. Lægreid (Eds.), *The Ashgate research companion to new public management* (pp. 147–161). Aldershot: Ashgate.
Byrkjeflot, H., & Angell, S. I. (2007). Dressing up hospitals as enterprises? The expansion and managerialization of communication in Norwegian hospitals. In *Mediating business, the expansion of business journalism*. Copenhagen: Copenhagen Business School Press.
Byrkjeflot, H., Christensen, T., & Lægreid, P. (2014). The many faces of accountability: Comparing reforms in welfare, hospitals and migration. *Scandinavian Political Studies, 37*, 171–195.
Charles, D., & Wilson, B. (2012). Managing regional engagement: The role of benchmarking. In R. Pinheiro, P. Benneworth, & G. A. Jones (Eds.), *Universities and regional development: A critical assessment of tensions and contradictions*. New York, NY: Routledge.
Christensen, T., & Lægreid, P. (2001). *New public management: The transformation of ideas and practice*. Ann Arbor, MI: Ashgate.
Clark, B. (1972). The organizational saga in higher education. *Administrative Science Quarterly, 17*, 178–184.
Clark, B. R. (1970). *The distinctive college*. New Brunswick, NJ: Transaction Publishers.
Clark, B. R. (1978). Academic differentiation in national systems of higher education. *Comparative Education Review, 22*, 242–258.
Clark, B. R. (1998). *Creating entrepreneurial universities: Organizational pathways of transformation*. New York, NY: Pergamon.
Clark, B. R. (2004). *Sustaining change in universities: Continuities in case studies and concepts.* London: Society for Research into Higher Education and Open University Press.
Claxton, K., Sculpher, M., & Drummond, M. (2002). A rational framework for decision making by the National Institute for Clinical Excellence (NICE). *The Lancet, 360*, 711–715.
Cohen, I. G. (2013). Transplant tourism: The ethics and regulation of international markets for organs. *The Journal of Law, Medicine & Ethics, 41*(1), 269–285.
Colyvas, J. A., & Powell, W. W. (2006). Roads to institutionalization: The remaking of boundaries between public and private science. *Research in Organizational Behavior, 27*, 305–353.
Czarniawska-Joerges, B., & Sevón, G. (2005). *Global ideas: How ideas, objects and practices travel in a global economy*. Copenhagen: Liber and Copenhagen Business School Press.
Daniels, N., Bryant, J., Castano, R. A., Dantes, O. G., Khan, K. S., & Pannarunothai, S. (2000). Benchmarks of fairness for health care reform: A policy tool for developing countries. *Bulletin of the World Health Organization, 78*, 740–750.
Deem, R. (1998). 'New managerialism' and higher education: The management of performances and cultures in universities in the United Kingdom. *International Studies in Sociology of Education, 8*, 47–70.
Deem, R. (2001). Globalisation, new managerialism, academic capitalism and entrepreneurialism in universities: Is the local dimension still important? *Comparative Education, 37*, 7–20.

Dimaggio, P. (1991). Constructing an organizational field as a professional project: US art museums, 1920–1940. In W. W. Powell & P. Dimaggio (Eds.), *The new institutionalism in organizational analysis*. Chicago, IL: University of Chicago Press.

Drori, G. S., Meyer, J. W., & Hwang, H. (2006). *Globalization and organization: World society and organizational change*. Oxford: Oxford University Press.

Drori, I., & Honig, B. (2013). A process model of internal and external legitimacy. *Organization Studies*, *34*, 345–376.

Enders, J., Kehm, B., & Schimank, U. (2015). Turning universities into actors on quasi-markets: How new public management reforms affect academic research. In D. Jansen & I. Pruisken (Eds.), *The changing governance of higher education and research* (pp. 89–103). Cham, Switzerland: Springer International Publishing.

Evleth, D. (1995). Vichy France and the continuity of medical nationalism. *Social History of Medicine*, *8*(1), 95–116.

Foss, N. J. (1997). *Resources, firms, and strategies: A reader in the resource-based perspective*. Oxford: Oxford University Press.

Frank, D. J., & Gabler, J. (2006). *Reconstructing the university: Worldwide shifts in academia in the 20th century*. Stanford, CA: Stanford University Press.

Fumasoli, T., Pinheiro, R., & Stensaker, B. (2015). Handling uncertainty of strategic ambitions: The use of organizational identity as a risk-reducing device. *International Journal of Public Administration*. [Online first]. doi:10.1080/01900692.2014.988868

Garman, A. N., & Johnson, T. J. (2015). Defining world-class care in academic medicine: Enablers and challenges. In S. C. Buttigieg, C. Rathert, & W. Von Eiff (Eds.), *International best practices in health care management* (Vol. 17, pp. 23–29). Advances in Health Care Management. Bingley, UK: Emerald Group Publishing Limited.

Gerschel, A., & Polsky, L. (2013). *Rapid retooling: Developing world-class organizations in a rapidly changing world*. Alexandria, VA: American Society for Training and Development.

Goes, J., Savage, G. T., & Friedman, L. H. (2015). International "Best Practices" in health care: The roles of context and innovation. In S. C. Buttigieg, C. Rathert, & W. Von Eiff (Eds.), *International best practices in health care management* (Vol. 17, pp. 31–35). Advances in Health Care Management. Bingley, UK: Emerald Group Publishing Limited.

Grant, R. M. (2003). Strategic planning in a turbulent environment: Evidence from the oil majors. *Strategic Management Journal*, *24*, 491–517.

Hazelkorn, H. (2009). Rankings and the battle for world-class excellence: Institutional strategies and policy choice. *Higher Education Management and Policy*, *21*, 1–22.

Heidemann, E. G. (2000). Moving to global standards for accreditation processes: The expert project in a larger context. *International Journal for Quality in Health Care*, *12*, 227–230.

Hetherington, R. W. (1991). The effects of formalization on departments of a multi-hospital system. *Journal of Management Studies*, *28*, 103–142.

High, P. A. (2009). *World class IT: Why businesses succeed when IT triumphs*. San Francisco, CA: Jossey-Bass.

Isaksen, A. (2009). Innovation dynamics of global competitive regional clusters: The case of the Norwegian centres of expertise. *Regional Studies*, *43*, 1155–1166.

Kehm, B. M., & Stensaker, B. (2009). *University rankings, diversity, and the new landscape of higher education*. Rotterdam: Sense Publishers.

Kipping, M., & Wright, C. (2012). Consultants in context: Global dominance, societal effect, and the capitalist system. In T. Clark & M. Kipping (Eds.), *The Oxford handbook of management consulting* (pp. 165–185). Oxford: Oxford University Press.

Krücken, G. (2003). Learning the 'new, new thing': On the role of path dependency in university structures. *Higher Education*, *46*, 315–339.

Krücken, G., & Meier, F. (2006). Turning the university into an organizational actor. In G. S. Drori, J. W. Meyer, & H. Hwang (Eds.), *Globalization and organization: World society and organizational change* (pp. 241–257). Oxford: Oxford University Press.

Llewellyn, S., & Northcott, D. (2005). The average hospital. *Accounting, Organizations and Society*, *30*, 555–583.

Maassen, P., & Olsen, J. P. (2007). *University dynamics and European integration*. Dordrecht: Springer.

Marquardt, M. J. (1999). *The global advantage: How world-class organizations improve performance through globalization*. Houston, TX: Gulf Publishing.

Martinsen, D. S., & Vrangbæk, K. (2008). The Europeanization of health care governance: Implementing the market imperatives of Europe. *Public Administration*, *86*, 169–184.

McKee, M., & Healy, J. (2002). The significance of hospitals: An introduction. In M. Mckee & J. Healy (Eds.), *Hospitals in a changing Europe* (pp. 3–13). Buckingham: Open University Press.

Meyer, J. W., Ramirez, F. O., Frank, D. J., & Schofer, E. (2007). Higher education as an institution. In P. Gumport (Ed.), *Sociology of higher education: Contributions and their context*. Baltimore, MD: Johns Hopkins University Press.

Meyer, J. W., & Schofer, E. (2007). The university in Europe and the world: Twentieth century expansion. In G. Krücken, A. Kosmützky, & M. Tork (Eds.), *Towards a multiversity? Universities between global trends and national traditions*. Berlin: Transcript-Verlag.

Montgomery, K. (2005). *How doctors think: Clinical judgment and the practice of medicine*. Oxford: Oxford University Press.

Morphew, C., & Huisman, J. (2002). Using institutional theory to reframe research on academic drift. *Higher Education in Europe*, *27*, 491–506.

Musselin, C. (2000). *The role of ideas in the emergence of convergent higher education policies in Europe: The case of France*. Working Paper Series, Center for European Studies, Harvard University.

Oakland, J. S. (2001). *Total organizational excellence: Achieving world-class performance*. Oxford: Routledge.

Oertel, S., & Soll, M. (2015). The transformaiton of German universities. Paper presented at the Comparative Workshop in the Graduate School of Education, Stanford University.

Olsen, J. P. (2007). The institutional dynamics of the European university. In P. Maassen & J. P. Olsen (Eds.), *University dynamics and European integration*. Dordrecht: Springer.

Pfeffer, J., & Salancik, G. R. (2003). *The external control of organizations: A resource dependence perspective*. Stanford, CA: Stanford Business Books.

Pinheiro, R. (2012). *In the region, for the region? A comparative study of the institutionalisation of the regional mission of universities*. Oslo: University of Oslo.

Pinheiro, R. (2013). Bridging the local with the global: Building a new university on the fringes of Europe. *Tertiary Education and Management*, *19*, 144–160.

Pinheiro, R. (2015). Humboldt meets Schumpeter? Interpreting the 'entrepreneurial turn' in European higher education. In S. Slaughter & B. J. Taylor (Eds.), *Competitive advantage: Stratification, privatization and vocationalization of higher education in the US, EU, and Canada*. Dordrecht: Springer.

Pinheiro, R., Aarevaara, T., Berg, E., Geschwind, L., & Torjesen, D. O. (forthcoming). Strategic mergers in the public sector: Comparing universities and hospitals. In S. Tarba, R. Cooper, & C. Sarala (Eds.), *Mergers and acquisitions in practice*. London: Routledge.

Pinheiro, R., Benneworth, P., & Jones, G. A. (Eds.). (2012). *Universities and regional development: A critical assessment of tensions and contradictions*. New York, NY: Routledge.

Pinheiro, R., & Stensaker, B. (2014). Designing the entrepreneurial university: The interpretation of a global idea. *Public Organization Review*, *14*, 497–516.

Preker, A. S., & Harding, A. (2003). A conceptual framework for the organizational reforms of hospitals. In A. S. Preker & A. Harding (Eds.), *Innovations in health service delivery: The corporatization of public hospitals*. Washington, DC: The World Bank.

Ramirez, F. O. (2010). Accounting for excellence: Transforming universities into organizational actors. In L. Portnoi, V. Rust, & S. Bagely (Eds.), *Higher education, policy, and the global competition phenomenon* (pp. 43–58). Basingstoke: Palgrave.

Ramirez, F., & Tiplic, D. (2014). In pursuit of excellence? Discursive patterns in European higher education research. *Higher Education*, *67*, 439–455.

Ramirez, F. O., & Christensen, T. (2013). The formalization of the university: Rules, roots, and routes. *Higher Education*, *65*, 695–708.

Redecker, C., Ala-Mutka, K., & Punie, Y. (2010). Learning 2.0 – The impact of social media on learning in Europe. Policy brief. JRC Scientific and Technical Report. EUR JRC56958 EN. Retrieved from http://bit.ly/cljlpq. Accessed on February 6, 2011.

Reisner, E. H. (1927). *Nationalism and education since 1789*. New York, NY: MacMillan.

Risse, G. B. (1999). *Mending bodies, saving souls: A history of hospitals*. New York, NY: Oxford University Press.

Rooney, D., Hearn, G., & Ninan, A. (2008). *Handbook on the knowledge economy*. Cheltenham: Edward Elgar.

Sahlin-Andersson, K., & Engwall, L. (2002). *The expansion of management knowledge: Carriers, flows, and sources*. Stanford, CA: Stanford University Press.

Sahlin, K., & Wedlin, L. (2008). Circulating ideas: Imitation, translation and editing. In R. Greenwood, K. Sahlin-Andersson, & R. Suddaby (Eds.), *The Sage handbook of organizational institutionalism* (pp. 218–242). London: Sage.

Schwartzman, S., Pinheiro, R., & Pillay, P. (2015). *Higher education in the BRICS countries: Investigating the pact between higher education and society*. Dordrecht: Springer.

Scott, J. (2006). The mission of the university: Medieval to postmodern transformations. *The Journal of Higher Education*, *77*(1), 1–39.

Scott, W. R. (2008). *Institutions and organizations: Ideas and interests*. London: Sage.

Scott, W. R., Martin, R., Mendel, P. J., & Caronna, C. A. (2000). *Institutional change in healthcare organizations: From professional dominance to managed care*. Chicago, IL: University of Chicago Press.

Secord, H. (2003). *Implementing best practices in human resources management*. Toronto: CCH Canadian.

Slaughter, S., & Rhoades, G. (2004). *Academic capitalism and the new economy: Markets, state, and higher education*. Baltimore, MD: Johns Hopkins University Press.

Sollish, F., & Semanik, J. (2011). *Strategic global sourcing best practices*. New York, NY: Wiley.

Stachowiak, K., Pinheiro, R., Sedini, C., & Vaatovaara, M. (2013). Policies aimed at strengthening the ties between universities and cities. In S. Musterd & Z. Kovács (Eds.), *Place-making and policies for competitive cities*. London: Blackwell.

Starr, P. (1982). *The social transformation of American medicine*. New York, NY: Basic Books.

Stensaker, B., & Norgård, J. D. (2001). Innovation and isomorphism: A case-study of university identity struggle 1969–1999. *Higher Education*, *42*, 473–492.

Swayne, L. E., Duncan, W. J., & Ginter, P. M. (2012). *Strategic management of health care organizations*. New York, NY: Wiley.

Temple, P. (2011). *Universities in the knowledge economy: Higher education organisation and global change*. London: Taylor & Francis.

Thornton, P. H., Ocasio, W., & Lounsbury, M. (2012). *The institutional logics perspective: A new approach to culture, structure, and process*. Oxford: Oxford University Press.

Timmermans, S., & Berg, M. (2003). The practice of medical technology. *Sociology of Health & Illness*, *25*(3), 97–114.

Trow, M., & Burrage, M. (2010). *Twentieth-century higher education: Elite to mass to universal*. Baltimore, MD: Johns Hopkins University Press.

US Army. (1996). *World-class research and development: Characteristics for an army research, development, and engineering organization*. Washington, DC: National Academies Press.

van Lent, W. A., de Beer, R. D., & van Harten, W. H. (2010). International benchmarking of specialty hospitals. A series of case studies on comprehensive cancer centres. *BMC Health Services Research*, *10*(1), 253.

Voelker, K. E., Rakich, J. S., & French, G. R. (2001). The balanced scorecard in healthcare organizations: A performance measurement and strategic planning methodology. *Hospital Topics*, *79*, 13–24.

Walgenbach, P., & Hegele, C. (2001). What can an apple learn from an orange? Or: What do companies use benchmarking for? *Organization*, *8*(1), 121–144.

Wang, Q., Cheng, Y., & Liu, N. C. (2013). *Building world-class universities: Different approaches to a shared goal*. Rotterdam: Sense Publishers.

Wangenge-Ouma, G., & Langa, P. (2010). Universities and the mobilization of claims of excellence for competitive advantage. *Higher Education*, *59*, 749–764.

Weick, K. E. (1995). *Sensemaking in organizations*. London: Sage.

Weick, K. E. (2009). *Making sense of the organization*. Chichester: Wiley.

Wellstein, B., & Kieser, A. (2011). Trading "best practices"—A good practice? *Industrial and Corporate Change*, *20*(3), 683–719.

Wright, C., Sturdy, A., & Wylie, N. (2012). Management innovation through standardization: Consultants as standardizers of organizational practice. *Research Policy*, *41*(3), 652–662.

Wright, J. S. F. (2009). The regulatory state and the UK Labour Government's re-regulation of provision in the English National Health Service. *Regulation and Governance*, *3*, 334–359.

REFORMED OR DEFORMED? THE UNENDING RENEWAL OF THE PUBLIC UNIVERSITY BETWEEN UNINTENDED CONSEQUENCES AND UNEXPECTED CHALLENGES

Jürgen Deeg

ABSTRACT

University reforms have been pervasive in European higher education over decades. Analyses of these reforms are still incomplete, however. To find a more comprehensive approach in explaining the relentless transformation of public universities, this paper suggests a novel, interactionist point of view. Drawing on ideational aspects of universities as institutions, the paper first explores the differentiation of basic, influential ideas of change. A recently developed typology is then used to further elaborate upon the composition and relation of these ideas. Finally, evidence is provided that supports a non-linear dynamic consisting of reciprocal influences, which overall indicates a recursive

Towards a Comparative Institutionalism: Forms, Dynamics and Logics Across the Organizational Fields of Health Care and Higher Education
Research in the Sociology of Organizations, Volume 45, 59–80

ISSN: 0733-558X/doi:10.1108/S0733-558X20150000045014

contingency between institutional context and coexistent frames of change.

Keywords: Frames of change; institutional transformation; interactionist approach; recursive contingency; university reform

INTRODUCTION

In recent decades, manifold changes in the national and global political, social, cultural, and economic context have initiated a widespread restructuring of the European higher education sector and its institutions (cf. Bolden, Petrov, & Gosling, 2008). This transformation process, being primarily tangent to technical and administrative functions as well as to teaching in many respects, does not leave the organization of academic research untouched anymore (e.g., Whitley & Gläser, 2007). It thus contributes to the overall process of "tightening up of loose coupling" in the organization(s) of higher education (cf. Lutz, 1982). All respective reform efforts have been based on the idea that the adaptability of universities to an ever rapidly changing, dynamic and globalized environment needs to be enhanced. Accordingly, the organizational restructuring of public universities – like other typical change approaches and strategies in higher education (cf. Bolden et al., 2008, p. 26) – has followed the dual imperatives of governmental regulation and market pressures. However, in contrast to the apparently cohesive ideology of Neo-Liberalism and New Managerialism (cf. Deem & Brehony, 2005) as main drivers of these processes, the results of university reforms have been rather inconsistent and unsettled. Hence, many and manifold forms (and faces or facets) of reform exist, due to the diversity of influencing forces (cf. Christopher, 2012) and differing pathways of development (cf. Pritchard, 2011).

Against this backdrop, the transformation of the field of higher education is often conceived as an exemplary case of a concomitant institutional transformation, that is, the transformation of the university institution (e.g., Frølich, Huisman, Slipersæter, Stensaker, & Pimentel Botas, 2013). Typically, such approaches are based on the assumption of a close connection between the field-specific dynamic and direction and the institutional dynamic constituted by the diffusion and adoption of a certain kind of (institutional) logic (Lounsbury & Boxenbaum, 2013; Thornton, Ocasio, & Lounsbury, 2012). However, given the increasing non-linearity in the dynamics of change, the linearity in the mode of action underlying typical arguments of cross-sectorial transgression and transformation might be, at least in part, a misrepresentation of the actual nature of change (cf. Bromley & Meyer, 2014). For instance, Bromley and Powell (2012), after delineating and discussing different forms of decoupling depicted in hierarchically ordered ways of unidirectional influence (pp. 491, 497), nevertheless argue for an extension of the approach through feedback processes, so far poorly understood from their point of view. While robust evidence on how in turn institutional responses shape the field is fairly limited, Frølich et al. (2013) consequently conclude that it is a "continuing challenge for higher education research [...] to build and renew the analytical bridges between environmental changes and organisational dynamics" (p. 80). Particularly against the powerful image of "institutional imperialism" (Meyer & Höllerer, 2014, p. 3), that is, the conquest of institutional spheres by extraneous rationalities or organizational forms, reciprocal or interactionist explanatory models are still rare at the moment. Accordingly, Deroy and Clegg (2015) have recently called for introducing the concept of *recursive contingency* into institutional theory in order to make significant improvements in theorizing institutional change and transformation. By joining US institutional theory with German social theory of Luhmann (1995), the authors intend to improve analyzing and explaining change both in pluralistic organizations and in multiple institutional systems. With this in mind, it appears worthwhile to apply such an approach to public universities as higher education institutions as these are exhibiting both features at the same time and thus form a truly unique object of study.

Evidently, university reforms are a natural subject for institutional analysis and theory. At the same time, these reforms have multiple angles and avenues that can give rise to exploring different lines of thought and argument. Apart from the typical focus on the translation of exogenous patterns into endogenous processes and structures, particularly a closer look at the *mobilizing potential*, that is, the forces that create and modify the dynamics of both institutions and their fields (cf. Meyer, 2010), might be worth considering. For that purpose, the *ideational aspects of institutions* serve as a reasonable starting point, as the "structure of ideas and their proliferation" are regarded as important foci in studies of institutional development and change (Lewis & Steinmo, 2012, p. 335). In general, this would imply targeting main ideas ("*Leitideen*") at the inter-institutional level (Meyer & Höllerer, 2014, p. 6), providing whole societies with guidance via value orientations and criteria of rationality. More specifically, (cognitive) frames function as the very basic fabric of institutions (*constituent*) as well a driving force ("*movens*") in institutional development and evolution (Werner & Cornelissen, 2014, pp. 1451, 1467; see also Berger & Luckmann, 1966 for prioritizing previously the cognitive over the normative aspect as starting point of institutional development). In general, such frames are used to explore vertical linkages between a macro-social level of cognitive schemas and a micro-level of individual actors (Werner & Cornelissen, 2014, p. 1453). However, in order to take a novel path, a horizontal perspective is preferred at this point, combined with a closer examination of the contents of scripts and their interaction.

The overall purpose of this paper is to contribute to the *theory of institutional development* by focusing on *basic ideas of change* underlying university reforms and shaping their potential impact. These ideas are interpreted as being part of the *institutional change context* (see Andrews, 2013, pp. 41–59), which is crucial for the resulting impact of institutional reforms. In particular, such ideas can be seen as *initiators* of processes capable of institutional transformation (cf. Deroy & Clegg, 2015, p. 76), while being non-deterministic in their effects. As a consequence thereof, institutional dynamics are conceived as a *qualitative development* characterized by emergent properties. Accordingly, cumulative and intermittent, conjunctive and disjunctive processes can be observed (see Bergek & Onufrey, 2014). In such cases, change takes place both between coexisting ideas and the creation of novel, radically different ideas. Apart from their need of interpretation, ideas can be characterized according to their impact on (the change of) institutional design through their interdependence and recursiveness – similar to the relations between actors making use of them (cf. Murdoch & Gays, 2014). This implies that existent ideas are, at least in part, influenced by their precursors, which concurrently constitutes the interplay of ideas. Further, an initial idea that is transformed later on might in turn affect the original idea due to its revised content (i.e., having a recursive influence). Consequently, contexts of institutional change are probably never an empty space or *tabula rasa*. Rather, they represent a fairly differentiated and difficult terrain, filled with relational forces. Due to the fact that inter-relatedness can be given both diachronically and synchronically (Meyer & Höllerer, 2014, p. 8) and can be studied by retrospective and prospective glances (Deroy & Clegg, 2015, p. 74), fairly different avenues of analysis exist.

In order to realize the intent of the paper, the analysis subsequently carried out is based on two successive steps: First, the differentiation of ideas of change underlying university reform is explored in more detail. Starting with the basic idea of reforms, two further extensions are identified – namely reforming the public university via the concept of New Public Management and, then the idea of the entrepreneurial university as a new self-proclaimed "pathway of transformation" (cf. Clark, 1998). In this way, different fields of research and strands of discussion, which have thus far remained largely discrete and separate from one another, are successively analyzed. The depiction given in this section is based on existent literature, and at the end, it is considered to which extent the potential of a recursive contingency is already incorporated. Second, the core ideational elements of the three basic ideas of change, being central results of the initial differentiation, are then compared and analyzed. To this end, a typology recently proposed by Werner and Cornelissen (2014) is used to demonstrate the composition and relation of these ideas. From this, it emerges that the dynamics of university reforms can be delineated as a multifarious development. Specifically, it can be demonstrated how basic ideas of change, serving as drivers of institutional development via respective frames, are generating cumulative and intermittent as well as conjunctive and disjunctive movements. Some inherent limitations of the typology used are then briefly discussed, and important results and implications of the analysis are pointed out, while different interpretations of the overall picture are compared. Finally, the paper returns to a more fundamental vantage point, drawing general conclusions regarding institutional reform.

THE DIFFERENTIATION OF IDEAS OF CHANGE

In general, it is beyond debate that university reforms are a recurrent phenomenon (Wright & Rabo, 2010, p. 1). Unsurprisingly, changes to the governance and management of higher education institutions inclusive of their reasons and effects have been the subject of a vast discourse and numerous studies over the last 30 years (Jones, 2014, p. 129). While it is beyond the scope of this paper to give a complete and detailed analysis, the debate can be characterized by two extreme positions: First, there is a notion in literature that universities are in a state of constant change (e.g., Altmann & Ebersberger, 2013). Such continuous change, having taken place ever since their inception in medieval times, is interpreted as an unmediated response to changing societal, economic, and political contexts. This argument is usually exemplified by looking at major changes in the university system (cf. Brockliss, 2000). From this point of view, institutional reforms are common and similar, despite that they occur in different cases or take shape in varying contexts (see Andrews, 2013, p. 7) – ultimately becoming almost routine (cf. Brunsson, 2009). Moreover, their impact is sometimes regarded as fairly limited. For example, Maassen et al. (2012, p. 9) have noted that several decades of reform have seemingly not resulted in a comprehensive transformation in European higher education. While in this perspective university reforms are often depicted as a kind of gradual, additive change hardly affecting institutional persistency (Manhart, 2014, p. 265) or resilience (cf. Olsen, 2007; Wittrock, 1985), the cumulated effects of various interrelated (re-)reforms are considered as having a greater impact in the long run (see also Deem, Hillyard, & Reed, 2007, pp. 24–25). Finally, the "nothing much has changed" position has overlooked the extraordinary growth of universities and university enrollments in Europe and throughout the world (Schofer & Meyer, 2005).

The opposite position claims that the present "reform movement" is far beyond an episodic nature of change and that the reiteration of reform initiatives has actually led to a permanent continuation of reforms (e.g., Hoyle & Wallace, 2007). With that said, the novel character and pervasive influence (see Andrews, 2013, p. 4) of the "frenzy of university reforms" (Wright & Rabo, 2010, p. 1) is regularly stressed. Also, as reforms are in many cases prone to the non-attainment of goals (e.g., Boucher, 2011), they are perceived as "unfinished business" (Hoyle & Wallace, 2007, p. 10) stimulating a relentless reiteration. In the end, every "new" reform starts at the (presumed) deficits of the last reform, giving only the occasional opportunity to further reforms (Boyer, 2009, p. 76). From this point of view, reforms consist of a vicious circle of readapting, rearranging, or restarting purposes over and over again, while either exhibiting no substantial effects or even aggravating problems and complicating the situation. For example, de Boer, Enders, and Leisyte (2007) have illustrated how various reforms and re-reforms in Dutch higher education – stepping back and forward – created a compound jumble of reforms in effect. Hence frequently, destructive effects of excessive reforming are highlighted. These are not only weakening the substance of universities as institutions, but while undermining their identity and diminishing their impact, endangering higher education in its entirety (e.g., Alvesson, 2013).

In this context, it might be helpful to reconsider the basic idea of reforms in order to disentangle the complex discussion on this matter. In retrospect, the idea of reforms seems to have been a constant companion of the public university for most of the 20th century, apparently intensifying with accelerated societal change and technical progress toward its end. Nevertheless, university reforms represent a specific idea of change as they are enacted or initialized in order to remedy detected shortcomings (Kieser, 2012, p. 245). These can be given either in society as such or in its specific subsystems or sectors with their specific institutions and organizations. In this regard, public universities, like other organizations, were typically conceived of as subunits of the national state (Meyer, 2009, p. 254) and thus represented a fundamental object of reform efforts. Regardless of whether reforms were intended for an adaptation to changed realities or to new ideas (Luhmann, 2006, p. 336), the root of problems has equally been seen as located in the institutional design itself (cf. Arellano-Gault & Lepore, 2011, p. 1033) inducing the need of its restructuring. As a consequence of this approach, reforms mainly consist of conscious design efforts that are based on goal directedness, future orientation, and planning. Under these circumstances, the change of structures is regarded as a means or procedure holding out prospects of a better future (Luhmann, 2006, p. 339). Additionally, this aspired-for future is in turn portrayed as already present in other cases, that is, other organizations, institutions, systems, societies, or countries (*ibid.*). Hence, interdependent processes of revaluation and devaluation are already characteristic of the overall idea of reform. Moreover, these opposite poles constitute an area of tension, providing a fertile ground for the emergence of recursive contingency.

Yet in older institutional theory, the impetus for institutional reforms was seen as resulting from emerged deviations in the realization of the fundamental institutional idea or ideal (Blänkner & Jussen, 1998; Schelsky, 1971) – consequently influencing the institution's capacity to maintain rigor and fidelity for example. In this sense, reforms were usually regarded as a response to an occasional crisis, while the need for institutional renewal (or survival) served as the most powerful rationale in many cases. However, according to Schelsky (1971, p. 49) such a notion of reform implies the enforcement of an old institutional idea by adopting new means and new tasks only. From this perspective, existing institutions are given a new "spirit" via reforms (Schelsky, 1971, p. 51), while leaving their fundamental pillars intact. They modify at best the form but not the contents of the institution, that is, its subject matters of action or patterns of cooperation (Musselin, 2006, p. 73), or other fundamental elements. By contrast, institutional change in a broader sense has later on been seen as induced from the exterior (exogenous) (cf. Würmseer, 2010, pp. 89–127). This was opening up a much wider gateway for dynamic forces, gaining momentum beyond the transient character of change in former times. Already at this stage, characterized by the general notion of reform, attractive prototypes have been derived by cross-sectoral comparisons. This implies re-evaluating the performance of public educational institutions by the aspiration level of more advanced economic structures and activities. Such orientation can be interpreted as representing the first step in an ongoing process of synchronization and equalization, where universities are about to lose their specificity and are increasingly considered as normal organizations (Logue, 2014, p. 175; see also Ramirez, Byrkjeflot, & Pinheiro, forthcoming). In this respect, it is worth noting that historically the classical public university is much older than modern formal organizations existing today (Manhart, 2014, p. 261). Measured against the considerable capabilities of design and control that many contemporary organizations can make use of, the university has represented almost inevitably an unsatisfactory entity, which further supports the need for its improvement. However, gaining on with more progressive and efficient forms of organization via structural adaptation can prove to be a most difficult undertaking for public universities, as these might make further or even faster progress at the same time.

Possibly, the latter insight could have given rise to a rethinking of reforms. And indeed, over time the general idea of reform, briefly outlined earlier, has undergone major extensions, as well as refinements: Starting in the last quarter of the 20th century (cf. Hoyle & Wallace, 2007, p. 9), public sector reforms in many countries have prompted public universities together with other public and non-profit institutions and organizations, to become more efficient, accountable, and transparent through various, diverse actions and measurements taken within the overall idea of New Public Management (NPM) (cf. Tahar, Niemeyer, & Boutellier, 2011). Particularly, such reforms have implied an increased autonomy and flexibility for universities through a reduction of government's decision-making competencies at the operative level in order to develop them toward being more integrated and closed entities (*ibid.*, p. 290). Evidently, the fundamental concern of this movement toward management ideas has been to govern and control higher education systems and institutions like other publicly funded services and organizations (cf. Ferlie, Musselin, & Andresani, 2008, p. 326). In this sense, Deem and Brehony (2005) characterize NPM in general as "the implementation of a particular form of regulatory governance of public services by state agencies" (p. 219). The primary objective of NPM has been to give public sector organizations a *new orientation* in order to change the way they operate (cf. Dieffenbach, 2009, p. 894). However, research has shown that there has not only been a wide range of diversity in the actual implementation of NPM reforms in Europe, but many of these reforms have not led to radical change (e.g., Pollitt, van Thiel, & Homburg, 2007). Consistent with the overall problems of reforms as a pattern of change, NPM reforms have been to a considerable extent a reaction to earlier reforms and their effects – whether unintended side effects or reverse consequential effects – rather than the implementation of the original design ideas (Wegrich, 2009, p. 137). Over the years, NPM has not only lost its newness with its progressive diffusion, but seems increasingly to lag behind the times (cf. Levy, 2010). Recently, while (post-NPM) alternatives are discussed (Pollitt & Bouckaert, 2011, p. 11), a concurrent restraint in reforming higher education can be observed, whereby cautious consolidation and incremental continuation of modernization are prioritized in European higher education policy (Maassen et al., 2012, p. 9).

A new, third phase of the reform discussion finally started at the turn of the millennium when terms such as the entrepreneurial university or academic capitalism/entrepreneurship (cf. Clark, 1998; Slaughter & Leslie, 1997, etc.) entered the stage. They stimulated a shift toward more corporate and entrepreneurial forms of organization in higher education (Bolden et al., 2008, p. 26). This recent wave of change encapsulates in a new term – "third academic revolution" (Etzkowitz & Viale, 2010) – pre-eminently driven by globalization and the simultaneous rise of the knowledge economy (cf. Bell & Stevenson, 2013; Olssen & Peters, 2005). Basically this turn implies a *changed attitude* toward higher education institutions as effected by external, environmental changes, consisting of financial or economic pressures, and resulting in changing perceptions about their role (Teixeira & Dill, 2011, p. xiv). Being near-global in its political reach and institutional effects, the marketization and privatization of public higher education institutions is still tied to the entire restructuring of the public sector (Wright & Rabo, 2010, p. 4). It denotes, however, the shift from quasi-markets in higher education to *quasi-economic higher education institutions* (Teixeira & Dill, 2011, p. xi) and thus reaches beyond the initial scope of NPM. Ultimately, universities are no longer seen as educational institutions (cf. Logue, 2014, p. 175) and are consequently regarded as an integral part of the commercial innovation system (Altmann & Ebersberger, 2013, p. 2). In addition to that, the new enterprise logic extends the internal focus of performance orientation – which NPM had already established – to a focus on an external, competitive market-orientation (Adcroft, Teckman, & Willis, 2010, p. 579). At the same time, interconnectedness and (market) interdependence have increased (*ibid.*, p. 585). Accordingly, at the core of the entrepreneurial university lies "the capacity to instigate a culture of flexibility and change" (Stensaker & Benner, 2013, p. 401). Thus, change is conceived as a steady state, aiming at an endless transition with no fixed endpoint in sight (Etzkowitz & Viale, 2010, p. 607). Conceivably, entrepreneurial logic has the potential for profoundly redesigning universities as institutions, with the model of internal governance clearly shifting to the transactional type (Wilkesmann, 2013) together with a "hard" managerialism based on contractual cost control (Olssen & Peters, 2005). Despite this, the entrepreneurial ideal may encourage both institutional transformation and institutional lock-in for universities (cf. Stensaker & Benner, 2013).

Overall, the review of the literature seems to confirm the notion of recursive contingency (see Deroy & Clegg, 2015, pp. 75–76) to a certain extent, as demonstrating several unintended consequences and unexpected challenges. This seems to apply particularly to the extension and refinement of the overall idea of reforms resulting from the introduction of NPM as a concept of institutional change. As has been noted repeatedly in the relevant literature, reforms are in many cases prone to the non-attainment of goals, manifested by the typical gaps, deviations, and derailments of reforms (see Aberbach & Christensen, 2014). However, according to Hoyle and Wallace (2007, p. 10), gaps between intention and outcome have even been exacerbated by the particular strategy of reform, for instance when educational reforms are generating further ambiguity rather than reducing existing ambiguity (*ibid.*, pp. 12–13). In this regard, O'Reilly and Reed (2011) have argued that instead of providing an organizational re-orientation, NPM has resulted in an "organizational re-tooling" (p. 1088), while Ferlie, Musselin, and Andresani (2008, p. 341) have noted that in many European countries higher education has been an important field of application of new tools for public management. At the same time, it has not only been argued that these new management techniques were seriously deficient (i.e., ineffective in increasing performance), but that many problems associated with the old bureaucratic structures have persisted and, to make things worse, several new maladies have emerged (Dieffenbach, 2009, p. 897). Moreover, while NPM reforms have been prevalent in Europe, their effects turned out be quite diverse and less radical than conceived at their setout (e.g., Pollitt et al., 2007). In conclusion, the previous observation that NPM reforms have been to a considerable extent a reaction to earlier reforms and their effects, rather than the implementation of the original design ideas can be taken as striking evidence for recursive contingency in the second phase of the university reform process.

Turning finally to the concept of the entrepreneurial university as the most recent step in the differentiation of ideas of change, some similar observations can be noted. For example, Stensaker and Benner (2013, p. 414) have argued that entrepreneurial universities may run the risk of becoming more, rather than less, ambiguous as an institution. While universities all over the world are being forcefully asked to "be useful" and are expected to account for their utility explicitly (Metcalfe, 2010, p. 6), the margin for misrepresentations is substantial. Obviously, the new enterprise logic is based on a competitive orientation (Adcroft et al. 2010, p. 579), the consequence being that traditional forms of cooperative collaboration are threatened with being replaced by serious frictions and adversaries. In addition to the risk of creating internal incoherence in this way, the entrepreneurial university has also to be aware of strained relations with its environment (Stensaker & Benner, 2013, p. 414). Hence, the often-quoted "triple helix" might not only constitute productive trilateral constellations of universities, industry, and government (Etzkowitz & Viale, 2010, p. 601) but also triple problems of translation and intricate entrapments. Among others, Altmann and Ebersberger (2013, p. 3) have pointed out the growing complexity of such settings, which are characterized by multiple interactions with various partners and their different rationales, cultures, development paths, and dynamics. Paradoxically, the entrepreneurial university might then increase the internal fractionalization of the university, while intensifying its external interlocking at the same time (Manhart, 2014, p. 261). To this extent, the gap between intention and results could widen further. Thus overall, the entrepreneurial ideal may encourage theoretically and practically both institutional transformation and institutional lock-in for universities (cf. Stensaker & Benner, 2013).

THREE FRAMES OF CHANGE IN COMPARISON

The stages described above can be distilled into core ideational elements and respective types of frames according to the way of structuring the dynamics of framing proposed by Werner and Cornelissen (2014, pp. 1455–1460). In their article, the authors delineate a basic typology of frames that is based on two dimensions: The first axis represents the degree to which a frame is (dis-)similar to prior schemas; the second axis indicates the extent to which a frame provides a minor or more significant change compared to previous schemas. As a result, four types of frames can be identified: moderate versus radical regarding the second axis and shifting versus blending regarding the first. In a similar manner, O'Reilly and Reed (2011) have identified and analyzed the main discourses of UK public services modernization, subdivided in residual, dominant, and emerging discourses, demonstrating the usefulness of such lines of inquiries for disclosing representations of (organizational) agency and deriving conclusions on impact. Based on a combination of both categorizations, the review of the ideas previously distinguished yields the following picture.

According to the basic idea of reform, the public university had been regarded as a *public institution*. Its inevitably recurrent reforms have been instances of an *induced change* – either through internal or through external forces. At the same time, classical reforms are an exemplary case of a "rewriting for reorganizational purposes" (Werner & Cornelissen, 2014, p. 1456), by questioning existent schemas and mobilizing alternatives and are thus typical of *frame shifting*. It is even more so the case when considering that reforms are regularly depicted as a means or procedure holding out the prospect of a brighter better future (Luhmann, 2006, p. 339). This intended future is in turn portrayed as already present in other cases, for example, other organizations, institutions, systems, societies, or countries (*ibid.*). Additionally, this idealization is almost necessarily collateral with a negative depiction of public organizations and institutions as isolated monopolies or monopsonies with little interest in responding to society (cf. Arellano-Gault & Lepore, 2011, pp. 1032–1033). Upon closer examination the reformist frame is a somewhat *blank frame* or *passe-partout*, as not only are occasions nearly endless, but also purposes and ends – taken to extremes in excessive reformism, where the (presumed) deficits of the last reform are setting off further reforms (cf. Boyer, 2009, p. 76). Given some recent restraint in reforming higher education (Maassen et al., 2012, p. 9), the basic frame of reform could be regarded as *residual*, but still persistent. Yet, a slow-down of reformative fervor is not necessarily induced by the failure of or disappointment with reforms (cf. Aberbach & Christensen, 2014).

In the next phase, marked by the advent of NPM, the public university has concurrently been construed as a *public service institution*. Its subsequent reforms represented an *imposed change*, originating from a strong disappointment with the scope, quality, and efficiency of the services provided by public sector organizations (Dieffenbach, 2009, p. 905). Thus, a particular form of regulatory governance by state agencies is subsequently implemented (Deem & Brehony, 2005, p. 219). This clearly demonstrates that employing the concept of NPM for reasons of university reform has gone far beyond the mere "incorporation of words" (cf. Werner & Cornelissen, 2014, p. 1456), as a typical characteristic of a *blended frame*. In essence, this frame is based on the transference of management ideas from the business sector, that is, trying to turn the university into a more flexible service organization (cf. Taylor, 2012, p. 11; Wright & Rabo, 2010,

p. 5). Considering that NPM has taken an indirect route via public administration to public higher education, it represents an extension of a frame that was blended previously and simply passed on. Nevertheless, its orientations have dramatically changed the very understanding of public services (Dieffenbach, 2009, p. 897). In this respect, the longer-term consequences of NPM for organizational restructuring and cultural re-engineering are likely to be substantial (Deem et al. 2007, p. 2). Given however the apparent aging and attenuation of NPM, its *dominance* can be called into question at the present day.

In the final phase, going beyond reform in the strictest sense, the university has been interpreted as a *(quasi-)economic institution* (cf. Logue, 2014, p. 175; Teixeira & Dill, 2011, p. xi). Compared to previous frames, this might be regarded as a *major change* and hence indicates a *radical type of frame*. At a glance, its terminology – academic capitalism, entrepreneurial university (cf. Slaughter & Leslie, 1997) – is determined by typical "hybrid" noun–noun combinations as well as by composed concepts, which are usually characteristic of *frame blending* (cf. Werner & Cornelissen, 2014, p. 1457). Given the many different connotations of the compound word "entrepreneurial university" and the overlap by adjacent concepts, however, this frame could just as well be labeled as *pluralistic*. In this sense, it is maybe less consisted of a balanced blend than a heterogeneous mixture. In addition, the new enterprise logic is very much based on a competitive orientation (Adcroft et al. 2010, p. 579), which is basically inconsistent with traditional forms of cooperative collaboration in higher education. Such a supplanting of pre-existent logic is more in accord with *frame shifting* (Werner & Cornelissen, 2014, p. 1459), however, and is exemplified by the disjunctive entrepreneurial language (*ibid.*, p. 1467). Strikingly, this frame propagates an *incorporated change*, as the public university is meant to acquire the capacity of flexible adaptation characteristic of the modern commercial enterprise, and to ultimately evolve into a self-changing entity. Turning finally to the issue of impact, the entrepreneurial university could be categorized as an *emerging frame* giving its recent origin at the turn of the millennium. While the entrepreneurial frame has the potential to profoundly redesign European public universities, the implementation of the overall idea is fragmentary. In addition, there is a variety of local adaptions to specific contexts (e.g., regional markets; Wright & Rabo, 2010, pp. 3–4) according to the typical translation of universal ideas by individual actors within institutional fields (cf. Sahlin & Wedlin, 2008).

DISCUSSION

Similar to the idea expressed in the title of Frølich et al. (2013), the assumption of multiplex settings (e.g., different environments) allows for a reinterpretation of the institutional change being observed within the field of higher education: Overall, delineating the dynamics of university reforms again by using the typology of key frames (cf. Werner & Cornelissen, 2014, p. 1458) exhibits a developmental direction from shifting to blending frames. Additionally, a radicalization of frames can be assumed, as the initial moderate frames are outshined by the last blended and presumably most radical frame. This can be regarded as evidence for the frequently voiced impression that the dynamics of change in higher education have accelerated over the past decades. However, this can just as well be accredited to the contents of the frames becoming more radical, and not only due to the rapidity of alternation. This is evident from both the bluntness of borrowing from the commercial sphere and the pointed emphasis of expressions like "private virtues vs. public vices" (Teixeira & Dill, 2011) for propagating the modern commercial enterprise as a (literally) shining example worth copying by the public university. The overall stark contrast is shrinking, however, when those frames chronically close are compared to each other directly. For example, the markedly mechanistic metaphors of the entrepreneurial frame in fact resemble NPM's instrumentalistic attitude – although only in a different guise. Hence, the same idea is just rephrased and in effect not superseded. While it is tempting to regard the frames as fixed against the background of the typology employed for analytical purposes, it would be more realistic to discuss them as being *in flux*. This is particularly the case of the entrepreneurial frame, which is signified precisely by the elements of flexibility and change (cf. Stensaker & Benner, 2013, p. 401). Even so, some caution is advised, as the first step in the analysis has concentrated on major moves or significant stages representing the relentless renewal of the public university over the more recent decades. Such a line of inquiry takes into account the conjuncture that overall rapid and social change that is being observed contemporarily is dominated by "very visible patterns" (Meyer, 2010, p. 6). However, it has to be called to mind that the differentiation of ideas is a constant movement and that such movements have no clear line of division (Deroy & Clegg, 2015, p. 74). Consequently, the depiction is based on an arbitrary classification probably providing no clear evidence of recursive influences on the level of ideas.

At the same time, reforms have mutated from being endemic (Bromley & Powell, 2012, p. 506) to pandemic (near-global) in their spread and reach. This shift from change as episodic to a steady state has presumably set the stage for the further proliferation and multiplication of frames, as any constant change is dependent on a continuous supply of ideas. As a result, an interactionist theorizing would assume a reciprocal stimulation of frames and change, rather than a linear-hierarchical causation. It might help to further elucidate why and how visible patterns provide a continuing basis for further mobilization (cf. Meyer, 2010, p. 15). Yet, the impetus could not only originate from gaps between overdrawn cultural depictions of the institutional capacity of action ("agency"; *ibid.*) or disclosed decoupling. Rather, unintended but *unwanted* outcomes can more directly motivate movements of mobilization (in contrast to disappointments at delusions of grandeur) – thus completing the circle. However, one significant blind spot in the model proposed by Werner and Cornelissen (2014) is to be noted. Interestingly, it does not take into consideration the potential self-destruction of frames as represented by the aforementioned autophagy of reforms or reform waves. Its logic suggests a continuous reframing of frames with an ensuing infinite "survival" that is inconsistent with selectionist approaches (cf. Deroy & Clegg, 2015, p. 76). Additionally, no genuine autopoietic emergence of frames is envisaged, as in this model all blended of shifted frames consist of (parts of) other existent frames – being inconsistent with the "reality of evolution" (Luhmann, 2006, p. 330).

In sum, the movements derived in the preceding analysis neither represent a "tinkering towards utopia" (gradual incremental change) nor a series of punctuated equilibria (punctual transformative change) – and thus belie different theoretical expectations originating from these opposing positions (Bromley & Powell, 2012, p. 506). Regarding the former, the entrepreneurial university can hardly rate as the ideal for the majority of the European academe. On the contrary, it is at a minimum almost a dystopia due to its numerous critics. There is also no inevitability/coerciveness for the ultimate emergence of the entrepreneurial frame – except as a reflex of entrepreneurial society, which is in turn more an idea than a reality. Any such replication of contingency theory must also not necessarily be a seminal coupling for institutional theory, as its inherent tendencies of reductionism are repeatedly criticized (Meyer & Höllerer, 2014, p. 8). To rebut the presumption of a saltatory development of the public university, following punctuated transformations in the field of higher education, the absence of clearly recognizable triggering events for the emergence of the very ideas needs to be acknowledged. Rather, the relentlessness of reform does not reveal proper periods of convergence that are usually typical for punctuated equilibrium – even so, the present is closely approaching. Thus the notion of a permanent disequilibrium (Lewis & Steinmo, 2012, p. 320) seems to become increasingly relevant. Given constant upheaval in the field, a common search for archetypes in institutional theory and research might be in vain or end up in a daunting complexity of forms (cf. Meyer & Höllerer, 2014, p. 6). There is also reason to the assumption of a self-created complexity, considering the jumble left over by inconsistent reforms and their results (cf. de Boer, Enders, & Leisyte, 2007), which further impedes the intended retrieval of clear structural response patterns.

Against this backdrop, the impression of an *incomplete evolution*, where many variations (e.g., numerous stylized gestalt models, cf. Pinheiro, 2013, p. 147) are followed by little selection or only arbitrary retention, is occurring. At least during the earlier stages of reform, universities have shown to be defensive (or immune) rather than being selective. It can further be argued that feedback loops to the environment have additionally contributed to the development of new models (Bromley & Powell, 2012, p. 518). Moreover, the dynamics of university reform might have resulted in (increasingly) fuzzy forms. It should be mentioned that particularly the entrepreneurial terminology and its various frameworks have been widely criticized as insubstantial and exhibiting unsystematic theoretical and conceptual underpinnings (Mars & Rios-Aguilar, 2010, p. 442). This has not only caused considerable confusion in academic debate, but has opened a wide range of nearly incommensurable implementations. In this regard, the issue of impact beyond a merely cognitive adoption (cf. Greenwood, Hinings, & Whetten, 2014, p. 6) is worth reconsidering. In general, it is beyond debate that university reforms comprise examples of institutional decoupling in both ways, as suggested by Bromley and Powell (2012), thus providing the crucial explanation for the absence of (practical) effects. Nevertheless, for instance, various NPM tools were – are least partly – put into practice and exhibited not only intended effects. The latter observation is challenging the assumption of a strict linear chain of cause and effect assumed in Bromley and Powell's model with institutional decoupling acting as a neutralizer or interrupting event. According to an interactionist approach, a *recoupling*, that is, reconnection and reconciliation of practices with policies and even super-ordinated frames and ideas that reshape the environment in turn, would be a logical conclusion. Certainly, innovative practices are the point of origin for emerging frames. Such practices, pressing upward, are in need of a framing in order to gain legitimacy – even before being adopted widely. In this respect, it is worth reconsidering that Clark (1998) conceptualized the entrepreneurial transformation of five

European research universities, by finding innovative methods for reducing heavy reliance on governmental support. Not least, cases of practices are powerful parts of designing frames more convincingly (e.g., case studies of best practice) – and hence are giving impetus to ideas *and* action equally.

CONCLUSIONS

This paper contributes to the theory of institutional change and development by searching new analytical bridges between the institution and its context. To this end, it has explored some different lines of thought quite uncommon to date in studies of the transformation process in higher education and its institutions. In particular, it has suggested an extension of current theorizing by providing a conceptualization of change, which incorporates the possibility of non-linear dynamics. Using the example of the European public university, it has been proposed that phenomena and instances of unintended agency, actions, and consequences (Bromley & Powell, 2012; Westphal & Park, 2012) are worth considering for the study of institutional change and might be a fruitful starting point for further analyses of the current state of higher education – and beyond (e.g., health care). Following Deroy and Clegg (2015), introducing the concept of recursive contingency might help to extend and elaborate the theory of institutional change and development. In particular, its inclusion could stimulate a shift from more simple uses of structural contingency theory to more complex approaches that fit better to the interior complexity of institutions and the vast variety of institutional responses to changes in respective fields (cf. Delbridge & Edwards, 2013; Greenwood, Raynard, Kodeih, Micelotta, & Lounsbury, 2011). In accord with this line of argument, the paper has challenged the assumption of coherent, unitary forces driving university reforms. For this purpose, it has contrasted the conventional idea of institutional imperatives with the idea of emergent dynamics in higher education (cf. Kondakci & Van den Broeck, 2009). In the same vein, O'Reilly and Reed (2011, p. 1080) have pointed out that particularly public sector modernization discourses have provided very different conceptions of how the driving forces of change are to be generated and sustained. As a consequence, university reforms, despite the existence of very similar agendas for restructuring the public sector, did not result in universal uniformity (e.g., Filippakou, Salter, & Tapper, 2012). In general, the diffuse character of the modern actor (Meyer, 2010, p. 14) notwithstanding, it can be concluded that many and manifold forms of reform (co)exist.

While it finally might be argued that institutional spheres have anyway no center (Deroy & Clegg, 2015, p. 78) and thus have no central point of control, ongoing processes of change at the ideational level still leave a mark on multiple institutional systems, when taking higher education institutions as an example. As seen from the latest tendencies beyond reform, the functional differentiation of institutions in the early modern era is displaced by a postmodern integration and hybridization of functions (Etzkowitz & Viale, 2010, p. 607). In the end, this culminates in the partial equalization of educational and economic institutions (Teixeira & Dill, 2011, p. xi), which incorporates not only the business rationale in universities (except perhaps the explicit profit motive or the pursuit of profit *maximization*) but also constant flux as a new constituent feature of organizing higher education. In addition, the coinstantaneous internal and external orientation of the entrepreneurial university aims at dissolving the traditional division of labor, where academics have priority over academic matters and external stakeholders over (all) other matters (Cummings, Fisher, & Locke, 2011, p. 2), as a balanced ideal of shared governance. Thus far such deliberate asymmetries are displacing the configurational coherency that universities were essentially based on the traditional institutional prototype is not only reformed, but perhaps deformed. This kind of reshaping of higher education can ultimately result in a genuine *trans*figuration of the university, giving occasion to further redefinitions in the future. In line with Deroy and Clegg (2015, p. 83), it is thus suggested that the public university will become less foreseeable in its further evolution and less stable in its composition. In this way, it might become indeed a truly unruly object of analysis for institutional studies – albeit in a different sense than has already been expressed (cf. Meyer & Höllerer, 2014, p. 3). This might give cause to carry out more subsequent comparative analyses, such as in this volume, as these analyses could represent an appropriate means for determining its observable dynamic in relation to other institutions and organizations – particularly since sectorial boundaries are increasingly blurred (Bromley & Meyer, 2014).

ACKNOWLEDGMENTS

I would like to thank the editors of this volume, first and foremost Rómulo Pinheiro, for their extremely helpful comments on earlier drafts of this paper and Lisa Blaschke and Wendelin Küpers for their valuable assistance at its final optimization.

REFERENCES

Aberbach, J. D., & Christensen, T. (2014). Why reforms so often disappoint. *American Review of Public Administration*, *44*, 3–16.

Adcroft, A., Teckman, J., & Willis, R. (2010). Is higher education in the UK becoming more competitive? *International Journal of Public Sector Management*, *23*, 578–588.

Altmann, A., & Ebersberger, B. (2013). Universities in change: A brief introduction. In A. Altmann & B. Ebersberger (Eds.), *Universities in change, innovation, technology and knowledge management* (pp. 1–6). New York, NY: Springer.

Alvesson, M. (2013). *The triumph of emptiness: Consumption, higher education, and work organization*. Oxford: Oxford University Press.

Andrews, M. (2013). *The limits of institutional reform in development, changing rules for realistic solutions*. Cambridge: Cambridge University Press.

Arellano-Gault, D., & Lepore, W. (2011). Transparency reforms in the public sector: Beyond the new economics of organization. *Organization Studies*, *32*, 1029–1050.

Bell, L., & Stevenson, H. (Eds.). (2013). *Organizing public education*. London: Sage.

Bergek, A., & Onufrey, K. (2014). Is one path enough? Multiple paths and path interaction as an extension of path dependence theory. *Industrial and Corporate Change*, *23*, 1261–1297.

Berger, P. L., & Luckmann, T. (1966). *The social construction of reality: A treatise in the sociology of knowledge*. New York, NY: Anchor Books.

Blänkner, R., & Jussen, B. (Eds.). (1998). *Institutionen und Ereignis: Über historische Praktiken und Vorstellungen gesellschaftlichen Ordnens*. Göttingen: Vandenhoeck & Ruprecht.

Bolden, R., Petrov, G., & Gosling, J. (2008). *Developing collective leadership in higher education*. London: Leadership Foundation for Higher Education.

Boucher, M. (2011). The gap between intention and results in the Bologna-based university system. In P. Hayes & J. El Gammal (Eds.), *Universitätskulturen* (pp. 215–231). Bielefeld: Transcript Verlag.

Boyer, D. (2009). What is driving university reform in the age of globalization? *Social Anthropology/Anthropologie Sociale*, *18*, 74–76.

Brockliss, L. (2000). Gown and town: The university and the city in Europe 1200–2000. *Minerva*, *38*, 147–170.

Bromley, P., & Meyer, J. W. (2014). They are all organizations: The cultural roots of blurring between the nonprofit, business, and government sectors. *Administration & Society* [Online first]. doi:10.1177/0095399714548268

Bromley, P., & Powell, W. W. (2012). From smoke and mirrors to walking the talk: Decoupling in the contemporary world. *The Academy of Management Annals*, *6*, 483–530.

Brunsson, N. (2009). *Reform as routine: Organizational change and stability in the modern world*. Oxford: Oxford University Press.

Christopher, J. (2012). Governance paradigms of public universities: An international comparative study. *Tertiary Education and Management*, *18*, 335–351.

Clark, B. R. (1998). *Creating entrepreneurial universities: Organizational pathways of transformation*. London: Pergamon Press.

Cummings, W. K., Fisher, D., & Locke, W. (2011). Introduction. In W. Locke, W. K. Cummings, & D. Fisher (Eds.), *Changing governance and management in higher education: The perspectives of the academy* (pp. 1–16). Dordrecht: Springer.

de Boer, H., Endres, J., & Leisyte, L. (2007). Public sector reform in Dutch higher education: The organizational transformation of the university. *Public Administration*, *85*, 27–46.

Deem, R., & Brehoney, K. J. (2005). Management as ideology: The case of new managerialism in higher education. *Oxford Review of Education*, *31*, 217–235.

Deem, R., Hillyard, S., & Reed, M. (2007). *Knowledge, higher education and the new managerialism: The changing management of UK universities*. Oxford: Oxford University Press.

Delbridge, R., & Edwards, T. (2013). Inhabiting institutions: Critical realist refinements to understanding institutional complexity and change. *Organization Studies*, *34*, 927–947.

Deroy, X., & Clegg, S. (2015). Back in the USSR: Introducing recursive contingency into institutional theory. *Organization Studies*, *36*, 73–90.

Dieffenbach, T. (2009). New public management in public sector organizations: The dark sides of managerial "enlightenment". *Public Administration*, *87*, 892–909.

Etzkowitz, H., & Viale, R. (2010). Polyvalent knowledge and the entrepreneurial university: A third academic revolution? *Critical Sociology*, *36*, 595–609.

Ferlie, E., Musselin, C., & Andresani, G. (2008). The steering of higher education systems: A public management perspective. *Higher Education*, *56*, 325–348.

Filippakou, O., Salter, B., & Tapper, T. (2012). The changing structure of British higher education: How diverse is it? *Tertiary Education and Management*, *18*, 321–333.

Frølich, N., Huisman, J., Slipersæter, S., Stensaker, B., & Pimentel Botas, P. C. (2013). A reinterpretation of institutional transformation in European higher education: Strategising pluralistic organisations in multiplex environments. *Higher Education*, *65*, 79–93.

Greenwood, R., Hinings, C. R., & Whetten, D. (2014). Rethinking institutions and organizations. *Journal of Management Studies* [Online first]. doi:10.1111/joms.12070

Greenwood, R., Raynard, M., Kodeih, F., Micelotta, E. R., & Lounsbury, M. (2011). Institutional complexity and organizational responses. *Academy of Management Annals*, *5*, 317–371.

Hoyle, E., & Wallace, M. (2007). Educational reform: An ironic perspective. Educational Management. Administration & Leadership, *35*, 9–25.

Jones, S. (2014). Distributed leadership: A critical analysis. *Leadership*, *10*, 129–141.

Kieser, A. (2012). Organisationen regeln – wer aber steuert Organisationen? In S. Duschek (Ed.), *Organisationen regeln* (pp. 227–251). Wiesbaden: VS Verlag.

Kondakci, Y., & Van den Broeck, H. (2009). Institutional imperatives versus emergent dynamics: A case study on continuous change in higher education. *Higher Education*, *58*, 439–464.

Levy, R. (2010). New public management: End of an era? *Public Policy and Administration*, *35*, 234–240.

Lewis, O. A., & Steinmo, S. (2012). How institutions evolve: Evolutionary theory and institutional change. *Polity*, *44*, 314–339.

Logue, D. M. (2014). Adoption and abandonment: Global diffusion and local variation in top management teams. In G. S. Drori, M. A. Höllerer, & P. Walgenbach (Eds.), *Global themes and local variations in organization and management* (pp. 175–188). Milton Park: Routledge.

Lounsbury, M., & Boxenbaum, E. (Eds.). (2013). *Institutional logics in action*. Research in the Sociology of Organizations (Vol. 39A + B). Bingley: Emerald Group Publishing Limited.

Luhmann, N. (1995). *Social systems*. Stanford, CA: Stanford University Press.

Luhmann, N. (2006). *Organisation und Entscheidung* (2nd ed.). Wiesbaden: VS Verlag.

Lutz, F. W. (1982). The tightening up of loose coupling in organizations of higher education. *Administrative Science Quarterly*, *27*, 653–669.

Maassen, P., Nerland, M., Pinheiro, M., Stensaker, B., Vabø, A., & Vukasović, M. (2012). Change dynamics and higher education reforms: Effects in education, research, governance and academic profession. In M. Vukasović, P. Maassen, M. Nerland, M. Pinheiro, B. Stensaker, & A. Vabø (Eds.), Effects of higher education reform: Change dynamics (pp. 1–18). Rotterdam: Sense Publishers.

Manhart, S. (2014). Organisiertes Veralten – veraltete Organisation? Zur Stabilität der Universität in den Neuerungsdynamiken von Wissenschaft und Reformen. In M. Göhlich (Ed.), *Das Neue in Organisationen* (pp. 259–269). Wiesbaden: Springer.

Mars, M. M., & Rios-Aguilar, C. (2010). Academic entrepreneurship (re)defined: Significance and implications for the scholarship of higher education. *Higher Education, 59*, 441–460.

Metcalfe, J. S. (2010). University and business relations: Connecting the knowledge economy. *Minerva, 48*, 5–33.

Meyer, J. W. (2009). *World society*. Oxford: Oxford University Press.

Meyer, J. W. (2010). World society institutional theories, and the actor. *Annual Review of Sociology, 36*, 1–20.

Meyer, R., & Höllerer, M. A. (2014). Does institutional theory need redirecting? *Journal of Management Studies* [Online first]. doi:10.1111/joms.12089

Murdoch, Z., & Geys, B. (2014). Institutional dynamics in international organizations: Lessons from the recruitment procedures of the European external action service. *Organization Studies, 35*, 1793–1811.

Musselin, C. (2006). Are universities specific organisations? In G. Krücken, A. Kosmützky, & M. Torka (Eds.), *Towards a multiversity? Universities between global trends and national traditions* (pp. 61–82). Bielefeld: Transcript Verlag.

Olsen, J. P. (2007). The institutional dynamics of the European university. In P. Maassen & J. P. Olsen (Eds.), *University dynamics and European integration* (pp. 25–54). Dordrecht: Springer.

Olssen, M., & Peters, M. A. (2005). Neoliberalism, higher education and the knowledge economy: From the free market to knowledge capitalism. *Journal of Education Policy, 20*, 313–345.

O'Reilly, D., & Reed, M. (2011). The grit in the oyster: Professionalism, managerialism and leaderism as discourses of UK public services modernization. *Organization Studies, 32*, 1079–1101.

Pinheiro, R. (2013). Bridging the local with the global: Building a new university on the fringes of Europe. *Tertiary Education and Management, 19*, 144–160.

Pollitt, C., & Bouckaert, G. (2011). *Public management reform: A comparative analysis* (3rd ed.). Oxford: Oxford University Press.

Pollitt, C., van Thiel, S., & Homburg, V. (Eds.). (2007). *New public management in Europe: Adaptations and alternatives*. Basingstoke: Palgrave Macmillan.

Pritchard, R. M. O. (2011). *Neoliberal developments in higher education: The United Kingdom and Germany*. Oxford: Peter Lang.

Ramirez, F., Byrkjeflot, H., & Pinheiro, R. (forthcoming). Higher education and health organizational fields in the age of world class and best practices. In R. Pinheiro, L. Geschwind, F. Ramirez, & K. Vrangbæk (Eds.), *Towards a comparative institutionalism: Forms, dynamics and logics across the organizational fields of health care and higher education*. Bingley: Emerald Group Publishing Limited.

Sahlin, K., & Wedlin, L. (2008). Circulating ideas: Imitation, translation and editing. In R. Greenwood, K. Sahlin-Andersson, & R. Suddaby (Eds.), *The SAGE handbook of organizational institutionalism* (pp. 218–242). London: SAGE.

Schelsky, H. (1971). *Einsamkeit und Freiheit* (2nd ed.). Düsseldorf: Bertelsmann Universitätsverlag.

Schofer, E., & Meyer, J. W. (2005). The worldwide expansion of higher education in the twentieth century. *Sociological Review*, *70*, 898–920.

Slaughter, S., & Leslie, L. (1997). *Academic capitalism: Politics, policies and the entrepreneurial university*. Baltimore, MD: John Hopkins University Press.

Stensaker, B., & Benner, M. (2013). Doomed to be entrepreneurial: Institutional transformation or institutional lock-ins of new universities? *Minerva*, *51*, 399–416.

Tahar, S., Niemeyer, C., & Boutellier, R. (2011). Transferral of business management concepts to universities as ambidextrous organisations. *Tertiary Education and Management*, *17*, 289–308.

Taylor, J. (2012). Fads and fancies: The use of management tools in UK universities. *Excellence in Higher Education*, *3*, 1–13.

Teixeira, P. N., & Dill, D. D. (2011). Introduction: The many faces of marketization. In P. N. Teixeira & D. D. Dill (Eds.), *Public vices, private virtues? Assessing the effects of marketization in higher education* (pp. vii–xxiii). Rotterdam: Sense Publishers.

Thornton, P. H., Ocasio, W., & Lounsbury, M. (2012). *The institutional logics perspective: A new approach to culture, structure, and process*. Oxford: Oxford University Press.

Wegrich, K. (2009). Public management reform in the United Kingdom: Great leaps, small steps and policies as their own cause. In S. F. Goldfinch & J. L. Wallis (Eds.), *International handbook of public management reform* (pp. 137–154). Cheltenham: Edward Elgar.

Werner, M. D., & Cornelissen, J. P. (2014). Framing the change: Switching and blending frames and their role in instigating institutional change. *Organization Studies*, *35*, 1449–1472.

Westphal, J. D., & Park, S. H. (2012). Unintended agency: Impression management support as a trigger of institutional change in corporate governance. *Research in Organizational Behavior*, *32*, 23–46.

Whitley, R., & Gläser, J. (2007). *The changing governance of the sciences: The advent of research evaluation systems*. Dordrecht: Springer.

Wilkesmann, U. (2013). Effects of transactional and transformational governance on academic teaching: Empirical evidence from two types of higher education institutions. *Tertiary Education and Management*, *19*, 281–300.

Wittrock, B. (1985). Dinosaurs or dolphins? Rise and resurgence of the research-oriented university. In B. Wittrock & A. Elzinga (Eds.), *The university research system: The public policies of the home of scientists* (pp. 13–38). Stockholm: Almqvist & Wiksell International.

Wright, S., & Rabo, A. (2010). Introduction: Anthropologies of university reform. *Social Anthropology/Anthropologie Sociale*, *18*, 1–14.

Würmseer, G. (2010). *Auf dem Weg zu neuen Hochschultypen: Eine organisationssoziologische Analyse vor dem Hintergrund hochschulpolitischer Reformen*. Wiesbaden: VS Verlag.

COMPARING THE INSTITUTIONALISATION OF PERFORMANCE MANAGEMENT SCHEMES FOR HOSPITALS IN DENMARK, GERMANY AND ENGLAND

Karsten Vrangbæk, John Appleby, Tanja Klenk and Sarah Gregory

ABSTRACT

Performance management (PM) has been developed to a central part of health care reforms. However, ideas of performance are traditionally contested in the health care sector and split up between a professional and a bureaucratic understanding of effective service delivery. With the rise of New Public Management, an additional layer of PM instruments has been put on the already existing structures. As a result, different PM regimes can be distinguished, which vary in the way they define performance, blame underperformance and design accountability instruments

Towards a Comparative Institutionalism: Forms, Dynamics and Logics Across the Organizational Fields of Health Care and Higher Education
Research in the Sociology of Organizations, Volume 45, 81–106

ISSN: 0733-558X/doi:10.1108/S0733-558X20150000045015

to ensure appropriate behaviour. The paper investigates the institutional design of PM schemes of three different cases – Denmark, Germany and England – which are representative for different PM regimes.

Keywords: Performance management; health care; institutional design; diffusion; translation

INTRODUCTION

During the last few decades, health care has been subject to what has been described as reform activism. With these reforms, we can see a transition from professional dominance to political control, management and market. Another dominant trend is captured by the concepts of *audit society* and *performance management* (PM) (Pollitt, 2011). However, global waves of reforms are rarely implemented in the same way across different institutional settings. More often, they are translated into local recipes and programmes with considerable variation across sectors, regions and countries (Czarniawska & Joerges, 1996; Sahlin & Wedlin, 2008). Preconditions for governance and the embedding of specific governance models differ across settings as a result of differences in institutional structures, culture and traditions. Moreover, even if many reforms have been argued for as ways of clarifying governance and organisation, they have largely added to institutional complexity and institutional ambiguity. This means that although the topical global themes clearly dominate recent reform agendas, fields are still characterised by multiple institutions, each with different implications regarding how to organise, govern and interpret what health care is and how it should be governed and developed. This chapter focuses on one of the dominant reform themes in recent decades, namely the introduction of PM (Bouckaert & Halligan, 2008). We compare the institutional translation of PM in three country cases: Germany, England and Denmark. These country cases are selected to provide variation on important underlying institutional characteristics within a setting of publicly managed health systems in Europe. We focus on hospital care, as this represents the bulk of health expenditures, but will also include examples of performance indicators directed at collaboration between hospitals and other parts of the health system.

PM has been characterised as an important part of the New Public Management (NPM) development, which has become a key reference point in much of the academic debate about public administration over the past three decades (Hood, 1991; Lægreid & Christensen, 2007). Several recent studies have discussed PM in a comparative light at the general level (Bouckaert & Halligan, 2008; Moynihan, 2008). There are national studies about the translation of the PM concept into national contexts (Blomgren, 2007), but there is very limited systematic comparative knowledge about such processes. We will provide a structured comparison of PM schemes in the three countries based on a point-in-time description of institutional design components. This will enable us to discuss field-level adaptations of 'templates' (Wedlin, 2007) and discuss implications for our theoretical understanding of the translation of transparency regimes into soft governance mechanisms in this era.

Guiding our analysis will be the following questions:

- *How has the general idea of PM in health care been translated into institutional field changes in England, Denmark and Germany?*
- *Do the PM schemes represent significant changes in the governance regimes of health care within the three countries?*

The rest of the chapter is organised in the following way. First, we discuss the relevant theories for the comparative analysis. Second, we offer a presentation of the methods for the comparison. Third, we present the results of the comparative analysis and a discussion about the broader implications for our understanding of translation processes in this field.

THEORETICAL PERSPECTIVES ON THE TRANSLATION OF PM IDEAS WITHIN HEALTH CARE

Diffusion and translation of ideas have been key topics within neo-institutional theory since the early 1990s (Sahlin & Wedlin, 2008). Early contributions developed the idea of imitation as a key mechanism for spreading institutionalised ideas within institutional fields (DiMaggio & Powell, 1983). The Scandinavian brand of neo-institutionalism has developed these ideas further and operates with the concepts of *translation* (Czarniawska & Joerges, 1996) and *editing* (Sahlin-Andersson, 1996) to signify the active process of reconstructing the meaning of general ideas within particular institutional contexts. 'Ideas do not diffuse in a vacuum but are actively translated in a context of other ideas, actors traditions and institutions' (Sahlin & Wedlin, 2008, p. 219). 'To imitate then is not just to copy, but also to change and to innovate' (*ibid.*, p. 219).

Early contributors such as Meyer and Rowan (1977) emphasised the ceremonial adoption of ideas and the ensuing tendency to decouple institutionalised ideas from organisational practice. Subsequent contributors have shown that decoupling is unlikely to be the end result, and that adopted ideas contribute to changes in individual organisations as well as broader organisational fields (Sahlin & Wedlin, 2008). Powerful ideas are spread by key carriers in 'broadcasting' and 'chain mode imitation' or are mediated by third party actors and organisations (e.g. consultancies or international organisations). In the process, they often become decontextualised, rationalised, scientized, and theorised (Strang & Meyer, 1993) before being reconstructed and translated into specific organisational ideas shaped by contextual contingencies and interests.

An interesting development in the neo-institutional research agenda is the shift from focusing on diffusion and translation of organisational prototypes presented as specific organisational components to 'templates' that signify 'frames or targets that actors use to compare or benchmark their activities, and to describe how success should be assessed' (Sahlin & Wedlin, 2008, p. 231). Templates suggest evaluation criteria, rankings, standards and widespread notions of what constitutes success. Transparency is a fundamental issue within modern day templates, along with governance, quality and performance. The drive for transparency is part of a tendency to develop new and softer forms of regulation and self-regulation in modern organisational fields (Hood, Scott, James, Jones, & Travers, 1999). Some of the mechanisms behind this development include growing distrust, a push for new types of responsibility and a search for control within 'regulatory markets' through pre-emptive adaptation and influencing of regulatory schemes. Contextual factors include the expansion and influence of scientific discourse, marketisation, new modes of democracy in the Internet era and a tendency to develop more formal organisations to assign explicit responsibilities (Blomgren, 2007; Sahlin & Wedlin, 2008, p. 234).

The objective of this paper is to investigate developments in institutionalised translation of transparency templates in three Northern European countries. We speculate that the specific institutional contexts with their specific carriers and translational modes will mean that the underlying ideas are translated somewhat differently, although it will probably also be possible to find many commonalities. Investigating similarities and differences across the countries will provide us with an indication of field-level translations within the current era in this particular sector.

To facilitate our systematic comparison of transparency regimes within health care, we combine institutional and public administration contributions. Taking the lead from Van Dooren, Bouckaert, and Halligan (2010, p. 33), we can define performance as the realisation of public values such as efficiency, effectiveness, equity and quality. *Performance measurement* is the process of acquiring performance information. The measurability of activities and their effects is a key concern. *PM* is the incorporation and use of performance information in decision-making and adjustment of organisational practices in order to ensure that practices support public values, goals and objectives.

The organisational psychologist Aubrey Daniels coined the term PM as a broad description of the managerial and technical processes involved in ensuring that the goals and objectives of organisations (and individuals, or indeed whole economic sectors) were met. Underlying the notion of PM is the implication that intrinsic or extrinsic motivations and incentives – such as professional pride, satisfaction in a job well done or the market-driven competitive threat of bankruptcy or unemployment – are not necessarily sufficient to ensure that organisations and individuals 'do the right thing' to ensure that organisational goals are met. Moreover, even when these incentives and motivations are all maximised and aligned with goals, knowledge of the best way to achieve objectives may be lacking. In these circumstances, some degree of active management of performance is needed. To manage performance in a systematic way, one must define the relevant dimensions and measuring points that are aligned with the goals of the organisation.

Public sector organisations are normally not dependent on markets for their survival and do not have a bottom line in the same way as private organisations. Instead, they are faced with several different goals related to their institutional roles in serving the public interest. These goals relate to delivering value for money, but also to serving broader societal objectives such as robustness, due process, transparency, promoting equity, preserving the long-term public interest and adhering to general public and democratic rules of operation (Jorgensen & Bozeman, 2007). Stated somewhat differently, they involve efficiency, equity, security, liberty and community 'goals' (Stone, 1997). Each of these goals must be defined in more detail for each public organisation and are likely to be subject to conflicting interpretations over time (Stone, 1997). As in the private sector, such general objectives may be broken down into operational goals. Performance in the public sector is thus a multifaceted issue related to goals that are reinterpreted and redefined in complex political processes. Translation, editing and activation of different 'templates' are important parts of this reconstruction process. Performance measurement is the institutionalisation of data collection to provide insight into the performance of public organisations in regards to the overall goals as they are defined at any given time. It follows from this that one can expect PM to be contested and subject to reinterpretation according to different formulations of values and objectives.

In a formal sense, we rely on definitions from the work of Van Dooren et al. (2010) and Daniels (2004). According to these scholars, *performance measurement* is defined as:

> (sub)system wide collection of standardized performance data using some type of common template. The collection of data is imposed through an authoritative (political) decision at some level, with the purpose of facilitating insight into performance.

PM is

> incorporation and use of performance information by internal management or external stakeholders for decision-making or intervention in order to ensure that practices support public values, goals, and objectives.

Taking the perspectives of values in addition to important issues about agency and methods in PM, we argue that there are three key dimensions of PM systems, each with their specific institutional features and assumptions:

As noted above, there is limited systematic comparative knowledge about the way PM ideas are translated into specific designs in specific sectors and national institutional settings, and even less information about the effects of such schemes in practice. The following sections present a preliminary illustration of the framework as set out in Table 1 through a comparison of key features of the PM schemes for hospitals in three Northern European countries. We conclude with a discussion about the linkages between underlying institutional design of the three health system and the specific PM schemes.

There are a number of challenges in developing a comparative analysis of PM schemes across countries. First, although the definitions are fairly clear at a general level, there is significant variation in the interpretation of the different elements in different countries and different sectors. Historical developments, political traditions and institutional contexts influence the development of particular PM regimes and the understanding of various PM terms. It can therefore be difficult to draw the line between what is PM and what is not. The definition presented above, and the categories outlined in the table, represents our guiding principles in the selection of phenomena to investigate. Second, analysing PM schemes is a 'moving target' as national systems tend to develop over time, sometimes dramatically in response to political decisions and compromises and sometimes gradually

Table 1. Dimensions for Descriptive Analysis of Performance Management Schemes.

What is the underlying rationale?	Purpose/objectives	• Financial viability and sustainability • Quality improvement (clinical and patient experience) • Avoidance of accidents and malpractice incidents • Value for money (activity/resources or quality/resources) • Maintenance of trust and legitimacy
	Mechanisms and assumptions about causality	• External (hierarchical) scrutiny and threat of interventions • Automatic sanctions • Benchmarking, 'naming and shaming' • Transparency to enable choice or selective contracting • Enable self-assessment and support organisational development
Who collects data? How is it collected?	Agencies and actors	• Which agencies and actors are responsible for collecting and using performance data?
	Scope and measurement	• What is measured: activity, process quality (compliance with predefined standards, guidelines or procedures for administrative and/or clinical activities), clinical outcomes, patient experiences, economic performance? • Which criteria are applied for assessment (averages, standards, targets, etc.)?
	Depth/unit	• Data collected at the individual or the organisational level? Who is responsible for delivering, collecting and using performance data?
How is data used for performance management?	Control/sanctioning	• Explicit or implicit sanctions related to the PM scheme? • Which agencies are responsible for control and intervention?
	Disclosure/publication	• How are data published (presentation, aggregation, composites, weighting)? Who has access to data? (public in general, public principals, peer organisations, own organisation, etc.).
	Economic incentives	• Are economic incentives (rewards/punishments) part of the PM scheme?

as a consequence of bottom–up decisions and the horizontal spread of ideas. In the next section, we explain how we attempt to handle these challenges.

METHODS

We are looking for schemes that fall within these definitions within the three countries. We use Internet searches and descriptions from official sources (ministries, agencies, quality assessment institutions, etc.) combined with expert assessments from the three countries to find the schemes, and we seek validation of our findings through peer-level presentations. This approach provides an overview of the formal institutionalisation of PM schemes at the field level, while we have limited information about the micro-level outcomes of the translation process.

The specific method in the paper then is to use the descriptive dimensions presented in the previous section to guide a systematic collection of written information about PM schemes in the three countries. The collection of data has been facilitated by the fact that all four authors are embedded in national research environments with experts in health systems analysis and performance assessment. The written (Internet) material has been structured and presented in descriptions of each of the three national PM schemes using the same dimensions and headlines for all three. These descriptions have been validated through presentations for national-level experts. They have subsequently formed the background for qualitative semi-structured interviews with key policy actors in the three countries to facilitate the interpretation of the different schemes and address questions about the translation and institutional implications of the schemes.

DESCRIPTIVE ANALYSIS OF PM SCHEMES

General Characteristics of the Field-Level Translation of PM Ideas in the Three Countries: Templates and Institutional Contexts

The *Danish* approach to PM reflects the multilevel governance structure with decentralised responsibility for health care delivery (regions and municipalities) and central state-level responsibility for general regulation, overall political strategy and coordination of public finances. PM in the form of quality assessment has been introduced gradually through negotiated agreements building on bottom–up experiments and pilot projects at the decentralised level. The role of the state has been to develop guidelines and standards, and to facilitate the development of an overall framework for collecting the different decentralised initiatives. The resulting Danish

Quality Assessment Model is based on self-assessment within hospitals combined with external accreditation and monitoring through clinical quality databases, patient satisfaction surveys, etc. The core philosophy is to support self-development at the hospital and regional levels. Yet, at the same time, the state has opted for publication of some quality data in national web portals. The publication of such data is supposed to facilitate the choice of (public) hospitals and create some level of reputational competition. The Danish Quality Assessment Model was developed and implemented from 2003 to 2015. Starting in 2015, it no longer applies to hospitals, as it has now 'served its purpose' of securing a common level of quality. The accreditation-based scheme will still exist for primary care and home care services, while the intention is to develop a new and more 'patient-value-based' system that emphasises results rather than processes and to link this more explicitly to economic incentives. This change is a reaction to complaints from health professionals and hospital managers about the burden of registering information and preparing for the accreditation process. The turn illustrates several dilemmas in PM schemes within health care: firstly, that the 'transaction costs' of collecting and processing data may be higher than the benefits, and secondly that although the purpose of PM schemes ultimately is to benefit the patients, it has previously been difficult to find good comparative measures for the value creation. This has led to a focus on process dimensions, which are not always perceived as relevant by health professionals and patients.

Clinical- and process-related quality data are used by national and regional authorities in Denmark for management and comparisons within regions and across regions. There are currently no explicitly stated or automatic sanctions related to quality performance at the national level, but such issues are normally part of the performance contracts for hospital- and department-level managers. The national authorities have the power to investigate quality breaches and may intervene in cases of poor performance. Yet, in most cases, this is handled at the regional level, which may react to negative performance measures by dismissing the hospital management or implementing more detailed monitoring and steering, and thus reducing the autonomy of the hospitals. In a general context of reductions in hospital facilities, another option for the regions is to close down departments or hospitals.

PM in regards to productivity is an integrated part of the economic steering system between the state and regions, and within regions (between regions, hospitals and general practitioners (GPs)). The activity level of hospitals and regions is measured through a diagnosis related groups (DRG) system and related to input resources to form hospital-level productivity measures that are published in national-level publications. While the bulk of the state financing of regions is in the form of block grants, a minor (5–10%), yet important, portion comes through activity-based funding. The regions will only receive this funding if their activity is above a certain target level. The target level is raised by 2% annually, pushing the regions and their hospitals to increase productivity. Most regions have opted for higher levels of activity-based financing for their internal management of hospitals. This is implemented through hospital-level steering contracts and agreements with hospitals. The level of activity-based financing often varies between different departments, with areas like orthopaedic surgery being most subjected to activity-based payment. See Fig. 1 for more details about the Danish PM scheme.

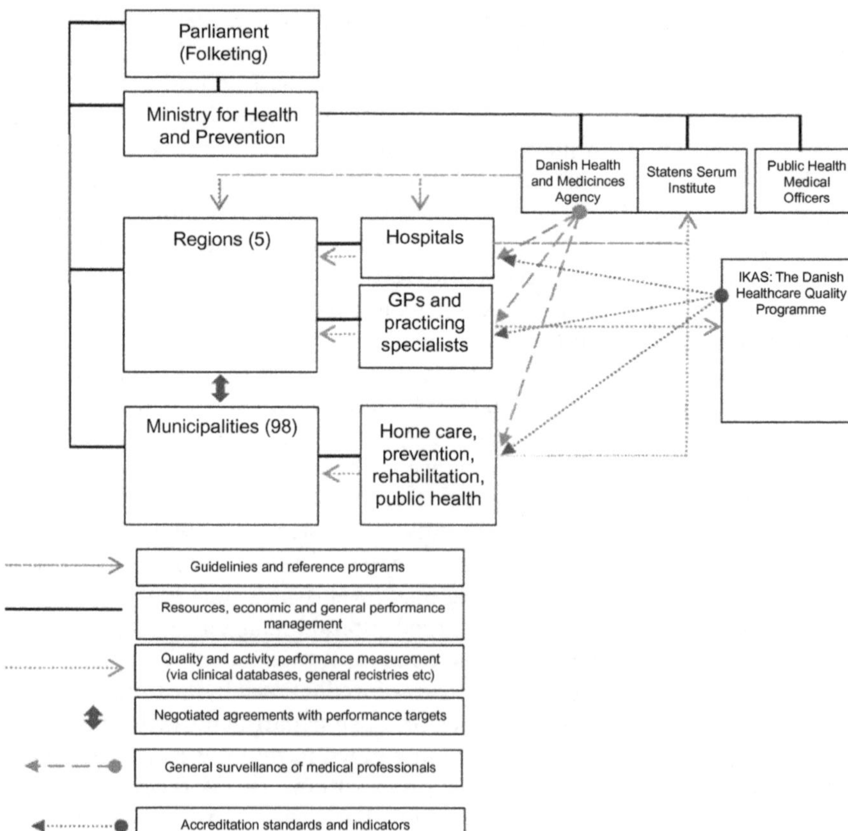

Fig. 1. Denmark.

The governance of the *German* hospital sector is characterised by a multicentred power structure emphasising relatively independent 'self-governing' relationships between sickness funds and providers. The multicentred power structure is also expressed in the relatively high degree of autonomy for the German Bundesländer. The 'self-governance' structure and the discretion the Länder enjoys in hospital policy means that national-level authorities have limited direct power to impose large-scale national systems, and that such systems must be negotiated with both the Länder and the actors of self-governance. Furthermore, the heterogeneity of provider organisations with private not-for-profit, public and private for-profit hospitals means that solutions must be adjusted and streamlined, and that compliance is less secure than in a 'command and control' system.

Cases of medical malpractice are handled within the complex system of self-governance and are thus non-transparent for the wider public. A new law on patients' rights was implemented in 2013, allowing patients to access their individual patient file and easing the burden of proof in cases of conflict. However, the major burden of proof still lies with the patients. As a result, incidents of poor quality are rarely discussed in regional or nationwide public media.

Accordingly, the general sentiment remains that the quality of the system is high (even though Germany is rarely placed among the top of the OECD or EU15 countries, but usually below the average; Busse & Blümel, 2014, p. xxvii). This means that politicians have not been pushed by a hot public debate to introduce new versions of quality assessment on a continuous basis as was the case in England. This, as well as the complex governance of the hospital sector, might explain why Germany is a latecomer in the field of national-level PM initiatives.

In recent years, however, performance and quality of inpatient care has entered the political agenda. As a result of the multicentred power structure, we find a variety of different actors who are active in the field of PM. PM schemes have been introduced by the actors of self-governance (health insurance funds, hospital umbrella organisations) as well as individual hospitals, particularly for-profit providers. Historically, many of the quality management schemes in Germany have been developed regionally or within particular groups of providers. Indeed, many of the current initiatives have the same characteristics, and they remain voluntary and limited in scope. Yet, the coalition government in 2014 announced its intention to put hospital quality in the centre of attention and has passed a hospital law in July 2015. At the present time (before the so-called hospital structure law becomes effective in 2016), the following PM schemes can be considered as the most important ones (see further in Fig. 2):

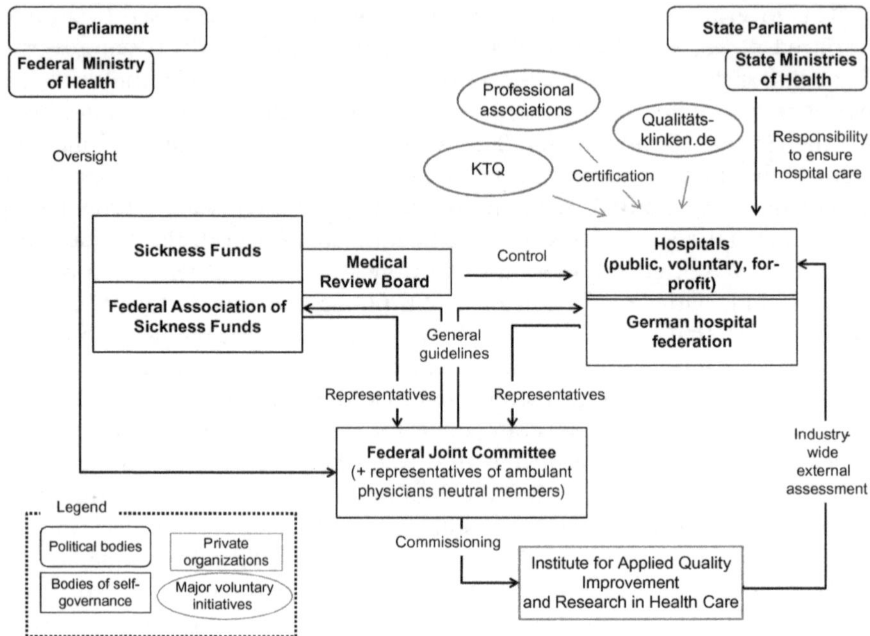

Fig. 2. Germany.

- *Legally required PM tools:* Hospitals are legally required to implement an internal quality management system (since 2000, § 135 a SGB V). In addition, since 2005 they are obliged to regularly publish quality reports (§ 137, 3 SGB V). Finally, hospitals are obliged to participate in an external and industry-wide comparative quality assessment (§ 137 a SGB V).
- *Voluntary assessments on the meso-level*, which are, for instance, conducted by professional associations or by joint initiatives of umbrella organisations of funders and providers (e.g. KTQ [*Kooperation für Transparenz und Qualität im Gesundheitswesen*, Cooperation for Transparency and Quality in Health Care]).
- *Voluntary initiatives by single hospitals*, for example, the online platform 'Qualitätskliniken.de'.

The *English* NHS is often considered a fairly centralised system with much power at the central level due to national-level public financing and state ownership of hospitals. Yet, the introduction of the commissioner/provider split, patient choice, and autonomous Foundation Trusts (FTs) has necessitated the development of an alternative PM framework to ensure the quality and financial viability of the trusts.

National-level administrative power is not as strong as might be expected. PM has been delegated to arms-length bodies (Monitor, Trust Development Authority (TDA)), and it is unlikely that power will ever shift back to the Department of Health. The result has been a process of continuous adjustment, with new institutions functioning on top of those that already exist. The complexity and inherent inconsistencies of the regulatory structure generate ongoing pressure for adjustment.

The high political salience of health care and relatively strong support for the NHS in the population present a dilemma for national-level politicians, as they are frequently held accountable for health system performance, but in fact no longer have the direct control over the commissioning and delivery of services. The institutional structure with relatively large (monopoly) hospitals exacerbates this need for control, as hospital failures would be unacceptable in many English cities.

The parliamentary system and the centralised ownership/governance structure means that majority governments have the power to introduce radical changes in PM schemes without extensive negotiations with opposition parties and interest groups. The general political salience of the health sector (the special status of the NHS) makes it important for politicians to signal that they have control over the NHS (financially and in terms of quality). Introducing new PM schemes can serve as a (symbolic) lever to achieve this.

The result is a PM setup composed of several institutions having somewhat overlapping mandates related to different and, to some extent, contradictory underlying objectives in the system. The system is further complicated by the fact that somewhat different regimes and institutional setups exist for 'FTs' and 'Non-FTs'. Furthermore, the institutional roles are divided between Monitor and the TDA and the Care Quality Commission (CQC) (see further in Fig. 3).

Looking across the three countries, we can conclude that PM schemes focusing on transparency and quality have been introduced in all three countries. However, the carriers and mechanisms for introduction are somewhat different, and both the timing and content of the general templates are adjusted according to the specific institutional conditions in the three countries. It is further important to note the layering structure of PM schemes. Rather than 'grand designs', we are observing the results of gradual and partly uncoordinated introductions and retranslations of PM components over time responding to new contingencies, events,

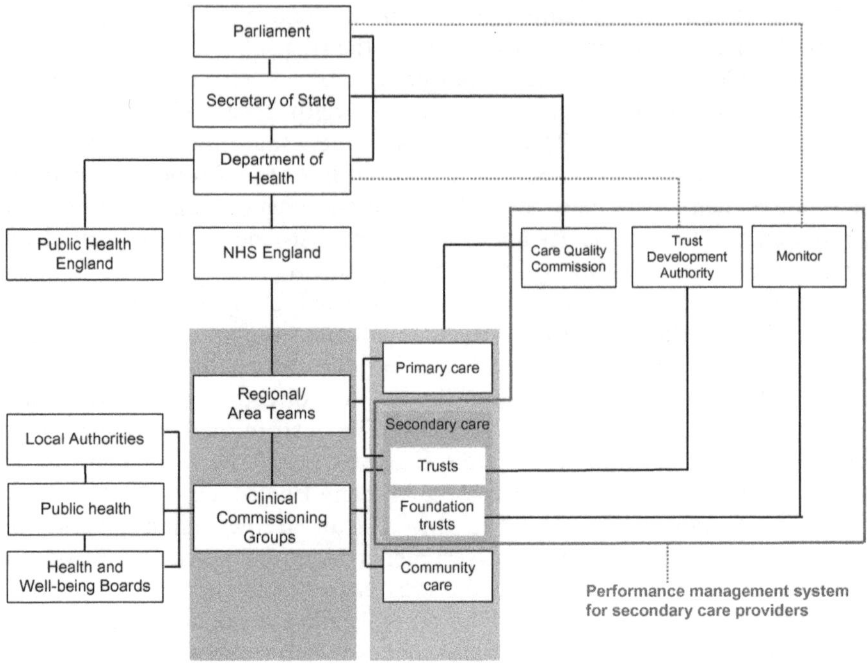

Fig. 3. England.

opportunities and actor interests. To understand these processes better, we will take a look at the stated rationales behind the three schemes.

How Are the Rationales Behind the Three Schemes Constructed?

The purpose of PM schemes in Denmark is to improve quality (clinical and patient-experienced), reduce the risk of accidents and malpractice incidents and evaluate that the regions and their hospitals deliver value for money.

The assumptions about mechanism and causality in Danish PM schemes are mixed and appear to be changing at the moment. This reflects the stepwise development and the need for compromises between national and regional levels and health professionals. The official rhetoric behind the Danish Quality Assessment Model was to enable self-assessment and support organisational development; yet, the process also enabled external (hierarchical) scrutiny with an implicit threat of interventions if hospitals failed the accreditation exercise or consistently fell behind on various parameters. The recent announcement of a turn towards a 'value-based assessment' and the abandonment of the accreditation scheme for hospitals (but not for GPs and municipalities) indicates a change in rationale from process to outcome. Furthermore, it implies a centralisation as the National Ministry is supposed to establish 'few, but carefully selected indicators of quality' that the hospitals will be measured up against. Performance in regards to these measures will be linked to economic incentives. We thus see a change in the overall template from reliance on organisational self-development combined with external scrutiny of adherence to (process) standards towards a result-oriented scheme reinforced by economic incentives. Similar developments can be found in the other Nordic countries (IVBAR in Sweden) and in England (P4P in primary care). The Danish case thereby appears to exemplify a gradual shift towards a new international template for organising PM in health care. The new template emphasises results/outcomes and reduces the attention to process standards. The new template also implies a weakening of the influence of international carriers such as the Joint Commission and their approach to standards-based accreditation.

So far, *Germany* has been characterised by many different PM schemes. This also means that there are several different underlying rationales. Seen from the perspective of health policy at the federal level, the primary objective of PM schemes is to improve quality and to avoid accidents and malpractice incidents. Health insurance organisations are obliged by law to cooperate with the German hospital federation in the Gemeinsamer Bundesausschuss (Joint Health Commission) and are charged with the development of guidelines for the national hospital performance schemes. However, as health insurance funds operate in a competitive market, they also have a strong interest in securing value for money, and thus have initiated additional schemes such as the AOK Routine data quality assessment. What's more, as competition has become fiercer not only on the side of the funders but also between providers, single hospitals have discovered performance as a competitive advantage, publishing performance data to demonstrate their clinical integrity. In particular, for-profit providers consider quality management as a mechanism to build trust and gain legitimacy. Even though their share (in terms of units) has exceeded the share of public hospitals in recent years, for-profit hospitals are still met with scepticism in large parts of the society and are thus in search of mechanisms to increase public confidence.

All initiatives, whether they have been introduced by the Joint Health Commission, by health insurance funds, or by single hospitals, are based on the idea of enabling self-assessment. There is a shadow of hierarchy behind the external and industry-wide comparative quality assessment.

According to § 137 a SGB V, an external inspection can follow in case the assessment reveals irregularities. In addition, the regular examinations by the Medical Review Board of the Statutory Health insurance Funds (MDK, see below) are an instrument of external hierarchical scrutiny with the according threat of interventions. However, in a comparative perspective, a fierce control and sanctioning philosophy, which is characteristic for the British NHS, is lacking in Germany. On the contrary, ideas of promoting organisational learning prevail.

Due to the proliferation of different PM schemes in *England*, it is hard to point to a single underlying rationale. Rather, the different systems reflect different underlying objectives and also a variety of different assumptions about mechanisms and causality. In comparison to Denmark and Germany, the explicit focus on financial viability and robustness stands out. In Denmark, such issues are part of the management obligations of the five regional authorities and are handled internally as a relationship between the hospital management and the regions. In Germany, financial issues are negotiated between (associations of) sickness funds and (associations of) providers.

Another feature that makes England different from Denmark and Germany is the top–down formulation of an explicit annual 'Mandate' from the government to NHS England, which is intended to set the strategic direction for the NHS. The decentralised nature of the Danish and German systems means that there is less tradition for legally binding directives issued at the national (Denmark) and federal (Germany) levels. Rather, the central level relies on framework legislation, while many specific issues are handled through negotiated agreements. However, there has also been a tendency in Denmark to formulate more explicit targets and to make them subject to monitoring schemes and implicit threats of economic sanctions against the regions.

But financial viability is not the only purpose of the English PM schemes. An equally important objective is to improve both clinical and patient-experienced quality and to increase value for money. Both of these purposes are pursued through the collection of quality data by the CQC, Monitor (for FTs) and the NHS-TDA (for non-FTs).

The assessments of CQC, Monitor and TDA exemplify the focus on several purposes in the sense that financial robustness, value for money, quality, and safety are emphasised.

How Are Data Used for PM?

In Denmark, information about activity, productivity, service and quality is collected by national authorities through national patient registries,

DRG payment systems and specific reporting by regional and local authorities. They also feed into a recently set-up system of 50 indicators covering broad areas of population health, treatment quality, patient experiences and efficiency. These indicators are published in regular reports (Ministry for Health and Prevention, 2014).

Selected indicators (waiting times and some quality indicators) are published on national-level websites with interactive facilities to enable comparison and choice (eSundhed.dk: Sundhedskvalitet.DK). eSundhed.dk also contains a set of 11 indicators that are specifically aimed at measuring the interaction between municipalities and regions (hospitals) on a number of process dimensions. Accreditation reports are published by IKAS.dk.

All of the five Danish regions use some level of performance data (activity, waiting times, some quality indicators) for their internal steering of hospitals. This may be formalised in written agreements (soft contracts) between hospital management and regional authorities specifying targets and incentives. Performance data are also used in steering interaction between state and regions and municipalities.

Activity information is also used to determine a minor part of the allocation of funds from the national level to the regions. This is based on target activity levels, which must be reached in order to obtain funding from specific activity funds (approximately 5% of regional income). Activity information is also used to determine the municipal co-financing of hospital treatment (approximately 20% of regional income).

There are no explicit incentives or sanctions related to service and quality indicators. However, they are part of the ongoing monitoring and steering of regional and municipal activities and are discussed in coordination forums. It is likely that more explicit economic incentive schemes related to service and quality will be developed in the future, as the Ministry and the regions have jointly announced a plan to go beyond the traditional 'negotiated' use of quality data. Comparative quality performance data are already used to monitor overall developments and to compare across different regions and municipalities. Furthermore, a system of 50 key indicators has been developed to facilitate a more systematic and multidimensional monitoring of performance in the coordination of care across regions (hospitals) and municipalities (home-based and elderly care).

Quality indicators are also used as part of the information base for making decisions about which hospitals are allowed to perform highly specialised treatment procedures.

Control and sanctioning of medical personnel is an integrated part of department- and hospital-level management. Issues of misconduct or malpractice may be evaluated through complaint procedures organised by national authorities. The National Board of Health and Medicine is responsible for the surveillance of medical conduct and can revoke licences to practice medicine.

In *Germany*, the AQUA institute collects outcome data for 30 selected treatment procedures. Since 2011–2012, patient surveys are used as an additional data source for external assessments. In 2013, the data set was enlarged by integrating data collected by health insurance funds into the external comparative assessments. Thus, the performance measurement scheme of the AQUA institute is rather ambitious. Yet, in terms of disclosure, the information is mostly published at the aggregate level and without direct possibility for comparison. Peers and public authorities and the public in general only have access to general information about how many problems have been identified, and not about which hospitals or regions do better or worse. This is probably a reflection of the 'negotiated' nature of the system with many stakeholders.

The structured quality reports, which hospitals are required to publish regularly, allow assessments of single hospitals. However, no direct comparison between hospitals is possible. The general idea of these reports is that quality data should be accessible to the general public (for patients) and public principals (health insurance funds, GPs/outpatient care, bodies of administrative oversight). Hospitals have to deliver their quality reports to a regulatory office (which is part of the umbrella organisation of the health insurance funds). However, only detailed information about input and process parameters are collected and published. The quality reports inform amongst other things about the size of the hospital in terms of the number of beds and employees, its technical equipment and its activities in terms of number of cases, but the reports do not give information on output or outcome.

In addition to these mandatory measures, there are several voluntary systems covering networks of providers in particular areas. KTQ and Qualitätskliniken.de (quality hospitals) are two well-established examples of such voluntary initiatives. KTQ performs quality certification; information on 63 indicators is gathered by self-assessment and external auditors (http://www.ktq.de/).

Qualitätskliniken.de, too, offers quality certification, thereby considering 400 indicators in different dimensions (e.g. medical quality, patient security, patient satisfaction, ethics). In contrast to KTQ, Qualitätskliniken.de puts strong emphasis on benchmarking and choice (http://www.qualitaetskliniken.de/). To increase transparency in the hospital sector and to foster patient choice, the quality results are published on an online platform, which also allows hospital comparison. While KTQ is a joint initiative of the Federal Association of Sickness Funds, the Federal Chamber of Physicians, the German Hospital Federation and the German Nursing Council, Qualitätskliniken.de is run by a consortium of private and voluntary hospital providers.

A third example of a voluntary quality assessment is Quality Assurance Based on Routine Data, which has been developed in close cooperation by the Scientific Institute of the General Regional Funds and the Helios Clinics. Secondary routine administrative data such as data concerning diagnoses, procedures or demographics contain information about long-term outcome (mortality, subsequent revision and the need for care following surgical treatment), and thus allow an assessment of the outcome of hospital treatment (Heller, 2008). Hitherto, the results of the assessments are only available for the hospitals themselves.

So far, sanctions related to poor quality results are rare in Germany, indicating that data collection is not guided by a control and sanctioning philosophy to the same extent as in England. Health insurance funds and umbrella organisations of the outpatient sector are allowed to compare hospitals, give recommendations for patients on the basis of the quality reports and publish their recommendations on their homepages (hospitals have to be informed before publication). Up to now, health insurance funds have been somewhat reluctant to publish hospital rankings. They rather provide online tools that enable the insured to search and assess hospitals according to the structured quality reports. However, as the structured quality reports contain information based mainly on input indicators, it is questionable whether these reports and the online tools are helpful instruments to give the general public sanctioning power in a competitive hospital market.

While the sanctions following the structured quality reports are limited in scope, sanctions related to hospital evaluations by the Medical Review Board of the Statutory Health Insurance (MDK, Medizinischer Dienst der Krankenversicherung) and to the external industry-wide quality assessment are more explicit. In case the MDK reveals situations of misconduct or malpractice, licences to practice medicine can be revoked by the responsible authority at the state level (§ 12, 4 BÄO). In addition, financial sanctions can be applied. Financial incentives also play a role in evaluation conducted by the AQUA Institute. All hospitals receiving remunerations from the health insurance system (in 2012: 1,658 hospitals, AQUA, 2013) are obliged to document the data and make them available for external assessment. Hospitals are expected to document 100% of the data of the agreed 30 procedures assessed by the AQUA Institute. If less than 80% of the data are made available for the AQUA Institute, financial sanctions are applied. In cases where the quality assessment reveals irregularities and hospitals are identified as underperforming, they are invited to enter a so-called structured dialogue (§ 10 QSKH-RL). In a first step, the hospital is requested to explain the irregularities. If the explanation is not compelling, the case is discussed with the hospital management. An inspection can follow, presuming the hospital management agrees. All in all, the sanction mechanism reflects very much the corporatist nature of the German hospital sector with its consensus-oriented decision-making style, which persists even though the system has experienced a shift towards market-based governance (Bode, Lange, & Märker, 2013).

England is characterised by different PM regimes for FT and non-FTs, which are governed by two different bodies. For FTs this is Monitor, and for non-FTs the TDA. A key task for the TDA is to work its way out of existence by helping non-FTs prepare to become FTs.

Monitor, meanwhile, has accreted a variety of regulatory roles over time – for example, setting prices for most secondary care services as part of the Payment by Results tariff regime, and, importantly, assessing trusts for FT status, then 'licensing' FTs (a new measure introduced by the Health and Social Care Act 2012 to set out new objectives/conditions for Monitor in relation to the way they performance manage FTs. Summary details are listed here) and involvement in assessment of possible anticompetitive behaviour and patient choice as part of the work of the Competition and Markets Authority (CMA – a body which oversees competition issues across the economy as a whole and which has recently come to oversee the NHS).

Monitor assesses trusts for FT status against three criteria:

- Whether a trust meets the required quality performance threshold (working closely with the CQC to determine this);
- How well-run the trust is;
- The financial viability of the trust to ensure it can continue to deliver high-quality care on a sustainable basis.

The idea of a 'licence' grew out of a need for someone, somewhere in the system (in this case Monitor), to have powers to routinely review/performance manage trusts once they had become FTs. Details of the provider licence can be accessed on the Internet (http://www.monitor-nhsft.gov.uk/home/news-events-publications/our-publications/browse-category/guidance-health-care-providers-and-commissioners/licensing-provid).

The power to licence trusts was extended to all NHS trusts (i.e., non-FTs) by the H&SC Act 2012 to enable Monitor to fulfil its powers as part of the licensing regime viz. the power to:

- Set prices for NHS-funded care in partnership with the NHS England;
- Enable integrated care;
- Safeguard choice and prevent anticompetitive behaviour, which is against the interests of patients;
- Support commissioners to protect essential health services for patients if a provider gets into financial difficulties;
- Oversee the way that NHS FTs are governed.

Monitor was encouraged to develop a compliance framework. This was a measurement of how well an FT was run, but the measures it contained include, for example, waiting times standards. This meant that poor performance against national standards and targets would lead an FT to be declared in breach of the compliance framework (i.e. badly run) and thereby open to intervention by Monitor. In general, Monitor modelled the compliance framework on the annual 'plan' for the NHS as set out in the operating framework (to 2013) and in the national planning rounds for NHS England (in 2013 and now). In theory, the compliance framework was only supposed to be temporary; however, it has yet to be removed.

NHS-TDA oversees the remaining trusts. NHS-TDA inherited many of the broad powers of Strategic Health Authorities and can directly intervene against trusts that it considers to be poorly performing, and has done so since its introduction – trusts are effectively in a line-management relationship with TDA.

Another key regulatory organisation in terms of PM is the CQC. The CQC is the latest of a long(ish) line of quality management/promotion organisations stretching back to the original 2001 'improvement' organisation, the Commission for Health Improvement (CHI, 2001–2004) (http://en.wikipedia.org/wiki/Commission_for_Health_Improvement). CHI was superseded by the Commission for Healthcare Audit and Inspection (CHAI), renamed the Healthcare Commission (2004–2009), which in turn was replaced by the CQC from 2009 onwards. All were/are non-departmental government bodies. The role of the CQC now is to:

- Regulate and inspect public and private health and social care services in England.
- Register all providers of care based on an ongoing demonstration that they meet or already meet various care standards (cf., http://www.cqc.org.uk/about-us/how-we-do-our-job for details on the CQC's role and process).

CONCLUSION AND DISCUSSION: CURRENT TRENDS IN INSTITUTIONAL TRANSLATION OF PM WITHIN HEALTH CARE

The case studies have shown many similarities, but also important differences, among performance measurement of hospitals in Denmark, Germany and England. Broadly speaking, there is a tendency toward increasing ambitions in regards to PM in all three countries. National-level systems have gradually been developed to supplement local or regional experiments, or to replace previous national schemes, as in England. There are similarities in the units of data collected and in the dual purposes of the schemes as both internal development tools and increasingly also instruments for external accountability.

However, there are also some differences in the way this international trend towards the implementation of encompassing PM schemes is translated into the national institutional landscapes of the three countries under consideration. Differences can be seen with regard to both the general logic of the performance measurement (focus on control and sanctioning vs. support of organisational learning) and the governance of performance measurement (centralised vs. decentralised solutions). In this respect, England and Germany can be considered as 'most dissimilar cases', with England having implemented several mandatory national systems with considerable powers to intervene in specific hospitals, while performance measurement of German hospitals relies on the idea of self-governance granting hospitals considerable room of manoeuver. The German system is characterised by trust in the hospital's own initiatives; organisational learning is not systematically enforced from 'above' with either positive or negative sanctioning instruments. Denmark is somehow in the middle between the models of England and Germany, combining powerful actors at the central level with the encouragement for individual organisational learning at the hospital level. Further research is needed to assess the effects of the different approaches on hospital performance.

Going back to the theoretical perspectives on diffusion and translation of ideas and templates, our comparative analysis of the three cases leads to several interesting observations.

First, we find strong support for the claim by Sahlin and Wedlin (2008) that there is a strong emphasis on transparency templates within this sector (p. xxx). All three countries have seen a strong emphasis on frames or targets that actors use to compare or benchmark their activities and describe how success should be assessed (*ibid.*, p. 231). The templates suggest evaluation criteria, rankings, standards and widespread notions of what constitutes success. We also find evidence for the claim from Nordic institutionalism that editing in local/national contexts can lead to significantly different solutions. It is clear from our cases that the institutional structure of national health systems, with their inherent power structures and distribution of power among stakeholders, facilitates particular translations in some national organisational fields rather than others. We can therefore confirm the observation that 'Ideas do not diffuse in a vacuum but are actively translated in a context of other ideas, actors traditions and institutions' (*ibid.*, p. 219). 'To imitate then is not just to copy, but also to change and to innovate' (*ibid.*, p. 219).

Some of the important contextual factors include: firstly, national characteristics with regard to the adoption of ideas of NPM, and secondly, national characteristics of the health care system. Following the comparative literature on NPM (Christensen, Laegreid, Roness, & Røvik, 2007; Pollitt & Bouckaert, 2003), it seems to be likely that countries with early and extensive implementation of NPM such as England are more open to comprehensive PM schemes with disclosure strategies to support contracting and choice, and with more emphasis on economic incentives than NPM latecomers like Germany. The differences in terms of scope, depth and the underlying rationalities of PM schemes we have found in the three countries are also supported by the literature on health care regimes (Blank & Burau, 2014). England with its integrated NHS system seems to be more likely to develop centrally driven PM systems than the fragmented German health care system, which grants actors of self-governance considerable room for manoeuver. However, an additional dynamic has been at play in England. As the emphasis over the past decades has shifted to decentralisation of power to 'arms-length' agencies (NHS England, Regional Development Authorities) and relatively autonomous hospital 'FTs' and 'non-FTs', there has been a push to establish several different PM institutions dealing with different aspects of performance and different types of delivery organisations. Furthermore, the different PM institutions have developed over time to accommodate the different political emphasis of shifting governments and as a result of 'institutional politics' and competition (from CHI to CQC and Monitor). The decentralisation has also created a need for explicit PM of economic viability in England. This task is assigned to Monitor for trusts and NHS-TDA for non-trusts. In the Danish case, this sort of economic performance assessment is an integrated part of the regional management, and in Germany, these issues have mostly been articulated at the national level, rather than in regards to economic viability of the individual hospitals, probably due to the stronger element of private providers.

Our cases also clearly show the importance of political-level decisions in the introduction of new templates. Although such decisions are usually negotiated between relevant stakeholders and may be pre-empted by developments and pilot projects in the field, it is clear that once a central-level political decision has been made, this has important implications for the development of PM schemes in this field. This is an important observation in comparison to much neo-institutional literature, which tends to downplay or even ignore the role of political decision-makers and their power to impose organisational templates in organisational fields. Our observations also lead to sensitivity for several stages in the process. Often there is a preliminary stage where traditional diffusion and translation mechanisms are dominant. This leads to local-, regional-, or network-based experiments and pilots. Such pilots may be taken up by powerful national-level stakeholders in search for solutions to various problems of control and legitimacy and subsequently fed into a decision process. In this decision process, new opportunities for translation occur as political negotiations enfold. This can lead to reformulation of the initial concepts, and typically contributes to the decontextualisation, rationalisation and theorisation identified by Strang and Meyer (1993). Once a decision has been reached, this feeds into a process of implementation with new opportunities for translation and adjustment of the template. However, all actors in the field must address the template as it is now backed by political coercive power. This means that the subsequent phases of translation are more structured and delimited than sometimes assumed in the organisation theory literature. Combining neo-institutionalist literature with public administration literature, therefore, provides significant benefits when analysing organisational fields such as health care, where public authorities play a significant role as regulators, funders and organisers of service.

We can also confirm the interpretation of transparency schemes as part of a tendency to develop new and softer forms of regulation and self-regulation in modern organisational fields (Hood et al., 1999). Some of the mechanisms behind this development include growing distrust, a push for new types of responsibility and a search for control within 'regulatory markets' through pre-emptive adaptation and influencing of regulatory schemes. Contextual factors include the expansion and influence of scientific discourse, marketisation, new modes of democracy in the Internet era and a tendency to develop more formal organisations to assign explicit responsibilities (Blomgren, 2007; Sahlin & Wedlin, 2008, p. 234).

Finally, our cases confirm the observation that public sector organisations have many, and sometimes competing goals, and that this has implications for the design of PM schemes. We therefore see rather broad PM schemes combining several different goals. However, we also see that a new generation of PM schemes is emerging, trying to combine results orientation with economic incentives in more sophisticated ways than before. Yet, it is also clear that there is a long way to go before such schemes have proven their robustness and superiority to other schemes.

REFERENCES

AQUA. (2013). German Hospital Quality Report 2012, Institute for Applied Quality Improvement and Research in Health Care GmbH, Göttingen, Germany.

Blank, R. H., & Burau, V. D. (2014). *Comparative health policy* (4th ed.). Basingstoke: Palgrave Macmillan.

Blomgren, M. (2007). The drive for transparency: Organizational field transformations in Swedish healthcare. *Public Administration*, *85*(1), 67–82.

Bode, I., Lange, J., & Märker, M. (2013). Qualitätsagenda im krankenhauswesen. Eine diffuse agenda und reichlich ambivalenz. *Sozialer Fortschritt*, *62*(12), 293–299.

Bouckaert, G., & Halligan, J. (2008). *Managing performance: International comparisons*. London: Routledge.

Busse, R., & Blümel, M. (2014). Germany: Health system review. *Health Systems in Transition*, *16*(2), 1–296.

Christensen, T., Laegreid, P., Roness, P. G., & Røvik, K. A. (2007). *Organization theory and the public sector: Instrument, culture and myth* (Vol. 1, pub 1). London: Routledge.

Czarniawska, B., & Joerges, B. (1996). Travels of ideas. In B. Czarniawska & G. Sevón (Eds.), *Translating organizational change* (pp. 13–48). Berlin: Walter de Gruyter.

Daniels, A. C. (2004). *Performance management: Changing behavior that drives organizational effectiveness* (4th ed., rev.). Atlanta, GA: Performance Management Publications.

DiMaggio, P., & Powell, W. (1983). The iron cage revisited: Institutional isomorphism and collective rationality in organizational fields. *American Sociological Review*, *48*, 147–160.

Heller, G. (2008). Zur messung und darstellung von medizinischer ergebnisqualität mit administrativen routinedaten in deutschland. *Bundesgesundheitsblatt – Gesundheitsforschung – Gesundheitsschutz*, *51*(10), 1173–1182. doi:10.1007/s00103-008-0652-0

Hood, C. (1991). A public management for all seasons? *Public Administration*, *69*(1), 3–19.

Hood, C., Scott, C., James, O., Jones, G., & Travers, T. (1999). *Regulation inside government*. Oxford: Oxford University Press.

Jorgensen, T., & Bozeman, B. (2007). Public values: An inventory. *Administration Society*, *39*(3), 354–381.

Lægreid, P., & Christensen, T. (Eds.). (2007). *Transcending new public management: The transformation of public sector reforms*. Aldershot: Ashgate.

Meyer, J. W., & Rowan, B. (1977). Institutionalized organizations: Formal structure as myth and ceremony. *American Journal of Sociology*, *83*(2), 340–363.

Ministry for Health and Prevention. (2014). *Indblik i sundhedsvæsenets resultater*. Retrieved from http://www.sum.dk/Aktuelt/Publikationer/Indblik-i-sundhedsvaesenets-resultater-maj-2014.aspx. Accessed on August 31, 2014.

Moynihan, D. P. (2008). The dynamics of performance management: Constructing information and reform. In *Public Management and Change Series*. Washington, DC: Georgetown University Press.

Pollitt, C. (2011). Performance blight and the tyranny of light. In M. Dubnick & H. G. Frederickson (Eds.), *Accountable governance: Problems and promises* (pp. 81–98). New York, NY: M.E. Sharpe.

Pollitt, C., & Bouckaert, G. (2003). Evaluating public management reforms: An international perspective. In H. Wollmann (Ed.), *Evaluation in public-sector reform: Concepts and practice in international perspective* (pp. 12–35). Cheltenham: Edward Elgar Publishing.

Sahlin-Andersson, K. (1996). Imitating by editing success: The construction of organizational fields. In B. Czarniawska & G. Sevon (Eds.), *Translating organizational change* (pp. 69–92). Berlin: Walter de Gruyter.

Sahlin, K., & Wedlin, L. (2008). Circulating ideas: Imitation, translation and editing. In R. Greenwood, C. Oliver, R. Subbady, & K. Sahlin (Eds.), *The SAGE handbook of organizational institutionalism* (pp. 217–241). London: Sage.

Stone, D. A. (1997). *Policy paradox: The art of political decision making*. New York, NY: W.W. Norton.

Strang, D., & Meyer, J. W. (1993). Institutional conditions for diffusion. *Theory and Society*, *22*, 487–511.

Van Dooren, W., Bouckaert, G., & Halligan, J. (2010). *Performance management in the public sector*. London: Routledge.

Wedlin, L. (2007). The role of rankings in codifying a business school template: Classifications, diffusion and mediated isomorphism in organizational fields. *European Management Review*, *4*(1), 24–39.

PART III
INSTITUTIONAL LOGICS IN HEALTH CARE AND HIGHER EDUCATION

STRATEGIC AND ENFORCED LOGICS HYBRIDIZATION: AN AGENCY VIEW WITHIN FRENCH HOSPITALS AND UNIVERSITIES

Corinne Grenier and Johan Bernardini-Perinciolo

ABSTRACT

Adopting an agentic positioning, we question and compare competing logics hybridization within French hospitals and universities facing major reforms inspired by new public management. In addition to the resulting forms of hybridization exposed in the literature (accepted or refused), we observe four additional modes: instrumentalized, uncomfortable, reformulated, and suffered. They all reveal the varied manner with which each professional faces reform. However, we develop a new argument: the ways professionals hybridize (or do not) their prevailing logic depends on an overarching mode of hybridization that characterizes the way their organization deals with reform. We identify two contrasting modes: overarching strategic logics hybridization and overarching enforced logics hybridization. They give insight into how actors decouple structure from practices. We contribute to the literature on logics hybridization by first analyzing the role of specific actors who act as either a

Towards a Comparative Institutionalism: Forms, Dynamics and Logics Across the Organizational Fields of Health Care and Higher Education
Research in the Sociology of Organizations, Volume 45, 109–144

ISSN: 0733-558X/doi:10.1108/S0733-558X20150000045016

translator-actor or a closure-actor to respectively facilitate appropriation of the reforms or to protect professionals against the growing dominance of the new logic introduced by the law; and secondly by discussing importance of articulating higher and lower organizational levels all involved in hybridization.

Keywords: Hybridization; translator-actor; closure-actor; institutional logics; hospitals; universities

JEL classifications: I23; I18; L30; I19

INTRODUCTION

Traditionally, universities and hospitals are viewed as ideal types of professional bureaucracies characterized by a strong autonomy of actors who are in a position to decree rules and norms for practices in line with their own professional culture and values (Mintzberg, 1996). For few decades, new public management (NPM) principles (Burau & Vrangbæk, 2008) have been spreading into professional organizational fields to introduce more efficiency and accountability (Brunsson & Sahlin-Anderson, 2000; Christensen & Lægreid, 2011). The idea is that negative consequences from the noted autonomy within professional organizations should be counterbalanced by managerial practices and new organizational arrangements serving the diffusion of NPM principles. Implementation of such NPM reforms have been studied in various ways (Amar & Berthier, 2007; Ferlie et al., 1996; Hood, 1991) but all have the aim of investigating to what extent and how professional organizations correspond to such changes, which are intended to modify the prevailing institutionalized habits (economic vs. professional efficiency, accountability to external bodies vs. appraisal by peers, etc.).

In this paper, we embrace the institutional pluralism that organizations face and mobilize the literature on institutional logics (Reay & Hinings, 2005; Thornton, Ocasio, & Lounsbury, 2012) and hybridization (Battilana & Dorado, 2010; Greenwood, Raynard, Kodeih, Micelotta, & Lounsbury, 2011; Skelcher & Smith, 2013). Taking its essence from the Latin *hibria* to qualify the offspring of a sow and a wild boar, this term means, in a common sense, the product of two or more different things (Gittell & Douglass, 2012). The existing literature questions hybridization at different levels of analysis or of interests: organization, context, logic, etc. Here, we consider that hybridization can lead to either hybridized practices and/or identities of actors, or to logics hybridization, both in a more or less balanced coexistence between logics (Daudigeos, Boutinot, & Jaumier, 2013; Reay & Hinings, 2009; Thornton et al., 2012; Van Gestel & Hillebrand, 2011). Generally, the literature investigates the various forms of hybridization and the facilitating conditions for such (more or less) alteration of the prevailing professional logics. We intend to contribute in a different way to the literature: we analyze hybridization (its content) to show what it reveals about why actors implement reforms. In doing so, we adopt an agentic position. Hybridization has often been viewed as a necessary response to external changes, as if actors have no choice other than integrating economic logic into their prevailing professional values and practices. We conversely consider that individuals or organizations can exercise some degree of strategic choice (Dorado, 2005) in the way they integrate hybrid logics (or do not). They do not just reproduce their logics or integrate new logics, but either adapt them to local contexts or are able to give predominance to one or the other logics according to the stakeholders they work with or depend upon.

Our contribution is based on how one French university and one French hospital implemented reforms inspired by NPM. These reforms present significant challenges to these two kinds of organizations because they introduced new objectives (excellence for universities, profitability for hospitals) and new managerial and governance principles (the "autonomy" of the university and the clinical services pole within hospitals). Both organizations are then confronted with potential competition between the prevailing professional logics and newly introduced economic logics (Christensen & Lægreid, 2001, 2011; Leicht & Fennell, 2008). We chose these organizations as a revelatory (or typical) case (Yin, 2003) for the original way hybridization has been appropriated and implemented, and then for contributing to the literature. Our methodological approach consists of identifying the controversies raised about the reforms and the solutions adopted by the actors, which give us access to how they have more or less hybridized their prevailing logics with an economic logic.

The paper is organized as follows. We first identify specific modes of hybridization that enrich the literature on institutional pluralism in two directions: hybridization per se and the ability of actors to deal with such reforms while trying to maintain professional logic at the core (an agentic perspective). Second, we sustain a new argument: the ways actors hybridize (or do not) their prevailing logic depends on an overarching mode of hybridization that characterizes the way the organization deals with reform.

We identify two contrasting modes: overarching strategic logics hybridization and overarching enforced logics hybridization. They give insight on the way actors decouple structure from practices and we depict them by analyzing the actors who act as either a translator-actor or *closure-actor*. We then propose a further research agenda.

THEORETICAL BACKGROUND

Institutional Logics and Logics Hybridization

Institutional logics provide detailed insights into how institutions shape actors' values and practices as well as how they make sense of situations (Dunn & Jones, 2010; Reay & Hinings, 2005). They give actors guidelines for action, recognition of appropriate goals to pursue, and describe means to achieve them (Pache & Santos, 2013). Because each logic represents a way of thinking and acting, the multiplicity of institutional logics can produce competition between stakeholders, thus resulting in difficulties of cohesion and management (Dunn & Jones, 2010; Edwards & Delbridge, 2011; Lounsbury, 2007). Additionally, in a competing institutional context, a hierarchy takes place between a dominant logic and the other(s) (Reay & Hinings, 2009). In this sense, an uncontrolled hybridity may cause changes and conflicts of domination between stakeholders (Kitchener, 2002; Scott, Ruef, Mendel, & Caronna, 2000) in terms of governance (Thornton, Jones, & Kury, 2005), organizational structure (Cooper, Hinings, Greenwood, & Brown, 1996; Tracey, Phillips, & Jarvis, 2011), and practices (Lounsbury, 2007) and, finally, can expose organizations to mission drift and to a loss of their main objective (Battilana & Dorado, 2010).

But conflict is not the only way; logics can coexist for a long time even if it is precarious. Thornton et al. (2012) state that sustainable hybridity can be achieved if the conflict and tension that emerge from competition of logics are managed. It then requires decoupling the strategies of stakeholders and/or their activities (Fiss & Zajac, 2006) or developing codependency relations (Reay & Hinings, 2009). Sustainable hybridization also seems possible by implementing identity hybridization with a strategy in which socialization and recruitment are critical (Battilana & Dorado, 2010; Battilana, Lee, Walker, & Dorsey, 2012; O'Connor & Smallan, 1995). Research has shown different ways of solving competing logics: maintaining the prevailing logic, replacing the prevailing logic with a new one, keeping the coexistence of multiple logics, and implementing hybridization between competing logics, which is when one logic (often the dominant one) integrates elements of other logics, resulting in a new logic that synthesizes several logics (Battilana & Dorado, 2010).

An Agentic Perspective on Logics Hybridization

The fundamental point of departure of the neo-institutional perspective is institutional isomorphism, because organizations seek legitimacy within their environment for sustaining their development and accessing the resources they need (DiMaggio & Powell, 1983). Recent literature, however, has focused on institution change. Hargrave and Van de Ven (2006) identify four process models of institutional innovation: the design, adaptation, diffusion, and collective action models. The first two processes focus on reproduction through evolutionary and adaptive processes, whereas the diffusion model examines changes by considering institutions as the level of analysis. The collective action model constitutes a kind of overarching model that considers the role of actors in changing institutions when they "break away from scripted patterns of behavior" (Dorado, 2005, pp. 387–388). Actors' agency within an institutional environment is then considered in different ways. Some works focus on the political dimension of institutional changes, because they result from "networks of distributed and partisan actors in an interorganizational field who are embedded in a collective process of creating or revising institutions" (Hargrave & Van de Ven, 2006, p. 867). Networking progressively sustains mobilization of actors in favor of changes, generally initiated by peripheral promoters of the field (Hargadon & Douglas, 2001) who raise endemic tensions and disputes. Such a process helps the production of aligned arguments in favor of change. A second, but linked, major focus of the literature relies on the cognitive dimension of institutional change, when actors frame institutional problems and develop theses and antitheses in favor of change. This process is viewed as change theorization, which refers to "self-conscious development and specification of abstract categories and the formulation of patterned relationships such as chains of cause and effect" (Strang & Meyer, 1993, p. 492). A third stream of literature highlights the role of social positions in the ability to conduct changes (Battilana, 2006; DiMaggio, 1988; Dorado, 2005). Individuals' social position that can be "determined by their position in this organizational field, on the one hand, and by their position in their organization, on the other hand" (Battilana, 2006, p. 660). In this way, individual's social position (social groups' status, individual's formal and informal position in organization, etc.) enables individuals to have the necessary resources but also enough legitimacy to do so (Battilana, 2006; Lawrence, 1999; Maguire, Hardy, & Lawrence, 2004; Seo & Creed, 2002). Thus, political and social cognitive sides help assert that organizations and individuals can exercise some degree of strategic choice whilst responding to institutional pressures (Pache & Santos, 2013; Seo & Creed, 2002). Oliver (1991) has offered a well-known typology of strategic responses to pressure: conformity, compromise, avoidance, defiance, and manipulation. In another way, Pache and Santos (2013) analyze strategic choices in institutionalized environments depending on the degree of adherence to competing logics. In this sense, actors can be *novice* when they have no adherence to the logic, *familiar* with the logic when they know what the logic means and can comply with it in practice but without values adherence, or *identified* with the logic if there is high adherence. Each level of adherence implies a level of hybridization that will be more or less high and more or less accepting of change.

RESEARCH FIELD AND METHODOLOGY

The Research Field

We investigate and compare hybridization within one French middle-sized hospital and one French middle-sized university, publicly funded and whose CEO and President (respectively) is nominated by the French government. Both leaders and organizations are obliged by the law to adopt major reforms based on NPM principles: the 2009 Hospital, Patients, Health, Territories (HPST) law and the 2007 Law on Rights and Responsibilities of Universities (LRU), respectively. Our case concerns three logics: two prevailing ones – the *academic* and the *medical* logics and the new logic (*economic*) introduced by the reform. The latter is said to undermine the existing professional logics, as it induces an heteronomous control (i.e., from outside the professional sphere) on professions reputed to be self-controlled (Paradeise, 2008; Parsons, 1951); and according to Mintzberg (2010), professionals "ignore" (*ibid.*, p. 331) the issues of the organization viewed as governed by managers. In line with Reay and Hinings (2005), the three logics are described in Table 1 below.

Table 1. Professional and Economic Logics.

Logic		Hospital Case	University Case
Professional logic	Values	Patient-focused	University strongly anchored in its local environment to better serve students and companies
	Practices	Restoring patient well-being whatever length of the duration at the hospital and practicing medical acts to deliver it	Customized curriculum programs
			Research activities derived from individual academic interest
Economic logic	Values	Framing medical acts and limiting duration at hospital for economic reasons	Fit the performance criteria imposed by the law (research volume and quality, student numbers, etc.)
	Practices	Using monitoring indicators, quality control, move toward staff, and equipment rationalization	Assess activities and develop accountability practices

The Hospital Case

The 2009 HPST law reinforces the move toward new hospital governance, which promotes performance development through efficiency and care quality. The spirit of the reform is to instill hybridization between medical and economic logics within hospitals, because it officially promotes the "medico-economic" logic. However, and especially because of the very bad financial situation of French hospitals, health professionals are strongly required to make economic considerations a quasi-priority in their decisions or activities: medical activities and investments have to be made and evaluated with regard to economic criteria before any others, and with regard to medical criteria when it does not lead to damaging the financial situation of the hospital. The clinical services pole is the locus targeted by the law in which both professional and economic logics have to be hybridized. The pole, which clusters clinical services, is headed by a gynecologist (i.e., clinical manager; Doolin, 2001), with the assistance of one senior nurse (in charge of managing nurses and organizing the delivery of care), and one management assistant (in charge of collecting and analyzing economic data). It has to integrate economic criteria into decision making on medical activities, including the way activities are performed. An internal system of contractualization (the pole contract) specifies the economic and medical objectives of the pole. Various tools, such as accounting instruments, budget control tools, and modes of fixing tariffs on activities, are at the disposal of the pole head to manage activities (including volume and categories of activities, modes of delivering, materials or staff recruitment, etc.). Among the 11 clinical services poles structured by the hospital, we report in this research analysis undertaken on the child-woman pole – which embraces the maternity ward, pediatrics, pediatric emergencies, obstetrics, and medically assisted procreation activities – and we then concentrate our analysis on how the head of the pole hybridizes (or not) professional logic when performing both managerial (as a manager) and clinical (as a doctor) duties. We chose this pole because, in the largest study (Grenier & Bernardini-Perinciolo, 2013), compared to the other poles of the hospital, the clinical manager and its management team acted in an original way to deal with the logics hybridization advocated by the HPST reform. We consider this case as revelatory or typical (Yin, 2003).

The University Case

French universities are experiencing ongoing implementation of performance-based approaches in their management to meet objectives of competitiveness in research and higher education at an international level (Enders & Musselin, 2008; Musselin, 2008). This approach of performance has been introduced in the French legal system by the 2007 LRU, and allows universities to independently manage their budgets. Through change in the university governance, the objectives of LRU are to make universities more attractive and increase their international visibility (placing French universities at the top of international rankings). Universities were given five years to voluntarily take on new responsibilities starting in 2009. In this context, academics have to be accountable with regard to their activities. Accountability is based on three changes: external evaluation; mandatory research evaluation, whereas before only voluntary candidates for promotion were submitted; and successful implementation of new tasks resulting from the evaluation (consisting of managing indicators that are not produced by those being evaluated). The above measures are thought to help strengthen the control of behavior and the use of time and resources (Enders & Musselin, 2008) with respect to aspects such as the execution of teaching tasks, expenses, incentive mechanisms for budget allocation, and so on. In this context, hybridization is reflected in how academic professionals collectively contribute to better organizational performance through specific collective teaching and research activities that target the *organization as a whole*.[1] Thus, we identify the university as our level of analysis.

More specifically, the study focuses on a middle-sized French university that has addressed the LRU requirements since 2009, at the very beginning of the LRU implementation (Grenier & Zeller, 2014), and we concentrate our analysis on how professional actors at one UFR[2] hybridize (or not) their professional logic when performing managerial tasks and teaching and research endeavors.

The Rationale for Comparison

Three main reasons sustain the relevance of comparing these two cases.

Similarities in how the reforms affect hospitals and universities:

- Both reforms attempt to achieve a balance between academic or medical logic and economic logic (toward profitability and excellence, respectively).
- Performing such objectives is achieved through major structural changes, against the collection of numerous loci of activities and their pluralistic nature: the pole against numerous services, and the whole organization against the quasi-autonomy of the UFR.
- The targeted levels of change (the clinical services pole and the top management of the university) are both managed by one professional actor (the president of the university has a PhD in management and still produces academic research; the head of the clinical pole is a specialized doctor in gynecology, and still does his job on a part-time basis) who is supposed to develop hybrid competencies (O'Connor & Smallan, 1995).

Differences in how the reforms affect hospitals and universities:

- Even though the HPST law came after the LRU law (respectively, 2009 and 2007), hospitals are facing a long-standing process of change driven by economic considerations even before the major reform of 1996. Conversely, the introduction of NPM principles within French universities is a much more recent phenomenon.
- Although the university is headed by a hybrid manager, who functions as a teacher-researcher and manager, the hospital is headed by a professional administrator educated at a specialized school (French School of Public Health).
- Reforms focus on two different levels of major change: the clinical services pole and the university as a whole. Consequently, the pole rests under the hierarchical authority of the hospital CEO, who himself has to

report directly to the ministry, whereas the president of the university is directly appointed by the ministry.

Similarities when considering the cases of hospital and university
In their respective fields, the hospital and university cases are both locals, middle-sized organizations and have confronted critical issues for their survival. Both organizations face a dire situation (rising financial debt, decrease in student numbers, difficulties in hiring academics) and are potential targets of a possible "forced merger" and even a closure threat in the case of the university.

The Research Methodology

For this investigation we pursued qualitative and comparative research based on a case study methodology (Yin, 2003). We collected primary data (interviews and some observation in situ) and secondary data (various reports, regulatory texts, other documents, etc.). Concerning primary data of the hospital field, we interviewed the three members of the so-called "trio" piloting the pole (the head, the senior nurse, and the management-assistant) as well as the head and the senior nurses of the two main medical services that compose the pole and eight other professionals, offering contrasting position facing the reform (see Table 2). Similarly, in the higher education case, we interviewed the president of the university, the head of the UFR as well as academics of varied statutes (professor and lecturer) associated with two disciplines represented in the UFR (law and management). Table 2 presents the actors interviewed.

We use Miles and Huberman's (2003) recommendations in analyzing and comparing data on a coding grid (for both primary and secondary data) based on our theoretical framework. Following Reay and Hinings (2005), we coded all materials using the two dimensions of institutional logics: *values and associated practices* (Table 1). The data analysis was organized around the following (three) steps. First, we identified critical episodes (termed "*controversies*") that relate to activities at the core mission of the professionals, which are ones the professionals perceived as the most challenged by the reform. Controversies are then organized according to relevant analysis units to investigate our research question on hybridization. In line with our theoretical framework, we consider that the way actors solve controversies relies on the way they succeeded (or not) in hybridizing competing logics in their local context. Tables 3 and 4 present the identified controversies; what the

Table 2. The Study Sample.

Research Field	Actors Interviewed	Function	
University (17)	Professor of ecology	Dean (and president)	
	Professor of law	Codirector of doctoral school	
		Director of laboratory	
		Codirector of master	
	Professor in law, lecturer in management	UFR department heads	
	Lecturer in management, lecturer in law	Program director heads	
	Lecturer in management	Advisor to the dean	
	Others: PhD, professor in law, two lecturers in law, two professors in management, four lecturers in management		
Hospital (18)	Gynecologist	Head of pole	Pole management team
	Senior nurse	Senior nurse of pole	
	Middle manager	Management assistant	
	Gynecologist, pediatrician	Heads of medical services	
	Pediatric senior nurse, senior midwife, two senior nurses	Senior nurses of medical services	
	Others: Two nurses, two midwives, two gynecologists, two pediatricians		
	The chief of the strategy and prospective department		

top-down reforms were intended to accomplish within both the university and hospital in the concerned activities domains (e.g., espoused changes; i.e., Orlikowski, 2002); and the local solutions for controversies and the kind of hybridization pursued (consult the case study analysis section below). Second, we identified the local solutions for controversies when negotiations for finding these solutions revealed tensions between both logics. Because these solutions derive from the ways actors have more or less hybridized the professional and economic logics they are embedded in, we present the solutions in terms of *values* and *practices*, the two dimensions of institutional logics. Third and finally, we analyzed the various forms of hybridization actors display when attempting to reconcile both logics or resist economic logic when solving (more or less) these controversies.

We resorted to various analytical tactics to secure the internal and external validity of the research (Drucker, Ehlinger, & Grenier, 2001). First, we enriched primary data with secondary data so as to enhance the level of validity (Eisenhardt, 1989). In addition, each author coded the data separately; comparison among coding enabled us to stabilize this analysis. Specific attention was put on: (a) the way the case study was presented in relation to the theoretical concepts; (b) the selection of data sets as to best contribute to a deep understanding of the ways actors hybridize (or not) logics (Tables 3 and 4). For each case, we present the local controversies (column 1) around which actors try to find accepted solutions and which reveal different kinds of hybridization (column 3). In column two, we describe the content of these controversies and in column four, the way either values or practices have been more or less hybridized. Finally, the main results were openly discussed with some key informants in either field.

ANALYSIS OF THE CASE STUDIES

We present the analysis of the cases separately and then discuss our results in the next part.

The University Case Study

Overview on Hybridization and Local Solutions for Controversies

Table 3 details the five controversies identified during our interviews with university actors. The findings are then compared to the intentions of the 2007 reform (e.g., espoused changes). We then identified local solutions for controversies since they reveal the kind of hybridization being pursued at the local level.

The Various Forms of Logics Hybridization

As described in the literature (Kraatz & Block, 2008; Pache & Santos, 2013), we observe that competition between logics leads to either hybridized values and associated practices (hybridization accepted in 5 out of 15 episodes) or values and practices still anchored in professional logics (hybridization refused in 5 out of 15 episodes).

Table 3. Controversies Raised and Local Solutions Developed through Logics Hybridization (University Case).

Local Controversies	Espoused Changes Expected from Reforms	Local Solutions for Controversies	
External evaluation of research	1. Using external and harmonized (at national level) grid of criteria 2. Mixed qualitative and quantitative criteria 3. Research evaluation done by one national agency (AERES[a]) 4. Impact of the AERES evaluation on financial allocation to the university	Hybridization refused	*Values*: Research evaluation must still be given by peers.
			Practices associated: Academics refuse to align their research with the criteria of the external agency.
		Hybridization accepted	*Values*: The academic job is based on research evaluation.
			Practices associated: Academics accept the need to alter their research activities in line with the AERES evaluation guidelines.
		Instrumentalized hybridization	*Values*: Evaluation is a valuable process to assess good use of "public funds," even if done using criteria academics cannot control.
			Practices associated: Academics orient their research in line with the AERES guidelines, but at the same time develop critical discourse on it.
Research agenda	1. Research agenda aligned with the president's strategic positioning for the university 2. Research labs in social sciences requested to work with external main labs in the region	Hybridization refused	*Values*: Research is driven by researcher interests.
			Practices associated: Academics continue to define their research agenda in line with their own interests.
		Hybridization accepted	*Values*: The survival of the university requires research reorientation in line with the strategic plan of the president.

Table 3. *(Continued)*

Local Controversies	Espoused Changes Expected from Reforms	Local Solutions for Controversies	
			Practices associated: Academics accept to integrate research themes as enumerated by the president into their own research agenda.
		Uncomfortable accepted hybridization	*Values*: Confidence is placed in some actors who assert that the survival of the university requires research reorientation in line with the strategic plan of the president.
			Practices associated: Academics would like as far as possible to integrate the research themes enumerated by the president; however, they express difficulties in making their agenda evolve.
Teaching evaluation by students	1. Conceiving and implementing process 2. Using teaching evaluation questionnaires	Hybridization refused	*Values*: Teaching cannot be evaluated because the diploma of academics (PhD) means competence in teaching.
			Practices associated: They refused to have their teaching evaluated.
		Hybridization accepted	*Values*: Teaching evaluation helps compare the university teaching quality with others, then helps prove its legitimacy.
			Practices associated: The academics deploy the evaluation process in their courses.

		Instrumentalized hybridization	*Values*: Teaching evaluation is a valuable process to prove the relevance of the strategic plan of the president.
			Practices associated: They accept teaching evaluation and even some of them deploy evaluation processes in their courses, but at the same time they maintain critical discourse on the relevance of criteria and on the way criteria are elaborated
Increasing professional placement of the students	1. Designing curriculum in line with local economic expectations 2. Developing collaboration with the local economic sphere	Hybridization refused	*Values*: Universities deliver courses based on academic debates.
			Practices associated: They do not integrate local or professional issues into their courses.
		Hybridization accepted	*Values*: Providing professional placement to good students helps legitimize the university in its local environment.
			Practices associated: They agree to integrate local and professional issues into their courses by developing stronger links with the professional sphere.
Being involved in corporate commissions	1. Entering electoral process 2. Participating in corporate commissions	Hybridization refused	*Values*: Academics career and legitimacy rely on research activities.
			Practices associated: They refuse to participate in such commissions.
		Hybridization accepted	*Values*: University survival requires being involved in corporate commissions to all work together toward shared objectives.

Table 3. *(Continued)*

Local Controversies	Espoused Changes Expected from Reforms	Local Solutions for Controversies	
			Practices associated: Despite academics' career and legitimacy always relying on research, they agree to spend time in community involvement.
		Instrumentalized hybridization	*Values*: Academics' career and legitimacy rely on research activities.
			Practices associated: Academics however find interests in participating in corporate commissions, either for their future career or because they expect to negotiate resources for their research activities.
		Reformulated hybridization	*Values*: University survival requires being involved in commissions to work all together toward shared objectives.
			Practices associated: For academic (expertise) and for personal reasons (career), academics demonstrate interest in being involved in the management of the sole commissions or departments dealing with research activities.

[a]AERES: Agence d'Evaluation de la Recherche et de l'Enseignement Supérieur; Agency for Evaluation of Research and Higher Education.

We therefore observe three additional logics interactions that enrich the existing literature:

- *Instrumentalized hybridization*: dissociation between values claimed and practices associated. Such hybridization helps academics to maintain compliance with their dominant logic (professional logic), either to maintain their own identity or to appear legitimate to their colleagues, while agreeing to modify their practices. Maintenance of a kind of coherence is exercised through critical discourse on the way of implementing the reform. We find two orientations for the instrumentalized hybridization:
  - *The corporate-oriented, instrumentalized hybridization*: when academics comply with the corporate discourse or positioning of the university, valuating the president's strategic plan which defends the role of the local and mid-sized university, against merger or closure threat. Academics then are willing to change their practices, but at the same time, they develop a critical discourse on behalf of the "good use of public funds" (close to a "public service mission" the university is supposed to deliver; Grenier & Zeller, 2014).
  - *The individual-oriented, instrumentalized hybridization*: when academics act for career or personal interest reasons.
- *Uncomfortable accepted hybridization*: even if actors accept hybridizing their values and practices, they do not develop adequate practices because they are missing competencies.
- *Reformulated hybridization*: Academics are ready to hybridize their practices in line with the economic logic facet of the 2007 regulation, but they interpret the reform to better comply (aligned) with their academic values.

Agentic Behavior Facing the Implementation of the 2007 Reform?

The 2007 reform aimed to help universities seek higher excellence in teaching and research and all the UFR were supposed to contribute to this objective. Obviously, the implementation of the reform six years after has not complied with the espoused reform, and the university has not yet acquired a proper and specific identification. The academic logic is still strongly considered legitimate within the university, making the prevailing UFR and research labs the legitimate places for discussions and the privileged social arenas to define research agendas and/or teaching content. However, the reform is not rejected per se, and for each of the domains represented by the controversies, we find actors who refuse hybridization as well as others who accept it or who develop specific kinds of hybridization. This position with regard to hybridization does not depend on the academic discipline of the professionals. That being said, it seems that younger actors (PhD students, young professors) as well as those already invested in collective actions for the benefit of the university prior to the reform are more favorable to hybridize their logics. We have observed an overarching sense-making process (Weber & Glynn, 2006; Weick, 1995; Weick, Sutcliffe, & Obstfeld, 2005) of the reform at the level of the entire university that reveals the agentic behavior of the actors involved, which we term the *overarching strategic hybridization.*

This overarching hybridization means that academics mainly support the strategic positioning of the president engaging with the LRU reform to make the university legitimate (DiMaggio & Powell, 1983; Meyer & Rowan, 1977; Scott, 1987; Suchman, 1995) and then to find resources for escaping threats of merger or closure. At the same time, they develop abilities to preserve as far as possible their prevailing logic. For instance, they express critical discourses on NPM or negotiate access to resources so as to be comfortable with keeping their values aligned with their academic logic while altering their practices in line with a more economic logic. Although very few academics were found to hybridize and align their identities and practices, we mainly observe an agentic posture based on decoupling identities (still mainly anchored in the academic logic) from practices that are altered to comply with the LRU prescriptions. For instance, when academics accept altering the curriculum to be more attractive to the local business sphere, align their research agenda with the president's strategic positioning for the university, etc. Because of their social position (Battilana, 2006) or ability to raise appropriate resources (Maguire et al., 2004), making them behaving in an agentic way, these academics are especially the ones whose research is of sufficient high quality (and recognized by external colleagues) so as not to be damaged by the AERES evaluation orientation; or are recognized as good teachers so they can resist modifying their courses to integrate local topics raised by the economic environment and local firms (for instance, to increase student placement).

The Hospital Case Study

Hybridization and Local Solutions for Controversies

Table 4 details the four controversies identified during our interviews with hospital personnel compared to the 2009 reforms intended to be introduced within the hospital (e.g., espoused changes). We then identified the local solutions for controversies because they reveal the kind of hybridization pursued.

Table 4. Controversies Raised and Local Solutions Developed through Logics Hybridization (Hospital Case).

Local Controversies	Espoused Changes Expected from Reforms	Local Solutions on Controversies	
Professionals hiring	1. Hiring costs covered by activities increase. 2. Hiring is justified by creation of activities if they are profitable.	*Suffered hybridization*	*Values*: Hiring is done to satisfy patient needs (competencies) and care quality (job excellence).
			Practices associated: Professionals have to conform to the rules of hiring anchored in economic logic: hiring for mainly profitable medical activities.
		Hybridization accepted	*Values*: Recruitment for profitable medical activities is a driving force of pole development to meet patient needs.
			Practices associated: Professionals are involved in or sensitive to assessment of medical activity profitability when requesting recruitment.
Activity profitability assessment	1. Price per activities 2. Profitability of care quality	*Suffered hybridization*	*Values*: Medical activities must target patient well-being.
			Practices associated: Professionals have to conform to the obligation to make medical activities profitable.
		Instrumentalized hybridization	*Values*: Objectives of profitability and well-being of patients are not incompatible through separate medical activities.
			Practices associated: Professionals accept the need to change their practices to enhance the profitability of some medical activities when they succeed in demonstrating the legitimacy of other activities that are less profitable.
		Reformulated hybridization	*Values*: The pole has to be financially balanced but not necessarily profitable because of the public statute of the hospital.
			Practices associated: Professionals demonstrate the well-balanced finances of the medical activities they would like to launch.

Table 4. *(Continued)*

Local Controversies	Espoused Changes Expected from Reforms	Local Solutions on Controversies	
The pole contract as a tool of governance	1. Autonomy of the pole 2. Allocating resources to the pole 3. Accountability principle	*Suffered hybridization*	*Values*: The pole contract is not the appropriate and legitimate tool to manage the hospital.
			Practices: The professionals have to conform with managerial and governance rules of the pole, even when they have great difficulties in having the means to behave as so (access to data, etc.).
		Instrumentalized hybridization	*Values*: Clinical services' pole logic of management is compatible with autonomous management of medical services.
			Practices associated: Even if medical services heads recognize the role and the legitimacy of the clinical services pole to address their request for hiring or activities development, they sometimes override the pole to negotiate with top management.
Professional involvement in medical activities management	1. In their activities management, professionals refer to the trio of the pole.	*Suffered hybridization*	*Values*: The clinical units' heads value their infra-managerial roles on behalf of the pole trio.
			Practices: They complain from not benefiting from the announced infra-autonomy to perform their duties. They are only then involved in daily operational tasks.
		Hybridization refused	*Values*: They make any effort to improve the well-being of patients.
			Practices associated: They mainly concentrated on only medical activities, refusing to perform any operational tasks.

The Logics Hybridization

As described in the literature (Kraatz & Block, 2008; Pache & Santos, 2013), we observe that competition between logics leads to hybridized values and practices (*hybridization accepted*), but in only one case among the nine controversy solutions we analyzed. In three cases, medical personnel were capable of manipulating the introduction of the economic logic in ways already described above (*instrumentalized and reformulated hybridization*), by dissociating practices and values. In four cases out of the nine controversies analyzed, professional actors behaved in a *suffered manner*, when they had to conform to the dominant economic facet of the HPST law (practices) while attempting to maintain their values embedded in the medical logic. However, in most cases, and contrary to the university case, hospital professionals were unable to escape the changes required by the law.

Agentic Behavior Facing the Implementation of the 2009 Reform?

The HPTS reform aims to fight against the collection of medical units within hospitals, which were quasi-autonomous and much more oriented toward medical rather than economic considerations in their way of being managed. A general target of the reform relies on the creation of the clinical services poles as an appropriate intermediate structural level (between top management and services), which has to mitigate professional and economic criteria to manage activities. A first glance reveals that the poles are in place. However, a more fine-grained analysis shows how the economic logic has spread (became institutionalized) throughout the entire hospital. In such contexts, professionals sometimes succeed in finding a proper level of hybridization by reformulating the terms of the reform or by instrumentalizing their adhesion to the economic orientation of the hospital. But, the dominant situation is one in which medical professionals do not really have the appropriate means to do their job; and we label this agentic behavior as an *overarching enforced hybridization*. Indeed, and similar to other French hospitals, this middle-sized hospital is unprofitable, putting the top leadership under strong pressure from the regional health agency. Any hiring or investment for developing medical activities is accepted if/when professionals can prove their profitability. Contrary to the university case, the reform is both relied on by internal and external hierarchies. As a consequence, functional departments such as HRM or IS departments are at the core of the profitability-oriented way of managing the hospital. They do not accept transferring a part of their jobs to the pole, which is not as autonomous as described in the HPST governance principle.

DISCUSSION

In the context of institutional pluralism, we question reform appropriation within professional organizations through the theoretical frame of institutional logics and agentic perspective. Our research design is based on the identification of controversies and the way professionals solve them. The analysis of solutions for controversies first makes visible debates raised about reform implementation within organizations, and second gives an account of the degree of agency of professionals when dealing with economic logic that competes with their professional (academic and medical) logics.

In both cases, and from a structural point of view, we have observed that structural changes have been implemented in line with the reforms requirements (the university considered as a whole organization developing its own strategic message, and the pole where medical activities are regulated) and anchored the spirit of the reform (excellence and profitability). However, at the same time we observed to what extent daily practices are more or less disconnected from what the reforms require. Some professionals refuse to hybridize their prevailing professional logics with economic logic; others find ways to make compromises between both logics (instrumentalized and reformulated hybridization); some change their practices but in a suffered manner (suffered hybridization).

All these behaviors give a varied picture of the more or less agentic ability of actors to deal with the reforms while working in the same organization (Clemens & Cook, 1999). The literature already offers many responses for explaining the ability of actors to deploy agentic behaviors in a context of institutional pluralism, for example through a social position (Battilana, 2006; Dorado, 2005) or via adherence to each institutional logic (Pache & Santos, 2013). Our case analysis reveals one additional explanation, that is, agency behavior of individuals sustained by a higher organizational level (the organization and its president, the pole and its head in the cases of the university and the hospital, respectively). Consequently, we articulate both individual (the professionals) and organizational (the organization or the pole representing the infra-organizational level) levels of analysis to explain agentic behaviors in a context of institutional pluralism. Our data sets help sustain a new argument to the existing literature: the ways actors hybridize (or do not) their prevailing logic and display agentic behavior depend on an overarching mode of hybridization that characterizes the way the organization (or any appropriate structural level they operate within daily) deals with change. We identify two contrasting manners in which the university and the pole deal with such change, which we term *overarching strategic logics hybridization* and *overarching enforced logics hybridization*, respectively.

In both cases, many professionals do not accept the requested changes. But in the case of the university, the president succeeded in turning the reform into a strategic interest for finding resources to escape threats of closure or merger (Pfeffer & Salancik, 1978). In this sense, external pressures of change have to be answered to gain legitimacy and to survive (DiMaggio & Powell, 1983; Meyer & Rowan, 1977; Scott, 1987). Seeking legitimacy in that way helps the university to gain autonomy and act more strategically (Oliver, 1991), or to become more entrepreneurial, and especially being able of addressing issues raised by various stakeholders (Pinheiro & Stensaker, 2014). This agentic organizational positioning offers academics enough supportive arguments and resources either to hybridize (even in different ways) their prevailing logic with the economic logic or to resist hybridization. Conversely, in the case of the hospital, the pole could *not* escape the strong move toward economic consideration and failed in asserting its autonomy against the top-management (itself under the strong pressure of the ministry) or the functional departments (having tools to manage profitability requirements). However, this case enlightens how such enforced hybridization could be *counterbalanced* by the specific role of the head of the pole, who helped professionals in their daily practices. Indeed, although the head of the pole declares himself to be a novice (Pache & Santos, 2013) with economic logic, he or she takes benefits from the management team members[3] by becoming familiar with it to combine medical and economic logics (Berg & Pinheiro, forthcoming; Pache & Santos, 2013; Zibler, 2002).

Overarching hybridization sustains ways actors make sense of the new regulations, helping how they interact to collectively reduce the ambiguity of a situation (Weick, 1995). Contrary to the dominant literature that considers an institution's imprint to be the cause of cognitive constraints and then ways of analyzing the environment, we follow Weber and Glynn's who explain that "internalized constraint works through the preclusion of potential alternatives" (2006, p. 1640), then leading actors to "make sense with institutions, not outside them or despite them" (2006, p. 1642). Sensemaking is managed by the very specific role of the head of the pole and of the president of the university (as explained in the sector about the translator-actor and the closure-actor). These roles are made possible especially because the actors continue to display their core professional tasks (publishing articles or making medical consultations). Table 5 describes the two overarching hybridizations. Both depict a specific form of decoupling within public organizations confronted with adopting reforms that

Table 5. Overarching Strategic and Enforced Logics Hybridizations.

	Overarching Strategic Logics Hybridization	Overarching Enforced Logics Hybridization
Purpose of the reform	The university as a whole organization Excellence	Clinical poles as autonomous in managing clinical activities Profitability
Reform implementation	Strategic agency of compliance with economic logic as a means to make the university legitimate to escape external threats	Enforced agency of being under pressure to integrate economic considerations Weak autonomy of the pole
Logic dominance	Professional logic	Economic logic
Driven forces	Accommodating the economic logic with professional logic Supportive process on the reason for implementing the reform	Escaping the economic logic Counterbalanced process helping professionals to save face
Decoupling	Symbolic adoption	Symbolic implementation
Critical actors	The president acting as a translator-actor	The pole head acting as a closure-actor

undermine prevailing logics. We will discuss them by turning back to the literature on decoupling and exploring the specific role of two actors, one of whom acted as a *translator-actor* and the other as a *closure-actor*.

Specific Modes of Decoupling Sustaining Overarching Hybridization

Among the five strategic responses to pressures (reforms in our contribution) actors can sustain, Oliver (1991) has identified the strategy of compromise or decoupling. Decoupling is the king of agentic behavior when actors try escaping or manipulating such pressures. It relies on the gap between structures and daily practices (Meyer & Rowan, 1977). Generally, *structures* (including organizational arrangements, procedures, tools, etc.) are the ones imposed by reforms whereas *practices* refer to the ways of acting that are embedded in the professional logics of the actors concerned. Decoupling helps explain why organizations respond to external pressures in a heterogeneous manner (Boxenbaum & Jonsson, 2008), implementing reforms with different degrees of impact on activities and structures. For instance Pinheiro, Ramirez, and Trondal (2014) show how "*efforts to enhance tight-coupling across university structures, functions and activities have the potential for reducing (rather than enhancing) adaptive capacity at the organizational level*" (*ibid.*, p. 2215). The literature has identified several reasons for decoupling: when actors (engineers as professional actors) interpret the reforms (the ISO norm implementation) as a threat to their own rationalized myths and practices they want to safeguard (Sandholtz, 2012); when academics in higher education do not perceive the reforms as efficient solutions for their organizations (Geschwind & Karlsson, 2014); when they do not trust the actors in charge of the implementation of the reforms, when reforms are ambiguous (Oliver, 1991); when they lack competences or supportive resources to adopt the reform (Lim & Tsutsui, 2012; Meyer & Rowan, 1977); or when they ignore its true content or objectives (Bromley & Powell, 2012). We also find that actors with high power in their organization (due to their hierarchical position or legitimacy) could more easily decouple to pursue their own strategic interests (Westphal & Zajac, 2001) or to maintain or gain power/autonomy in the case of hospitals (Kernand et al., 2014). Bromley and Powell (2012) have identified two forms of decoupling: *symbolic adoption*, when the adoption of the reform does not result in meaningful implementation, leading to persistence of prevailing practices; and *symbolic implementation*, when new practices are implemented and become routines but are still viewed as not contributing to the core goals of the organization, as perceived by professionals because of their own logics. The agentic behavior of the case academics and the medicals rely on these two forms of decoupling, but offer additional understanding of this mechanism.

In the case of the university, academics accepted the entry of their organization in the LRU process as labeled by their president: proving legitimacy of the university and finding arguments for escaping the threat of merger or closure. Some of them participated in top-level committees in which the strategy and the way of implementing the reform are discussed. But the reform remains ambiguous[4] (Gornitzka, 1999) and, for instance, academics could argue that the target of excellence (Pinheiro & Geschwind, 2014) could continue to be reached through prevailing habits (i.e., ritualistic compliance; Meyer & Rowan, 1977). Our university case offers a specific mode of decoupling as symbolic adoption because the meaningful label of the reform implementation is itself decoupled: a visible adherence to the reform as promoted by the ministry as well as a manipulated adherence (through instrumentalized and reformulated hybridization), which allows them to maintain some prevailing activities. This is similar to Huisman, Norgård, Rasmussen, and Stensaker (2002) as they earlier observed how academics adopt the identity labels of the reform, but not the meanings behind those labels, hence leading to weak institutionalization of new practices. In addition to the ambiguity of the reform already mentioned, we find three additional explanations of such symbolic adoption: (a) the ability of actors who benefit from enough resources or legitimacy to comfortably deal with their apparent opposition to the reform; (b) the legitimacy of the president (who continues to do research); and (c) the president's understanding of how such reform could disturb one's academic peers.

In the case of the hospital, and even if we acknowledge that any reform contains ambiguity (Gornitzka, 1999), the HPST reform states to the professionals two clear "desired outcomes" (*ibid.*, p. 17) without ambiguity: they are forced to adopt the reform, and its main objectives strongly state that profitability must be restored. Although the official statement of HPST is about deploying a "medico-economic" logic within hospitals, the professionals cannot ignore the economic logic in their decisions, which more and more prioritizes medical logic for any decision made concerning activities or medical investments (in consideration of the financial deficit of the hospital). Professionals are then requested to use various tools of accountability and profitability measurements. This case offers a specific mode of decoupling as a symbolic implementation, anchored in a counterbalanced mechanism that helps professionals maintaining a discourse or some practices anchored in their professional logic relating to patient services quality. This counterbalanced mechanism is portrayed by the specific role of the head of the pole who acts as a *closure-actor*, that is, he or she attempts to facilitate the daily activities of the professionals and moderate the quasi-dominance of the economic logic within the pole. This role contrasts with the way the president of the university manages the boundaries of his or her organization, as a *translator-actor* between the requirements of the external stakeholders and the professionals within the organization. Below, these two distinct roles are discussed in more detail.

Two Roles for Managing Boundaries: The "Translator-Actor" versus the "Closure-Actor"

A frame is an interpretive lens through which individuals perceive and interpret the world and occurrences in this world (Boxenbaum, 2006; Goffman, 1974), shaping and guiding action. Frames are legitimate and strongly stabilized because they are anchored in the institutional logics of professional fields. In our context, the LRU and HPST reforms offer frames (as previously described) that undermine the prevailing frames within the university and the hospital, and that the professionals value only partly. The acceptance of the new frames requires transformation through translation (Boxenbaum, 2006). Implementation of reforms requires that the latter are locally translated before being articulated with the prevailing practices, considering that translation is exercised with more or less success (Biggart & Guillén, 1999; Boxenbaum, 2006).

Translation consists of moving and transforming frames across boundaries to reach a (more or less) combined and accepted frame. It helps "to perceive a managerial practice from multiple perspectives and subsequently engage creatively with frames" (Boxenbaum, 2006, p. 941). The result is local grounding, consisting of hybrid elements (*ibid.*, p. 940) of the new practices promoted by the reforms with local (prevailing) practices. This end proceeds from two activities: "individual preference, [which] captures what each translator considered most meaningful and valuable within the managerial practice" and "strategic reframing, [which] refers to strategic considerations in terms of resource mobilization, implementation" (*ibid.*, p. 940). We focus on the role displayed by the president of the university and the head of the hospital pole as the crossing of the boundaries between the external and the internal boundaries of the organizational units under investigation (i.e., the university and the pole). The literature on boundary actor or spanner (Brown & Duguid, 1998, 2001; Cross, Ernst, & Pasmore, 2013) generally considers the translation (of reform, tool, managerial change, etc.) from one professional world (Carlile, 2004) to another. Our comparative case provides novel insights to one complementary role, namely, when the *mediator role* (Di Marco, Taylor, & Alin, 2010; Gray, 2008) not only consists of translating but also closing boundaries to prevent the entry of some change imposed by one professional world into another world.

The president acts as a "*translator-actor*" as he or she translates the reform entry as a mean to escape threats of closure or merger. This translation makes sense for all the professionals because he or she translates more specifically the main requirements of the reform (research excellence, relevance of program curriculum with the main stakes of the companies and other bodies the students are educated to work within) into research and curriculum aligned with the requirements of the local environment of the university, defending the value of small-sized universities truly anchored in their immediate environment to contribute to its development. This translation process facilitates alignment between higher (ministry) and lower (university and academics) institutional levels expectations and gives academics supportive arguments to deal with the reform in a way that helps them preserve (more or less) their prevailing logics. And although in the UFR there remains the legitimize locus where academics continue to discuss research and teaching and to refer to (against the reform which promotes the university as a whole), it is rather at this level that arguments in favor of the reform (to escape threat of merger or closure) and ways of implementing the reform in a more or less hybrid manner are discussed. In return, the academics feed the president with proper arguments to legitimate his or her strategic posture, without being weakening by the persistence of ancient practices.

Turning to the case hospital, we observe that the head of the pole displays such translation so that to favor the acceptance of the HPST law, for instance whilst negotiating recruitment or additional resources for developing activities with the hospital director or the functional departments (Quality, HRM, etc.). Yet, this field offers an additional and contrasting insight into the specific role of this individual as a "*closure-actor*," preventing a too strong an entry within the pole of the requirements of economic considerations, and, subsequently, producing a discourse in favor of the "medico-economic logic." Although this logic, officially stated by the HPST reform, is generally contested among professionals, the defense of such logic is a way for defending "Care against Figures," which then makes it possible for the head of the pole (the clinical manager) to assert professional values and to produce a discourse that counterbalances the growing economic pressure on the hospital and the quasi-dominance of the economic logic (Grenier & Bernardini-Perinciolo, 2013). Such a dual role is made possible through a well-accepted distribution of responsibilities within the pole's managerial team (the trio): the assistant-manager is devoted to accountability and the senior nurse is devoted to nurse and social worker management; forming all together a distributed leadership (Baker & Denis, 2011) based on mutual understanding and clear collaboration. This distributed trio helps the head of the pole to claim himself or herself being a novice (Pache & Santos, 2013) on the managerial and accounting instrumentations, continuing to be well perceived as a doctor among one's peers while, at the same time, familiar enough (*ibid.*) with the political issues of the hospital to raise the right arguments during negotiations.

Both actors display their "*translator*" and "*closure*" roles through critical discourse on the reforms: critical discourse for supporting hybridization (through decoupling the meaningful label of the reform according to the varied set of stakeholders) in the case of the university, and critical discourse for resisting enforced hybridization (through restoring the boundaries of the pole against the top-management and the functional departments so that to help medicals to save the face, and to help them display tasks in line with their medical logic) in the case of the hospital.

What is more, both actors develop such boundary roles according to the following reasons or rationale:

- Being able to demonstrate the rightness of their position, by producing some "tangible" proofs such as: some researchers of the university benefit from academic audiences at an international level (even if there are only a few!), programs attract students who commit to long-term internships in local companies; the pole offers a rather good financial balance (compared to the other poles of the hospital), the investments the head have made have sustained activity increase, etc.;
- Being legitimate in the eyes of external stakeholders, who are mainly the ministry in the case of the university and the CEO of the hospitals (considered here as external to the pole), as they have been appointed by them and not disputed since. Such external legitimacy (Suchman, 1995) has crucial influence on the ability of the university and the pole to be understood, sourced, and evaluated as expected. In line with Drori and Honig (2013), we find evidence of the critical insight of internal legitimacy, defined as "the acceptance or normative validation of an organizational strategy through the consensus of its participants, which acts as a tool that reinforces organizational practices and mobilizes organizational members around a common ethical, strategic or ideological vision" (*ibid.*, p. 347). This is consistent with Olsen (2007) who asserts that institutions are validated by outsiders (e.g., the state) but are defended by insiders.

The president of the university and the clinical manager of the pole search for internal legitimacy (among the academics or the members of the pole) to be sustained in their role of implementing the LRU and the HPST reforms: being legitimized as *translator-actor* or *closure-actor*. This legitimacy is achieved since they still continue to exercise their traditional professional tasks, that is, research and medical activities.

CONCLUSION AND FURTHER RESEARCH

We investigate implementation of reforms inspired by NPM in two professional organizations (hospital and university) through a hybridization of logics between the prevailing academic and medical logics and the economic logic imposed by the reforms, inspired by the NPM principles. Consistent with the literature (Kraatz & Block, 2008; Pache & Santos, 2013; Seo & Creed, 2002), we observe that some professionals refuse hybridization, and that others partly hybridize their prevailing logics. They do so by maintaining their ancient practices and identities, but mainly by decoupling professional identity from more hybrid practices, or finding compromises to accept the reforms although others adhere to the new logic. However, we have identified more nuanced process of hybridization that we label: *instrumentalized, reformulated, suffered,* and *uncomfortable accepted.*

In addition, we offer two distinctive explanations than those provided in the existing literature. First, we demonstrate that the ways actors hybridize (or not) their logics and display some kind of agentic behaviors is contingent upon an overarching mode of hybridization displayed at higher organizational level, and which, in turn, characterizes how these higher levels deal with changes, that is, in the form of overarching strategic and overarching enforced logics hybridizations. Second, we provide support to the fact that this double-level hybridization process is sustained by the specific role of actors located at the boundaries between the lower and the higher organizational levels, hence acting as "translator-actor" to facilitate appropriation of the reforms on the one hand, and/or as "closure-actor" to protect professionals against the growing dominance of the new logic introduced by the law.

We propose to pursue this analysis (future studies) by identifying the abilities of these translator- and closure-actors in acting as sense-makers (Gioia & Chittipeddi, 1991) influencing the manner the reform should be interpreted on the one hand, and on the other contributing to the work of Hope (2010) who has investigated some abilities such as controlling working agenda, recruiting experts, etc. Sense-making is a relational process in which actors elaborate on their own interests as to coordinate and collaborate efficiently and in light of local norms, traditions, and identities (Olsen, 2007). This, in turn, encourages us to mobilize Strauss, Bucher, Ehrlich, Schatzman, and Sabshin (1963) seminal work on Negotiated Order (NO). In our case study, we observe how the university as a whole (and not just the UFR) and the clinical pole (and not just the medical services) began being perceived as the organizational level of action by professionals. In such a context of institutional pluralism, we find it suitable for future studies to shed light on the extent and how negotiations about reforms make actors perceive themselves as dependent into a negotiated space institutionalized as separate from the rest of the organization. NO introduces the role of social interactions, which has often been neglected in institutional analysis (Hallett & Ventresca, 2006), these authors considering as important not only to focus on what people are doing to transform institutions but also on how they do it together. We will then contribute to theoretical stream that departs from social structures as given and emphasizes that social order results from negotiated and cooperative interactions between actors rather than "the reactions of participants to existing rules, as mechanistic and other traditional social control approaches claim" (Pasquero, 1991, p. 54).

NOTES

1. This expression is clearly anchored in our actor-wood perspective (coherent with our agentic perspective of behaviors of individuals in an institutional pluralistic context). It means that the university should be considered as a more complete organization (the LRU spirit) against the quasi-autonomy of its constituents (UFR), making the university a collection of programs or research agendas in a weak coherent manner.
2. UFR: *Unité de Formation et de Recherche*; Education and Research Unit. UFRs are legally autonomous and operate under their own statutes; they associate training departments and research centers or laboratories.
3. And especially the management assistant, who has a long professional experience as a medical secretary and, recently, has a Master in "Management of Health Organizations" and who is familiar (Pache & Santos, 2013) with managerial and economic considerations. Our data analysis could not qualify this management assistant as "identified" (*ibid.*) with the economic logic. He or she indeed displays a mitigated attitude toward too strong economic pressure on that hospital, which he or she considers to be a public organization in charge of public service (of health), resulting in his or her thinking that the medical logic should continue to be reinforced.
4. Ambiguity is first about the pressure to comply with the reform imposed by the ministry on the president of the university. Universities had five years to enter the LRU system, and because in a context of huge contests against the reform, the university in the study adopted it during the first year, and its president expected some indulgence on behalf of the ministry. In addition, the priority given to research excellence or to education is not clear and may offer some margins in the way of hiring new colleagues or evaluating professional activities.

ACKNOWLEDGMENT

The authors thank Christelle Zeller, PhD student at the CERGAM (IMPGT) Laboratory, Aix-Marseille University, for having collected the data for the university case study and for her contribution to the paper.

REFERENCES

Amar, A., & Berthier, L. (2007). Le nouveau management public: Avantages et limites. *Gestion ET Management Publics*, *5*, 1–14.

Baker, R., & Denis, J. L. (2011). Medical leadership in health care systems: From professional authority to organizational leadership. *Public Money and Management*, *5*, 355–362.

Battilana, J. (2006). Agency and institutions: The enabling role of individuals' social position. *Organization*, *13*(5), 653–676.

Battilana, J., & Dorado, S. (2010). Building sustainable hybrid organizations: The case of commercial microfinance organizations. *Academy of Management Journal*, *53*(6), 1419–1440.

Battilana, J., Lee, M., Walker, J., & Dorsey, C. (2012). In search of the hybrid ideal. *Stanford Social innovation Review*, *Summer 2012*, 50–55.

Berg, L., & Pinheiro, R. (2015). Handling different managerial logics in the public sector: Comparing management in Norwegian universities and hospitals. In R. Pinheiro, F. Ramirez, K. Vrabæk, & L. Geschwind (Eds.), *Towards a comparative institutionalism? Forms, dynamics and logics across health and higher education fields*. Research in the Sociology of Organizations. Bingley, UK: Emerald Group Publishing Limited.

Biggart, N. W., & Guillén, M. F. (1999). Developing difference: Social organization and the rise of the auto industries of South Korea, Taiwan, Spain, and Argentina. *American Sociological Review*, *64*(5), 722–747.

Boxenbaum, E. (2006). Lost in translation? The making of Danish diversity management. *American Behavioral Scientist*, *49*(7), 939–948.

Boxenbaum, E., & Jonsson, S. (2008). Isomorphism, diffusion and decoupling. In R. Greenwood, C. Oliver, K. Sahlin, & R. Suddaby (Eds.), *The Sage handbook of organizational institutionalism* (pp. 78–98). London: Sage.

Bromley, P., & Powell, W. (2012). From smoke and mirrors to walking the talk: Decoupling in the contemporary world. *Academy of Management Annals*, *6*, 483–530.

Brown, J. S., & Duguid, P. (1998). Organizing knowledge. *California Management Review*, *40*(1), 90–111.

Brown, J. S., & Duguid, P. (2001). Knowledge and organization: A social-practice perspective. *Organization Science*, *12*(2), 198–213.

Brunsson, N., & Sahlin-Anderson, K. (2000). Constructing organizations: The example of the public sector reform. *Organization Studies*, *21*(4), 721–746.

Burau, V., & Vrangbæk, K. (2008). Institutions and non-linear change in governance: Reforming the governance of medical performance in Europe. *Journal of Health Organization and Management*, *22*(4), 350–367.

Carlile, P. (2004). Transferring, translating, and transforming: An integrative framework for managing knowledge across boundaries. *Organization Science*, *15*(5), 555–568.

Christensen, T., & Lægreid, P. (2001). New public management. *The transformation of ideas and practice*. Aldershot: Ashgate.

Christensen, T., & Lægreid, P. (2011). Complexity and hybrid public administration—theoretical and empirical challenges. *Public Organization Review*, *11*(4), 407–423.

Clemens, E. S., & Cook, J. M. (1999). Politics and institutionalism: Explaining durability and change. *Annual Review of Sociology*, *25*, 441–466.

Cooper, D. J., Hinings, C. R., Greenwood, R., & Brown, J. L. (1996). Sedimentation and transformation in organizational change: The case of Canadian law firms. *Organization Studies*, *17*(4), 623–647.

Cross, R., Ernst, C., & Pasmore, B. (2013). A bridge too far? How boundary spanning networks drive organizational change and effectiveness. *Organizational Dynamics*, *42*, 81–89.
Daudigeos, T., Boutinot, A., & Jaumier, S. (2013). Taking stock of institutional complexity: Anchoring a pool of institutional logics into the interinstitutional system with a descendent hierarchical analysis. In M. Lounsbury & E. Boxenbaum (Eds.), *Institutional logics in action, Part B* (Vol. 39, pp. 319–350). Research in the Sociology of Organizations. Bingley, UK: Emerald Group Publishing Limited.
Di Marco, M. K., Taylor, J. E., & Alin, P. (2010). Emergence and role of cultural boundary spanners in global engineering project networks. *Journal of Management in Engineering*, *26*(3), 123–132.
DiMaggio, P. J. (1988). Interest and agency in institutional theory. In L. G. Zucker (Ed.), *Institutional patterns and organizations: Culture and environment* (pp. 3–21). Cambridge: Ballinger.
DiMaggio, P. J., & Powell, W. W. (1983). The iron cage revisited: Institutional isomorphism and collective rationality in organizational fields. *American Sociological Review*, *48*(2), 147–160.
Doolin, B. (2001). Doctors as managers. New public management in a New Zeeland hospital. *Public Management Review*, *3*(2), 231–254.
Dorado, S. (2005). Institutional entrepreneurship, partaking, and convening. *Organization Studies*, *26*(3), 385–414.
Drori, I., & Honig, B. (2013). A process model of internal and external legitimacy. *Organization Studies*, *34*(3), 345–376.
Drucker, C., Ehlinger, S., & Grenier, C. (2001). Validity and reliability. In R. A. Thiétart et al. (Eds.), *In doing management research – A comprehensive guide* (pp. 196–220). London: Sage.
Dunn, M. C., & Jones, C. (2010). Institutional logics and institutional pluralism: The contestation of care and science logics in medical education, 1967–2005. *Administrative Science Quarterly*, *55*, 114–149.
Edwards, T., & Delbridge, R. (2011). *Managing institutional complexity through multiple organizational arrangements: Negotiated order in the superyacht field.* Working paper. Cardiff Business School.
Eisenhardt, K. M. (1989). Building theories from case study research. *Academy of Management Review*, *14*(4), 532–550.
Enders, J., Musselin, C. (2008). Retour vers le futur? Les professions universitaires au XXIe siécle. Centre pour la recherche et l'innovation dans l'enseignement (Ed.). *L'Enseignement Supérieur L'Horizon*, *2030*, 131–160.
Ferlie, E., Ashburner, L., Fitzgerald, L., & Pettigrew, A. (1996), *New public management in action*. Oxford: Oxford University Press.
Fiss, P., & Zajac, E. J. (2006). The symbolic management of strategic change: Sense-giving via framing and decoupling. *Academy of Management Journal*, *49*(6), 1173–1193.
Geschwind, L., & Karlsson, S. (2014). *Why change? The rationale for major organisational change in higher education institutions*. Rotterdam: Egos colloquium.
Gioia, D., & Chittipeddi, K. (1991). Sensemaking and sensegiving in strategic change initiation. *Strategic Management Journal*, *12*, 433–448.
Gittell, J. H., & Douglass, A. (2012). Relational bureaucracy: Structuring reciprocal relationships into roles. *Academy of Management Review*, *37*(4), 709–733.

Goffman, E. (1974). *Frame analysis*. Cambridge, MA: Harvard University Press.

Gornitzka, Å. (1999). Governmental policies and organisational change in higher education. *Higher Education*, *38*(1), 5–31.

Gray, B. (2008). Enhancing transdisciplinary research through collaborative leadership. *American Journal of Preventive Medicine*, *35*(2), 124–132.

Greenwood, R., Raynard, M., Kodeih, F., Micelotta, E. R., & Lounsbury, M. (2011). Institutional complexity and organizational responses. *The Academy of Management Annals*, *5*(1), 317–371.

Grenier, C., & Bernardini-Perinciolo, J. (2013). La décision du chef de pôle hospitalier aux prises avec des logiques institutionnelles concurrentes: Vers un espace hybride décisionnel – Une recherche exploratoire. GEAP conference, Edinburg, September.

Grenier, C., & Zeller, C. (2014). La mobilisation collective face à un changement institutionnel imposé par le haut – Le cas d'une université de petite taille dans le contexte de mise en œuvre de la loi LRU. *RIMHE*, *10*, 93–113.

Hallett, T., & Ventresca, M. (2006). How institutions form: Loose coupling as a mechanism in Gouldner's patterns of industrial bureaucracy. *American Behavioural Scientist*, *49*, 908–924.

Hargadon, A., & Douglas, Y. (2001). When innovations meet institutions: Edison and the design of the electric light. *Administrative Science Quarterly*, *46*, 476–501.

Hargrave, T., & Van de Ven, H. (2006). A collective action model of institutional innovation. *Academy of Management Review*, *31*(4), 864–888.

Hood, C. (1991). A public management for all seasons. *Public Administration*, *69*, 3–19.

Hope, O. (2010). The politics of middle management sensemaking and sensegiving. *Journal of Change Management*, *10*(2), 195–215.

Huisman, J., Norgård, J. D., Rasmussen, J., & Stensaker, B. (2002). Alternative universities revisited: A study of the distinctiveness of universities established in the spirit of 1968. *Tertiary Education and Management*, *8*(4), 316–332.

Kernand, W. N., Ovbiagele, B., Black, H. R., Bravata, D. M., Chimowitz, M. I., Ezekowitz, M. D., ... Wilson, J. A. (2014). On behalf of the American heart association stroke council, council on cardiovascular and stroke nursing, council on clinical cardiology, and council on peripheral vascular disease. Guidelines for the prevention of stroke in patients with stroke and transient ischemic attack: A guideline for healthcare professionals from the American Heart Association/American Stroke Association. *Stroke*, *45*, 2160–2236.

Kitchener, M. (2002). Mobilizing the logic of managerialism in professional field: The case of academic health centre mergers. *Organization Studies*, *23*(3), 391–420.

Kraatz, M., & Block, E. (2008). Organizational implications of institutional pluralism. In R. Greenwood, C. Oliver, K. Sahlin, & R. Suddaby (Eds.), *Sage handbook of organizational institutionalism* (pp. 243–275). London: Sage.

Lawrence, T. B. (1999). Institutional strategy. *Journal of Management*, *25*(2), 161–188.

Leicht, K. T., & Fennell, M. L. (2008). Institutionalism and the professions. In R. Greenwood, C. Oliver, K. Sahlin, & R. Suddaby (Eds.), *The Sage handbook of organizational institutionalism* (pp. 431–448). London: Sage.

Lim, A., & Tsutsui, K. (2012). Globalization and commitment in corporate social responsibility: Cross-national analyses of institutional and political-economy effects. *American Sociological Review*, *77*, 69–98.

Lounsbury, M. (2007). A tale of two cities: Competing logics and practice variation in the professionalizing of mutual funds. *Academy of Management Journal*, *50*, 289–307.

Maguire, S., Hardy, C., & Lawrence, T. B. (2004). Institutional entrepreneurship in emerging fields: HIV/AIDS treatment advocacy in Canada. *Academy of Management Journal, 47*(5), 657–679.

Meyer, J. W., & Rowan, B. (1977). Institutionalized organizations: Formal structure as myth and ceremony. *American Journal of Sociology, 83*(2), 340–363.

Miles, M. B., & Huberman, M. (2003). *Analyse des données qualitatives* (2nd éd.). Bruxelles: De Boeck & Larcier.

Mintzberg, H. (1996). Managing government, governing management. *Harvard Business Review, May–June*, 75–83.

Mintzberg, H. (2010). Structure et dynamique des organisations, 21ème édition, Editions d'Organisation.

Musselin, C. (2008). *Les universitaires*. Paris: Edition La Découverte.

O'Connor, G., & Smallan, C. (1995). The hybrid manager: A review. *Management Decision, 33*(7), 19–28.

Oliver, C. (1991). Strategic responses to institutional processes. *The Academy of Management Review, 16*(1), 145–179.

Olsen, J. P. (2007). The institutional dynamics of the European university. In P. Maassen & J. P. Olsen (Eds.), *University dynamics and European integration* (pp. 25–54). Dordrecht: Springer.

Orlikowski, W. (2002). Knowing in practice: Enacting a collective. *Organization Science, 13*(3), 249–273.

Pache, A. C., & Santos, F. (2013). Embedded in hybrid contexts: How individuals in organizations respond to competing institutional logics. In M. Lounsbury & E. Boxenbaum (Eds.), *Institutional logics in action, Part B* (Vol. 39, pp. 3–35). Research in the Sociology of Organizations. Bingley, UK: Emerald Group Publishing Limited.

Paradeise, C. (2008). Autonomie et régulation: Retour sur deux notions-clés. In T. Le Bianic & A. Vion (Eds.), *Action publique et légitimités professionnelles* (pp. 249–277). Paris: Lextenso éditions, pp. 289–296.

Parsons, T. (1951). *The social system*. Glencoe, IL: The Free Press.

Pasquero, J. (1991). Supraorganizational collaboration: The Canadian environmental experiment. *Journal of Applied Behavioral Science, 27*, 37–64.

Pfeffer, J., & Salancik, G. (1978). *The external control of organizations: A resource dependence perspective*. New York, NY: Harper & Row Publishers.

Pinheiro, R., & Geschwind, L. (2014). Rising the summit or flattening the agora? The elitist turn in science and higher education policy in Northern Europe. Paper presented at the ECPR, Glasgow, 3–6 September.

Pinheiro, R., Ramirez, F., & Trondal, J. (2014). Loose-or tight-coupling? Exploring the interplay between decoupling, slack and resilience in universities. 7th Annual EuroMed Conference of the EuroMed Academy of Business – The future of entrepreneurship.

Pinheiro, R., & Stensaker, B. (2014). Designing the entrepreneurial university: The interpretation of a global idea. *Public Organization Review, 14*(4), 497–516.

Reay, T., & Hinings, C. R. (2005). The recomposition of an organizational field: Health care in Alberta. *Organization Studies, 26*(3), 351–384.

Reay, T., & Hinings, C. R. (2009). Managing the rivalry of competing institutional logics. *Organization Studies, 30*(6), 629–652.

Sandholtz, K. W. (2012). Making standard stick: A theory of coupled vs. Decoupled compliance. *Organization Studies, 33*(5–6), 655–679.

Scott, W. R. (1987). The adolescence of institutional theory. *Administrative Science Quarterly, 32*, 493–511.

Scott, W. R., Ruef, M., Mendel, P. J., & Caronna, C. A. (2000). *Institutional change and healthcare organizational*. Chicago, IL: University of Chicago.

Seo, M., & Creed, W. E. D. (2002). Institutional contradictions, praxis and institutional change: A dialectical perspective. *Academy of Management Review*, *27*(2), 222–247.

Skelcher, C., & Smith, S. R. (2013). Hybridity and institutional logics: Framing a comparative study of UK and US nonprofits. Public Management Research Association Conference, University of Wisconsin-Madison, WI.

Strang, D., & Meyer, J. (1993). Institutional conditions for diffusion. *Theory and Society*, *22*, 487–511.

Strauss, A. L., Bucher, R., Ehrlich, D., Schatzman, L., & Sabshin, M. (1963). The hospital and its negotiated order. In E., Freidson (Ed.), *The hospital in modern society* (pp. 147–168). New York, NY: Free Press.

Suchman, M. C. (1995). Managing legitimacy: Strategic and institutional approaches. *Academy of Management Review*, *20*, 571–610.

Thornton, P. H., Jones, C., & Kury, K. (2005). Institutional logics and institutional change in organizations: Transformation in accounting, architecture, and publishing. In C. Jones & P. H. Thornton (Eds.), *Special issue: Transformation in cultural industries* (Vol. 23, pp. 125–170). Research in the Sociology of Organizations. Bingley, UK: Emerald Group Publishing Limited.

Thornton, P. H., Ocasio, W., & Lounsbury, M. (2012). *The institutional logics perspective: A new approach to culture, structure, and process*. New York, NY: Oxford University Press.

Tracey, P., Phillips, N., & Jarvis, O. (2011). Bridging institutional entrepreneurship and the creation of new organizational forms: A multilevel model. *Organization Science*, *22*(1), 60–80.

Van Gestel, N., & Hillebrand, B. (2011). Explaining stability and change: The rise and fall of logics in pluralistic fields. *Organization Studies*, *32*(2), 231–252.

Weber, K., & Glynn, M. A. (2006). Making sense with institutions: Context, thought and action in Karl Weick's theory. *Organization Studies*, *27*(11), 1639–1660.

Weick, K. E. (1995). *Sensemaking in organization*. Thousand Oaks, CA: Sage.

Weick, K. E., Sutcliffe, K. M., & Obstfeld, D. (2005). Organizing and the process of sensemaking. *Organization Science*, *16*, 409–421.

Westphal, J. D., & Zajac, E. J. (2001). Decoupling policy from practice: The case of stock repurchase programs. *Administrative Science Quarterly*, *46*(2), 202–228.

Yin, R. K. (2003). *Case study research, design and methods, 3rd ed.* London: Sage, Applied Social Research Methods Series, 5.

Zibler, T. B. (2002). Institutionalization as an interplay between actions, meaning and actors: The case of a rape crisis center in Israel. *Academy of Management Journal*, *45*(1), 234–254.

HANDLING DIFFERENT INSTITUTIONAL LOGICS IN THE PUBLIC SECTOR: COMPARING MANAGEMENT IN NORWEGIAN UNIVERSITIES AND HOSPITALS

Laila Nordstrand Berg and Rómulo Pinheiro

ABSTRACT

In this study, we are addressing changes in managerial logics after the introduction of New Public Management (NPM)-reforms in two public sectors in Norway, namely the hospital and the university sectors. These sectors were previously dominated by professional and political logic in management, and the focus is on professionals in managerial positions. We are asking: How do professionals in managerial positions across universities and hospitals mediate between previous and newly introduced logics in management after NPM-reforms? *We have chosen to compare changes in management across the hospital and the university sectors. Both sectors are largely publicly owned and dominated by*

Towards a Comparative Institutionalism: Forms, Dynamics and Logics Across the Organizational Fields of Health Care and Higher Education
Research in the Sociology of Organizations, Volume 45, 145–168

ISSN: 0733-558X/doi:10.1108/S0733-558X20150000045018

professions, but their mission differs. The empirical material comprises interviews with formal leaders from dissimilar professional backgrounds, at different levels in the organisations in two cases. The findings show that management influenced by the market logic has been introduced, but in a hybrid version. The professional logic has however not been left behind, but expanded and supplied by a neo-bureaucratic logic. Leadership is functioning as a 'catalyst' to handle the different logics. The originality of this paper is a comparison of management in health care and higher education related to a model of hybrid management.

Keywords: Institutional logics; hybrid management; higher education; universities; hospitals; Norway

INTRODUCTION

In Norway, as in other western countries, the public sector has been the subject of administrative reforms influenced by New Public Management (NPM). The ideological foundation behind NPM asserts that public sector organisations can improve their overall performance by introducing managerialism, technology and values emanating from the private sector (Pollitt & Bouckaert, 2011). The NPM-influenced reforms have taken different trajectories in different countries, but their purposes and approaches are rather similar, namely: (1) increased efficiency; (2) enhanced accessibility for clients/users; (3) reduced public consumption and (4) increased managerial accountability (Christensen & Lægreid, 2011). This paper focuses on the last aspect, that is, on how public sector managers are dealing with the new institutional frameworks introduced by these reforms. Management, or the lack of it, is seen as one of the *problems* but also as a *solution* to the different problems facing the sector (Degeling & Carr, 2004).

We have chosen to compare changes in management across two relatively distinct sectors of the economy that have, in recent years, been infused with different ideas emanating from NPM. The university (HE) and hospital sectors are, to a large extent, dominated by professionals and they both inhabit a highly institutionalised environment laden with both formal (regulations) and informal (values, norms, identities, etc.) rules. The main missions of universities are education and research (and increasingly, societal roles as well), whilst cure and care are central to hospitals. Hospitals are also involved in research and education of professionals (e.g. doctors and nurses). The Norwegian university and hospital sectors are largely publicly owned and managed. Over the last few decades, NPM has been a central driving force in the modernisation of these two societal sectors or organisational fields.

Due to their multiple roles and functions, universities and hospitals can be seen as hybrid organisations, that is, 'multifunctional entities combining different tasks, values and organizational forms' (Christensen & Lægreid, 2010). By using the concept of hybridity, we address potential tensions and inconsistencies between the elements of culture and structure. The term 'hybridity' refers to a combination of disparate (often existing) elements which form a new phenomenon (Battilana & Lee, 2014). The specific tensions and inconsistencies addressed in this paper pertain to management.

Given the rise of the market logic, introduced by NPM, and the emphasis placed on efficiency, economic control and management (Scott, Ruef, Mendel, & Caronna, 2000), we expect public universities and hospitals to have responded strategically to handle rising environmental complexity (Hrebiniak & Joyce, 1985; Oliver, 1991). For the university sector, the starting point for our analysis is that of the 2003/2004 Quality Reform (QR), which had significant effects on both organisational and funding matters (Gornitzka, 2006). In Norwegian universities, professional management is institutionalised by a dual management structure, in which academics and professional administrators co-exist (Gornitzka & Larsen, 2004). Funders and providers are increasingly occupied with strategic issues such as research excellence (world class), external partnerships and resource allocation, including attracting external funds (Frølich, Huisman, Slipersæter, Stensaker, & Bótas, 2013). Leaders are either appointed by the board or elected by their peers. In the hospital sector, unitary management (HOD, 1999) was introduced by a reform in 2001 (HD, 2001), replacing troika management (Kirchhoff, 2013). Managerial positions became profession neutral and available to doctors as well as nurses and others. Following this hospital reform there was stronger centralisation and the hospitals came under ministerial control, with health regions and an enterprise model. The organisation of hospitals moved from professional bureaucracy to divisions of medical specialties as clinics for medicine, surgery, psychiatry, etc. (Berg & Byrkjeflot, 2014).

Public sector reforms are characterised by increasing hybridity (Peters & Savoie, 1998), and this development is (still) poorly understood (Christensen & Lægreid, 2010). More research is needed on the importance of institutional frames for management across different sectors and professions, and, in turn, on how this is influencing the development of the public sector as a whole. The overarching research problem addressed in this paper is: *How do professionals in managerial positions across universities and hospitals mediate between previous and newly introduced logics in management after NPM-reforms?*

Thus, the paper illuminates how public sector organisations in one Nordic country are responding to changing technical and institutional environments. In so doing, it provides new insights into how professionals in managerial positions based at public universities and hospitals cope with and make sense of (reflexivity) and rationalise such internal changes. This is viewed in the light of strategic imperatives and against the backdrop of taken for granted universal (professional) and local (organisational) norms, values and identities.

In Norway, as in other Nordic countries, the higher education (HE) and health care sectors have been the target of major government-led reform in the last decade or so. Yet, to date, few studies have undertaken a cross-sectorial comparative analysis of the effects of such reforms on key internal aspects such as management. As a case, Norway is an insightful one since both sectors have historically been characterised by a heavy reliance on professionals – doctors and academics – to run internal affairs. What is more, there is a growing awareness in both policy and academic circles that, after a series of bold reforms, and partly as a result of the gradual move towards post-NPM approaches (Pollitt & Bouckaert, 2011), it is now time to 'bring back the professionals'. In this context, it is imperative to take stock of the changes resulting from the first wave of NPM-inspired reform in the management of Norway's hospitals and universities.

NORWAY

Norway is a unitary state, run with parliamentary, multi-party and mostly minority governments. Norwegian values are rather egalitarian and collectivist and include well-developed corporatist arrangements. Consensus orientation is embedded in culture and governance, and the level of conflict in society is rather low (Christensen, 2003; Christensen & Lægreid, 2010). The Norwegian welfare state can be described as fitting the 'Scandinavian model' (Esping-Andersen, 1990) with universalism and high levels of public participation. Equity and equality (of opportunity/access) are central tenets of the system, and this is reflected in the development of the public education and health care sectors (Magnussen, Vrangbæk, Saltman, & Martinussen, 2009; Pinheiro & Antonowicz, 2015).

The hospital sector is dominated by public hospitals with free inpatient treatment and equal access for all citizens. The costs are covered by national insurance and there is no specific health tax (Johansen, 2006). The finances are assigned through DRGs[1] (Byrkjeflot & Torjesen, 2010), covering 50% of the budget (DKF, 2013). The extended use of day surgery and outpatient treatment is partly covered by out-of-pocket payments (Brenne, 2006). The Norwegian higher education sector, which is mostly publicly run, is based on a binary divide (which is gradually eroding) between universities and non-university institutions, and could be seen as being aligned with the so-called 'Nordic Model' (Gornitzka & Maassen, 2011). Provision across the public sector is tuition-free, and free access (on both socio-economic and regional grounds) has long been a cornerstone of the system (Pinheiro & Antonowicz, 2015).

THEORETICAL BACKDROP

The term 'hybrid management' can be used to describe how managers cope with challenges posed by a changing technical and institutional environment after reforms on the one hand, and the need to motivate and involve professionals across the board on the other hand. Hybrid indicates a combination of institutional logics that are not normally combined under one organisational roof or sub-unit. In this section, we introduce the actual professional groups and dominant logics characterising management in the sectors.

Institutional Logics amongst Professional Groups

Due to the high level of expertise and task complexity, the occupational groups in hospitals (nurses, doctors, etc.) and universities (academics) are considered to be *professionals* (Freidson, 2001), who are thought to be key actors in the modern welfare state (Kuhlmann, 2006). They are given autonomy and professional self-regulation and the right to serve clients and patients (Molander & Terum, 2008). Professionals can also be viewed as political actors (Scott, 2008) with the power to act as mediators between the state and citizens, and through this they can pursue their own interests and become a political problem (Abbott, 1988). What is more, professionals play an important role in the implementation of government-led reforms (Eymeri-Douzans, 2011).

The work of professionals is embedded in the norms and values of both the organisational structures and the institutions (formal and informal rules) they inhabit, but also originates from their early socialisation whilst undertaking formal training (Scott, 2008). Different professional groups are embedded with various values and norms. These can be viewed as different 'institutional logics', defined as taken for granted principles that guide and motivate actions for groups and individuals in organisations (Friedland & Alford, 1991; Thornton & Ocasio, 2008). Different logics can work side by side in an organisation, yet logics are often conflicting and competitive (Greenwood, Raynard, Kodeih, Micelotta, & Lounsbury, 2011). That said, within a given local setting – hospital or university – institutional logics serve the critical function of binding together the work undertaken by different professionals (Byrkjeflot, 1997b). Yet, at the same time, professional logics are rooted in the normative framework of a given profession (Scott et al., 2000), thus tensions are likely to emerge when logics are combined or mixed.

In the context of universities and hospitals, *professional logics* are not irrelevant. Across both sectors, there are multiple types of professionals, possessing distinct ideals on how to practice management (Abbott, 1988; Freidson, 1994). Professional management, which is essentially about planning daily and strategic activities, builds on a platform of knowledge developed through education and training (Byrkjeflot, 1997b). Following this line of thought, the presence of a professional logic in the Norwegian health care and higher education sectors would imply a strong focus on preserving the interests of colleagues or peers with the same professional background in addition to (daily and strategic) planning in accordance with the internal dynamics, priorities, values and identities of a given professional group (e.g. doctors, nurses, academics). Indicators of this logic can be focus on planning of shifts and schedules connected to professionals and operational activities related to patients and students. Another central issue is focus on quality of the services offered and professional development. Decision-making is consensus oriented and bottom-up.

As part of the public sector, hospitals and universities seek legitimacy (internal and external) in order to operate (Deephouse & Suchman, 2008), and are characterised by a *political logic*, framed around just or equal access to public services (Clark, 1983; Scott et al., 2000) and the fair (re-) distribution of common goods (Thornton, Ocasio, & Lounsbury, 2012; Vrangbæk, 1999). Administrative procedures are important to ensure equal treatment (Hood, 1991; Osborne, 2011). Hence, the political logic amongst

Norwegian health care and higher education managers would place a strong emphasis on aspects like equity (access to services) and equality (equal treatment amongst patients/students). Indicators of this logic could be emphasis on following internal and external rules and legal systems, documentation and a hierarchical orientation in decision-making.

The so-called 'logic of management' was introduced by NPM-inspired reforms. Rational planning and distribution of tasks from the leader to the follower are seen as crucial processes (O'Reilly & Reed, 2010, 2012). This, in turn, results in an emphasis on the division of labour and hierarchical relations (Rost, 1993). Management by objectives or MBO (Pollitt & Bouckaert, 2011) is central. The main focus is on efficiency (Flynn, 2002), that is, the management of resources and economic control (Pollitt, 1993; Strand, 2007). In contrast to academics, who are first and foremost loyal to the disciplinary fields to which they belong and in which they have been socialised (Teichler, Arimoto, & Cummings, 2013; Welch, 2005), professional managers are loyal to their own organisations (and in the case of public bureaucracies, to the state as well) and develop activities according to emerging objectives and environmental shifts (Byrkjeflot, 1997b). Indicators of the managerial logic in Norwegian health care and higher education include changes in organisational structures with an emphasis on hierarchy and line management, focus on efficiency and economy, strategic management of resources (both human and financial) and MBO.

A common feature of these new logics is that they can be viewed as 'impersonal' (Berg, 2015). Differences are shown through different authority bases: the logics are rooted in the professional, political and market systems.

METHODS

In this study, we have chosen a comparative approach which Yin (2014) refers to as a multiple-case, replication design, and the aim is to test and further develop theory. The cases from the hospital and university sectors are chosen because they are suitable for highlighting the theories and examine how managerial logics develop after reforms, and to investigate indicators derived from the theories. As written in the 'Introduction' section, the NPM-reforms influence both organisation and management in the sectors, although different solutions are selected. By having selected two middle-sized public institutions, we have enhanced the comparative dimension, albeit the considerable differences in contextual circumstances. A comparison of two cases offers a more robust image than a single-case design (Yin, 2014), and gives a deeper knowledge of how influential the reforms are on logics in management. What is more, the possibility for analytical generalisation increases if the findings are corroborating (*ibid.*).

We strategically invited participants who we expected could add knowledge and information to our project. The empirical material comprises semi-structured interviews ($N = 36$) with formal leaders at different levels in the organisations in two cases. From the hospital case, we interviewed 18 doctors and nurses in managerial positions in a medium-sized general hospital in Norway. Organisationally, they were managers at the three levels below the CEO: the clinic, department and unit levels. The managers were responsible for clinical treatment and related personnel in their units (not only personnel from their own profession). From the university case, we interviewed 18 managers, of whom eight were located in the central administration (Rector, Vice Rector and Administrative Directors) and 10 were at the sub-unit level (Dean and Department Heads). The managers were from different scientific fields. By interviewing managers from different professions and scientific fields, we open up for a variety of interpretations of management. The interviews (site visits) were undertaken by the authors between 2009 and 2012.

One methodological limitation of the study pertains to the fact the interviews were not undertaken simultaneously and used different interview guides, since the scope of the research projects in question differed somewhat (both were integral components of the doctoral dissertations of the authors). That said, both studies were comparative in nature (design) and adopted a similar conceptual framework with special attention given to patterns of change and adaptation within professional, public organisations in Norway (consult Berg, 2015; Pinheiro, 2012a). The common themes related to tensions arising from changes in managerial logics after the introduction of new governance structures and funding schemes.

LOGICS AND TENSIONS FACING THE HOSPITAL AND UNIVERSITY SECTORS

In the following sections, we highlight the interplay between different institutional logics professional managers face across the two sectors at local level.

The Hospital Sector

Historically there has been a difference in the perceptions of management held by nurses and doctors. For both professions, management is about responsibility for a function and planning daily activities (Degeling, Maxwell, Kennedy, & Coyle, 2003), but in the nursing tradition administrative functions were part of the role and managerial qualifications were central in the selection of managers (*ibid.*). Amongst doctors, the best amongst equals was traditionally appointed as the leader (Degeling et al., 2003), and the selection of managers took place using professional criteria. This latter way of viewing management has been deeply challenged by the reforms – not without protests from the doctors. Polemics in the newspapers and doctors leaving their positions followed nurses becoming leaders of doctors in the early years of the reforms (Johansen, 2005). The conflicts burned out, and in our empiric material, we can detect a change of attitude in reports from managers; now the best manager is wanted for a managerial position, not the best professional. Both doctors and nurses have entered the profession neutral management positions following the reforms. In 2012, 37% of the CEOs of Norwegian hospitals were doctors and 21% had a nursing background (Kjekshus & Bernstrøm, 2013). At the clinic/division level, 57% of managers were doctors and 34% were nurses, whilst at the department level 48% were doctors and 40% were nurses (*ibid.*).

Focusing on how managers defined management and on their managerial work (content and approach), the data show that managers focused on aspects like MBO, management of resources, loyalty towards a given financial framework and cost consciousness – elements that are intrinsically associated with a managerial logic (Byrkjeflot, 2011). Tensions related to the hierarchical dimension (Rost, 1993) were also mentioned. Both nurses and doctors emphasised the importance of being available for their staff, in addition to the fact that the introduction of line management organisation and hierarchical (top-down) steering had had a considerable impact on the daily management of the hospital. Another organisational characteristic after the introduction of new divisional organisation and changes in governance systems in line with managerial logic (Christensen & Lægreid, 2002), is a demand for more cooperation and coordination, resulting in an exponential increase in staff meetings.

Changes in, for example, administrative procedures and workload, can be traced back to technological developments, new accounting methods and altered workforce composition, thus making it rather difficult to determine the real cause(s) of change. In this respect, hospital managers reported that, following the reforms, the administrative workload had increased tremendously, including internal transaction costs associated with the introduction of multiple new systems and procedures. The managers expressed some understanding of the need for documentation according to a political logic (focus on equity and equality), but also questioned the use of resources and expensive routines.

Despite the reformers' wish to purify the managerial focus, the professional logic (Byrkjeflot, 1997a) has not been left behind. There seems to be a strong focus on quality and professional development amongst the unitary managers from both health professions, at all levels, but the focus has expanded to include groups other than their own profession. This quote from a middle manager illustrates this aspect:

> … [management is about] choosing the direction, how to build the personal resources so they [staff] have the needed competences, how can we recruit new competences? Make sure that we are in the frontline. (Doctor)

Surprisingly, the hospital managers stressed personal characteristics, both in their definitions of management and in their descriptions of managerial work, and in the light of core tenets from the literature on leadership (Ferlie, 2012). Essential features of leaders were included in definitions of management from both professions:

> … I think it is about being a good example … But also having good manners, being nice and behaving properly. (Doctor, middle manager)

> I think very simple about management. It is about being available for the employees. And good management is, for me, ordinary politeness and taking the personnel seriously. (Nurse, first-line manager)

The notion of the leader as a visionary (providing a direction to follow) and focused (on selected areas and results) individual is also related to classic leadership traits (*ibid.*). The managers suggested that it was important to influence staff and motivate them in the chosen directions. The managers' motivation to be in a leadership position was also central. They enjoyed being in a position where they had a say, and were able to choose what to work with, and influence their own professional development.

The University Sector

Similarly, professional management has become a fully institutionalised feature of Norwegian universities (Frølich, 2005). The rise in management has resulted in a dual structure, where academics and professional administrators co-exist, albeit in two different (line management) domains of the organisation. As a result of increasing rationalisation, initiated prior to but intensified by the 2003/4 QR, Norwegian universities have been transformed into more complete organisational forms (Ramirez, 2006). A series of new internal tensions or conflicts have emerged. The first pertains to increasing academic bureaucratisation, as a result of administrative bureaucratisation (Gornitzka, Kyvik, & Larsen, 1998). The second pertains to tensions resulting from the centralisation of decision-making procedures (e.g. the allocation of funds) at both the central and sub-unit levels (Pinheiro, 2012a, 2012b). This latter tension is particularly salient since it is seen by many as threatening traditional academic values and traditions based on egalitarianism and collegiality (Tapper & Palfreyman, 2010). A third tension between academics and university managers pertains to rising instrumentality (Pinheiro, 2015) and the increasing focus on measuring (research) performance, university rankings and benchmarking (Charles & Wilson, 2012; Hazelkorn, 2009). Most importantly in the context of this paper, Norwegian academics are increasingly being pressured to adopt the market logic, focusing on efficiency, entrepreneurial mind-set, links with external actors (e.g. funders), etc., whilst remaining truthful to the 'old' logic focusing on the 'public good', equity, egalitarianism, openness, collaboration, etc. The following interview quotes – from managers at different organisational levels – illustrate some of these tensions.

> To combine traditional academic ethos with a spirit of enterprise or outreach is not easy but it can be done! It takes time, and you have to have patience. (Senior academic administrator, central administration)

> It is a problem [for universities], if you want to compete you have to be elitist! It is a paradox; in (winter) sports Norway is very successful. We have a fabric of elite sportsmen and that is considered to be very nice and successful. But, in academia and politics, it is not good to talk about elitism! (Senior academic administrator, faculty level)

> Yes, there are challenges … these are different times, simply. Today you have to produce more, it's a requirement. Personally, I do not have much of a problem [with this orientation]. We need those requirements [pressures] here, otherwise we would relax and some other university, maybe [the University of] Oslo, would not … We would wake up one day and be in the back seat. (Senior academic administrator, departmental level)

Academic managers perform a very important mediating task in their attempt to bridge and mediate between conflicts emanating from the different logics. This, in turn, has resulted in the rise of what some have termed the 'third way' (Whitchurch, 2008), a hybrid orientation amongst academic professionals that encompasses aspects linked to the market – a focus on excellence and efficiency – with more traditional conceptions of the academic profession (e.g. respect for autonomy) and the notion of knowledge as a public good rather than a private commodity (see Slaughter & Rhoades, 2004). In certain circumstances, and to some extent, the professional logic has even been strengthened, for example, by reinforcing the importance of academic freedom and democratic decision-making as a means of counterbalancing the 'logic of the marketplace' associated with NPM-inspired reforms.

When it comes to the interplay between meritocratic and egalitarian behaviour, we also identify a series of tensions that academic managers are struggling to cope with. On the one hand, the logic of the marketplace (Pinheiro, 2015), associated with the strategic attention paid to world-class rankings, external funding, etc., clashes with the traditional notion of a 'community of equals' (Olsen, 2007), substantiated around the subsidisation of weaker fields (like the humanities) by stronger ones (like the sciences). What is more, there is a growing tension between instrumentalist logics focusing on the *exploitation* of existing assets (linked to the rise of strategic science regimes within universities) at the expense of the more long-term *exploration* of future possibilities (in all 'relevant' fields) intrinsically associated with science and the University as fiduciary and relatively autonomous social institutions (*ibid.*).

> Our main task is to teach and to do basic research. If that is compatible with the rest [external demands] fine, but I am not willing to sacrifice [our core activities], I should not, for the demands of a local or regional business. (Senior academic administrator, central administration)

DISCUSSION

In this section, we review our findings in the light of the literature. To describe the increasing institutional complexity, we first discuss the evidence of the market logic in the two fields, thereafter different logics in management. We also suggest ways of interpreting the reactions to strategic responses to the reforms.

The market dimension is visible in both organisation and management. The move from hospitals being public administrative bodies to being hospital enterprises (Byrkjeflot & Guldbrandsøy, 2013) and establishing a clinic structure with increased accountability for managers is in line with the market orientation. This way of altering the organisation of hospitals can be interpreted as a way to influence management through redesigning formal structures and changing the conditions for managers (Borum, 2003; Christensen & Lægreid, 2002). Line management through hierarchical levels can also be viewed as a central feature of management (Pollitt & Bouckaert, 2011), and is stressed by the managers. Similarly, in the university field, the gradual but steady move towards more instrumental (market-based) perspectives has resulted in substantial changes in the organisation of academic activities in Norway, for example, a move from elected to appointed leaders as well as the inclusion of external stakeholders in the internal governance structures of universities.

The market dimension is also visible through the logics which characterise the managers in both sectors, but this is described according to missions in the sectors. After the NPM-reforms in the hospital sector, managers focus on efficiency (Flynn, 2002) – management of resources and costs are central aspects of the managerial logic (Byrkjeflot, 2011; Pollitt, 1993; Pollitt & Bouckaert, 2011; Strand, 2007). Likewise, MBO (Kaufmann & Kaufmann, 2003; Pollitt & Bouckaert, 2011), which is emphasised by the managers, is a central dimension of managerialism (Pollitt & Bouckaert, 2011) due to the perception that all aspects of organisational life need to be managed to reach the organisations' goals (O'Reilly & Reed, 2012). Some of the managers also viewed management as generic and not connected to professional management, and this is also in line with the NPM view of management (Boston, 2011). Acting according to managerial logics can be interpreted as a strategic response (Greenwood, Díaz, Li, & Lorente, 2010; Pache & Santos, 2013). The managers must act according to these logics in order to be allowed to be managers in the new system. The emphasis on these seemingly conflicting logics can also be seen as a result of logic institutionalisation (Cooper, Ezzamel, & Willlmott, 2008), and thus successful hybridisation (Battilana & Lee, 2014).

Reforms in the university sector included many aspects associated with NPM, namely, a strong emphasis on quality, accreditation and accountability (Stensaker & Harvey, 2011); changes in the distribution of public funding for teaching and research, with a performance element (Pinheiro, Geschwind, & Aarrevaara, 2014); a focus on efficiency (Gornitzka et al., 2004); the rise of strategic planning and 'strategic science' regimes (Pinheiro & Stensaker, 2014); and the institutionalisation of a professionalised managerial structure (in tandem with traditional academic structures) within universities (Gornitzka & Larsen, 2004). These 'innovations' have, amongst other things, led to stronger rationalisation, increasing competition, and the centralisation of decision-making procedures, thus setting in motion a series of related tensions and dilemmas around the ways in which university systems and institutions are steered by government and internally governed by managers (cf. Pinheiro et al., 2014).

The introduction of the market dimension can be viewed as a means of scaling back the public sector (Christensen & Lægreid, 2010). However, managers from both sectors questioned whether the market dimensions were efficient in scaling back, due to the increase in administrative work which followed the introduction of new systems for planning, reporting, benchmarking and so on. The vast amount of new administrative routines were too time consuming for most of the managers, and in the hospital sector managers reported that assistant manager roles had been created at all hierarchical levels to deal with these new bureaucratic tasks. Similarly, HE, many university respondents referred to the increasing administrative workload resulting from the implementation of new structures and procedures, confirming earlier insights that administrative bureaucratisation leads to academic bureaucratisation (Gornitzka & Larsen, 2004). This is, to a large degree, a function of the emphasis reform processes have placed on delegation (enhanced institutional autonomy), which has resulted not only in increasing professionalisation but also in more attention being paid to accountability (reporting, consulting, assessing, etc.). The increase in administrative routines can be interpreted as a new form of bureaucracy associated with a 'neo-bureaucratic logic' (Byrkjeflot & Jespersen, 2014), which has developed under the enterprise model. This logic is characterised by increased regulatory management and indirect control which distinguishes the neo-bureaucratic logic from the previous public administrative regime and political logic in which hierarchy and centralised regulations were important (Scott et al., 2000). Professional work is more regulated and the managers are performing indirect control through different reporting and quality systems (Byrkjeflot & Jespersen, 2014). That said, our data suggest that the managers (across the health sector) were not completely negative about the new routines, but realised that they could use the new systems to justify new investments (e.g. in equipment, locations, new staff).

Hybridity in organising (Battilana & Lee, 2014) is also reflected in the organisation of the sectors. For example, in the health care sector, modification is shown both through the introduction of the clinic structure and in the meetings that are required when different professions are cooperating, as there is an increasing need for coordination of complex tasks. The focus on contact with external stakeholders in relation to additional funding streams is less evident amongst hospital managers, but is a key feature of reform processes targeting the university sector (Frølich, 2005; Pinheiro et al., 2014).

In addition to the rise of the managerial and neo-bureaucratic logics (highlighted above), the professional logic was also found to be evident across both sectors or organisational fields.. As indicated earlier, professional logics are rooted in the norms from the profession (Scott et al., 2000). However, in the hospital sector, this focus has expanded and managers are now taking responsibility for the different professions and occupations in their unit. This can be interpreted in the light of professional management as following up the development of the competence of the professionals (Freidson, 2001). The strong emphasis on professional management can, in addition, be interpreted as managers' strategic response to the reforms (cf. Oliver, 1991), maintaining external legitimacy with the wider public and showing that hospital values are still at stake (Kirchhoff, 2013). Furthermore, the strong focus on professional development can be interpreted as a strategic posture by the hospital owners to enhance the implementation of the reform. But, in contrast to the previous regime based on dual management, the managers now have unitary responsibility for all professions. This can also be interpreted as a hybridisation of professional management. The reformers can try to influence the content of management through the way the work is organised, with new framework conditions which intend to influence managerial practices and postures (Christensen & Lægreid, 2002; Christensen, Lægreid, Røvik, & Roness, 2007; Scott, 2008). The managers are forced to expand their centre of attention through new organisational structures and new logics, which is evident through planning, reporting, benchmarking, budgeting, etc., and this is forcing managers from different professions to become more alike. Similarly, in universities, the emphasis on professional management has not necessarily eroded traditional academic norms and identities, which still remain well rooted (Vabø & Aamodt, 2008). Instead, academic managers (particularly at the sub-unit level) find themselves in the challenging position of having to mediate between different logics (e.g. efficiency vs. equity), often engaging in processes of 'local translation' (Sahlin & Wedlin, 2008) in order to infuse meaning to local audiences (academic peers) in the light of changing contextual circumstances.

Surprisingly, 'leadership' and 'leaderism' seem to be an important aspect of management in hospitals and universities after the reforms. Leaderism (O'Reilly & Reed, 2010, 2012) is a development of managerialism and stresses equality between the leader and the follower. The relationship between the leader and the employee is a central aspect of leadership (Ladegård & Vabo, 2010). The basic assumption is that leaders and followers have common goals, and that the postures of both leaders and followers need to be strategically adjusted to the goals and that together leaders and followers can create a good social environment (O'Reilly & Reed, 2010, 2012). The leaders influence the norms and values in the organisation (Schein, 2010). The evidence of leadership arises from interviewees' definitions and descriptions of management, in which the personal characteristics of the leader were important, and this leads the interpretation towards leadership (Degeling & Carr, 2004). The visionary and targeted leader (Byrkjeflot, 1997b; Johnsen & Døving, 2010; Viitanen & Konu, 2009) can be illustrated by a description of the leader as a person who set the direction, which the staff follows with great loyalty. We also stress that motivation, both to lead and influence the staff and the inner motivation to be in a position where they (the leader) has a say, are important aspects of leadership (Ladegård & Vabo, 2010). This emphasis on leadership can be interpreted as a strategic response to handling the tensions between competing logics (Fjellvær, 2010) in the hybrid organisation, and the ambiguity which arises in changing circumstances (Noordegraaf, 2012). The managers emphasise leadership as a 'catalyst' for implementing the different logics.

CONCLUDING DISCUSSION: FROM PURIFIED TO HYBRID MANAGEMENT

The aim of this paper was to analyse how public sector organisations are responding strategically to the challenges brought by increasing institutional complexity. More specifically, we investigated how managers from the hospital and university sectors mediate between different institutional logics.

The overall intention of the Norwegian management reforms was to purify management from a NPM-logic, but the introduction of a market-logic into public organisations already laden with several professional logics and a well-entrenched public administrative logic was found to be problematic. The findings from this study indicate that, across both sectors, management has been introduced but not in a pure form. The term 'hybrid management' describes the combination of logics uphold by managers within the organisation to accomplish daily tasks and strategic objectives. The professionals involved (academics, nurses, doctors, etc.) are not leaving previous logics behind, but instead are developing them further, through hybridisation (Greenwood et al., 2010).

Interestingly, our study also found that, contrary to the primary aim of the architects of NPM-inspired reforms, management efficiency has been constrained as a result of rising bureaucratisation and hospital and university managers are also influenced by a 'neo-bureaucratic' logic. Managers – at least in the hospital sector – suggested that this logic was not solely negative: it may also be used as a tool to support professional and other types of requests. Finally, the data suggest that both hospital and university leaders emphasise the relational aspects between the leader and the employee, with the former acting as mediators or *brokers* between the different logics and their respective identities (Kodeih & Greenwood, 2014), which are also increasingly hybrid in nature. Based on this, we could tentatively argue that across both sectors, leadership – at various levels – acts as a catalyst to handle the different logics in management. At the local level, new sets of tensions and volitions have emerged regarding management jurisdictions (Abbott, 1988) amongst different professionals and managerial groups, with managers increasingly expected to resolve tensions by taking into account the collective goals of the organisation whilst being truthful to and respectful towards the needs, aspirations, values and identities of the different professionals involved. In contrast to traditional bureaucracies, where functional and hierarchical relations play a rather prominent role (Blau, 1972), the rise of managerial and professional hybridity puts an emphasis on leaders' personal characteristics and social relations. This observation is aligned with earlier findings showing the increased complexity in management as previous ('old') logics are not left behind (Arman, Liff, & Wikstrøm, 2014; Scott et al., 2000), which is in itself an indicator of institutionalisation on the one hand (Zucker, 1991) and organisational resilience on the other hand (Pinheiro & Trondal, 2014).

From the logics evident in our empirical material (two cases), we developed a model (Fig. 1). The hybrid managerial role can be conceived as

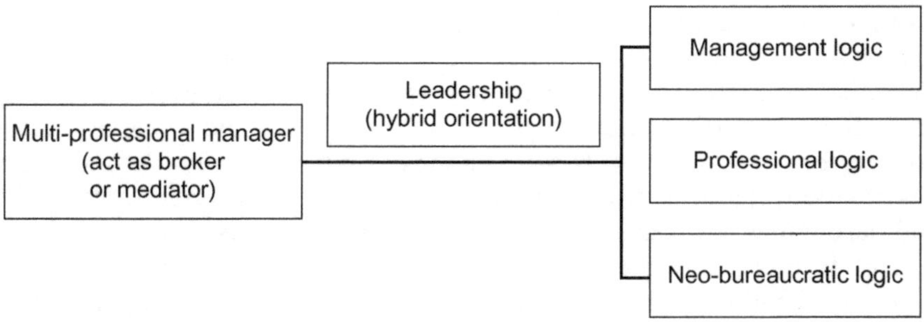

Fig. 1. The Multi-Professional Manager: Hybrid Leadership as a Means of Coping with Multiple Logics. *Source*: Adapted from Berg (2015).

multi-professional (Berg, 2015), simultaneously containing logics emanating from management and the professions, in addition to a neo-bureaucratic logic, and with leadership acting as a catalyst to handle the different institutional logics. What is more, the aforementioned leadership role also encompasses mediating logics and tensions across different levels, for example, between policy and strategic imperatives at the national (government) and institutional (central administration) levels, and in the 'heartland' composed of academic and health professionals.

On the right-hand side of our model are the three major logics identified in our study as being present following the implementation of NPM-reforms across the two sectors. In the middle of the figure is the leadership logic, which managers at universities and hospitals use as a means of mediating the tensions resulting from competing dimensions associated with the three dominant logics (Fjellvær, 2010), in addition to the ambiguity associated with management more generally (Noordegraaf, 2012).

Our comparative study reveals that, despite the fact that both sectors have historically been affected by conflicting external pressures and that, as a result, some degree of hybridity has traditionally been identified at public hospitals and universities, as public organisations they seem to be evolving in ways that are contrary to the initial expectations of the so-called 'rationalisers' (i.e. towards logic coexistence rather than replacement). What is more, *path-dependencies* (Beckert, 1999; Hay & Wincott, 1998), *social positions* (Battilana, 2006) and *agency* (e.g. resistance) (Beckert, 1999) were found to play an increasingly important role in the determination and co-evolution of new and existing (old) formal and informal structures and behavioural patterns.

The adoption of new organisational designs or *archetypes* (Greenwood & Hinings, 1993) – such as divisional organisation in the hospitals or the dual management structure in universities – has resulted in growing demand for planning and coordination, hence increasing internal transaction costs (meetings, etc.). This, in turn, has led to increasing rationalisation, and, somewhat ironically, to enhanced bureaucratisation (reporting, assessing, controlling, etc.) (Gornitzka et al., 1998). Thus, we could say that, across both sectors, we are currently seeing a move from one type of hybrid – the old situation, characterised by the coexistence of different professional logics and decoupling – towards hybridised forms that are based on a combination of features associated with each of the logics in question. This is a means of handling internal tensions and a way of addressing the need for organisational coherence, access to scarce resources and, not least, legitimacy.

As we move from NPM towards a post-NPM era (Pollitt & Bouckaert, 2011), future studies could, for example, identify the degree of durability associated with the newly identified hybrid logics and their consequent effects on internal structures, individuals' roles (included but not limited to formal leaders), professional identities and 'real' behavioural postures, as well as the extent to which hybridisation: (a) contributes to patterns of convergence (isomorphism) versus divergence (polymorphism); (b) affects the performance of core versus more peripheral tasks; and (c) affects the overall resilience (ability to adapt and change) of public sector organisations operating in highly institutionalised environments or organisational fields.

NOTE

1. DRG, *Diagnosis-Related Group*, is a system to group illnesses based on diagnoses and treatment procedures. Surgical procedural code, diagnosis code, gender, age and discharging routines are coded. The system was introduced by the reform in 1997 (Byrkjeflot & Torjesen, 2010).

ACKNOWLEDGEMENTS

Earlier versions of this paper were presented at the 2014 EUROMED-conference, Kristiansand, 18–19 September 2014, a Brown Bag seminar hosted by the Department of Political Science and Management, University of Agder, 13 May 2015, and the 2015 EGOS-conference, Athens, 2–4 July 2015. The authors would like to thank the participants for useful comments. We also thank the volume's editors and reviewers for insightful suggestions, which have vastly improved the paper. Any remaining errors are our own.

REFERENCES

Abbott, A. (1988). *The system of professions*. Chicago, IL: University of Chicago Press.

Arman, R., Liff, R., & Wikstrøm, E. (2014). The hierarchization of competing logics in psychiatric care in Sweden. *Scandinavian Journal of Management*, *30*, 282–291.

Battilana, J. (2006). Agency and institutions: The enabling role of individuals' social position. *Organization*, *13*, 653–676.

Battilana, J., & Lee, M. (2014). Advancing research on hybrid organizing – Insights from the study of social enterprises. *The Academy of Management Annals*, *8*, 777–799.

Beckert, J. (1999). Agency, entrepreneurs, and institutional change. The role of strategic choice and institutionalized practices in organizations. *Organization Studies*, *20*, 777–799.

Berg, L. N. (2015). *Multifaglig ledelse – Hybridisering av sykehusledelse etter NPM-reformer*. Ph.D. thesis, Universitetet i Bergen.

Berg, L. N., & Byrkjeflot, H. (2014). Management in hospitals – A career track and a career trap. A comparison of physicians and nurses in Norway. *International Journal of Public Sector Management*, *27*(5), 379–394.

Blau, P. M. (1972). *The dynamics of bureaucracy: A study of interpersonal relations in two government agencies*. Chicago, IL: University of Chicago Press.

Borum, F. (Ed.). (2003). *Ledelse I sygehusvæsenet*. København: Handelshøjskolens forlag.

Boston, J. (2011). Basic NPM ideas and their development. In T. Christensen & P. Lægreid (Eds.), *The Ashgate research companion to new public management*. Farnham: Ashgate.

Brenne, A.-H. (2006). Norway. In R. Bernd, C. A. Dubois, & M. McKee (Eds.), *The healthcare workforce. Learning from experience*. European Observatory on Health Systems and Policies. Wiltshire: The Cromwell Press.

Byrkjeflot, H. (1997a). Fra ledelse til management? In H. Bykjeflot (Ed.), *Fra styring til ledelse*. Bergen: Fagbokforlaget.

Byrkjeflot, H. (1997b). *Fra styring til ledelse*. Oslo: Fagbokforlaget.

Byrkjeflot, H. (2011). Healthcare states and medical professions: The challenges from NPM. In T. Christensen & P. Lægreid (Eds.), *The Ashgate research companion to new public management*. Farnham: Ashgate.

Byrkjeflot, H., & Guldbrandsøy, K. (2013). Både hierarkisk styring og nettverk. En studie av utviklingen i styringen av norske sykehus. *Tidsskrift for samfunnsforskning*, *54*, 463–492.

Byrkjeflot, H., & Jespersen, P. K. (2014). Three conceptualizations of hybrid management in hospitals. *International Journal of Public Sector Management*, *27*(5), 447–458.

Byrkjeflot, H., & Torjesen, D. O. (2010). Managerial innovation in health care. The introduction, translation and use of the American DRG system in the hospital sectors in Norway and Denmark. In H. Knudsen, J. Falkenberg, K. Grønhaug, & Å. Garnes (Eds.), *Mysterion, strategica og kainotomia*. Oslo: Novus forlag.

Charles, D., & Wilson, B. (2012). Managing regional engagement: The role of benchmarking. In R. Pinheiro, P. Benneworth, & G. A. Jones (Eds.), *Universities and regional development: A critical assessment of tensions and contradiction*. Milton Park: Routledge.

Christensen, T. (2003). Narrative of Norwegian governance: Elaborating the strong state. *Public Administration*, *81*, 163–190.

Christensen, T., & Lægreid, P. (2002). Reformer og lederskap. Omstilling i den utøvende makt. Oslo: Universitetsforlaget.

Christensen, T., & Lægreid, P. (2010). Complexity and hybrid public administration – Theoretical and empirical challenges. *Public Organization Review*, *11*, 407–423.

Christensen, T., & Lægreid, P. (2011). *The Ashgate research companion to new public management*. Farnham: Ashgate.

Christensen, T., Lægreid, P., Røvik, K. A. A., & Roness, P. G. (2007). *Organization theory and the public sector: Instrument, culture and myth*. London: Routledge.

Clark, B. R. (1983). *The higher education system: Academic organization in cross-national perspective*. Los Angeles, CA: University of California Press.

Cooper, D., Ezzamel, M., & Willmott, H. (2008). Examining 'institutionalization': A critical theoretic perspective. In R. Greenwood, C. Oliver, K. Sahlin, & R. Suddaby (Eds.), *The SAGE handbook of organizational institutionalism*. London: Sage.

Deephouse, D., & Suchman, M. (2008). Legitimacy in organizational institutionalism. In R. Greenwood, C. Oliver, K. Sahlin, & R. Suddaby (Eds.), *The SAGE handbook of organizational institutionalism*. London: Sage.

Degeling, P., & Carr, A. (2004). Leadership for the systemization of health care: The unaddressed issue in health care reform. *Journal of Health Organization and Management*, *18*, 399–414.

Degeling, P., Maxwell, S., Kennedy, J., & Coyle, B. (2003). Medicine, management, and modernisation: A "dance macabre"? *British Medical Journal*, *326*, 649–652.

DKF. (2013). Endring av Prop. 1 S (2013–2014) Statsbudsjettet 2014. *Prop. 1 S Tillegg 1 (2013–2014) Proposisjon til Stortinget (forslag til stortingsvedtak)*, Det Kongelige Finansdepartement.

Esping-Andersen, G. (1990). *The three worlds of welfare capitalism*. Cambridge, MA: Polity Press.

Eymeri-Douzans, J.-M. (2011). NPM reforms legacy. A common praxeologic, a variety of acclimatizations, a renewed bureaucratization. In J.-M. Eymeri-Douzans & J. Pierre (Eds.), *Administrative reforms and democratic governance*. London: Routledge.

Ferlie, E. (2012). Concluding discussion: Paradigms and instruments of public management reform – The questions of agency. In C. Teelken, E. Ferlie, & M. Dent (Eds.), *Leadership in the public sector: Promises & pitfalls*. London: Routledge.

Fjellvær, H. (2010). *Dual and unitary leadership: Managing ambiguity in pluralistic organizations*. Bergen: Norges Handels Høyskole.

Flynn, R. (2002). Managerialism, professionalism and quasi-markets. In M. Exworthy & S. Halford (Eds.), *Professionals and the new managerialism in the public sector*. Buckingham: Open University Press.

Freidson, E. (1994). *Professionalism reborn: Theory, prophecy, and policy*. Chicago, IL: University of Chicago Press.

Freidson, E. (2001). *Professionalism: The third logic*. Cambridge, MA: Polity Press.

Friedland, R., & Alford, R. R. (1991). Bringing society back in symbols, practices, and institutional contradictions. In W. Powell & P. Dimaggio (Eds.), *The new institutionalism in organizational analysis*. Chicago, IL: University of Chicago Press.

Frølich, N. (2005). Implementation of new public management in Norwegian universities. *European Journal of Education*, *40*, 223–234.

Frølich, N., Huisman, J., Slipersæter, S., Stensaker, B., & Bótas, P. (2013). A reinterpretation of institutional transformations in European higher education: Strategising pluralistic organisations in multiplex environments. *Higher Education*, *65*, 79–93.

Gornitzka, Å. (2006). What is the use of Bologna in national reform? In V. Tomusk (Ed.), *Creating the European area of higher education*. Dordrecht: Springer Netherlands.

Gornitzka, Å., Kyvik, S., & Larsen, I. M. (1998). The bureaucratisation of universities. *Minerva*, *36*, 21–47.

Gornitzka, Å., & Larsen, I. M. (2004). Towards professionalisation? Restructuring of administrative work force in universities. *Higher Education*, *47*, 455–471.

Gornitzka, Å., & Maassen, P. (2011). University governance reforms, global scripts and the "Nordic Model". Accounting for policy change? In J. Schmid, K. Amos, J. Schrader, & A. Thiel (Eds.), *Welten der Bildung? Vergleichende Analysen von Bildungspolitik und Bildungssystemen*. Baden-Baden: Nomos Verlagsgesellschaft.

Gornitzka, Å., Stensaker, B., Smeby, J.-C., & De Boer, H. (2004). Contract arrangements in the Nordic countries: Solving the efficiency-effectiveness dilemma? *Higher Education in Europe*, *29*(1), 87–101. doi:10.1080/0379772041000167331 9

Greenwood, R., Díaz, A. M., Li, S. X., & Lorente, J. C. (2010). The multiplicity of institutional logics and the heterogeneity of organizational responses. *Organization Science*, *21*, 521–539.

Greenwood, R., & Hinings, C. (1993). Understanding strategic change: The contribution of archetypes. *Academy of Management Journal*, *36*, 1052–1081.

Greenwood, R., Raynard, M., Kodeih, F., Micelotta, E. R., & Lounsbury, M. (2011). Institutional complexity and organizational responses. *The Academy of Management Annals*, *5*, 317–371.

Hay, C., & Wincott, D. (1998). Structure, agency and historical institutionalism. *Political Studies*, *46*, 951–957.

Hazelkorn, H. (2009). Rankings and the battle for world-class excellence: Institutional strategies and policy choice. *Higher Education Management and Policy*, *21*, 1–22.

HD. (2001). *Sykehusreformen. Ot. prp. nr. 66*. Oslo: Sosial- og Helsedepartementet.

HOD. (1999). §3-9. *Ledelse i sykehus*. Retrieved from http://www.lovdata.no/all/hl-19990702-061.html#3-9

Hood, C. (1991). A public management for all seasons? *Public Administration*, *9*(1), 3–19.

Hrebiniak, L., & Joyce, W. (1985). Organizational adaptation: Strategic choice and environmental determinism. *Administrative Science Quarterly*, *30*, 336–349.

Johansen, J. R. (2006). Health systems in transition. Norway. *European Observatory on Health Systems and Policies*, *8*(1), 1–169.

Johansen, M. S. (2005). Penga eller livet? *Lederutfordringer i det reformerte norske helsevesenet*. Bergen: Rokkansenteret.

Johnsen, Å., & Døving, E. (2010). Ledelse og styring i organisasjonsteoriens klassikere. In G. Ladegård & S. I. Vabo (Eds.), *Ledelse og styring*. Bergen: Fagbokforlaget.

Kaufmann, G., & Kaufmann, A. (2003). *Psykologi i organisasjon og ledelse*. Bergen: Fagbokforlaget.

Kirchhoff, R. (2013). *Tyske sykehusleger i Norge i et institusjonelt perspektiv*. Bergen: Universitetet i Bergen.

Kjekshus, L. E., & Bernstrøm, V. (2013). Helseforetakenes interne organisering og ledelse. Intorg 2012. *Helseøkonomisk forskningsprogram ved Universitetet i Oslo. HERO 2013*. Oslo: Universitetet i Oslo.

Kodeih, F., & Greenwood, R. (2014). Responding to institutional complexity: The role of identity. *Organization Studies*, *35*, 7–39.

Kuhlmann, E. (2006). *Modernising health care: Reinventing professions, the state and the public*. Bristol: The Policy Press.

Ladegård, G., & Vabo, S. I. (2010). Ledelse og styring: – Teoretisk rammeverk. In G. Ladegård & S. I. Vabo (Eds.), *Ledelse og styring*. Bergen: Fagbokforlaget.

Magnussen, J., Vrangbæk, K., Saltman, R. B., & Martinussen, P. E. (2009). Introduction: The Nordic model of health care. In J. Magnussen, K. Vrangbæk, & R. B. Saltman (Eds.), *Nordic health care systems. Recent reforms and current policy challenges*. Berkshire: Open University Press.

Molander, A., & Terum, L. I. (2008). Profesjonsstudier – En introduksjon. In A. Molander & L. I. Terum (Eds.), *Profesjonsstudier*. Oslo: Universitetsforlaget.

Noordegraaf, M. (2012). The making of professional public leaders. Leadership as a practical myth. In C. Teelken, E. Ferlie, & M. Dent (Eds.), *Leadership in the public sector*. London: Routledge.

Oliver, C. (1991). Strategic responses to institutional processes. *Academy of Management Review*, *16*, 145–179.

Olsen, J. P. (2007). The institutional dynamics of the European university. In P. Maassen & J. P. Olsen (Eds.), *University dynamics and European integration* (pp. 25–54). Dordrecht: Springer.

O'Reilly, D., & Reed, M. (2010). 'Leaderism': An evolution of managerialism in UK public service reform. *Public Administration*, *88*, 960–978.

O'Reilly, D., & Reed, M. (2012). 'Leaderism' and the discourse of leadership in the reformation of UK public services. In C. Teelken, E. Ferlie, & M. Dent (Eds.), *Leadership in the public sector. Promises and pitfalls*. London: Routledge.

Osborne, S. P. (2011). Public governance and public services: A 'brave new world' or new wine in old bottles? In T. Christensen & P. Lægreid (Eds.), *The Ashgate research companion to new public management*. Farnham: Ashgate.

Pache, A.-C., & Santos, F. (2013). Inside the hybrid organization: Selective coupling as a response to competing institutional logics. *Academy of Management Journal*, *56*, 972–1001.

Peters, G., & Savoie, D. J. (1998). *Taking stock: Assessing public sector reforms*. Quebec: McGill-Queen's University Press.

Pinheiro, R. (2012a). *In the region, for the region? A comparative study of the institutionalisation of the regional mission of universities*. Ph.D. dissertation, University of Oslo.

Pinheiro, R. (2012b). University ambiguity and institutionalization: A tale of three regions. In R. Pinheiro, P. Benneworth, & G. A. Jones (Eds.), *Universities and regional development: A critical assessment of tensions and contradictions*. Milton Park: Routledge.

Pinheiro, R. (2015). Citius, altius, fortius: Mobilising the university for the 'Europe of knowledge'. In B. Culum, F. Robeiro, & Y. Politis (Eds.), *New voices in higher education research and scholarship*. Hershey, PA: IGI-Global.

Pinheiro, R., & Antonowics, D. (2015). Opening the gates or coping with the flow? Governing access to higher education in Northern and Central Europe. *Higher Education*, *70*(3), 299–313. doi:10.1007/s10734-014-9830-1

Pinheiro, R., Geschwind, L., & Aarrevaara, T. (2014). Nested tensions and interwoven dilemmas in higher education: The view from the Nordic countries. *Cambridge Journal of Regions, Economy and Society*, *7*(2), 233–250. doi:10.1093/cjres/rsu002

Pinheiro, R., & Stensaker, B. (2014). Designing the entrepreneurial university: The interpretation of a global idea. *Public Organization Review*, *14*(4), 497–516. doi:10.1007/s11115-013-0241-z

Pinheiro, R., & Trondal, J. (2014). *Loose- or Tight- Coupling? Exploring the interplay between decopling, slack and resilience in universities*. Paper presented at the European Forum for Studies of Policies for Research and Innovation, Manchester, 18–20th June.

Pollitt, C. (1993). *Managerialism and the public services: Cuts or cultural change in the 1990s?* Oxford: Blackwell.

Pollitt, C., & Bouckaert, G. (2011). *Public management reform: A comparative analysis – New public management, governance, and the neo-Weberian state*. Oxford: Oxford University Press.

Ramirez, F. O. (2006). The rationalization of universities. In M.-L. Djelic & K. Sahlin-Andersson (Eds.), *Transnational governance: Institutional dynamics of regulation*. Cambridge, MA: Cambridge University Press.

Rost, J. C. (1993). *Leadership for the twenty-first century*. Westport, CT: Greenwood Publishing Group.

Sahlin, K., & Wedlin, L. (2008). Circulating ideas: Imitation, translation and editing. In R. Greenwood, K. Sahlin-Andersson, & R. Suddaby (Eds.), *The Sage handbook of organizational institutionalism* (pp. 218–242). Los Angeles/London/New Delhi/Singapore: Sage.

Schein, E. H. (2010). *Organizational culture and leadership*. San Francisco, CA: Jossey-Bass.

Scott, W. R. (2008). *Institutions and organizations*. Los Angeles, CA: Sage.

Scott, W. R., Ruef, M., Mendel, P. J., & Caronna, C. A. (2000). *Institutional change and health care organizations: From professional dominance to managed care*. Chicago, IL: University of Chicago Press.

Slaughter, S., & Rhoades, G. (2004). *Academic capitalism and the new economy: Markets, state, and higher education*. Baltimore, N.J.: Johns Hopkins University Press.

Stensaker, B., & Harvey, L. (2011). *Accountability in higher education: Global perspectives on trust and power*. New York, NY: Taylor & Francis.

Strand, T. (2007). *Ledelse, organisasjon og kultur*. Bergen: Fagbokforlaget.

Tapper, T., & Palfreyman, D. (2010). *The collegial tradition in the age of mass higher education*. Dordrecht: Springer.

Teichler, U., Arimoto, A., & Cummings, W. K. (2013). *The changing academic profession: Major findings of a comparative survey*. Dordrecht: Springer.

Thornton, P., & Ocasio, W. (2008). Institutional logics. In R. Greenwood, C. Oliver, S. K. Andersen, & R. Suddaby (Eds.), *Handbook of organizational institutionalism*. Los Angeles, CA: Sage.

Thornton, P., Ocasio, W., & Lounsbury, M. (2012). *The institutional logics perspective: A new approach to culture, structure, and process*. Oxford: Oxford University Press.

Vabø, A., & Aamodt, P. O. (2008). Nordic higher education in transition. In T. Tapper & D. Palfreyman (Eds.), *Structuring mass higher education. The role of elite institutions* (pp. 57–72). New York & London: Routdlege.

Viitanen, E., & Konu, A. (2009). Leadership style profiles of middle – Level managers in social and health care. *International Journal of Health Care Quality Assurance Incorporating Leadership in Health Services*, *22*, 108–120.

Vrangbæk, K. (1999). New public management i sygehusfeltet – Udformning og konsekvenser. In E. Bentzen, F. Borum, G. Erlingsdottir, & K. Sahlin-Andersson (Eds.), *Når styringsmbitioner møder praksis. Den svære omstillingen af sygehus- og sundhedsvæsenet i Danmark og Sverige*. Munksgaard: Handelshøyskolens Forlag.

Whitchurch, C. (2008). Shifting identities and blurring boundaries: The emergence of third space professionals in UK higher education. *Higher Education Quarterly*, *62*(4), 377–396.

Welch, A. R. (2005). *The professoriate: Profile of a profession*. Dordrecht: Springer.

Yin, R. K. (2014). *Case study research. Design and methods*. Los Angeles, CA: Sage.

Zucker, L. G. (1991). The role of institutionalization in cultural persistence. In W. W. Powell & P. DiMaggio (Eds.), *The new institutionalism in organizational analysis* (pp. 83–107). Chicago and London: University of Chicago Press.

DECISION-MAKING POWER AND INSTITUTIONAL LOGIC IN HIGHER EDUCATION INSTITUTIONS: A COMPARATIVE ANALYSIS OF EUROPEAN UNIVERSITIES

S. Kubra Canhilal, Benedetto Lepori and Marco Seeber

ABSTRACT

The aim of this paper is to analyze responses of public universities to the introduction of New Public Management (NPM) as the outcome of balancing between the managerial logics endorsed by NPM and the academic professional logics. Building on the institutional logics approach, we develop a framework concerning how universities will achieve compliance to conflicting claims by strategies like compartmentalization and blending stipulations of both logics. Empirical results based on a large-scale survey of 26 universities in eight European countries display how compatibility is

Towards a Comparative Institutionalism: Forms, Dynamics and Logics Across the Organizational Fields of Health Care and Higher Education
Research in the Sociology of Organizations, Volume 45, 169–194

ISSN: 0733-558X/doi:10.1108/S0733-558X20150000045019

achieved through highly differentiated adoption of logics that depends on the task considered. The results reveal that the strength of NPM pressures strongly affects the adoption of managerial practices within universities yet has no significant effect on the academic characteristics.

Keywords: Decision-making; institutional logics; higher education

INTRODUCTION

In the last 30 years, there have been changes in the way public policies manage public services. The idea of such reforms is rooted back to the 1980s with Margaret Thatcher and Ronald Reagan. Namely New Public Management (NPM) reforms introduced certain policy narratives explaining how public organizations should operate, regardless of the characteristics of their particular sector of activity (Brunsson & Sahlin-Andersson, 2000; Ferlie, Musselin, & Andresani, 2008). These narratives emphasize the importance of economic values and objectives and foresee that public organizations should be managed like private companies.

However, empirical evidence indicates that the responses of public sector organizations to NPM reforms are more differentiated than isomorphic compliance to policy pressures (Ashworth, Boyne, & Delbridge, 2009; Bovaird & Downe, 2006) and are influenced by organizational characteristics like history, tasks, and position with respect to the state (Lægreid, Roness, & Rubecksen, 2007). Moreover, not only do responses vary between organizations, but compliance is selective with respect to different organizational features (Andrews, 2011).

Responses are particularly complex in sectors such as education and healthcare, which are characterized by resilient professional cultures which establish different modes of managing such organizations with respect to the private sector (Leicht & Fennell, 2008; Thornton, Ocasio, & Lounsbury, 2012). When public policies are coercive in implementing NPM, this would risk generating conflict and jeopardizing key elements of the professional culture, like the importance of trust and the autonomy of professionals, which is considered central to the performance of these organizations (Adler, 2008). In those cases, resistance from the organization is expected (Townley, 1997).

In this paper, we aim to investigate responses to the introduction of NPM policies in the case of public universities in Europe. Our analysis builds on the theoretical perspective of institutional logics. In this context, the aim of this paper is to investigate how the interaction between managerial and academic logic shapes responses from European public universities to NPM pressures. We hypothesize that rather than selecting one competing logic, universities are likely to develop more differentiated strategies to achieve some level of compatibility and to avoid conflict, adopting the core practices of the managerial logic, while keeping some central features of the academic logic and resorting to compromise in case of conflict.

For this aim, we investigate the adoption of two sets of practices, related respectively to the managerial and academic logic. The introduction of an organizational hierarchy and rule system represents two key stipulations of managerial logic (Brunsson & Sahlin-Andersson, 2000), while collegial decision-making and the participation of academics in decision-making are two core features of the academic logic. Accordingly, we expect that the considered cases, when subject to NPM pressures, will introduce hierarchy and rule systems, but try at the same time to maintain collegial decision-making and academic participations especially for those tasks considered central to the academic logic, such as the management of teaching and research. When stipulations of the two logics conflict on the same tasks, universities are expected to achieve some level of compatibility by compromising: for example, top-hierarchical positions might be occupied by academic leaders holding also professional authority, while the consultation and involvement of academics in decisions could be maintained also within a hierarchical and rule-based structure.

The contribution of this paper is twofold. On the one hand, we provide a more nuanced understanding of the public organization's response to NPM pressures quantitatively, particularly when the field is characterized by the presence of a strong professional culture. On the other hand, these results hint at the possibility that the introduction of managerial practices does not necessarily lead to the dysfunctional outcomes feared by some authors, like jeopardizing trust and demotivation of employees (Diefenbach, 2009). It suggests that the presence of a strong academic culture might allow universities to be selective in adopting managerial practices, while keeping some central elements of the academic logic which are functional to the characteristics of their activities.

INSTITUTION LOGICS AND RESPONSES TO INSTITUTIONAL PRESSURES

Institutional logics are socially constructed, historical patterns of assumptions, values, beliefs, rules and material practices by which individuals produce and reproduce their material subsistence, organize time and space, and provide meaning to their social reality (Thorton & Ocasio, 1999, p. 804). Logics provide cognitive and practical templates to organizations on how to perform certain tasks. Research has provided extensive evidence that many organizational fields are characterized by lasting institutional pluralism, that is, by the enduring presence of legitimate alternative logics (Friedland & Alford, 1991; Kraatz & Block, 2008).

Earlier institutional studies assumed that organizations would comply with one single logic and resist the other (Greenwood & Hinings, 1993). Namely, it was argued that blending institutional logics would jeopardize the identity of the organization, lead to conflicts at the level of activities, and generate uncertainty and ambiguity for the employees. Professional organizations would then have to decide whether to resist NPM pressures or become managerially orientated. In turn, decoupling would be an alternative strategy (Meyer & Rowan, 1977), which is risky when pluralism is long lasting, as audiences over time may become aware of the purely ritual character of compliance.

Recent research has shown that both blending and hybridity are more widespread than assumed, and that organizations can be intentional and goal-oriented in this process (Greenwood, Diaz, Li, & Lorente, 2009). Responses can be broadly classified into two groups (Greenwood, Raynard, Kodeih, Micelotta, & Lounsbury, 2011). On the one hand, structural responses aim to reduce tensions by creating subunits following different logics, for example, a technical department with a public-service mission and a sales department with a marketing mission (Jarzabkowski, 2004). Compartmentalization implies the adoption of intact groups of practices from individual logics (Pache & Santos, 2013). For instance, universities might adopt managerial practices for management tasks, while keeping academic practices for tasks more directly related to teaching and research. On the other hand, blending and compromising responses have been identified, where organizations combine elements of different logics by exploiting their compatibility (Jay, 2013) and, thereby, develop original sets of practices. For instance, when pressured by NPM to introduce a stronger hierarchical structure, universities might introduce elements of it, but soften it through participative arrangements and by avoiding any overt use of power. While managerial and professional logics might be incompatible at the level of general principles and values, it is possible that at the level of specific tasks, compatibility is achieved through case-by-case solutions. Further, it has been highlighted that organizations can be highly strategic in managing their legitimacy and, therefore, be selective in coupling with institutional logics (Pache & Santos, 2013). This means that, strategically, organizations will respond to a conflict between the logics by selectively complying with those stipulations considered central by each individual logic, in order to enhance legitimacy towards audiences.

Beyond the simple opposition between managerial and professional logics, this discussion first suggests that to understand how public organizations cope with pluralism, a highly differentiated analysis of the content of each logic and of the centrality of the different practices is needed. Second, it suggests that public organizations are more likely to seek compatibility through strategies like compartmentalization and blending, than to overtly oppose managerial logics, as this strategy would allow conflicting legitimacy claims to be better managed.

Achieving Compatibility

In our empirical investigation the focus is on two central stipulations of the managerial logic, that is, the introduction of hierarchy and rationality (Brunsson & Sahlin-Andersson, 2000), and two central stipulations of the academic logic, that is, decision-making by consensus (collegiality) and participation of individual academics to decision-making. A straightforward selective coupling argument would lead to the expectation that, in order to be compliant with both managerial and academic logic, universities would introduce *hierarchy* and *rationality*, while keeping at the same time collegiality and participation. However, things are not so simple, as these principles might contradict each other and, therefore, organizations are obliged to choose or to compromise. Therefore, a more careful analysis is required. In the managerial logic, organizational *hierarchy* is structural and is based on the definition of layers of leaders and followers (de Boer, Enders, & Leisyte, 2007); central control and vertical coordination with leaders defining goals and strategies and subordinates implementing them. Hierarchy should be enforced through formalized assignments of responsibilities and the definition of formal decision-making procedures. These principles would contradict an academic conception of hierarchy, which is based on professional authority, and where horizontal coordination prevails (hence rectors and deans are considered *primus inter pares*).

We suggest two approaches to limit conflicts in the introduction of a managerial hierarchical structure: on the one hand, focusing on those organizational activities which are not core in the academic understanding of a university, like administrative tasks, logistics, and resourcing. On the other hand, for those activities which are core to academia, like teaching and research, universities might reduce the cognitive distance between management and individual academics by empowering faculty leaders rather than university leaders; further, even within a hierarchical structure, they might reduce the power asymmetry by foreseeing consultation and participation of academics to decision-making and by preferring the construction of consensus against the overt use of hierarchical power.

In terms of rationality, the managerial logic endorses a conception where human action should be goal-oriented and based on the systematic evaluation of its consequences, emphasizing efficiency and precise measurement of outcomes as key values. In formal and practical terms, it draws on the adoption of planning instruments in decision-making and the diffusion of routines as tools to solve day-to-day problems in a predefined way (Brunsson & Sahlin-Andersson, 2000; Townley, 2002). Therefore, rationality is a complex and multi-layered concept which includes both an interpretive framework on the reality (theoretical rationality), a set of values which should direct the action (substantive rationality), and recipes on how to deal with day-to-day problems (practical rationality; Kalberg, 1980; Townley, 2002).

These distinctions allow for a more precise identification of points of conflict and elements of compatibility with the academic logics. Namely, the academic logic is not necessarily contrary to the adoption of simple rules in order to perform some tasks, like the repartition of the budget or the execution of managerial tasks. Stronger resistance from organizations is expected when rule systems involve judgments by the organizational leadership concerning the quality of academics, respectively, an understanding that the goal of a university should be to become more efficient.

Collegiality, as a core component of the academic logic, emphasizes the autonomy of professionals and their equal value, as well as a world where action should be driven by academic values and by the search for novelty, related to the unpredictability of scientific inquiry. In formal and practical terms, it emphasizes decision-making based on consensus. Academics who hold prestigious positions are often involved in the governance of the universities' tasks related to teaching and research, therefore academic merit usually has influence on university politics (Bergquist, 1992). Similarly, participation is about the involvement of academics and their power in the decision-making process and design of control instruments (Adler & Borys, 1996). On the one hand, such participatory arrangements are likely to be more acceptable in terms of the characteristics of academic work; on the other hand, rule systems co-shaped with professionals will enjoy a higher level of legitimacy and will meet less opposition and thus be more effective (Courpasson, 2000) (Fig. 1).

Accordingly, when hierarchy is introduced, compliance or compromise will depend on whether the task in question is a core or a non-core academic

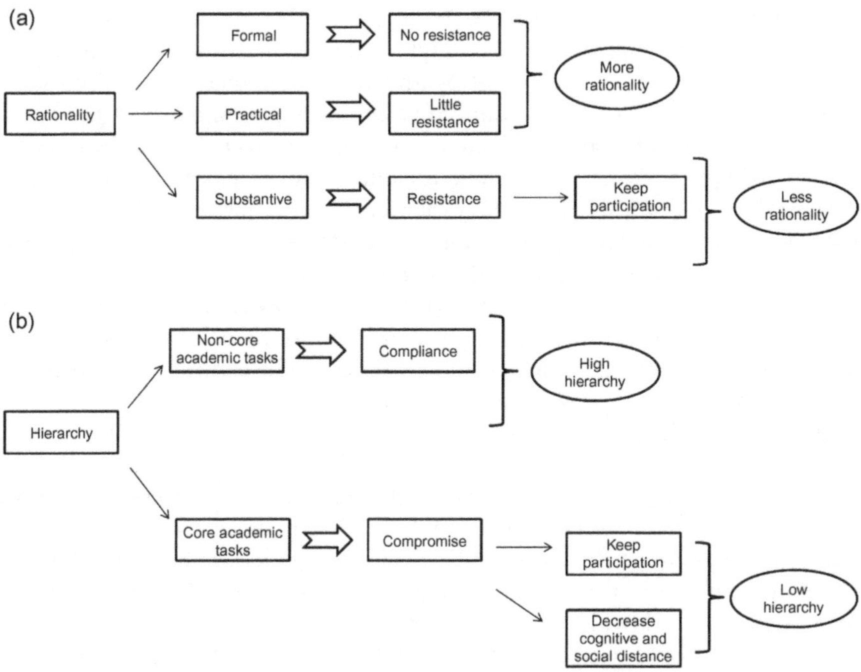

Fig. 1. Interaction of NPM with Hierarchy and Rationality. *Source*: Prepared by the Authors.

task. The expected behavior is that for the core academic tasks there will be a compromise, and in our case participation will be kept in tandem with a reduction of the cognitive distance between the various organizational subunits. Concerning rationality, we predict that substantive rationality will meet more resistance because it is connected to value, therefore compromise is needed to balance between the two logics by keeping the participation of individual academics to the creation of the evaluation tools.

INSTITUTIONAL LOGICS: CASE OF HIGHER EDUCATION

Public universities in Europe can be considered as a prototypical case of organizations subject to conflicting stipulations from a professional logic and from a managerial logic (Albert & Whetten, 1985). On the one hand, they were traditionally considered to be highly specific organizations, characterized by loose coupling (Weick, 1976) and the dominance of the profession (Mintzberg, 1979). The professional logic of academia emphasizes the specific nature of research activities, which cannot be controlled from the outside, and accordingly provides a rationale for autonomy of research and the lack of central control (Musselin, 2007). Moreover, it considers scientific disciplines to be the central cognitive and social structure of academia (Becher, 1994) through which professional careers are managed, and accordingly, results into decentralized universities (Becher & Trowler, 2001; Clark, 1983). Finally, it considers peer-to-peer coordination and collegial decisions based on consensus and formal equality of academics, to be central components of the decision-making process (Thornton & Ocasio, 1999).

On the other hand, in the past three decades universities in Europe have increasingly been subject to pressures to become similar to other organizations, to introduce a formal organizational structure, and to become "rational organizations" with well-defined goals and strategies (Ramirez, 2009). Normative pressures to align with the corporate model are part of a broader process of diffusion of a global organizational template, where all organizations compete worldwide, while characteristics related to individual sectors and countries should disappear (Meyer, Boli, Thomas, & Ramirez, 1997).

While in the United States this process began before1960s, in Europe public universities were protected from managerial pressures by an alliance between the State and the profession, built on an understanding that public organizations in general, and universities in particular, had different goals and ways of functioning when compared to companies (Ramirez & Christensen, 2013). Competition between universities has been a fact in the American ecology of higher education for a very long time. Universities are engaged in raiding faculty from other universities and in shielding themselves from other university efforts to seduce their faculty. External offers are a mechanism through which one may improve one's salary. On the other hand, in the European context, the institutional environment of European universities profoundly changed in the 1980s with the introduction of NPM narratives in public policies (Ferlie et al., 2008; Paradeise, Reale, Bleiklie, & Ferlie, 2009), which promoted an understanding that public organizations should also be managed like private companies, and specifically, develop a clear identity and introduce hierarchy and rationality in their structure (Brunsson & Sahlin-Andersson, 2000). Normative pressures were also accompanied by coercive interventions from the State and thus became more forceful, albeit with significant differences across countries in terms of the pace and extent of reforms (de Boer, Enders, & Schimank, 2007; Paradeise et al., 2009). Policies were implemented through regulatory changes, like granting more autonomy to universities, the introduction of market arrangements in funding (Teixeira, Jongbloed, Dill, & Amaral, 2004), and the diffusion of evaluation systems at the national level (Whitley & Glaser, 2007).

Table 1 displays how the academic and managerial logic provide widely different stipulations on how universities should be managed (Thornton & Ocasio, 1999). The managerial logic conceives universities as corporate actors oriented towards market competition and that performance should be managed through a well-defined hierarchy, where authority rests on the top management and it is legitimized by hierarchical relationship. The managerial logic foresees the centralization of decisions and their implementation through command and rule systems guiding employees in their activities. In contrast, the academic logic considers a university as a "community of scholars," whose main mission is to produce scholarly knowledge and maintain its reputation among peers. Authority is based on professional seniority and academic reputation, whereas decisions should be taken by consensus, and autonomy of academics should be guaranteed.

Table 1. Dimensions of the Academics and Managerial Logics.[a]

	Managerial	Academic
Economic system	Performance-based	Membership-based
Sources of identity	University as a corporate organization	University as professional organizations
Sources of legitimacy	Hierarchical position	Scholarly reputation
Sources of authority	Top management	Academic profession
Basis of mission	Increase organizational performance	Produce scholarly knowledge
Basis of attention	Performance measures	Peers judgment
Basis of strategy	Positioning in market niches	Constructing university reputation
Logic of investment	Focus on activities where the university enjoys a competitive advantage	Provide large freedom of research and teaching to the professorial body
Governance mechanism	Managerial decisions by top-hierarchy	Collegial principle

[a]Based on the dimensions of Thornton and Ocasio (1999).

Since the introduction of NPM reforms in Europe, it has been highly contested whether public policies would be able to transform universities into corporate organizations, with some scholars arguing that because of the characteristics of their activities and structural conditions related to the profession, transforming universities into organizational actors was not possible, and if so, it would be highly dysfunctional (Whitley, 2008).

Empirical evidence reveals a complex situation as well. On the one hand, policy pressures are changing European universities from being administrated organizations towards being managed organizations, with stronger central leadership and strategic capability (Krücken, Kosmützky, & Torka, 2007), where principles of efficiency, cost-effectiveness, and central strategic control are introduced (Christopher & Leung, 2015; de Boer, Enders, & Leisyte, 2007; Enders, Kehm, & Schimank, 2015; Kogan, Bauer, Bleiklie, & Henkel, 2006). On the other hand, there is a great deal of variation in this process (Sahlin, 2012), and changes are rather gradual and incremental (Musselin, 2007). The so-called World Class Universities have maintained traditional characteristics: they are internally decentralized, governance is co-shared between the faculty and the administration, and a high level of socialization among academics is maintained (Paradeise & Thoenig, 2011). Instead, universities grasping for the elite, the "wannabes," centralize power in managers, reduce both the power of deans and room for shared governance, and in doing so they downplay the community principles (Paradeise & Thoenig, 2013; Tuchman, 2009). Comparative analysis displays a systematic association between the strength of NPM pressures and the introduction of managerial elements like hierarchy and rationality (Seeber et al., forthcoming), but also that universities respond to the dilemma between central control and professional autonomy by combining formal and informal mechanisms of control (Bleiklie, Enders, & Lepori, forthcoming).

METHODOLOGY

Sample

The sample of universities was purposefully constructed in order to mirror some central dimensions of diversity in European universities, in terms of age, size, international reputation, and disciplinary concentration. Accordingly, the sample includes a rather heterogeneous set of universities in terms of size (number of students ranges from 2,000 to 90,000), age (foundation year between the middle-age and the late 1990s), international reputation (some universities in the sample being among the first 100 in international rankings, others not included at all) and finally, discipline concentration, as the sample includes both generalist universities and highly specialized technical universities. Moreover, the sample covers countries which are very different in terms of their politico-administrative systems (Bleiklie & Michelsen, 2013), as well as the strength and timing of the introduction of NPM policies (Bleiklie, Enders, Lepori, & Musselin, 2011; Paradeise et al., 2009).

The survey resulted in 687 respondents and a response rate of 48%. At the university level, the number of respondents ranged from 7 to 55, with response rates between 26% and 79%. In terms of the category of respondents, we collected 246 questionnaires from senate members (response rate 45%), 235 from middle managers (48%), 162 from board members (50%), 20 from central administrators (74%), and 24 from rectors (89%). In terms of roles, the composition of our respondents is thus rather similar to the original population.

Constructs

In order to test our hypothesis, we use a survey delivered to people occupying five different roles in 26 European universities. These are: members of the university board, members of the senates, rector or president, the person responsible for infrastructure and management (the "central administrator") and, finally, faculty deans. All survey questions were closed, most of them using 5-point Likert scales, with the exception of some questions which used a 3-point scale. Since not all questions were included in the questionnaires given to all groups, the number of respondents varies between questions (see Table 2 for all constructs and questions used).

Hierarchy

In order to analyze hierarchical structure, we used a survey question concerning the actual level of decision-making power for 13 different items and for three organizational levels inside universities (central level, faculty, and shopfloor which refers to the academic heartland; Clark, 1998). This question is suitable for our investigation because it deals with actual power and not just with formal competences, and it provides a fine-grained view by a large number of items. Moreover this question allows us to analyze the decision-making power of each organizational level by looking at different tasks (e.g., core and non-core academic and managerial tasks). Factor

Table 2. Constructs Table.

Constructs	Survey Question	Scale	Category Respondents	Items	*N*	Alfa	ICC[a]
H1: Hierarchy: managerial	Please indicate the extent to which actors within your university have actual decision-making power for the listed issues	3-point	All	Average score for 8 items by three levels (central, faculty, leadership)	583	.715	.10
Max (leadership, faculty)-shopfloor						.742 .743	.12 .07
H2: Hierarchy: academic	Please indicate the extent to which actors within your university have actual decision-making power for the listed issues	3-point	All	Average score for 5 items by three levels (central, faculty, leadership)	580	.740	.13
Max (leadership, faculty)-shopfloor						.712 .742	.13 .06
R1: Rule-based allocation	How important is each of the following factors in resource allocation to units?	5 point	Central administrator, senate, middle management	3 items referring to formula allocation	434	.701	0.22
R2: Comparison between units	For which of the following activities does your university systematically compare different units?	3 choices	Central administrator and middle management	Average score for 5 items	217	.850	0.11
R2: Evaluation of individuals	For which of the following activities does your university systematically compare individuals	3 choices	Central administrator and middle management	Average score for 5 items	192	.807	0.15
P1: Participation in the strategy	Importance of cooperation in realizing the university strategy	5 point	Rector, Central administrator, senate, board	Average score for 3 items	364	.768	0.06

C1: Collegiality	Do you agree with the following statements concerning your university?	5 point	All		675	.594	0.05
PA1: Power of the individual academics (shopfloor) – managerial tasks	Please indicate the extent to which actors within your university have actual decision-making power for the listed issues	3-point	All	Average score for 8 items by three levels (central, faculty, leadership)	583	743	.07
PA2: Power of the individual academics (shopfloor) Academic tasks	Please indicate the extent to which actors within your university have actual decision-making power for the listed issues	3-point	All	Average score for 5 items by three levels (central, faculty, leadership)	580	.742	.06

[a]The Intraclass correlation coefficient (ICC) measures the proportion of variance between groups. Values below 0.10 are indicative of no meaningful variations (Snijders & Bosker, 2012).

analysis run separately on the three levels provides convergent results and allows for the classification of items into two broad groups.

The first group includes the items related to the power concerning the nomination of hierarchical positions and management issues: (1) selecting leadership, (2) selecting the head of units, (3) setting the goals of units, (4) defining the budget of units, (5) setting employment conditions for a new chair, (6) setting rules and procedures for the evaluation of units, (7) defining policies for the management of academic staff, (8) setting study places for each curriculum.

The second group includes the items related to teaching, research, and academic appointments: (1) establishing the profile of a new position, (2) selecting the candidate for a new chair, (3) establishing new teaching programs, (4) evaluating individual academic performance, and (5) establishing research programs. Having these two groups allows us to measure hierarchy in terms of the power of each organizational level for academic and managerial tasks. We construct two measures of hierarchy as managerial hierarchy (see H1 in Table 2) and academic hierarchy (see H2 in Table 2). In order to measure managerial and academic hierarchy we construct it by taking the maximum between the leadership level and the faculty level, and subtract it from the shopfloor level.

Rationality

To analyze rationality we use the questions related to the introduction of rule systems. The first question is concerned with the use of criteria for the internal allocation of resources. Three items refer to formula allocation based on students, graduates, and external funding, which load onto a single factor. We construct a variable for *rule-based allocation* (see R1 in Table 2) as the average score for these three items.

The second question measures the two variables concerning whether the university systematically compares its units, respectively, subunits and individuals, for five dimensions (teaching performance, teaching process, research performance, research process, and non-academic affairs). The five items for each of the two questions load onto a single factor in the factor analysis and display a high level of consistency. We construct two distinct variables, one variable for units and one variable for subunits and individual comparisons (see R2 in Table 2).

Collegiality, Participation, and the Power of Individual Academics

In order to measure collegiality, we measure the decision-making power of the shopfloor level (see PA1 and PA2 in Table 2). Therefore, we use the same question of hierarchy; however, we analyze the power of the shopfloor. The question includes 13 items. Additionally, to measure participation, we use a question about cooperation with three items, regarding: (a) the importance of cooperation and participation in the creation of the universities' strategy; (b) the power of the individual academics (shopfloor level) for managerial tasks like nomination of heads, and (c) power of individuals regarding budgets and employment conditions. While in a purely collegial setting these tasks should be managed by academics as well, they are not central to the notion of academic autonomy per se.

New Public Management Reform Pressures
In order to analyze the impact of NPM, a variable has been constructed measuring the strength and duration of NPM policies on an indexed scale from 0 to 1. Four main criteria were considered: *timing*, which measures how long the NPM narrative has influenced the reform discourse in higher education; *competition* considers the share of public funds allocated via competitive streams of formula and projects; *accountability* is a proxy for the relevance of teaching and research evaluations promoted by ministries and agencies; *autonomy* is estimated by how leadership is selected (appointed or elected), and what is the power of the university to reorganize itself, for example, by changing the statute, creating new faculties or courses (Paradeise et al., 2009). Table 3 provides the NPM scores of each country involved in this study.

Data Analysis

First, we compare the means of the respondent's answers inside each university; since differences in responses by groups of respondents are non-significant for most of the questions we use, this procedure is robust against differences in the composition of the sample. We use a paired *t*-test in order to compare whether observed differences in the average of university means are statistically significant.

Secondly, in order to analyze the impact of NPM pressures on our variables, we perform multi-level analysis using as dependent variables the scores for each individual respondent. Independent variables include the level of NPM and organizational controls, as well as dummies for respondent's roles. Our model consists of responses from individuals within the universities. We model individual scores as an outcome of both individual

Table 3. Level of NPM Pressures.

	Timing of NPM Reforms	Funding		Accountability: Top-Down Evaluation of HEIs Research and Teaching Performance[a]	Autonomy: Leadership Selection, Decision-Making on Organization and Profile[a]	Overall NPM Influence
		Share of formula in core budget[b]	Share of project[b]			
Norway	From 2000 (2)	45% (2)	20% (2)	Evaluation system based on reports produced by HEIs (2); teaching program externally evaluated (2)	Appointed leaders at faculty and department Level (2); HEIs have the right to decide on internal organization (3)	0.45
Portugal	From 2000	90% (2)	3% (1)	Research evaluation and assessment and accreditation of HEIs and their study cycles done by independent agencies (2)	Mostly elected leaders (2). Power to reorganize within the legal framework, creation of courses submitted to the accreditation agency (2)	0.27
Italy	From 2000	7% (1)	3% (1)	Research assessment but limited impact (1); central accreditation (2)	Leaders elected by academics (1); HEIs can reorganize, teaching courses must satisfy law requirement (2)	0.00
Germany	From 2000	Federal funding (2)	12% (2)	*excellenz* initiative (2) accreditation agencies (2)	Leaders can be appointed top-down; most are still academics (1) reorganization power limited (1)	0.18
France	From mid-2000 (1)	Performance contracts (2)	30% (2)	Recent establishment of agencies for HEIs evaluation (2); timid evaluation of courses (1)	Leaders elected by academics (1), reorganization power is limited, although growing (2)	0.00
Switzerland	From 2000 (2)	Federal funding (2)	21% (2)	No HEIs wide teaching or research evaluation, which are up to each HEI (1)	Rectors appointed but often limited powers (2); some liberty to reorganize but also strong state intervention capability (2)	0.18

UK	From 1980s (3)	59% (3)	29% (3)	Research assessment exercise with strong impact (3); market-oriented accreditation (2)	Strong university leadership (appointed by board) and autonomy to reorganize (3)	1.00
The Netherlands	From mid-1980s (3)	90% (3)	10% (2)	Research evaluation for internal allocation (2); central accreditation (2)	Vertical system of appointment (3), within given national boundaries HEIs are free to reorganize (3)	0.82

For individual items we use a three-point scale 1 = low; 2 = medium; 3 = high. Total score is calculated as the average of the four items, rescaled from 1 (highest NPM influence) to 0 (lowest NPM influence).

[a]Paradeise et al. (2009).

[b]Share of funding allocated via formula and project (Chinchilla-Rodriguéz, Ferligoi, Miguel, Kronegger, & de Moya-Anegón, 2012; Lepori, Benninghoff, Jongbloed, Salerno, & Slipersaeter, 2005; Reale & Seeber, 2011).

level and university level variables. We treat the responses as continuous and use OLS. We calculate it as:

$$y_{ij} = \beta_1 + \beta_2 x_i + \beta_3 x_j + u_i + \varepsilon_{ij}$$

More specifically, we use j as the respondent and i as the university, and u_i as the observations at the individual level within the same university. We use this variable because these observations are not independent.

In terms of organizational controls, we use *the level of disciplinary concentration*, which is calculated by the Herfindahl index of the share of students enrolled in each of the nine subject domains of educational statistics. *Size* is measured through the number of students at the concerned university. Size is relevant since smaller organizations might be easier to manage through informal processes and thus display a lower level of formal hierarchy and rationality. *Age* is measured by the foundation year of the university. Finally, an indicator of *international reputation* has been derived from the Scimago Ranking (2011), the most complete world ranking in terms of organizational coverage that includes more than 1,000 Western European research organizations.

RESULTS

Descriptive Analysis

The results are consistent with our expectations that variations IN the managerial logic characteristics are higher than the variations IN the academic logic's characteristics, such as participation and collegiality with respect to rationality and hierarchy. When analyzing the measure of involvement of academics and of the collegial nature of the university, a noteworthy feature is that these characteristics are more uniform across the whole sample than those of hierarchy and rationality. The same applies for the intraclass correlation coefficient, showing that less than 6% of the responses' variance is at the university level. The only other indicators displaying such limited variation between universities, are those of shopfloor power, which can be largely interpreted as a similar measure of the involvement of academics in decision-making. This supports the assumption that the involvement of academics represents a common feature of the universities considered, which is rather uniform and less influenced by differences in national policies, as well as in the extent of NPM pressures.

Table 4. Paired Sample *T*-test Results.

	Paired Differences			t	df	Significance (Two-Tailed)
	M	SD	SEM			
Rationality formula-based allocation Rationality comparison between units	.13065	.14373	.02819	4.635	25	.000
Rationality comparison between units Rationality evaluation of individuals	.04016	.11513	.02303	1.744	24	.094
Hierarchy managerial Hierarchy academic	.23501	.11727	.02300	10.219	25	.000
Power academic shopfloor power Power management shopfloor	.22936	.10780	.02114	10.849	25	.000

With regard to the relationship among the variables, the results confirm our expectations. Fig. 2 demonstrates that rationality in resource allocation is higher than rationality when comparing units and individuals, respectively; furthermore, resource allocation is more formal than evaluating units and individuals, therefore, it is more applicable. More specifically, evaluating individual academics is quite contrary to the academic logic, therefore, it is not surprising to see that it has the lowest score among the other aspects of rationality. In the case of hierarchy, the results show that hierarchy for managerial tasks is higher than the hierarchy for academic tasks, which was also expected with the introduction of NPM reforms.

Lastly, the data reveal that the power of individual academics is higher in academic tasks than in management tasks. Therefore, competing logics do not require compliance for all their stipulations and do not oppose each other concerning all organizational activities (Greenwood et al., 2009; Jay, 2013). Descriptive statistics concerning the differences are statistically significant (t-test on paired samples, $p < 0.001$). However, the difference between units and individuals cannot be confirmed, as it is only marginally significant (Table 4).

Impact of NPM

In order to analyze the impact of NPM, we ran multi-level analysis (see Table 5). Accordingly, we tentatively conclude that there is no impact of NPM on collegiality and participation (see Table 5 for the results of the regression). In our models, the effect of NPM on the indicators we have presented in order to measure academic logic; collegiality, participation,

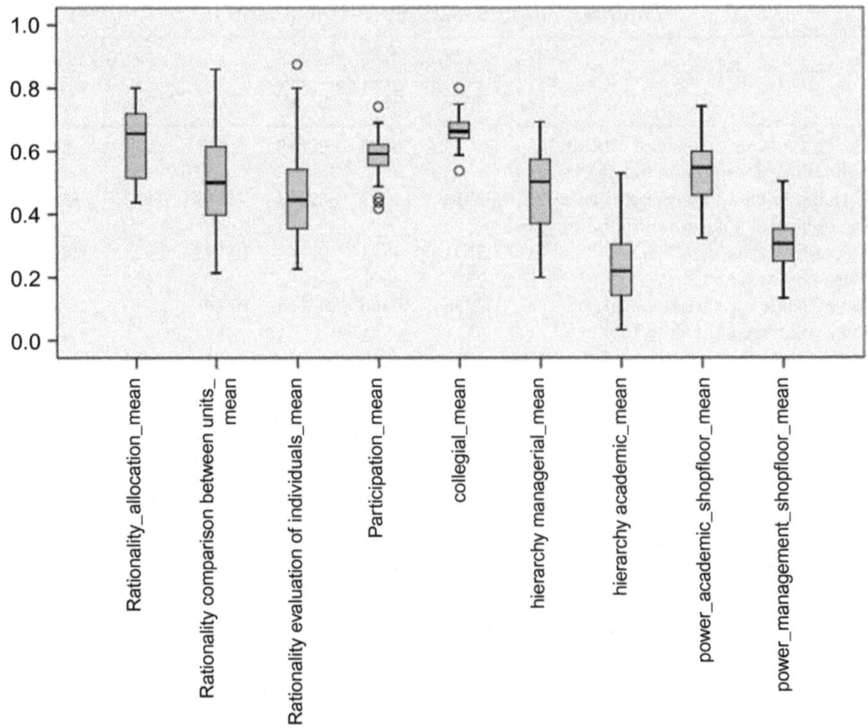

Fig. 2. Boxplots of Means of Responses Inside Individual Universities, $N = 26$.

and power of individual academics are found to be non-significant. This is an important finding since the demise of collegiality is often assumed in the literature that is critical of new public management. This also supports the insight that the involvement of academics represents a common feature of the universities considered, which is rather uniform and less influenced by differences in national policies, as well as in the extent of NPM pressures. On the other hand, the results reveal that NPM coefficients are fairly large and highly significant for hierarchy in managerial tasks as well as the variables within rationality (formula-based allocation, comparison between units and individuals) (Fig. 3).

We also run a multi-level regression separately for each dimension related to managerial logic. A stronger NPM (i.e., value of 1, corresponding to the level of the United Kingdom) generates a clear increase in the level of hierarchy and rationality, but in a way that is compatible with

Table 5. Multi-Level Regression Results.

Response	Hman_Full Hierarchy managerial	S.E.	Hacad_Full Hierarchy academic	S.E.	R1_Full Rationality formula-based allocation	S.E.	R2_Full Rationali ty comparison between units	S.E.	R3_Full Rationali ty evaluation of individuals	S.E.	P_Full Participation	S.E.	C_Full Collegial	S.E.	Sfac_Full Power_ academic	S.E.	Sf_Manfu Power_ management	S.E.
Fixed part																		
Cons	0.478	0.286	0.053	0.35	0.859***	0.195	−0.274	0.312	0.739*	0.319	0.692*	0.202	0.611***	0.127	0.609*	0.301	0.173	0.171
NPM	0.239***	0.054	0.171**	0.067	0.295***	0.037	0.212**	0.066	0.339***	0.069	0.036	0.039	−0.025	0.024	−0.002	0.057	−0.155	0.035
Disciplinary conc.	−0.133	0.084	−0.082	0.104	0.127*	0.053	0.122	0.1	0.124	0.106	0.103	0.059	0.07	0.038	0.126	0.088	0.131**	0.053
Size	−0.002†	0.001	−0.002	0.002	−0.001	0.001	0.004**	0.001	−0.001	0.001	0.001	0.001	.	0.001	0	0.001	0.001	0.001
Age	−0.032	0.108	0.009	0.131	−0.072	0.073	0.287*	0.118	−0.105	0.119	−0.045	0.076	−0.02	0.047	−0.036	0.114	0.066	0.062
Int. reputation	0.029	0.079	0.079	0.096	−0.167**	0.054	0.027	0.09	−0.168	0.095	−0.032	0.057	0.053	0.035	−0.014	0.082	−0.006	0.05
Rector	0.006	0.055	0.003	0.07	.	.	.	.	.	.	.	.	0.116***	0.032	−0.029	0.056	0.027	0.047
Central administrator	−0.032	0.062	−0.017	0.079	0.046	0.043	0.095	0.062	.	.	−0.004	0.045	0.068	0.036	0.014	0.063	0.102	0.053
Senator	0.004	0.031	0.063	0.039	0.017	0.02	.	.	.	.	.	0.023	−0.022	0.016	−0.054	0.031	0.009	0.025
Board member	0.054	0.035	0.13**	0.044	.	.	.	.	.	.	.	.	0.011	0.018	−0.076**	0.035	0.004	0.029
Random part																		
Level: institution																		
Cons/cons	0.003	0.002	0.004	0.003	0.001	0.001	0	0	0	0	0.001	0.001	0	0	0.004	0.002	0	0.001
Level: caseID																		
Cons/cons	0.073	0.005	0.118	0.007	0.036	0.003	0.07	0.007	0.064	0	0.038	0.003	0.026	0.001	0.074	0.005	0.053	0.003
−2*loglikelihood empty model	157,655																	
−2*loglikelihood:	131,474		391,383		−199,199		38,657		17,454		−154,979		−542,283		−26,951		155,586	
DIC:																		
pD:																		
Units: institution	26		26		26		26		25		26		26		26		26	
Units: caseID	538		539		434		217		192		364		675		540		538	

***<0.001, **<0.01, *<0.05, †<0.1, df = $N-1-$(variables).

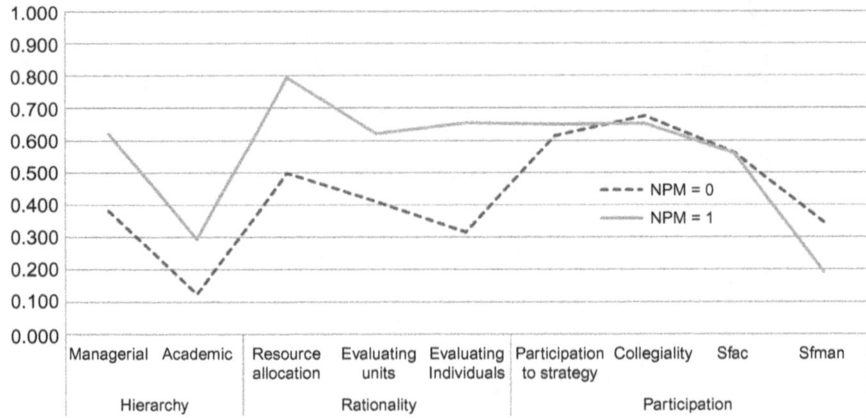

Fig. 3. The Impact of NPM.

the academic logic, since participation and collegiality are not affected. In the following section, we discuss the implication of our findings.

DISCUSSION AND CONCLUSION

In this paper, we show the effect of the NPM-inspired reforms on European universities by focusing on hierarchy and rationality from managerial logic and participation and collegiality from academic logic. We do so by looking at different tasks as well as different working groups in a university in order to be able to construct our measures. Our results provide a nuanced understanding of responses of public universities to managerial pressures enforced through NPM policies. On the one hand, we found evidence that NPM is associated with the introduction of hierarchy and rationality inside the case universities – more specifically, a stronger NPM pressure is correlated with a steeper hierarchy and differences in the level of power between leaders as foreseen by the managerial logic. The type of measures used, which refer directly to decision-making and power rather than to formal structure, makes it unlikely that these responses are purely ritualistic in nature (Meyer & Rowan, 1977). On the other hand, we also found that compliance is highly selective and strongly influenced by the presence and characteristics of the academic logic, like the participation of academics in decision-making processes; as there seems to be no significant association with NPM pressures. Thus, we found evidence of the phenomenon of compartmentalization (Pache & Santos, 2013).

These results are consistent with institutional theory, and particularly recent work on organizational responses to institutional pluralism (Kraatz & Block, 2008). When subject to conflicting institutional pressures, universities will try to find ways to simultaneously comply with managerial pressures and with the academic logic by developing highly differentiated responses according to the type of tasks. This way, this paper also contributes to the growing literature on hybridization and the co-existence of logics within the organizations (Battilana & Dorado, 2010; Jay, 2013).

Consequently, we would like to highlight two implications of our findings in the context of a better understanding of organizational change processes within public organizations as well as when it comes to the design of public policies. The empirical findings support previous studies suggesting that, under increasing NPM pressures, public organizations are indeed moving towards managed and more complete organizations and introducing some managerial element of hierarchy and rationality (Seeber et al., forthcoming). At the same time, the data show that this does not necessarily imply moving towards the corporate model of organizations, but rather moving in the direction of models found in other professional and knowledge-intensive organizations, like soft bureaucracies (Courpasson, 2000) or "enabling bureaucracies" (Adler & Borys, 1996). However, in certain cases, the emergence of *an enabling bureaucracy* does not occur for all the organizations. In certain cases, there are some individual universities in which the introduction of rationalization has been accompanied by stronger negative perceptions, arguably because the approach was less consensual (Ramirez, 2006). This might point to an interesting venue for future research, that is, under what ideal conditions do more hierarchy and rationality result into the development of an enabling bureaucracy. Importantly, the presence of a strong academic logic was central to this process and, accordingly, we might argue that it plays a key role in maintaining some characteristics of the professional work when introducing managerialism and in avoiding some of the most negative consequences of NPM reforms, like demotivation of workers, weakening of trust, and loss of flexibility and autonomy. In turn, this would suggest that public authorities should not consider professional logics as opponents to managerial reforms, which should be curbed. These should rather be considered as useful counterbalances that help to avoid the negative consequences of managerialism by taking into account the specific characteristics of the field.

REFERENCES

Adler, P. S. (2008). Professional work: The emergence of collaborative community. *Organization Science*, *19*(2), 359–376.

Adler, P. S., & Borys, B. (1996). Two types of bureaucracy: Enabling and coercive. *Administrative Science Quarterly*, *41*(1), 61–89.

Albert, S., & Whetten, D. A. (1985). Organizational identity. *Research in Organizational Behavior*, *7*, 263–295.

Andrews, M. (2011). Which organizational attributed are amenable to external reform? An empirical study of African financial management. *International Public Management Journal*, *14*(2), 131–156.

Ashworth, R., Boyne, G., & Delbridge, R. (2009). Escape from the iron cage? Organizational change and isomorphic pressures in the public sector. *Journal of Public Administration Research and Theory*, *19*(1), 165–187.

Battilana, J., & Dorado, S. (2010). Building sustainable hybrid organizations: The case of commercial microfinance organizations. *Academy of Management Journal*, *53*(6), 1419–1440.

Becher, T. (1994). The significance of disciplinary differences. *Studies in Higher Education*, *19*(2), 151–161.

Becher, T., & Trowler, P. R. (2001). *Academic tribes and territories. Intellectual enquiry and the culture of disciplines Ballmoor*. Buckingham: The Society for Research into Higher Education and Open University Press.

Bergquist, W. H. (1992). *The four cultures of the academy. Insights and strategies for improving leadership in collegiate organizations*. San Francisco, CA: Jossey-Bass Inc.

Bleiklie, I., Enders, J., Lepori, B., & Musselin, C. (2011). New public management, network governance and the university as changing professional organization. In T. Christensen & P. Lægreid (Eds.), *Ashgate research companion to new public management*. Aldershot: Ashgate.

Bleiklie, I., & Michelsen, S. (2013). Comparing HE policies in Europe. *Higher Education*, *65*(1), 113–133.

Bovaird, T., & Downe, J. (2006). N generations of reform in UK local government: Compliance and resistance to institutional pressures. *International Public Management Journal*, *9*(4), 429–455.

Brunsson, N., & Sahlin-Andersson, K. (2000). Constructing organizations: The example of the public sector reform. *Organization Studies*, *2*(14), 721–746.

Chinchilla-Rodriguéz, Z., Ferligoi, A., Miguel, S., Kronegger, L., & de Moya-Anegón, F. (2012). Blockmodeling of co-authorship networks in library and information science in Argentina: A case study. *Scientometrics*, *93*(3), 699–717.

Christopher, J., & Leung, P. (2015). Tensions arising from imposing NPM in Australian public universities: A management perspective. *Financial Accountability & Management*, *31*, 171–191.

Clark, B. R. (1983). *The higher education system. Academic organization in cross-national perspective*. Berkeley, CA: University of California Press.

Clark, B. R. (1998). *Creating entrepreneurial universities: Organizational pathways of transformation*. New York, NY: Pergamon.

Courpasson, D. (2000). Managerial strategies of domination. Power in soft bureaucracies. *Organization Studies*, *21*(1), 141–161.

de Boer, H., Enders, J., & Leisyte, L. (2007). Public sector reform in Dutch higher education: The organizational transformation of the university. *Public Administration*, *85*(1), 27–46.

de Boer, H., Enders, J., & Schimank, U. (2007). On the way towards new public management? The governance of university systems in England, the Netherlands, Austria, and Germany. In D. Jansen (Ed.), *New forms of governance in research organizations – Disciplinary approaches, interfaces and integration* (pp. 137–154). Dordrecht: Springer.

Diefenbach, T. (2009). New public management in the public sector: The dark side of managerialistic 'enlightenment'. *Public Administration*, *87*(4), 892–909.

Enders, J., Kehm, B., & Schimank, U. (2015). Turning universities into actors on quasi-markets: How new public management reforms affect academic research. *The Changing Governance of Higher Education and Research Higher Education Dynamics*, *43*, 89–103.

Ferlie, E., Musselin, C., & Andresani, G. (2008). The steering of higher education systems: A public management perspective. *Higher Education*, *56*(3), 325–348.

Friedland, R., & Alford, R. (1991). Bringing society back in: Symbols, practices and institutional contradictions. In W. W. Powell & P. J. DiMaggio (Eds.), *The new institutionalism in organizational analysis* (pp. 232–263). Chicago, IL: The University of Chicago Press.

Greenwood, R., Diaz, M., Li, X., & Lorente, J. (2009). The multiplicity of institutional logics and the heterogeneity of organizational responses. *Organization Science*, *21*(2), 521–539.

Greenwood, R., Raynard, M., Kodeih, F., Micelotta, E. R., & Lounsbury, M. (2011). Institutional complexity and organizational responses. *The Academy of Management Annals*, *5*(1), 317–371.

Greenwood, R., & Hinings, C. R. (1993). Understanding strategic change. The contribution of archetypes. *The Academy of Management Journal*, *36*(5), 1052–1081.

Jarzabkowski, P. (2004). Strategy as practice: Recursiveness, adaptation, and practices-in-use. *Organization Studies*, *25*(4), 529–560.

Jay, J. (2013). Navigating paradox as a mechanism of change and innovation in hybrid organizations. *Academy of Management Journal*, *56*(1), 137–159.

Kalberg, S. (1980). Max Weber's types of rationality: Cornerstones for the analysis of rationalization processes in history. *American Journal of Sociology*, 1145–1179.

Kogan, M., Bauer, I., Bleiklie, I., & Henkel, M. (2006). *Transforming higher education. A Comparative Study*. Dordrecht: Springer.

Kraatz, M. S., & Block, E. S. (2008). Organizational implications of institutional pluralism. In R. Greenwood, C. Oliver, K. Sahlin, & R. Suddaby (Eds.), *The SAGE handbook of organizational institutionalism* (pp. 243–275). London: Sage.

Krücken, G., Kosmützky, A., & Torka, M. (2007). *Towards a multiversity? Universities between global trends and national traditions (science studies)*. Bielefeld: Transcript.

Lægreid, P., Roness, P. G., & Rubecksen, K. (2007). Modern management tools in state agencies: The case of Norway. *International Public Management Journal*, *10*(4), 387–413.

Leicht, K. T., & Fennell, M. L. (2008). Institutionalism and the professions. In *The Sage Handbook of Organizational Institutionalism*. London: Sage.

Lepori, B., Benninghoff, M., Jongbloed, B., Salerno, C., & Slipersaeter, S. (2005). Changing patterns of higher education funding: Evidence from CHINC countries.

Meyer, J. W., Boli, J., Thomas, G. M., & Ramirez, F. O. (1997). World society and the nation-state. *American Journal of Sociology*, *103*(1), 144–181.

Meyer, J. W., & Rowan, B. (1977). Institutionalized organizations: Formal structure as myth and ceremony. *The American Journal of Sociology*, *83*(2), 340–363.

Mintzberg, H. (1979). *The structuring of organizations*. Englewood cliffs, NJ: Prentice Hall.

Musselin, C. (2007). Are universities specific organisations? In G. Krücken, A. Kosmützky, & M. Torka (Eds.), *Towards a multiversity? Universities between global trends and national traditions* (pp. 63–84). Bielefeld: Transcript.

Pache, A., & Santos, F. (2013). Inside the hybrid organization: Selective coupling as a response to conflicting institutional logics. *Academy of Management Journal*, *56*(4), 972–1001.

Paradeise, C., Reale, E., Bleiklie, I., & Ferlie, E. (2009). *University governance. Western European comparative perspectives*. Dordrecht: Springer.

Paradeise, C., & Thoenig, J. C. (2011). The road to world class university. Elites and wannabes. In *Organization studies workshop, 'bringing public organizations back in'*. Les Vaux de Cernay.

Paradeise, C., & Thoenig, J. (2013). Academic institutions in search of quality: Local orders and global standards. *Organization Studies*, *34*(2), 189–218.

Ramirez, F. O. (2006). The rationalization of universities. In *Transnational governance: Institutional dynamics of regulation* (pp. 224–245). Cambridge: Cambridge University Press.

Ramirez, F. O. (2009). Accounting for excellence: Transforming universities into organizational actors. In *Higher education, policy, and the global competition phenomenon and the global competition phenomenon and the global competition phenomenon*. New York, NY: Palgrave.

Ramirez, F. O., & Christensen, T. (2013). The formalization of the university: Rules, roots, and routes. *Higher Education*, *65*(6), 1–14.

Reale, E., & Seeber, M. (2011). *The transformation of steering and governance in higher education: Funding and evaluation as policy instruments*. Working Paper CNR-CERIS, Vol. 2, pp. 1–36.

Sahlin, K. (2012). The interplay of organizing models in higher education institutions: What room is there for collegiality in universities characterized by bounded autonomy? In B. Stensaker, J. Välimaa, & C. S. Sarrico (Eds.), *Managing reform in universities: The dynamics of culture, identity and organizational change* (pp. 198–221). London: McMillan, Palgrave.

Teixeira, P., Jongbloed, B., Dill, D., & Amaral, A. (2004). *Markets in higher education. Rhetoric or reality?* Dordrecht: Kluwer Academic Publishers.

Thornton, P. H., & Ocasio, W. (1999). Institutional logics and the historical contingency of power in organizations: Executive succession in the higher education publishing industry, 1958–1990 1. *American Journal of Sociology*, *105*(3), 801–843.

Thornton, P. H., Ocasio, W., & Lounsbury, M. (2012). *The institutional logics perspective: A new approach to culture, structure and process*. Oxford: Oxford University Press.

Townley, B. (1997). The institutional logic of performance appraisal. *Organization Studies*, *18*(2), 261–285.

Townley, B. (2002). The role of competing rationalities in institutional change. *Academy of Management Journal*, *45*(1), 163–179.

Tuchman, G. (2009). *Wannabe U: Inside the corporate university*. Chicago, IL: The University of Chicago Press.

Weick, K. (1976). Educational organizations as loosely coupled systems. *Administrative Science Quarterly*, *21*(1), 1–19.

Whitley, R. (2008). Constructing universities as strategic actors: Limitations and variations. In L. Engwall & D. Weaire (Eds.), *The university in the market* (pp. 23–37). Colchester: Portland Press Limited.

Whitley, R., & Glaser, J. (2007). The changing governance of the sciences. *The advent of research evaluation systems*. Dordrecht: Springer.

THE QUEST FOR PROMOTING INTEGRATED CARE IN THE SCANDINAVIAN COUNTRIES – RECENT REFORMS, POSSIBILITIES AND PROBLEMS

Dag Olaf Torjesen, Gro Kvåle and Charlotte Kiland

ABSTRACT

Integration between primary and secondary healthcare services and institutions has been at the core of health policy in Scandinavian countries over the last decade. This paper is based on an explorative case study of recent reforms in the healthcare sector and their outcomes in Denmark, Norway and Sweden. We discuss the possibilities of and problems for integrating the healthcare sector through the coordination mechanisms of hierarchy, market and network. The paper also discusses whether the institutional logic of the healthcare field is moving from a dual logic of 'cure' and 'care' towards a unifying logic of 'integrated care'. We find that although the organisational principles that regulate the relationship between actors in the healthcare field in the three countries have changed, the challenge of achieving a mix of coordinative

Towards a Comparative Institutionalism: Forms, Dynamics and Logics Across the Organizational Fields of Health Care and Higher Education
Research in the Sociology of Organizations, Volume 45, 195–213

ISSN: 0733-558X/doi:10.1108/S0733-558X20150000045026

mechanisms that promote, rather than weaken, integration remains. However, the new organisational and regulative arrangements are an arena for increased interaction and collaboration between the actors, and thus a foundation for change towards the institutional logic of integrated health care.

Keywords: Scandinavia; health care; coordination; integration

INTRODUCTION

In the post-Second World War period the hospital sector has been the citadel of the healthcare system, and the general hospital taken for granted as the primary building block in Scandinavian healthcare systems. A heavily hospital centred system evolved, which monopolised investments, personnel and technology, as well as patients, at the expense of primary health care (Haave, 2006). Scandinavian countries have been struggling with rising costs in the hospital sector and a growing elderly population. Consequently primary health care has received more attention from policy makers. In line with other countries in the western world (Evans, Baker, Berta, & Barnsley, 2013) and recommendations from the World Health Organization or WHO (WHO, 2001; Gröne & Garcia-Barbero, 2001), the Scandinavian countries have reformed their healthcare sectors towards 'de-hospitalisation' (Ahgren & Axelsson, 2011; Romøren, Torjesen, & Landmark, 2011; Wadmann, Strandberg-Larsen, & Vrangbæk, 2009). De-hospitalisation is intended to ensure that patients stay in hospital for shorter periods and get more of the health-related services they need closer to home. This means that hospitals concentrate on medical treatments that require highly specialised medical expertise and high-tech equipment. Patients are discharged once the specialised treatment is finished, and the municipalities are responsible for continued treatment and follow-up and daily care of patients. However, due to earlier discharge from hospital and increasing life-expectancy, the care of potentially sicker and weaker patients requires more expertise, new kinds of services and other resources in the local primary care institutions and services. Furthermore, there has also been a transfer in the amount and types of services in primary care, with wide variation in patient groups, from substance abuse and treatment of chronic diseases, to home care for the elderly and preventive health and rehabilitation.

These changes in responsibilities within the healthcare field place new demands not only on the municipalities' ability and capacity to provide services (Gautun & Syse, 2013) but also on the ability of primary and secondary healthcare institutions to cooperate and integrate their actions (Calnan, Hutten, & Tiljak, 2006). Many actors, professionals and institutions increasingly *share* the responsibility for patients, often with complex diagnoses and chronic conditions. They are increasingly expected to appear and operate as *one integrated system* and to produce '*seamless services*'.

Given this background, the purpose of this paper is to examine how the logic of *integrated health care* manifests itself in the Scandinavian healthcare field. In order to do this we will investigate the following research questions:

(1) What organising principles are in place to promote integration between the actors?
(2) What are the possibilities and problems associated with the chosen coordinating measures for achieving more integrated health services?

In the following section we describe and discuss our analytical framework, based on the institutional logics perspective, and the coordination mechanisms of hierarchy, market and network. We then sketch out our research design, and give a description of the organisation of the healthcare systems in Denmark, Norway and Sweden, and their moves towards integrated health care. We then discuss problems which have been experienced and which may emerge in the future and consider the possibilities for establishing integrated healthcare services and whether an integrated healthcare logic has developed in the Scandinavian healthcare field.

INTEGRATION OF INSTITUTIONAL LOGICS BY MEANS OF COORDINATION

What we are observing is probably a movement from a differentiated healthcare system with hospitals as its cornerstone towards a system with more integration between primary and specialist health care (hospitals). Until recently these two systems were considered different worlds (sets of activities and ways of organising) and unreconciled mind-sets (Gloubman & Mintzberg, 2001). Specialist health care has traditionally been regarded as the world of *cure*, while primary health care has been viewed as the world of *care*. In Scandinavian health care these two worlds have traditionally had distinct governance structures, patient perspectives, ideologies and professional cultures (Vrangbæk, 2011). These separated worlds could be interpreted as multiple and even competing institutional logics, that is '*the symbolic and material constructions which constitute the organizing principles and which are available to organizations and individuals to elaborate*' (Friedland & Alford, 1991, p. 248; Thornton, Ocasio, & Lounsbury, 2012, p. 8). The question being investigated here is *how* these two distinct institutional logics of health care can *merge* into a new logic of integration.

Integration can be broadly defined as, '*the act of making a whole out of parts; the co-ordination of different activities to ensure harmonious functioning*' (Gröne & Garcia-Barbero, 2001, p. 7). In health care, the concept of 'integrated care' is defined by the WHO as '*bringing together inputs, delivery, management and organization of services related to diagnosis, treatment, care, rehabilitation and health promotion*' (*ibid.*, pp. 7–8). Integration is therefore a means to improve services in terms of access, quality, user satisfaction and efficiency. In other words, both the general and healthcare specific definitions point to the need for critical organisational, coordinative measures to achieve integration.

The three main types of mechanism lying behind coordination processes are hierarchy, market and network (Bouckaert, Peters, & Verhoest, 2010). These categories are well-known from *intra-organisation* studies (Ouchi, 1980), but are just as, or perhaps even more, relevant to *inter-organisational* coordination. Coordination by *hierarchy* is based on legitimate authority, and achieved by processes of mandating and commanding, persuasion and encouragement. The *market* mechanism achieves coordination through transactions, competition and economic incentives that make coordination profitable for the actors involved. In a *network*, actors are integrated through cooperation and solidarity, mutual interests, and shared norms and responsibilities. The three modes of coordination can also be empirically connected or combined, even if they are theoretically and analytically separated (Bouckaert et al., 2010; Torjesen & Vabo, 2014). Bouckaert et al. (2010) have developed an analytical framework in which the main mechanisms of coordination, that is hierarchy, market and network, are used to classify and discuss various structural and managerial instruments to promote integration in the public sector. Inspired by this, we use two main analytical categories to describe and classify integrative measures in the healthcare field across Scandinavia. These are, firstly, the *regulations* imposed by central government in order to coordinate the actors and integrate services, which could be legislation mandating cooperation (hierarchy) or economic incentives (market). Secondly, we look at *organisational* instruments that are designed to facilitate coordination by network, that is collaboration between actors and development and reinforcement of shared goals, norms and knowledge. These could include managing the flow of information within the network, the management of the chain of production within the network, and the assignment of specific cooperation roles and positions.

RESEARCH DESIGN

Based on empirical observations we have chosen the Scandinavian countries – Denmark, Norway and Sweden – as our field of enquiry. These are often referred to as following the 'Scandinavian welfare model' with parallel development of health and welfare services (Esping-Andersen, 1990). The study uses an explorative case study methodology (Yin, 2014) to investigate how different coordinating measures have an impact on the constellation of the two different logics. It thereby casts light on the possibilities of and problems for achieving more integrated healthcare services. Based on this research approach, we have analysed each case, focusing on our research questions, given that the organisational field of health care in these cases is characterised by de-hospitalisation and integration. By choosing three countries instead of one we also expand the empirical foundation of the study.

A hospital centred tradition and movement towards an integrated healthcare sector are common features of the three cases. George and Bennett (2005, p. 67) emphasise the advantages of focusing attention on a small number of aspects of a case. In this study we concentrate on the aspect of *integration* within the field of health care. The descriptions and discussions are based on recent research literature on the topic (integrative reforms and/or policies) in the three countries. Our objective was to identify different ways of executing pro-integration measures, for example collaboration, cooperation, coordination, consolidation etc. Works that we define as pivotal in the field include Wadmann et al. (2009), Vrangbæk (2011), Ahgren (2010) Ahgren and Axelsson (2011), Romøren et al. (2011) and Torjesen and Vabo (2014). Finally, we use the concepts of *hierarchy*, *network* and *market* to compile and categorise examples of a broad range of coordination arrangements in order to seek a better understanding of the field of integrated health care in Scandinavia. This, in turn, enables us to deepen insight and better understand the possibilities and possible challenges associated with the chosen coordinating measures.

INTEGRATIVE MEANS AND MEASURES IN THE SCANDINAVIAN COUNTRIES

Denmark

The Danish state funds specialist health care through block grants and activity-based funding (ABF) given to the country's five administrative regions. The regions own and operate the hospitals, which are funded by a combination of global budgets and ABF based on diagnosis related group rates (DRGs). In 2007 the ownership and operation of the hospitals was handed over from the counties to five political-administrative regions. The Structural Reform, as it was called, also reduced the number of municipalities from 271 to 98. The main idea behind the reform was to strengthen the municipalities and give them increased responsibility for healthcare tasks such as prevention; rehabilitation of patients discharged from hospitals; home care; substance abuse care; social psychiatry; municipal dental health and co-payment for hospital services. General practitioners (GPs) operate as privately owned businesses, but receive most of their funding from public sources in a combination of capitation (1/3) and ABF (2/3). Much of the struggle for better structural integration focuses on discharge and admission of patients between hospitals and their residential municipality. The interfaces between hospitals and primary care are regulated by formal legislation and agreements based on the Health Act of 2007. It is also mandatory to establish regional consultative committees to secure continuous integrated health care for patients. Regions and municipalities have to sign health agreements covering a range of topics, including discharge and admission of patients, rehabilitation plans, and coordination of tasks and activities between the hospitals and municipalities. In addition, the Health Act states that regional authorities are responsible for developing rehabilitation plans for the patients at the time of hospital discharge (Wadmann et al., 2009). As an economic incentive, municipal co-payment has been introduced and amounts to approximately 20% of hospital treatment costs (cf. Vrangbæk & Sørensen, 2013). There are also penalty fees for not being able to receive discharged patients.

The Structural Reform also reintroduced Local Health Care Centres, a flexible organisational concept intended to facilitate coordinated health promotion and prevention services (Waldorff, 2010). In order to facilitate coordination and integration between national, regional and local actors, digitalisation of healthcare services has been on the agenda since 2007 (Wadmann et al., 2009). A cross-governmental organisation has been set up to establish a national e-health system, and the various actors and authorities have to develop their own IT-solutions in accordance with national demands (*ibid.*). With regard to production chains, evidence-based 'cancer packages' have been developed, with standards for treatment, time-limits, monitoring of patient pathways and a named contact person for each patient etc. (*ibid.*). Chronic diseases should be treated in accordance with a pathway programme. Finally, in terms of liaison positions, Denmark has 'general practitioner consultants', which means that a GP is hired by a region or hospital for a certain amount of hours per month to provide and exchange information about primary and specialist health care, and to help with developing procedures to manage the interface between hospital and municipal care (Wadmann et al., 2009).

Norway

Specialist health care (hospitals) in Norway is owned by the state and run by four regional health enterprises. Hospitals are funded by a mix of ABF/DRG and block grants, while GPs operate as private enterprises and are funded through contracts, ABF and out of pocket money. Primary health care is the responsibility of 428 municipalities.[1] In The Coordination Reform, (Stortingsmelding nr. 47 2008–2009), the main principles were to decentralise the expensive Norwegian hospital centred health system; discharge patients from hospitals earlier and handle a greater proportion of patients through primary, intermediate and long-term care instead of in hospitals. To improve interaction between hospitals and the municipalities, mandatory agreements were implemented as a key instrument for developing seamless health care and frictionless patient flow between hospitals and municipal health care. Local medical centres are about to become a common solution, as an arena for joined-up projects between hospitals and local healthcare authorities (Torjesen & Vabo, 2014). Between 2012 and 2015 an economic incentive system of co-funding was in operation, which meant that the municipalities had to pay 20% of the costs of hospital treatments alongside a penalty fee (approx. 440 euros per day) if they were unable to receive patients in primary care after discharge from hospital. This was meant to stimulate cooperation and the development of new local health services, for example low threshold wards (short-term monitoring and treatment), as an alternative to hospital services. However, co-payment was terminated in 2015, and so far it has not been replaced by any other economic incentive to promote coordination/integration (Stortingsmelding no. 2 2013–2014). From 2016 municipalities are required by law to establish units for emergency treatment. The new healthcare legislation gives the municipalities greater autonomy around organising and addressing the statutory tasks, and fulfilling their new responsibilities. Nevertheless, this is a heavy challenge for the many small Norwegian municipalities. In their efforts to try and overcome this, the municipalities have joined up and increased their resources through inter-municipality cooperation (Stortingsmelding nr. 47 2008–2009; Kalseth & Paulsen, 2008).

Digitalisation and e-health is also on the Norwegian agenda, as a means to improve the infrastructure for coordination and integration. A so-called knowledge centre for IT in health care (*Kith*) has been established to support the Coordination Reform (Torjesen & Vabo, 2014). As in Denmark, a system of general practitioner consultants acting as liaisons between hospitals and primary care has developed, with gradual implementation since the 1990s. Patient pathways and treatment chains are also emphasised in the Coordination reform (Fineide & Ramsdal, 2014; Torjesen & Vabo, 2014). Cancer-packages are being developed, more or less using the Danish solution as a blueprint, and such packages are supposed to be implemented for 30 cancer diagnoses in 2015 (Stortingsmelding no. 2 2013–2014)

Sweden

In Sweden, both primary and specialist health care are under the jurisdiction of the country's 20 counties. Specialist health care is publicly funded by contracts between counties and hospitals, and a mix of block grants and ABF. GPs are mainly employed by the counties; only 20% are privately employed. Approximately 1,000 local primary health care centres (PHCC) are operated by the counties. The PHCCs have an interdisciplinary profile, employing GPs, nurses, physiotherapists, midwifes etc. (Karlberg, 2008). A total of 290 municipalities are responsible for care and nursing for the elderly, the disabled, long-term care for the mentally ill, and patients discharged from hospitals.

Integration of healthcare services in Sweden consists of two main components: *local health care* and *chains of care*. The local healthcare concept, developed in a national action plan for health and social services, can be described as upgraded family and community oriented primary care, supported by specialists from the hospital sector. To date it has been implemented in two-thirds of the counties, covering 80% of the Swedish population (Ahgren, 2010; Ahgren & Axelsson, 2011; Wadmann et al., 2009). There is no single standard model for organising local care services. Due to different local needs and conditions within the counties and communities, it is a question of combining existing resources and competences for the healthcare needs of the local population (Ahgren, 2010; Wadmann et al., 2009). This task may entail drawing up joint operational plans, setting up joint organisations or providing joint measures for groups with particular needs. Local health care is usually not a matter of particular organisational units set up for this purpose, but rather a quite loosely integrated network-structure, developed to implement and operate chains of care (Ahgren & Axelsson, 2011). However, a common feature of local healthcare practices in Sweden is that specialist nurses are often put in charge of the coordination of services within their area of specialisation (Wadmann et al., 2009).

Within Scandinavia, Sweden has been at the forefront of developing comprehensive chains of care concepts (Ahgren, 2010; Ahgren & Axelsson, 2011; Romøren et al., 2011). According to Ahgren and Axelsson (2011), the chains of care are developed with inspiration from manufacturing organisations with an emphasis on integration of production processes. Thus, the chains of care in Swedish health care could be described as: all the services directed at particular patient groups or diseases/diagnoses within a given geographical location. The integration within the chains of care is based on formal and informal agreements between the providers and professionals. However, it is mandated by law that hospital doctors must inform other providers and organise the release and rehabilitation of patients (Wadmann et al., 2009). The content of the services is based on nationally developed and agreed upon guidelines (Ahgren & Axelsson, 2011; Karlberg, 2008). Finally, as in other countries, information technology is supposed to facilitate the coordination and integration of healthcare services, and has been on the policy agenda in Sweden for quite some time. A public company has been commissioned to develop and implement a comprehensive e-health strategy, which was launched in 2006, while the counties are responsible for putting it into local use (Wadmann et al., 2009).

EMPIRICAL FINDINGS

With respect to mandatory arrangements and incentive structures, the Norwegian health authorities are making use of hard steering measures (market incentives and mandatory agreements) in their efforts to encourage the municipalities and hospitals to cooperate and undertake new tasks. The incentives and administrative measures found in neighbouring Denmark are more or less a blueprint for this. Network-based instruments have been developed, but to a great extent they have been developed and implemented from the top-down in both Denmark and Norway. In this way, the health policy for improving integration has been changed from a mainly voluntary network form of cooperation based on a local bottom-up task oriented strategy towards a harder, top-down administrative, regulative strategy, with market incentives and hierarchy as key instruments for enhancing integration (Romøren et al., 2011).

In Sweden, the regulative agreements between specialist health care and primary care, so prominent in both Norway and Denmark, are lacking. The Swedish system for integration of healthcare services is a product of development and dissemination between counties over time, in accordance with the decentralised system of financially autonomous counties and municipalities. The local healthcare concept, PHCC and chains of care are the main features of Swedish integration of health services. Versions of chains of care, for example similar cancer packages, were first introduced in Denmark (2009), and later adopted (2015) in Norway. This might be a result of the popularity of the *lean production* concept in general (Røvik, 2007), and is a common trend in Scandinavian health care (Fineide & Ramsdal, 2014). Local medical centres are becoming increasingly popular in Norway. Whilst a solution mainly stimulated by the national authorities, they are also related to the Swedish PHCCs.

Table 1 offers an overview of the regulations and organisational instruments used to promote integration of health care in the three Scandinavian countries.

It is important to note that some regulative and organisational measures are difficult to categorise as market, hierarchy or network. Some of the measures have characteristics emanating from different categories. Many of the integrative measures labelled as network-based are in reality mandated by the state, but may be implemented in the form of network structures. Likewise, mandatory health agreements are hierarchically imposed, but are essentially implemented as network-like structures in the Danish regions

Table 1. Integrative Health Policy Measures between Primary and Secondary Health Care in Scandinavia.

	Hierarchy	Market inspired Incentives	Network
Denmark	Mandatory health agreements between regions and municipalities	Municipal co-payment for hospital treatment	National strategy for digitalisation of the DK healthcare services by a cross gov. organisation (SDSD)
	Mandatory consultative committees	Penalty fees for not receiving discharged patients in municipal health care	Chronic disease patient pathway programmes
	Mandatory, top-down cancer-packages launched by the National Board of Health	Some incentives for GPs (fees for following up patients)	GP consultants Danish Quality Assessment Scheme, contact persons for patients Local healthcare centres
Norway	Mandatory health agreements between hospitals and municipalities.	Municipal co-payment for hospital treatment (2012–2015)	National committee for e-health architecture National Main journal Knowledge centre for IT in the health sector (Kith)
	Mandatory, top-down cancer-packages (from 2015)	Penalty fees for not receiving discharged patients in municipal health care	Patient pathway descriptions developed by national health authorities
		No incentives for GPs	GP consultants Cancer coordinators in hospitals (mandatory) Liaison positions in health enterprises and inter-municipal regions Local medical centres
Sweden	Mandatory for hospital physicians to inform municipal authorities and GPs about hospitalisation and develop rehabilitation plans at discharge	No incentives for hospital or health centres	National strategy for e-Health developed by a cross governmental organisations (Carelink) Patient pathway descriptions developed in most counties Coordinator nurses in health centres in relation to disease specific patient groups National coordinator for psychiatry appointment by the Swedish government

and Norwegian municipalities. These measures can thus be regarded as *hybrid* coordinative mechanisms (Torjesen & Vabo, 2014). However, the question could also be raised of whether these combinations suggest that networks operate in 'the shadow of hierarchy' (Du Gay, 2002; Scharpf, 1997).

POSSIBILITIES OF AND PROBLEMS FOR INTEGRATED HEALTH CARE

All three Scandinavian countries have been active in setting up systems, structures and solutions in order to facilitate integration and cooperation in the healthcare sector. The question is how useful the different approaches and instruments are in achieving actual integration. In this section we discuss the possibilities of and problems with the chosen coordinative measures. We refer to, and rely on, empirical research on experiences of the arrangements, to the extent that such research exists and has been published. Otherwise, our discussion adopts a more generic and theoretical orientation.

Formal agreements between actors and authorities have been used to change the practice of healthcare services. In an analysis of healthcare agreements in Denmark, Vrangbæk (2011) shows that they function as arenas for dialogue where themes are discussed, coordination is planned and a common ground is developed. The agreements have, over time (period 2007–2011), become more concrete and formal. In Norway there has also been a change from the first agreement negotiations. Initially the negotiations were open-minded and constructive, focusing on shared responsibilities and common ground between equal partners. Later, there has been a tendency towards more self-centred and strategic bargaining between hospitals and municipalities (Torjesen & Vabo, 2014). The agreements function as a focal point of cooperation on a general level (Vrangbæk, 2011). However, these tools are no guarantee of changes in practice at the operational level in either the municipalities or the hospitals (*ibid.*). Agreements are legal instruments, developed and signed far from communities dealing with professional clinical work. Cooperation and collaboration through networks and partnerships is complicated and it takes time before results are obvious. An extensive number of professionals are tied up in meetings, round-table discussions and other cooperative activities, instead of spending their time on operational and patient centred activities

(Torjesen & Vabo, 2014). At the same time, networks and partnerships have the advantage of producing *negotiated agreements* which can reduce transaction costs at the beginning of a cooperation process and on commencement of new tasks (Agranoff, 2007; Andersen, 2010).

Implementing economic incentive structures (market-like coordination mechanisms) has been one of the Danish and Norwegian governments' main strategies for steering municipalities to coordinate services. But these incentive structures do not guarantee common efforts and cooperation. Municipal co-financing might equally result in strategic gaming activities instead of better cooperation and integration of services (Byrkjeflot, Christensen, & Lægreid, 2014). The municipalities and hospitals belong to two different levels of administration, with distinct professional logics (Gloubman & Mintzberg, 2001; Thornton et al., 2012) and budget systems and contrasting organisational structures (Vrangbæk, 2011). In both Norway and Denmark different regulatory frameworks and incentive structures in hospitals and primary care might result in a strategy to 'send the bill to the opponent' instead of focusing on cooperation in light of what is best for the patient (Romøren et al., 2011; Vinge & Kjellberg, 2009).

Extensive use of economic (market-inspired) incentives in the healthcare sector seems to lead to silo thinking, de-integration and strategic gaming where patients are handed back and forth between the various healthcare levels (Ahgren, 2010; Ahgren & Axelsson, 2011; Romøren et al., 2011). In Denmark, the incentives do not function as planned, as they seem too weak to influence municipalities' choices in the desired direction (Pedersen, 2005; Vrangbæk & Sørensen, 2013). In Norway, investing in and developing municipal specialist health care seems to be considered too high risk, and the municipalities find it less risky to buy hospital services from the secondary healthcare level (Torjesen & Vabo, 2014). For the hospitals, treatment of patients not included in the hospitals' economic incentive structures can be too expensive. For the municipalities, it is far too expensive to take over tasks without receiving ear-marked state funding (Veggeland, 2013). The Norwegian health authorities abolished co-financing in 2015, but maintained the penalty fees, without replacing the co-financing with incentives to reward more holistic and coherent patient trajectories, as has been recommended in Denmark to improve the incentive system (Vrangbæk, 2011).

In Denmark and Norway, and in the wake of the ongoing local government reforms, the boundaries between primary and secondary health care are constantly shifting. An increasing number of tasks are being transferred to the municipalities and GPs as these are supposed to play a more important role in the treatment of older patients (Vrangbæk, 2011). A challenge in the Danish case, as in the Norwegian, is to encourage GPs to participate in, and commit to, collaboration, since GPs run their own private businesses. This is in contrast to Sweden, where the vast majority of GPs are employed by the counties and operate in connection with the health centres. Due to the fact that there are few economic incentives to take part in coordination and collaboration, Danish and Norwegian GPs tend to prioritise their own businesses and are somehow placed on the sidelines of the coordination system (cf. Kristoffersen, 2013). Hence, there is a challenge in defining GPs as an integral part of the overall Danish and Norwegian healthcare systems, as they are in Sweden. The exception is the system with GP consultants.

Despite the attention that the digitalisation of health services and e-health have gained in recent years, the results and effects on integration are rather low. There are both legal and technical barriers to full scale sharing of patient data (Karlberg, 2008; Wadmann et al., 2009). Due to a lack of integrated technology based information and communication solutions between the primary and secondary healthcare services, communications between the different levels of the system (hospitals and municipalities) are characterised by information asymmetries regarding patient transfer processes and medication (Vrangbæk, 2011). Netteland and Naustdal (2014) show that it is not only inadequate IT-systems that are an obstacle to integration, the main problem is the lack of knowledge and will to use them. According to Romøren et al. (2011), Norway has been lagging behind the other Scandinavian countries in this respect.

With the introduction of local health care in Sweden, the provision of integrated care for the elderly and mentally ill has been improved, and gaps between different service providers reduced (Ahgren & Axelsson, 2011). Furthermore, the overall quality of care has benefited from multi-professional collaboration within the local healthcare framework (*ibid.*). However, a market inspired reform in 2010, granting every patient a choice of care, has resulted in fiercer competition and fragmentation instead of coordination and integration (Ahgren, 2010). It is also not obvious that the patient pathway descriptions and chains of care are have been unambiguously successful. Studies show that the Swedish counties are not entirely satisfied with their development, which seems to have been resisted by professionals opposing top-down implementation, an issue that has also been noted in relation to the transfer of care for the elderly to the municipalities on the one hand and the whole local healthcare concept on the other (Ahgren & Axelsson, 2011). In Sweden there are also worries that primary care faces problems with respect to the recruitment of physicians (Karlberg, 2008).

DISCUSSION AND CONCLUSION

The aim of this paper has been to examine how integrated health care is manifested in the Scandinavian healthcare field, in terms of what organising principles have been established and what experiences of the solutions have been to date. To sum up our findings we can conclude that the chosen coordinative mechanisms and structures have moved the healthcare sectors in the three Scandinavian countries towards a more integrated system. There have also been some promising changes in terms of effects: more patients are getting earlier discharges from hospitals and we observe a slow change in patient traffic from hospitals to home nursing and local medical centres (Hagen, 2014), with more patients treated in primary health care (Ahgren & Axelsson, 2011).

However, one main challenge we have uncovered pertains to how the *mix* of different coordination mechanisms (Sarapuu, Lægreid, Randma-Liiv, & Rykkja, 2014) and regulative and organisational instruments may weaken integration effects. The mix of coordinating mechanisms manifested in the instruments being adopted in Denmark and Norway lean heavily towards a hierarchy-network hybrid, supported by market-inspired incentives. In contrast, Swedish integration of health services seems more true to the pure (bottom-up) network mode of organising and coordination, but with a parallel use of market-like models. Economic incentives can both reinforce and weaken the effect of the other coordinating mechanisms. They can be too weak or too strong. On the one hand, the marginal role and incentives for GPs, municipal co-payment and penalty fees seems to be too weak to strengthen integration in Norway and Denmark. On the other hand, as in the choice of care in Sweden, they can be too strong and thereby possibly undermine integration.

Nonetheless, changes in the societal logics and resource environments (Thornton et al., 2012) in terms of promulgations from the WHO and ongoing integrative health policy reforms, are also slowly changing the institutional logic – the theories and frames, narratives and vocabulary (*ibid.*) – in the field of Scandinavian health care. The pre-existing cure and care logic can now better coexist in the Scandinavian healthcare field. Focus is slowly but steadily changing from single actors, differentiation and silo organising towards a holistic approach, centred on the interplay of the different parts, their functions, institutions and professions (Gröne & Garcia-Barbero, 2001, p. 1). The material manifestations of this logic in the implementation of various regulative and organisational instruments will probably also slowly change *practice* in the healthcare field in Scandinavia, towards integration. This happens not least because coordinative mechanisms are blending (Thornton et al., 2012) the cure logic of the hospitals and the care logic of local health services together in a more symbiotic and mutually dependent manner. Market instruments can however be a challenge to integration, stimulating strategic, egocentric behaviour, or interfering with other coordinative mechanisms, as has been experienced in the Scandinavian healthcare field. Conversely, networks – inclusive clinical pathways – represent a logic that ties actors together through dialogue, exchange of information, and shared norms and commitments. Networks, as a potent integrative mechanism, contribute to the development of ongoing relations and common understanding between actors in primary health care and hospitals, as in the case of Norway and Denmark. In Sweden, the concept of local health care – co-localisation in health centres with tight collaboration between several health professions – facilitates integration and the coexistence of diverse institutional practice of cure and care. From the literature on multiple institutional logics we know that interaction and collaboration in itself can be an important mechanism for institutionalisation and promote change in institutional logics (Reay & Hinings, 2009; Thornton et al., 2012).

Our focus here has mainly been on the tangible or material and structural dimensions underpinning health care coordination in Scandinavia. In order to better understand how the modes of coordination and policy changes and instruments for integration work at the operational level and on a day-to-day basis, an approach that also takes the normative and cognitive aspects (i.e. changes in cognitive maps and belief systems of the actors in the healthcare field) of healthcare institutions into account would be appropriate, and an important topic for future studies.

NOTE

1. In 2014 the Norwegian government initiated a voluntary merger process for municipalities that will probably lead to fewer, bigger and more robust units before 2017. The 'new' and bigger municipalities are meant to take over responsibility for healthcare services including rehabilitation, dental services and psychiatry.

REFERENCES

Agranoff, R. (2007). *Managing within networks: Adding value to public organizations*. Washington, DC: Georgetown University Press.

Ahgren, B. (2010). Competition and integration in Swedish health care. *Health Policy*, *96*, 91–97.

Ahgren, B., & Axelsson, R. (2011). A decade of integration and collaboration: The development of integrated health care in Sweden 2000–2010. *International Journal of Integrated Care*, *9*(11). Retrieved from http://www.ijic.org

Andersen, O. J. (2010). Sammen er vi sterke, men det kan også gå på tverke. Regional samstyring som mulighet og problem. *Norsk statsvitenskapelig tidsskrift*, *26*(1), 5–25.

Bouckaert, G., Peters, G. B., & Verhoest, K. (2010). *The coordination of public sector organizations. Shifting patterns of public administration*. Basingstoke: Palgrave Macmillan.

Byrkjeflot, H., Christensen, T., & Lægreid, P. (2014). When culture strikes back. Challenges of accountability in a multi-level healthcare service reform. Paper for When Health Policy Meets Everyday Practices, 9th International Organisational Behavior in Healthcare Conference, April 23–25, 2014, Copenhagen.

Calnan, M., Hutten, J., & Tiljak, H. (2006). The challenges of coordination: The role of primary care professionals in promoting integration across interface. In R. B. Saltman, A. Rico, & W. Boerma (Eds.), *Primary care in the drivers´s seat? Organizational reform in European primary care* (pp. 85–104). Berkshire: Open University Press/McGraw Education.

Du Gay, P. (2002). A common power to keep them all in awe: A comment on governance. *Cultural Values*, *6*(1/2), 11–27.

Esping-Andersen, G. (1990). *The three worlds of welfare capitalism*. Princeton, NJ: Princeton University Press.

Evans, J. M., Baker, G. R., Berta, W., & Barnsley, J. (2013). The evolution of integrated health care strategies. *Annual review of health care management: Revisiting the evolution of health systems organization* (Vol. 15, pp. 125–161). Advances in Health Care Management. Bingley, UK: Emerald Group Publishing Limited.

Fineide, M. J., & Ramsdal, H. (2014). Prosesstenkning – Standardisering av standardiserte pasientforløp og behandlingslinjer. In S. I. Vabo & M. Vabø (Eds.), *Organisering av velferd* (pp. 108–121). Oslo: University Press.

Friedland, R., & Alford, R. R. (1991). Bringing society back in: Symbols, practices and institutional contradictions. In W. W. Powell & P. J. DiMaggio (Eds.), *The new institutionalism in organizational analysis* (pp. 232–263). Chicago, IL: University of Chicago Press.

Gautun, H., & Syse, A. (2013). *Samhandlingsreformen*. NOVA Rapport, 2013 (8). Retrieved from www.nova.no/asset/6986/1/6986_1.pdf

George, A. L., & Bennett, A. (2005). *Case studies and theory development in the social sciences*. Cambridge, MA: Harvard MIT Press.

Gloubman, S., & Mintzberg, H. (2001). Managing the care of health and the cure of diseases – Part 1. *Health Care Manage Review*, *26*(1), 56–92.

Gröne, O., & Garcia-Barbero, M. (2001). Integrated care: A position paper of the WHO European office for integrated health care services. *International Journal of Integrated Care, June 1*. Retrieved from https://www.ijic.org/

Haave, P. (2006). The hospital sector. A four-country comparison of organisational and political development. In N. F. Christiansen, K. Pedersen, N. Edling, & P. Haave (Eds.), *The nordic model of welfare. A historical reappraisal* (pp. 215–242). Copenhagen: Museum Tusculanum Press, University of Copenhagen.

Hagen, T. P. (2014). Reinventing the "cottage hospital": Did implementation of municipal acute bed units reduce the demand for hospital admissions? Nordic Political Science Association. August 12–14, 2014.

Kalseth, B., & Paulsen, B. (2008). Strategisk samhandling på papir og i praksis? En kartlegging av lokale samarbeidsavtaler mellom kommuner og helseforetak per oktober 2008,

Sintef-Helse, Trondheim. Retrieved from http://www.sintef.no/project/Samdata/rapporter/Rapport%20A8640%20Samhandling.pdf

Karlberg, I. (2008). Sweden. In E. Nolte, C. Knai, & M. McKee (Eds.), *Managing chronic conditions. Experience in eight countries. Observatory studies No 15* (pp. 115–130). Copenhagen: European Observatory on Health Systems, WHO Regional Office for Europe.

Kristoffersen, J. E. (2013). Utfordringer i fastlegeordningen. In N. Veggeland (Ed.), *Reformer i norsk helsevesen* (pp. 111–142). Oslo: Veien videre, Akademisk forlag.

Netteland, G., & Naustdal, A. G. (2014). Risikofaktorar ved pasientovergangar. In O. Bukve & G. Kvåle (Eds.), *Samhandling og kvalitet i helseorganisasjonar* (pp. 117–136). Oslo: University Press.

Ouchi, W. G. (1980). Markets, bureaucracies, and clans. *Administrative Science Quarterly, 25*(1), 129–141.

Pedersen, K. M. (2005). *Kommunal medfinansiering av sundhetsvæsenet – en ide på sandgrund?* Odense: Syddanske University Press.

Reay, T., & Hinings, C. R. (2009). Managing the rivalry of competing institutional logics. *Organizational Studies 2009, 30*(06), 629–652.

Romøren, T. I., Torjesen, D. O., & Landmark, B. (2011). Promoting coordination in Norwegian health care. *International Journal of Integrated Care, 11*(7). Retrieved from http://www.ijic.org

Røvik, K. A. (2007). *Trender og translasjoner. Ideer som former det 21. Århundrets organisasjoner.* Oslo: University Press.

Sarapuu, K., Lægreid, P., Randma-Liiv, T., & Rykkja, L. H. (2014). Lessons learned and policy implications. In P. Lægreid, K. Sarapuu, L.-H. Rykkja., & T. Randma-Liiv (Eds.), *Organizing for coordination in the public sector. Practices and lessons from 12 European countries* (pp. 263–277). Basingstoke: Palgrave Macmillan.

Scharpf, F. W. (1997). *Games real actor plays. Actor-centred institutionalism in policy research.* Boulder, CO: Westview Press.

Stortingsmelding no. 2. (2013–2014). Revidert nasjonalbudsjett 2014, Finansdepartementet, Oslo.

Stortingsmelding nr. 47. (2008–2009). Samhandlingsreformen. Rett behandling – på rett sted – til rett tid, Helse- og omsorgsdepartementet, Oslo.

Thornton, P. H., Ocasio, W., & Lounsbury, M. (2012). *The institutional logics perspective. A new approach to culture, structure and process.* Oxford: Oxford University Press.

Torjesen, D. O., & Vabo, S. I. (2014). Samhandlingsreformen – virkemidler for koordinering. In S. I. Vabo & M. Vabø (Eds.), *Organisering av velferd* (pp. 138–157). Oslo: University Press.

Veggeland, N. (2013). Samhandlingsreformen – en bærekraftig reform? In N. Veggeland (Ed.), *Reformer i norsk helsevesen. Veien videre* (pp. 81–107). Oslo: Akademisk forlag.

Vinge, S., & Kjellberg, J. (2009). Kommuner får pisk, mens almen praksis og sygehuse får gulerødder. In M. Vestergaard (Ed.), *Skammekrogen – Debatbog om medicinske patienter* (pp. 113–127). København: Dagens Medicin Bøger.

Vrangbæk, K. (2011). Regioner og kommuners samarbeide om ældre medicinske patienter. Fokus, Forum for kvalitet og udvikling i offentlig service, July, No. 44.

Vrangbæk, K., & Sørensen, L. M. (2013). Does municipal co-financing reduce hospitalisation rates in Denmark? *Scandinavian Journal of Public Health, 41*(6), 616–622.

Wadmann, S., Strandberg-Larsen, M., & Vrangbæk, K. (2009). Coordination between primary and secondary healthcare in Denmark and Sweden. *International Journal of Integrated Care*. Retrieved from http://www.ijic.org

Waldorff, S. B. (2010). *Emerging organizations: In between local translation, institutional logics and discourse*. PHD series No. 10.2010, Copenhagen Business School.

WHO. (2001). European Office for Integrated Health Services, Integrated Care. Working definitions.

Yin, R. K. (2014). *Case study research: Design and methods*. (5th ed.). London: Sage.

PART IV
RESISTANCE AND TRANSFORMATION

INSTITUTIONAL ISOMORPHISM AND QUALITY MANAGEMENT: COMPARING HOSPITALS AND UNIVERSITIES

Tanja Klenk and Markus Seyfried

ABSTRACT

Quality management is high on the reform agenda of both universities and hospitals. This paper studies how quality management is implemented: who is responsible for QM and which instruments are used? The guiding research question is whether these two very distinct professional organizations respond in similar or different ways to a common reform trend. To analyze the extent of isomorphic tendencies a cross-sectoral, descriptive data analysis with data from 135 hospitals and 83 universities in Germany has been conducted. The results show that QM in hospitals is more elaborated in terms of quality instruments and at the same time more standardized. Universities, in contrast, follow quite individualistic ways to organize quality management.

Keywords: Quality management; implementation; institutionalism; universities; hospitals; cross-sectoral analyses

Towards a Comparative Institutionalism: Forms, Dynamics and Logics Across the Organizational Fields of Health Care and Higher Education
Research in the Sociology of Organizations, Volume 45, 217–242

ISSN: 0733-558X/doi:10.1108/S0733-558X20150000045020

INTRODUCTION

Quality has become an increasingly important issue in public sector reform, and despite the problems of defining quality (see Harvey & Green, 1993; Lindsay, 1992), organizations delivering public goods and services are these days expected to have encompassing quality management systems implemented.

This is also true for hospitals and universities in Germany (e.g., for higher education, see Stensaker, 2007; for hospitals, see Bode, Lange, & Märker, 2013; Offermanns, 2011). While quality has been on the German hospital policy agenda since the early 1990s, quality management is still a comparatively new issue in higher education. However, universities have caught up, in particular when it comes to quality management in teaching.

Even though universities and hospitals are both professional organizations, they are in literature considered as distinct and somewhat exceptional organizations, which can only be understood by taking their historical trajectories into account. Against this background, we wonder what happens when universities and hospitals are confronted with a similar reform trend: do they follow different quality management implementation paths? Or can we observe isomorphism, this being the alignment of actors and instruments of quality management (structural alignment)?

At a first glance, similarities prevail. Traditionally, professionals have been largely responsible for regulating their own conduct in the interest of higher standards (Donabedian, 1978, p. 861). Hence, doctors as well as university lecturers have been granted a high degree of discretion with regard to quality management. However, with public resources becoming scarce and with the rise of ideas of New Public Management, quality management and quality control at the organizational level – in addition to professional self-regulation – has been considered necessary (Klauber, Geraedts, Friedrich, & Wasem, 2011). Furthermore, universities and hospitals are confronted with increasing external demands regarding accountability and transparency. For both organizations, this implies a "loss of traditional forms of autonomy" (Dent & Whitehead, 2002; Kuhlmann & Saks, 2008; Lange, 2008, p. 243; Schimank, 2005, p. 362).

However, besides these similarities, there are also important differences between universities and hospitals. In Germany, hospitals are operating these days in a highly competitive field, especially in densely populated areas. Competition between universities, to the contrary, is still limited. While competition for research funds has indeed become fierce, German universities do not compete for students, even though they are supposed to do so (Krücken, 2008; Winter, 2012). Compared to universities, the hospital field is not only characterized by "more market," but at the same time also by "more rules." Thus, the traditional professional logic in hospitals is challenged by the equally strong logic of market and hierarchy.

We expect the particular attributes of hospitals and universities and of the environment in which they are located to make a difference. In the following, we study how the commonly shared trend towards quality management is translated within different institutional settings. What similarities and differences in the structures of quality management can be observed in these two different types of professional organization? What quality management instruments are typically applied and who is responsible for conducting quality management? Understanding the spread of quality management among public sector organizations as a process of institutionalization – hence as a social process by which structures, policies, and programmes attain "rule-like-status" as legitimate elements of the organization (Meyer & Rowan, 1977; Zucker, 1977) – we are also interested in what processes of coercive, mimetic, and normative isomorphism work within and across the two organizational fields (DiMaggio & Powell, 1983): How *do* differences between hospitals and universities influence structural organizational alignment (isomorphism)?

To analyze these two research questions, the paper proceeds as follows. In the next section, we describe our theoretical framework, thereby identifying those attributes of the organization and the environment in which it is located which are likely to shape the quality management model adopted by the organization. Subsequently, the research design, the dataset, and selected methods are described, followed by the presentation of the theoretical assumptions. The final section summarizes the most important results, from which research desiderata and further research perspectives are concluded.

THEORY AND ASSUMPTIONS

The theory of isomorphism has its seed in the seminal work of DiMaggio and Powell (1983). Concluding that "today [...] structural change in organizations seems less and less driven by competition or by the need of efficiency [...]" (DiMaggio & Powell, 1983, p. 147), they developed an approach to organizational change based on the concept of homogenization in the sense of isomorphism, driven by the quest for legitimacy. The authors identify three mechanisms of institutional isomorphic change, namely *coercive isomorphism*, *mimetic isomorphism*, and *normative isomorphism* (DiMaggio & Powell, 1983, p. 150).

Following their definitions, *coercive isomorphism* occurs when organizational change results from external pressure. The organization reacts to the demands of its (legal) environment, which can, for example, be formulated by a mandate of the government. External pressures can be exerted by other actors upon which the organization is dependent. However, external pressures arise also – in more informal and subtle ways – from cultural expectations (DiMaggio & Powell, 1983, p. 150f.). Thus, coercive isomorphism is not necessarily "direct" or "explicit" (DiMaggio & Powell, 1983, p. 151). The concept of *mimetic isomorphism* allows deviations from the coercive logic. In this case, uncertainty resulting from unclear solutions, causes, and consequences for organizational problems plays a crucial role. Organizations facing environmental uncertainty, and thus being in a vulnerable position, tend to copy similar organizations which appear to be successful. By doing so, they try not only to find answers for ambiguous situations, but also to gain additional legitimacy. On the other hand, mimetic isomorphism results in a severe lack of strategic thinking about institutional design (DiMaggio & Powell, 1983, p. 152). Finally, DiMaggio and Powell describe the mechanism of *normative isomorphism*, defining this concept in close relationship to professionalization. They identify two important sources of isomorphism. First, formal education combined with cognitive legitimacy; and second, the elaboration and growth of networks as providers of new ideas, models, or narratives (DiMaggio & Powell, 1983, p. 152). Studying quality management through the lens of isomorphism, we assume that different forms of isomorphism have occurred in both sectors. While the hospital sector is strongly dominated by coercive isomorphism, the higher education sector is dominated by a mixture of mimetic, normative and coercive isomorphism, leading to distinct organizational structures in quality management.

Isomorphism has a strong focus on the conformity, the similarity, and the stability of organizational arrangements, neglecting thereby the question as to why organizations respond to external demands differently even though they are exposed to the same institutional pressures. However, more recent contributions to neo-institutionalism have further elaborated the theory to strengthen its ability also to explain organizational differences and organizational change (Greenwood & Hinings, 1996). From the perspective of this strand of literature, neo-institutionalism is a model to link the organizational environment with the features of the organization. To understand how organizations adapt to external demands and why they respond differently to similar external pressures, two factors have to be taken into account: first, the structure of the field in which they are operating; and second, the particular characteristics of the organization under consideration (Greenwood, Raynard, Kodeih, Micelotta, & Lounsbury, 2011, p. 324). The institutional pressures to which an organization is exposed are crucially shaped by the structure of the field in which the organization is located. It is at this level where significant reference audiences, such as accreditation agencies or governmental institutions exerting regulatory powers, can be found.

Yet, how an organization perceives, interprets, and reacts to such external demands depends very much on organizational characteristics, which filter the institutional complexity outside the organization and shape the receptivity of the organization to multiple logics (Greenwood et al., 2011, pp. 339–348). Important filters in this respect are, for instance, primary task characteristics or organizational governance, particularly with regard to the relative influence of different groups and actors within the organization (e.g., the room for manoeuvre of professionals compared to the management of the organization).

Against this background we argue that the particular models of quality management adopted by universities and hospitals, respectively – in terms of the instruments applied and the actors responsible for conducting quality management – are a result of both differences at the level of the two organizational fields and at the level of organizations. To understand the adoption of quality management and to operationalize our argument, we consider the following features of the organization and its environment as crucial. With regard to the differences at the field level, we follow Meyer and Scott's seminal contribution and focus on the degree of fragmentation and the degree of centralization of the field (Meyer & Scott, 1983). Concerning organizational attributes, we take three different aspects into account. First these are the characteristics of the organization's primary task. Organizational studies have shown that management practices are highly context-sensitive (Mintzberg, 1979; Pollitt, 2006), with the tasks of an organization being an important aspect in this regard. For instance, tasks which are standardizable and clearly measurable require different management practices compared to non-standardizable tasks. With respect to our field of interest – professional organizations in the era of New Public Management (Dent & Whitehead, 2002) – we take, second, the degree of professional autonomy into consideration, as well as, third, the role of the management of the organization, which can be understood as a "countervailing power" to professional governance, restricting professional influence on quality management.

Governance of the Organizational Field

The concept of the organizational field is central for institutional analyses (Scott, 2001). It describes the actor constellations in which the actions of an organization are embedded and can comprise organizations, government and public administration, as well as competitors, funding sources or professional associations. From this institutional environment, normative, regulative, and cognitive expectations emerge, providing meaning for the organization and defining the set of legitimate organizational actions (Wooten & Hoffman, 2008, p. 130). The governance of the organizational fields of both higher education and hospital care is today characterized by a mix of professional, market, and state logics. Hence, pressures for isomorphic tendencies can stem either from competitive pressures (i.e., to gain a comparative advantage by implementing new standards in the field) or from regulative requirements which set common standards defined either by professional associations or by public bodies. Whether external regulatory requirements trigger processes of regulative isomorphism depends very much on the power position of the external regulator, be it a private accreditation agency or a unit of public administration. Are they able to impose their demands on the organization and do they have access to sanction mechanisms to reward or to criticize organizational action? Regarding competitive forces, we assume that higher market pressures and vulnerable market positions lead to higher levels of isomorphism: organizations struggling with their market position try to copy their successful competitors, thereby setting in motion processes of mimetic and normative isomorphism. Organizations exposed to low market pressures (i.e., in cases of excellence, or traditionally high reputation), in contrast, can resist isomorphic tendencies.

To compare different organizational fields, institutional theory considers two factors as important, namely the degree of fragmentation and the degree of centralization of the field (Scott & Meyer, 1991). While fragmentation describes the number of actors – regulators, competitors, professional associations – with each of them having different institutional expectations of the organization, centralization refers to the distribution of power among these external stakeholders. We assume that there is a relationship between the degree of centralization and fragmentation of the field and isomorphism, presuming that a higher degree of centralization and lower fragmentation of the field corresponds with higher tendencies of coercive isomorphism (assumption 1).

Characteristics of the Services Provided

Quality is perhaps one of the most frequently used words in the language of public sector reform, but also one of the most ambiguous. It can be considered as what Pollitt and Hupe (2011) have termed a "magic concept": the very high degree of abstraction and the notion's solely positive normative connotations overcome any opposition. However, its blurriness also means that defining and implementing a framework in the attempt to "manage" quality is rather challenging. The management of quality presupposes that it is clear what needs to be managed. Therefore, a definition of the quality concept is essential. While the measurement of quality in general is very difficult and needs precise definition, this is in particular true for professional service delivery. Defining the quality of services such as teaching, doing research, curing, and caring is particularly challenging as the user of those services is a co-producer. Hence, competing and conflicting understandings of "quality" are characteristic in the field of higher education and inpatient care. Quality can be defined as excellence, minimum standards, fitness for purpose and many others (for more definitions, see Harvey & Green, 1993, pp. 11–27). This is different from the field of industrial goods and products, where clear and rather standardized techniques cause high levels of isomorphism (Westphal, Gulati, & Shortell, 1996). We therefore expect lower levels of isomorphism for the fields of hospitals and universities, where services are unstandardized and difficult to assess. However, there are also important differences between universities and hospitals. Even though there are some global standards and trends in higher education, universities at the local level are prone to interpret and implement quality management approaches on their own (Paradeise & Thoenig, 2013, p. 196). Compared to higher education, global standards have become more common and accepted in the healthcare sector as, for instance, the diffusion of case-mix accounting has shown impressively (Covaleski, Dirsmith, & Michelman, 1993). Due to the fact that skilled practice plays an eminent role in both our fields, mimetic isomorphism seems to be the dominant form of procedural adaptation (DiMaggio & Powell, 1983, p. 151). Nevertheless, normative isomorphism might also be of importance, in particular when we take the crucial role of professional associations in higher education and hospital care into account. Thus, the characteristics of services provided influence the extent of the different types of isomorphism: standardized procedures correspond with higher degrees of isomorphism, and vice versa – we assume that the higher the complexity of services and the more techniques are unclear to provide these services, the lower are the levels of isomorphism (assumption 2).

Professional Autonomy

Even though the definition of quality is contested in the field of inpatient care and academic teaching, once a start has been made and quality criteria have been defined, the implemented instruments of quality management trigger processes of standardization and routinization. These processes might result in tendencies toward de-professionalization, as they are thought to streamline the decisions and actions of the professionals (Seyfried & Pohlenz, 2013, pp. 54–55). On the other hand, it is a core feature of professional identity to place emphasis on the singularity and particularity of the work, inherent to the interaction of a teacher with his or her students and the interaction between a doctor and a patient, and to refuse standard solutions and best practice models. Thus, we can assume that professionals are reluctant to accept externally imposed best practice models if they impose tight restrictions on their practice. They are unlikely to capitulate when confronted with standardization, but try to resist (for resistance in higher education institutions, see Anderson, 2006, 2008). Following these arguments, we assume that, in general, higher degrees of professional autonomy prevent isomorphic tendencies in order to avoid processes of de-professionalization resulting from routinization or standardization. On the other hand, we assume that where isomorphism takes place, it exerts its influence mainly through processes of mimetic and normative isomorphism (assumption 3).

Organizational Responsibility for Quality Management

Our final general assumption refers to the organizational responsibility for quality management: who are the main actors taking responsibility for conducting quality management within the organization? As professional bureaucracies (Mintzberg, 1979), hospitals and universities are shaped by both the logic of professionalism and the logic of administration and management. In theory, the professional bureaucracy emphasizes authority of a professional nature and relies in terms of coordination on the power of expertise. The strategies of the professional bureaucracy are mainly developed by the individual professionals within the organization and by professional associations on the outside. The empirical reality of hospitals and universities, however, is characterized by contentions and conflicts between the two logics. There are constant power struggles between the management and the professionals when it comes to the design of organizational processes and structures. The competing and conflicting logics of professionalism on the one hand and administration and management on the other hand shape the structure and processes of quality management. Quality management can be implemented in centralized ways, with the top management of the organization being responsible for quality management, or in decentralized ways, leaving more room for manoeuvre to the individual professionals. We assume that isomorphic tendencies are higher when quality management is a responsibility of the top management of the organization and highly centralized (and no longer lies in the responsibility of individual professionals), as ideas of "best practice" and of studying the models of successful competitors are a core feature of the managerial logic, while the professional logic emphasizes the individuality and incomparability of each single case (assumption 4). Hence we assume normative and mimetic isomorphism as the main processes of adaptation and convergence.

Table 1 summarizes the groups of characteristics presented above and the different types of isomorphism they are expected to influence. Each "X" indicates that a distinct type of isomorphism is likely to be associated with particular features of the governance and organization of the field.

Table 1. Features of the Organization and the Organizational Field and Mechanisms of Isomorphism.

	Features of the Organization and the Organizational Field		
	Governance of the field	Characteristics of services	Organizational responsibility
Isomorphism			
Coercive	X		
Normative	X	X	X
Mimetic	X	X	X

Source: Own illustration.

Hence, we assume that the governance of the field could promote or suppress all three types of isomorphism, while the characteristics of services and the internal organization of quality management are only associated with normative and mimetic processes of isomorphism.

CASE SELECTION, DATA AND METHODS

From an international comparative perspective, Germany is a latecomer in terms of New Public Management. While Anglo-Saxon countries have implemented many encompassing performance and quality management schemes, this process is still ongoing in Germany. Taking Germany as an example allows us to study the quality management schemes "in nascendi," which makes it an ideal case for cross-checking and further developing theories of isomorphism. This study has an explorative character. Therefore, its main purpose is to describe each feature and discuss the results under consideration of our assumptions concerning their influence on structural organizational alignment (isomorphism), which could serve as a starting point for future research.

Universities and hospitals are both professional organizations. However, they are embedded in an organizational field which is not only characterized by professional logics, but also by professional and market logics. As both academic teaching and inpatient care are considered in Germany as public services, universities and hospitals are subjected to intensive public regulation, challenging the autonomy of the professionals inside the organization. With regard to quality management, hospitals are, for instance, legally required to set up a system of internal quality management. In addition, the quality of service delivery is monitored by an external private agency, commissioned by the central government; hospitals are obliged to provide data for this obligatory external assessment and can be sanctioned in case of non-compliance. In the case of universities, the quality of academic teaching is high on the political agenda, too. However, compared to hospitals, statutory requirements for quality management are so far less institutionalized.

The differences with regard to the regulative institutionalization of quality management in the two fields under consideration might be explained by different governance settings. In federal Germany, both universities and hospitals are regulated by federal *and* state law. However, when comparing the two fields, the higher degree of centralization in the hospital field is striking. Not only funding, but also the general framework for quality management in hospitals is decided at the central level. Higher education (like education in general), in contrast, is one of the core activity fields of state government, which are very preoccupied with maintaining their competences and avoiding central influence, although in higher education policy, close horizontal and vertical ties are also existent. They should guarantee uniform educational chances, general quality standards and mobility (see Lanzendorf & Pasternack, 2008). Nevertheless, the regulatory framework for universities is much more fragmented compared to hospitals.

In line with the idea of academic teaching and inpatient care as public goods, funding for both services (still) stems predominantly from public sources. While funding is public, we find more variety when it comes to service provision. In particular, in the hospital case, welfare mix-solutions – meaning the co-existence of public, private non-profit and private for-profit service providers – are a core feature of the governance regime. In the university case, the variety of ownership structures is less pronounced; here, the field is dominated by public organizations operating in a public legal form.

The strengthening of the market logic, triggered by tight public budgets and cost-containment strategies, comes in particular to light in the hospital case, where the share of private for-profit companies has skyrocketed in the last two decades. In addition and similar to universities, hospitals have been subjected to internal marketization through the introduction of instruments of New Public Management (Schimank, 2005, p. 362; for universities as competitors, see Hasse & Krücken, 2013, section two). As a result of the more intense market logic in the hospital field compared to university teaching, the idea that service users (patients and students respectively) should be considered "customers" is more widespread in the hospital case. In contrast, it is an ongoing debate in Germany whether students are customers of universities. These differences with regard to the dominant field logics also have implications for quality management. Quality management in hospitals is much more stakeholder-oriented compared to universities. Therefore, customer surveys and complaint management tools are basic elements of hospital quality management systems. Furthermore, hospitals are much more willing to publish quality records, as private providers consider this a strategy to gain and maintain legitimacy. Sure enough, in the university case there are plenty of surveys as well. However, they focus on different groups of students and different topics; moreover, the results are often only used for descriptive ritualized purposes and are not published in a systematic, transparent and even standardized way (Charlton, 2002; Power, 1997).

With regard to our dataset, we have selected hospitals and universities in Germany. In order to reduce extraneous variance, we have focused on big organizations offering the full range of possible services. Hence, we have selected large hospitals with 400–500 healthcare beds, and large universities, which offer all graduate degrees: Bachelor's, Master's, doctorate, and Habilitation. Thus, our sample comprises 135 hospitals and 83 universities (for additional descriptive statistics, see Table 2).

Our data sources are manifold. For hospitals, we collected all biannually published quality records, which are required by law. We refer to the 2010 volumes, which are the most recent volumes available for the hospitals under consideration. We added information provided by the short profiles of the hospitals. Furthermore, we collected data from the hospitals' annual reports and homepages, as well as from the Federal Office for Statistics Germany, thereby focusing in particular on the time span from 2012 to 2014.

While encompassing data for hospitals are collected centrally by the *Deutsche Krankenhausverzeichnis* (DKV), the German Hospital Directory – an online presentation platform for all German hospitals – access to data is less convenient in the case of universities. In contrast to hospitals,

Table 2. Descriptive Statistics of Hospitals and Universities.

Hospitals			Universities		
Indicator	*n*	Mean	Indicator	*n*	Mean
Number of hospital beds	135	447	Number of students	82	18,616
Annual surplus 2010 in mill. €	88	2	Budget without medical faculties 2012 in mill. €	75	220
Total case number of fully inpatient treatments	135	15,733	Number of graduates	83	2,726
Total case number of semi-inpatient treatments	134	523	–	–	–
Total number of physicians (without external doctors with a hospital affiliation)	135	110	Scientific and non-scientific staff (without third party funds and medical faculties)	67	3,688
Total number of nurses (with a three year apprenticeship)	135	256	–	–	–
Percentage of hospitals with QM as part of executive management	127	96%	Percentage of universities with QM as part of executive management	82	27%

Source: Own dataset.

universities are not obliged to provide quality reports and information about the organizational structure of their quality management through standardized reporting schemes. Thus, we have collected data on quality management of universities by studying their internet homepages. We have focused on all sources providing information about the organizational structure of quality management (i.e., charts of the organization, quality manuals, quality reports). Furthermore, we have added data provided by the *Hochschulrektorenkonferenz* (HRK), the German Rectors' Conference, which is a "voluntary association of state and state-recognized universities and other higher education institutions in Germany" (BMBF, 2008, p. 110). Here, we used the most recent dataset which was available online (2014). Unfortunately, for universities it was not possible to get large-scale information on the structure and processes of quality management dating back to 2010 as was possible in the hospital case. As a result, we have a small time gap between both cases; however, we consider this still acceptable.

Simple descriptions were used to characterize the context of our sample in which isomorphism might influence the organizational structures and selected instruments of quality management. Our context variables for investigating and assessing isomorphic tendencies are the governance of the field (i.e., market forces or regulations by law); the characteristics of services (i.e., reflected in the diversity of measurement approaches or instruments); the professional autonomy; and, finally, the organizational responsibility for quality management.

With regard to "governance of the organizational field," we considered in particular the number of regulations and the intensity of market forces. The university sector is mainly regulated by state law, while hospital quality is mainly regulated at the central level. However, in addition to these regulations, which apply to all hospitals and universities, respectively, there are further regulations which are valid only for particular organizations. In the hospital field, some states have implemented additional laws, further intensifying the regulatory requirements for hospital quality management. In the case of universities, additional obligations could be introduced by target agreements between the State Ministry for Education and single universities. We categorize "additional regulation" as being where quality management is part of additional state law (hospitals) or target agreements (universities). In the university case, we focused on target agreements which were in force in 2012 to ensure time consistency within our dataset for the higher education sector. If the state laws or target agreements contain no particular statements on quality management, we categorize them as "standard regulations."

Market force considers the market position of each hospital and university. This variable is composed of the average of several z-transformed parameters measuring performance and staff (raw data presented above, see Table 2). Performance of universities is measured by the z-transformed number of graduated students; in the hospital case, z-values of inpatient and day care cases were included. The coding procedures for the staff are similar: we calculated z-scores for the available staff at universities, without medical staff and staff financed by third parties. In the hospital case, data on staffing levels is much more detailed. We therefore decided to calculate z-scores for the two main groups of staff, namely doctors and nurses. Finally, we divided the sum of all z-scores with the number of indicators, which were included in that index. We assume that positive z-scores indicate a "positive market position" with higher output and more staff and thus a higher performance, while negative z-scores indicate a "negative market position" with lower output and lower staff and thus a lower performance.

As for the characteristics of the services provided, we refer to a simple qualitative dichotomy. The central argument is that in the hospital case, skills and knowledge, and hence techniques for patient treatment, are more standardized compared to the techniques of academic teaching. This is in particular a result of the power of external professional associations, which is much higher in the hospital case. Here, the definition of knowledge and skills by medical associations has a long history, and at the same time recommendations for treatment techniques developed by these associations enjoy a much higher esteem than guidelines for academic teaching developed by academic professional organizations.

For professional autonomy, too, we propose a simple qualitative dichotomy, distinguishing between "low" for hospitals and "high" for universities, assuming that professionals in higher education in Germany have more discretionary power to organize quality management compared to professionals in hospitals. This coding is based on a qualitative assessment of the regulation of professionalism in the two policy fields, taking into account the number of rules and codes as well as their levels of detail and the possibilities of sanctions.

Our last variable documents the internal responsibility of quality management in universities and hospitals. Here, we assess to what extent quality management has become part of the bureaucratic core of the organization and is the responsibility of the management (instead of the individual professional), for example, through the establishment of quality departments or quality managers. The variable "organizational responsibility" obtains a value of 0 if there is no quality management or functional equivalent at all, which is only relevant for universities. The variable receives a value of 1 if quality management is part of diverse and somewhat unclear structures of the organization and a value of 2 if is part of the line organization. We award a score of 3 if the quality management unit is part of the executive management, signaling the highest possible hierarchical position (see Table 2, where the share of organizations with quality management as part of the executive management is presented).

One of our central dependent variables to assess isomorphism and the level of conformity within and across the two organizational fields is labeled "organizational actors of quality management." This is measured as the number of different actors who are involved in organizational quality management. For universities, we used a proxy-measure because the actors involved in quality management are not documented in a standardized way. Therefore, we focused on internal evaluations of teaching and learning as one of the core procedures of quality management in higher education. Due to the fact that internal evaluations are more and more a matter of regulation, the actors responsible for evaluation are recorded in the universities' evaluation statutes. The evaluation statutes are publicly available, which facilitates data collection. We do not claim that all these actors have the same position in the quality management system; neither do we assert that the mere number of actors provides information about the actors' potential to shape quality management structures. However, this number allows an assessment of the diversity of actors occupied with quality issues. Furthermore, it gives evidence on the extent of implementation, with a high number of different organizational levels being involved in quality management indicating a higher degree of organizational implementation. Another important advantage is that the variety measure based on the number of actors is easily comparable to quality management in higher education, while measuring the quality of actors (in terms of their hierarchical position and their possibilities to shape organizational decision making) would have created serious problems of comparability.

In addition, we counted the number of instruments applied in quality management so as to have an additional measure to assess the scope of conformity and the degree of organizational implementation. For this purpose, we listed all quality management instruments written down in the DKV hospital quality reports, in quality manuals, and on websites in the case of universities, respectively. Data collection proved to be challenging, especially in the case of universities. Since there is no standardized information on quality management, it was difficult to get a harmonized data base.

In spite of the comprehensive data sources being used, our study material also has limitations. A comprehensive understanding of the adoption of quality management in hospitals and universities requires insight into the broader perspective, including the main formal procedures of quality management (i.e., monitoring, reporting, controlling). Moreover, the qualifications and the educational background of quality managers are decisive. As quality management is a rather new phenomenon in both sectors, there are severe qualification gaps, and processes of professionalization are still ongoing, in particular in the case of universities (see Blümel, Kloke, & Krücken, 2011).

PROVIDING CONTEXT AND SUBSTANTIATING THE THEORETICALLY DERIVED ASSUMPTIONS

In this paper, we give particulars on the context in which isomorphism takes place and which influences the structures and the instruments of quality management in hospitals and universities have. Table 3 displays the main results of our contextual variables. The results are aggregated data and can be interpreted as verbalized summaries of frequency distributions. Where certain features – as presented above – apply for more than 60% of the cases within either the hospital or the university group, we labeled the whole group with this dominant feature. This process of categorization allowed us to obtain a broad snapshot of the main contextual features, which, in turn, provided an insight into the isomorphism of structures and instruments of quality management of hospitals and universities.

Governance of the field: As shown in Table 3, the governance of inpatient care in Germany is more centralized compared to higher education. For instance, hospitals are required by national law to conduct quality management. Higher education, in contrast, is regulated at the state level (Lanzendorf & Pasternack, 2008, p. 49), which entails variations in the regulatory regimes. What's more, some of the state regulations are rather vague with respect to quality management, allowing universities to develop individual quality management systems (Nickel, 2007, p. 19, 2008, p. 20ff.). Hospital care in Germany is not only more centralized compared to higher education, but at the same time more exposed to market forces. In the past years, hospital care in Germany has become a market with fierce competition and a high share of private for-profit providers (Bode, 2010; Stein,

Table 3. Features of the Organization and the Organizational Field.

	Features of the Organization and the Organizational Field			
	Governance of the field	Characteristics of services	Professional autonomy	Organizational responsibility
Hospitals	Additional regulations High competition	Techniques clear	Lower (compared to universities)	Mainly top management
Universities	Standard regulations Low competition	Techniques unclear	High	No clear tendency

Source: Own dataset.

2009). With increasing competition in the inpatient sector, single hospitals have discovered quality as a competitive advantage, publishing now overabundant data to demonstrate their clinical integrity (Gosfield, 1997).

Coming back to our assumptions about the impact of the governance of the field on the structure of quality management – *the more an organization is confronted with centralized regulation and the more vulnerable its market position, the higher are the levels of isomorphism* – we expect similarities in actors and instruments of quality management to be more common for hospitals than for universities. Here, the more centralized and at the same time more competitive structure of the hospital field has triggered processes of mimetic isomorphism.

Characteristics of the services provided: As for the characteristics of the services provided, we expected lower levels of isomorphism when the complexity of services is high and when techniques are unclear. Although "magic" and blurry concepts such as quality management provide an excellent precondition for isomorphic diffusion among organizations, structural organizational alignment becomes much more difficult when we consider its implementation in the day-to-day workplace. This holds true in particular when the characteristics of the primary task of an organization and related techniques vary. In the case of hospitals, quality failure has more fatal implications (death, irreparable health and body damages due to grave errors in medical treatment) than in universities (unemployment, students who change universities or study programmes, dropout rates, etc.). This implies that the characteristics and outcomes of techniques and possible quality failure are directly measurable in hospitals, but not in universities, where a variety of approaches, instruments, and concepts exist. Thus, quality management can be – and is – taken more seriously in hospitals than in universities. It is considered as a legitimate practice and therefore can shape the organizational procedures in a decisive way. In the case of universities, in contrast, measurement of the quality of techniques and possible quality failure is rather difficult and unclear. Accordingly, we expect isomorphic tendencies in the process of implementation to be lower (in terms of quality instruments and quality actors) in the case of universities. Here, actors and organizations have to cope with a variety of outputs, outcomes, conflicting goals, etc., which hamper standardization and routinization and maintain organizational diversity.

Professional autonomy: Another argument which is closely related and supports this view is that hospitals have a clearer defined consensus on professional standards for nearly all of their services. In contrast, in universities there is still an ongoing debate about what quality in teaching and learning is (Harvey & Williams, 2010, p. 85ff.). While standard procedures and pre-defined organizational pathways limiting professional autonomy are typical for hospitals, university teachers enjoy more room for manoeuvre in their everyday work. In line with our third assumption elaborated in the theory section above – the higher the professional autonomy within an organization, the lower the levels of isomorphism – we expect quality management to be implemented in hospitals in a top-down approach, with standard solutions for the internal organization of quality management. For universities, in turn, we expect a higher variation in organizational models of quality management, resulting from the different preferences of autonomous professionals (Deem, 2010, p. 38; Fredman & Doughney, 2012, p. 45; Schimank, 2005, p. 363).

Organizational responsibility for quality management: Given the fact that efforts to strengthen the managerial logic in professional bureaucracies have started much earlier in hospitals and are much more advanced, managers with a non-professional (economic or administrative) background are more influential in hospitals than in universities. According to the literature, the newly introduced quality management-related job positions, for example, quality managers, who work "in-between" and bridge the traditional professions within the administrative sphere, undergo three phases to become established and accepted: contestation, reconciliation, and reconstruction (Whitchurch, 2010). While most hospitals have already entered a different phase in establishing quality managers (e.g., reconciliation or reconstruction), universities are still coping with contestation and reconciliation. Accordingly, we expect a higher level of isomorphism in the hospital case due to the adoption of best practice models or the copying of successful competitors.

In a nutshell, while the contextual information on universities (governance of the field and characteristics of services provided, professional autonomy and the role of management) suggests limited tendencies of isomorphism, we can assume higher levels of isomorphism for hospitals. Therefore, we expect greater similarities with regard to actors and instruments of quality management between hospitals than between universities. For the latter, we expect much more diversity for actors and instruments of quality management.

RESULTS

The first evidence for these assumptions is provided by our data on relevant actors and applied instruments in quality management, which are described in the following section. These empirical findings cannot be regarded as a classical statistical test, but rather as a plausibility check. And another caveat remains: the investigation of isomorphism presupposes longitudinal data to see how structures or instruments converge. Unfortunately, there are no longitudinal data on quality assurance structures and instruments in higher education or for hospitals. Hence, we use our dataset as a snapshot which describes the state of convergence for the selected point of time. Although the evidence is restricted for a time series, it allows first conclusions from a cross-sectional perspective.

Tables 4 and 5 show the frequency distributions of quality management actors (variety in organizational actors of quality management) and of the quality measurement instruments. As presented above, we use the concept of isomorphism and the described contextual attributes to understand variety in organizational structures or instruments. Further specification is needed to understand developments over time.

As can be seen in Tables 4 and 5, we have categorized actors and instruments to avoid confusion and to facilitate the detection of structure. Already this structuring process uncovers interesting results. Before re-grouping, the original dataset contained more than 60 different actors, groups, and organizational units, etc., for 135 hospitals. The huge extent of organizational variety is even more evident in the university case: here, 160 different names of actors, etc., were coded for only 83 universities. The re-categorization process led to 10 categories for universities and eight for hospitals (see Table 4), indicating that, although hospitals reveal a considerably higher number of cases, the organizational variety seems to be lower

Table 4. Variety of Quality Management Actors (Categorized).

Universities			Hospitals		
Actor	*n*	%	Actor	*n*	%
Hospital management	3	2	University management	31	37
QM – Staff section	56	41	Vice president	11	13
QM – Department	11	8	Senate	5	6
QM – Manager (central level)	67	50	Deans/directors, etc.	48	58
QM – Manager (decentralized levels)	66	49	Faculties, departments	34	41
QM – Commissions	128	95	Central QM units	15	18
QM – Teams	91	67	Commissioners, appointees	13	16
Top-down steering through superior unit (holding, concern, foundation)	7	5	Commissions	23	28
Support through superior unit (holding, concern, foundation)	15	11	Students	4	5
			Others	3	4
Number of cases	135		Number of cases	83	

Source: Own dataset.

Table 5. Instruments of Quality Management (Categorized).

Hospitals			Universities		
Instrument	*n*	%	Instrument	*n*	%
Occupancy management	28	21	Survey[a]	84	101
Innovation management	34	25	Controlling/figures	8	10
Internal audit	116	86	Accreditation	45	54
External audit	97	72	Internal/external evaluation[a]	88	106
Benchmarking/peer review	53	39	Benchmarking	2	2
Complaint management	128	95	Complaint management	3	4
Staff survey	101	75	Ranking	3	4
Case conference	49	36	Monitoring	3	4
Incident conference	88	65	Personnel development	3	4
Patient survey	131	97	Others	13	16
Referring doctor survey	84	62			
Hygiene management	68	50			
Others	4	3			
Number of cases	135		Number of cases	83	

Source: Own dataset.

[a]Percentages might exceed values of 100% because of aggregated data – for example, within universities, several types of survey are applied (alumni, graduates, beginners, etc.) and they were summarized as one single "survey" category.

than for universities. As expressed in our assumptions, we find higher levels of isomorphism in the case of hospitals.

Regarding actors of quality management in universities, the results show that there is a dominance of university management (president, vice president, and senate). Besides, deans and faculties are relevant, followed by commissions and central staff units. Surprisingly, students – the "customers" – play only a negligible role. For hospitals, the management board turned out to be the standard actor, followed by quality management teams, commissioners, and staffers (see Table 4). Thus, unlike universities, we find quality management actors comparatively evenly spread over all organizational levels of hospitals. Each level is involved, beginning with the management board and commissions at the central level, followed by central staff units, quality managers on both central and decentralized levels, and finally ending with quality teams at the operational levels of specialist departments. In the standard model of quality management organization in hospitals, the overall responsibility of the implementation of quality management lies with the management board, while commissions at the central level representing all relevant actors of hospitals are involved in strategic decision making. Central staff units provide support for both the management board and the operational actors on the lower levels. The implementation of quality management is organized in a hierarchical line organization, with a quality manager at the central level, several quality managers at the ward level, and numerous quality teams at the lowest organizational level.

Similar results have been detected for measurement instruments of quality management (see Table 5). Again, the overall number of instruments which were categorized and recoded is much higher for universities (number of categories = 74) than for hospitals (number of categories = 33). After re-categorization, we ended up with 10 categories for universities and 13 for hospitals, although their number of cases is nearly four times higher. The frequency distribution provides two results: first, hospitals apply more instruments; second, there are standard instruments which are applied in nearly all hospitals, that is, internal audits, complaint management or employee surveys, etc.

Again, we find the assumptions developed above approved: levels of isomorphism are higher in the field of hospitals. Hospitals apply more instruments, but in a much more standardized way. This holds true in particular for quality measurement instruments. If we take again the ratio of all mentioned instruments and all cases, we get 3.0 instruments per university and 7.6 instruments per hospital (see Table 5). Although this is a crude measure, it provides further evidence that universities develop rather fewer and individualistic approaches, whereas hospitals implement manifold solutions, but all of them are much more standardized.

As already mentioned, the results are different when we focus on relevant actors because the average number of actors is nearly the same. Here, universities reveal a ratio of 2.3 actors per organization and hospitals a ratio of 3.3. Taking contextual information into account, these results support the view that quality management is well established and much more standardized in German hospitals in contrast to universities, where quality assurance is a rather new phenomenon and far away from being institutionalized. Nevertheless, empirical tests need to be done.

SUMMARY

This paper contributes to a better understanding of how a parallel trend – the increasing importance of quality management – is implemented in two different fields. Our research interest has focused on the organizational structures of quality management in universities and hospitals. We wanted to understand, first, what similarities and differences in the structures of quality management in the two types of organization can be observed.

To study this question, we conducted a cross-sectoral analysis. The analysis shows that there are indeed major differences between the organizational structures of quality management in universities and in hospitals. Quality management in German hospitals is much more elaborate in terms of quality instruments and at the same time much more standardized. In universities, in contrast, there is no common route to quality management. Universities rather follow quite individualistic ways to organize quality management. Thus, dissimilarities persist, albeit both types of professional organization are subject to a similar reform trend. Ironically, it seems that the field where professional associations are more powerful and have a greater say in policy making, namely the hospital sector, corresponds with lower levels of autonomy for the individual professional and thus with a loss of professional degrees of freedom.

To explain such differences and similarities, we have suggested consideration of the impact of the governance of the field, the nature of the services provided, the degree of the autonomy of professionals, and the power relation between bureaucrats and professionals. In the section "Providing Context and Substantiating the Theoretically Derived Assumptions," we have provided a preliminary assessment of our assumptions, given the available data. In the light of this preliminary assessment, we can conclude that levels of isomorphism are indeed higher when organizations are faced with centralized regulation and fierce competition, when techniques are clear and when professional autonomy is restricted, for instance by powerful positions of bureaucrats.

However, the limitations of our study and the available data should be kept in mind. So far, these reflections are only assumptions – they require further empirical testing to fully understand the forms, dynamics, and logics of quality management within and across health and higher education fields. In future empirical studies, however, our assumptions can also be applied to other types of organization which are considered to be "somewhat special." Maybe our assumptions can be refined, operationalized, and tested as hypotheses in quantitative analysis. Therefore, we consider our research as a general and important contribution to the study of the seemingly incomparable, which takes efforts to provide a framework for comparative institutionalism in social sciences a step further.

REFERENCES

Anderson, G. (2006). Assuring quality/resisting quality assurance: Academics' responses to 'Quality' in some Australian universities. *Quality in Higher Education*, *12*(2), 161–173.

Anderson, G. (2008). Mapping academic resistance in the managerial university. *Organization*, *15*(2), 251–270.

Blümel, A., Kloke, K., & Krücken, G. (2011). Professionalisierungsprozesse im hochschulmanagement in deutschland. In A. Langer & A. Schräder (Eds.), *Professionalisierung im nonprofit management* (pp. 105–127). Wiesbaden: VS Verlag für Sozialwissenschaften.

BMBF. (2008). *Status and recognition of non-formal and informal learning in Germany within the framework of the OECD activity 'Recognition of non-formal and informal learning'*. Bonn: Federal Ministry of Education and Research.

Bode, I. (2010). Der Zweck heil(ig)t die mittel? Ökonomisierung und organisationsdynamik im krankenhaussektor. In M. Endreß & T. Matys (Eds.), *Die ökonomie der organisation – Die organisation der ökonomie* (pp. 63–92). Wiesbaden: VS Verlag für Sozialwissenschaften.

Bode, I., Lange, J., & Märker, M. (2013). Qualitätsagenda im krankenhauswesen: Eine diffuse agenda und reichlich ambivalenz. *Sozialer Fortschr*, *62*, 293–299.

Charlton, B. G. (2002). Audit, accountability, quality and all that: The growth of managerial technologies in UK universities. In S. Prickett & P. Erskine (Eds.), *Education! Education! Education! Managerial ethics and the law of unintended consequences*. Exeter: Imprint Academic.

Covaleski, M. A., Dirsmith, M. W., & Michelman, J. E. (1993). An institutional perspective of case-mix accounting systems and health care organizations. *Accounting, Organizations and Society*, *18*(1), 65–80.

Deem, R. (2010). Herding the academic cats: The challenges of 'managing' academic research in the contemporary UK university. *Perspectives: Policy and Practice in Higher Education*, *14*(2), 37–43.

Dent, M., & Whitehead, S. (Eds.). (2002). *Managing professional identities: Knowledge, performativity and the "New" Professional*. London: Routledge.

DiMaggio, P. J., & Powell, W. W. (1983). The iron cage revisited: Institutional isomorphism and collective rationality in organizational fields. *American Sociological Review*, *48*(2), 147–160.

Donabedian, A. (1978). The quality of medical care. *Science*, *200*(4344), 856–864. doi:10.1126/science.417400

Fredman, N., & Doughney, J. (2012). Academic dissatisfaction, managerial change and neoliberalism. *Higher Education*, *64*(1), 41–58.

Gosfield, A. G. (1997). Who is holding whom accountable for quality? Health Affairs *(Millwood)*, *16*(3), 26–40.

Greenwood, R., & Hinings, C. R. (1996). Understanding radical organizational change: Bringing together the old and the new institutionalism. *Academy of Management Review*, *21*(4), 1022–1054.

Greenwood, R., Raynard, M., Kodeih, F., Micelotta, E. R., & Lounsbury, M. (2011). Institutional complexity and organizational responses. *Academy of Management Annals*, *5*(1), 317–371. doi:10.1080/19416520.2011.590299

Harvey, L., & Green, D. (1993). Defining quality: Assessment and evaluation in higher education. *Assessment and Evaluation in Higher Education*, *18*(1), 9–34.

Harvey, L., & Williams, J. (2010). Fifteen years of quality in higher education (Part Two). *Quality in Higher Education*, *16*(2), 81–113.

Hasse, R., & Krücken, G. (2013). Competition and actorhood: A further expansion of the neo-institutional agenda. *Sociologica Internationalis*, *51*(2), 181–205.

Klauber, J., Geraedts, M., Friedrich, J., & Wasem, J. (2011). *Krankenhausreport 2011: Qualität durch wettbewerb*. Stuttgart: Schattauer.

Krücken, G. (2008). Zwischen gesellschaftlichem Diskurs und organisationalen Praktiken. Theoretische Überlegungen und empirische Befunde zur Wettbewerbskonstitution im Hochschulbereich. In K. Zimmermann, M. Kamphans, & S. Metz-Göckel (Eds.), *Perspektiven der hochschulforschung* (pp. 165–175). Wiesbaden: Verlag für Sozialwissenschaften.

Kuhlmann, E., & Saks, M. (Eds.). (2008). *Rethinking professional governance: International directions in healthcare*. Bristol: Policy.

Lange, S. (2008). New public management und die governance der universitäten. *Der Moderne Staat – Zeitschrift für Public Policy, Recht und Management*, *1*(1), 235–248.

Lanzendorf, U., & Pasternack, P. (2008). Hochschulpolitik im ländervergleich. In J. Bogumil & R. G. Heinze (Eds.), Neue steuerung von hochschulen. Eine zwischenbilanz (pp. 13–28). Berlin: edition sigma.

Lindsay, A. (1992). Concepts of quality in higher education. *Journal of Tertiary Education Administration*, *14*(2), 153–163.

Meyer, J. W., & Rowan, B. (1977). Institutionalized organizations: Formal structure as myth and ceremony. *American Journal of Sociology*, *83*(2), 340–363.

Meyer, J. W., & Scott, W. R. (1983). *Organizational environments: Ritual and rationality*. Beverly Hills, CA: Sage.

Mintzberg, H. (1979). The structuring of organizations: A synthesis of *the research*. Englewood Cliffs, NJ: Prentice Hall.

Nickel, S. (2007). Institutionelle QM-Systeme in universitäten und fachhochschulen Konzepte–Instrumente–Umsetzung, Centrum für Hochschulentwicklung (CHE), Arbeitspapier Nr. 94.

Nickel, S. (2008). Qualitätsmanagementsysteme an universitäten und fachhochschulen: Ein kritischer Überblick. *Beiträge zur Hochschulforschung*, *30*(1), 16–38.

Offermanns, G. (2011). Qualitätsmanagement im krankenhaus. In *Prozess- und Ressourcensteuerung im gesundheitssystem* (pp. 173–249). Heidelberg: Springer-Verlag.

Paradeise, C., & Thoenig, J.-C. (2013). Academic institutions in search of quality: Local orders and global standards. *Organization Studies*, *34*(2), 189–218.

Pollitt, C. (2006). Performance management in practice: A comparative study of executive agencies. *Journal of Public Administration Research and Theory*, *16*(1), 25–44.

Pollitt, C., & Hupe, P. (2011). Talking about government. *Public Management Review*, *13*(5), 641–658. doi:10.1080/14719037.2010.532963

Power, M. (1997). *The audit society: Rituals of verification*. Oxford: Oxford University Press.

Schimank, U. (2005). 'New public management' and the academic profession: Reflections on the German situation. *Minerva*, *42*, 361–376.

Scott, W. R. (2001). *Institutions and organizations*. Thousand Oaks, CA: Sage.

Scott, W. R., & Meyer, J. W. (1991). The organization of societal sectors: Proposition and early evidence. In P. J. DiMaggio & W. W. Powell (Eds.), *The new institutionalism in organizational analysis* (pp. 108–140). Chicago, IL: Chicago University Press.

Seyfried, M., & Pohlenz, P. (2013). Entwicklungen und professionalisierung im bereich der evaluation an Hochschulen – Zwischen kontrolle und akademischer selbstreflexion. In J. Hense, S. Rädiker, W. Böttcher, & T. Widmer (Eds.), Forschung über evaluation: Bedingungen, prozesse und wirkunge*n* (pp. 43–61). Münster: Waxmann.

Stein, R. (2009). Privatisierung des krankenhauses in berlin-Buch. In N. Böhlke, T. Gerlinger, K. Mosebach, R. Schmucker, & T. Schulten (Eds.), *Die privatisierung von krankenhäusern in deutschland und ihre auswirkungen auf beschäftigte und patienten* (pp. 153–163). Hamburg: VSA.

Stensaker, B. (2007). Quality as fashion: Exploring the translation of a management idea into higher education. In D. F. Westerheijden, B. Stensaker, & M. J. Rose (Eds.), Quality assurance in higher education: Trends in regulation, translation and transformation (pp. 99–118). Dordrecht: Springer Netherlands.

Westphal, J. D., Gulati, R., & Shortell, S. M. (1996). The institutionalization of total quality management: The emergence of normative TQM adoption and the consequences for organizational legitimacy and performance. In J. B. Keys & L. N. Dosier (Eds.), *Academy of Management Best Papers Proceedings 1996* (pp. 249–253). Statesboro, GA: College of Business Administration at Georgia Southern University.

Whitchurch, C. (2010). Optimising the potential of third space professionals in higher education. *Zeitschrift für Hochschulentwicklung*, *5*(4), 9–22.

Winter, M. (2012). Wettbewerb im hochschulbereich. In M. Winter & C. Würmann (Eds.), Wettbewerb Und Hochschulen. 6. Jahrestagung der Gesellschaft für Hochschulforschung in Wittenberg 2011. *Die Hochschule*, *21*(2), 17–45.

Wooten, M., & Hoffman, A. J. (2008). Organizational fields: Past, present and future of a core construct. In R. Greenwood, C. Oliver, R. Suddaby, & K. Sahlin-Andersson (Eds.), *The SAGE handbook of organizational institutionalism* (pp. 130–147). London: Sage.

Zucker, L. G. (1977). The role of institutionalization in cultural persistence. *American Sociological Review*, *42*(5), 726–743.

TRANSFORMING PROFESSIONAL BUREAUCRACIES IN HOSPITALS AND HIGHER EDUCATION INSTITUTIONS

Teresa Carvalho and Rui Santiago

ABSTRACT

The reforms that have been promoted in public organisations in developed countries since the 1970s are said to impose changes in professional bureaucracies by promoting self-governance and institutional autonomy and by challenging professionals' status and their values and standards. Taking the specific case of Portugal, this paper intends to contribute to understanding to what extent professional bureaucracies, like hospitals and Higher Education Institutions (HEIs), have been affected by changes in state policies and how the professionals involved have responded to these organisational changes. Based on an empirical qualitative study the paper concludes that there are significant differences in the way the state changed the regulatory framework and the professional archetypes in hospitals and HEIs and that professionals give heterogeneous responses to these changes.

Keywords: Professional bureaucracies; institutionalism; doctors; nurses; academics

Towards a Comparative Institutionalism: Forms, Dynamics and Logics Across the Organizational Fields of Health Care and Higher Education
Research in the Sociology of Organizations, Volume 45, 243–269

ISSN: 0733-558X/doi:10.1108/S0733-558X20150000045021

INTRODUCTION

Since the end of the 1970s, transformations occurring in public sectors in advanced capitalist societies have not only been submitted to intense national and international academic debates but also to broader discussions among political and administrative elites, and even within society at large. Although the question about changes in the public sector generates much controversy, it is undeniable that present transformations were designed and implemented by a state which centrally planned and executed a specific socio-political agenda (Deem, Hillyard, & Reed, 2007), aiming to modernise the state and to impose a new institutional and organisational order in the public sector, especially in more developed countries.

This so-called modernisation has usually been described under diverse epithets with the most popular being: New Public Management (NPM), *managerialism*, entrepreneurialism or governance. Even if some differences are evidenced between them, they all attempt to characterise political initiatives that emphasise the imperatives of efficiency and efficacy, the orientation to the users' – now mainly signified as customers or clients – needs and the extension of market (or quasi-market) mechanisms to the public systems and institutions responsible for steering mechanisms (Ferlie, Ashburner, Fitzgerald, & Pettigrew, 1996; Hood, 1991; Pollitt & Boukaert, 2000). Public organisations have a fundamental role in the implementation of NPM/managerialism since they represent the main mediators used to promote the intended transformations in the public sector. In this context, the traditional way public organisations were organised – based on the hierarchical and bureaucratic structures and processes – has been severely questioned. Hierarchy and bureaucracy, as theorised by Max Weber (1995), have been represented as corporatist, static and inefficient (Hayek, 2014) and considered to be an obstacle to the enactment of a new *modus operandi* which organisations are compelled to assume so as to be in line with the new competitive environment and social demands. Subsequently, the advocates of NPM stressed the alleged virtues of flexibility and adaptability and called for political action to (re)programme organisational structures, power architecture, decision-making channels and the role and work of professionals.

In Portugal, the modernisation of the public welfare system started to be a popular subject in the late 1990s, when NPM was politically selected as the *magnum opus* in policy formation and implementation towards the reconfiguring of the public sector. The target was firstly the health system

(Carvalho, 2009) and, as expected, it was also extended to Higher Education (HE) (Carvalho & Santiago, 2010). Efficiency, competition, entrepreneurialism, market, consumers' choice and consumers' satisfaction became a dominant rhetoric in political and institutional discourses (Amaral, Magalhães, & Santiago, 2003; Carvalho, 2009; Magalhães & Santiago, 2012; Santiago, Magalhães, & Carvalho, 2005). Subsequently, since the beginning of the 2000s, the ideological support for substantial transformations in power structures and decision-making processes in health and Higher Education Institutions (HEIs) has come to the fore. The concentration of policy and strategic power at the central level, the decentralisation of operations to the intermediate levels and the deployment of line management represented the major traces in the attempts to institutionalise a new organisational order in health (especially in hospitals) and in HE. These attempts aimed to reconfigure the traditional bureaucratic professional structures and processes that were considered to be mainly serving corporatist interests and, at the same time, to have a static and inefficient character (Carvalho & Santiago, 2010; Clarke & Newman, 1997). Tendencies to implement NPM/managerialism political and organisational principles in Portugal were also recognised in other developed countries. Some comparative social policy studies (Carvalho & Bruckmann, 2014; Pollitt & Boukaert, 2000) have tried to analyse public reforms framed by NPM/managerialism and respective organisational responses by comparing different national initiatives and countries. Less emphasis has been devoted to changes in the public institutions' organisational heartland or, in other words, in their internal structures, processes and professionals' behaviour, as well as into cross-sector differences in these topics. Taking the specific case of Portugal, this paper addresses the following questions:

- To what extent have professional bureaucracies like hospitals and HEIs been affected by changes in state policies?
- How have the professionals involved interpreted and responded to these organisational changes?

The paper is structured as follows. First, an overall synthesis of the 'state of the art' related to professional bureaucracies and the changes that have been occurring within it is presented. Then, an account of the methodological aspects of the study is given, followed by the presentation of the findings on changes in the regulatory pillar and its impact on organisations. Finally, the main conclusions of the study are presented along with new guidelines for further research and the improvement of knowledge in this field.

PROFESSIONAL BUREAUCRACIES

The welfare state model, embedded in European democratic societies, was constructed through the association between bureaucracy and specialised professional knowledge. Weber (1995) was the first to analyse this symbiotic connection by linking the expansion of the bureaucracy, as the organisational rational basis sustaining the development of capitalist societies, with expert professionals. For Weber (1989, 1995) the legitimacy for taking decisions at the institutional level could be based on appointment or on a collegial-based regime legitimated through election. The bureaucratic-collegial regime, as a singular form of bureaucracy, allowed professionals to become co-producers of the local rules and to define the general conditions under which professional work was developed. This was expressed in the presence of professionals in the institutions' governing bodies, with deliberative power, as well as in their control of the institutions 'heartland'. Based on the legitimacy of standardised qualifications (Mintzberg, 1994) professionals also enjoyed much autonomy. Furthermore, professional careers were also structured under the bureaucratic logic following three of its basic traces, namely hierarchy; merit (linked to technical competency) and the ideal of calling or vocation (McKinlay, 2012).

Hospitals and universities were an illustrative example of these co-determination mechanisms, as well as of the strategic alliance that historically has been established between the bureaucratic and professional logics (Mintzberg, 1994). Whether renamed as professional bureaucracies (Mintzberg, 1994) or professional organisations (Greenwood & Hinings, 1993) this specific type of bureaucracy started to be under strong attack in the last three decades and was severely questioned in Western countries.

In Portugal, this phenomenon became particularly visible in the beginning of the 2000s. Parallel to questioning the welfare state principles, the limitations and disadvantages of professional bureaucracies were also emphasised. The dominant narrative stressed the idea that professional bureaucracies were unable to maintain equity, to ensure freedom of choice, to set priorities according to other interests beyond their own, to produce the expected results, to be more flat and oriented to society and to accept evaluation and external control (Clarke & Newman, 1997). It was assumed that only by replacing collegial or professional bureaucratic structures and implementing new forms of decision-making would it be possible to have more flexible and adaptable public organisations. This was perceived as an important endeavour in order to orient services delivery to results, focused on user interests and demands, and to make public organisations more accountable (open to social and economic control).

On the ground, the policy attempts to promote this replacement impelled public organisations to the sphere of the private enterprise/entrepreneurial-like model. NPM intended to promote a rupture with the past, stimulating the vertical integration of organisations, as to transform them into unified and complete entities. Decentralisation and delegated autonomy were expected to turn hospitals and HEIs into sort of complete organisations (Enders, De Boer, & Leisyle, 2008), through the unification of their structures and decision-making channels (Carvalho & Santiago, 2010; Magalhães & Santiago, 2012). To enable this vertical integration, and based on widespread beliefs about their inefficiency and corporatist interests, political initiatives were developed to limit professionals' power and autonomy.

Transforming Bureaucracies

The first theoretical developments surrounding the new (neo-)institutionalism in the social sciences put an emphasis on the external forces towards organisational homogenisation to the detriment of internal ones. According to DiMaggio and Powell (1983, 1991; see also Powell & DiMaggio, 1991), organisations tend to be more homogenised than diverse, not as a result of the competitive pressures stimulating the expansion of an universal model of bureaucracy (competitive isomorphism) towards efficiency attainment, as Weber (1995) suggested, but instead, from state, professions and social classes' practices translating into institutional isomorphism. According to this approach, organisations are conceptualised as institutionalised structures of power and authority that overlap with actors' micro-level practices (Reed, 1999). In other words, the internal processes of institutionalisation, other than the actors' selective reproduction of the scripts, values and beliefs present in the political, social and cultural environment, were not taken into account, namely the conflicts, negotiations and bargain events, as well as the inter- and intra-professional groups' power relations. That is why more recent strands of new institutionalism tend to emphasise the role of power and social skills in the construction of an organisational field (Fligstein, 1999; Lounsbury & Ventresca, 2003).

However, this construction is not only a process developed at the macro or meso levels but also at the micro organisational level. The specific field of an organisation is an important locus of the institutionalisation processes. The 'old' institutionalism complements some important conceptual elements and analytical concerns raised by the new institutionalists, due to the particular attention it gives to the ways in which myths, symbols and social cognitions are locally constructed and negotiated (Selznick, 1996). The combination of the 'old' and new institutionalism can be especially pertinent in the analysis of the outcomes resulting from the external and internal environments' interactions, enabled by the construction of meanings of its different elements, as well as in the role these outcomes can have in organisational stability and change.

The analysis of the effects of health and HE reforms at the institutional level cannot be taken as a matter of direct top-down influence. Changes involved in reforms are not only a game played between the macro environmental stimulus, oriented to produce structural and cognitive-cultural changes in organisations (Scott, 2001; Zucker, 1991), and their responses to it. This game is more complex, being played also at the meso and micro levels, that is through the ways in which organisations interact and professionals interpret and respond to both the macro pressures as well as the ways these are locally translated, in particular by local leadership structures (Carvalho & Santiago, 2010). In this context, the conceptual relevance of new institutionalism stems from its concerns with the presence of two analytical dimensions in the dual but interconnected dynamic of *de-institutionalisation* and *re-institutionalisation*: the external constraints, particularly those emanating from the state, social groups and professions and the internal, human factors, including actors' inter-subjectivity, values, beliefs, cognitive schemas and institutional scripts (Oliver, 1991; Olsen, 2007; Scott, 2001).

As professional bureaucracies, hospitals and HEIs are privileged arenas in influencing institutionalisation from a bottom-up perspective (Cohen, March, & Olsen, 1972). As these institutions are framed by different areas of specialised professional knowledge and expert skills (Freidson, 2001) which operate under different logics and often are loosely connected, professionals in these areas/fields engage in strategic action movements, based on the interpretation of their own and others' situations which influence a specific institutionalisation process. The neo-institutionalism approach (Greenwood & Hinings, 1993), based on its proposal around the archetype concept, can be rather useful to understand the intersection between two main forms of professional actors' sense-making mechanisms: (a) as reproducers of the institutionalised elements present in the environment, including the organisational field and (b) as producers of new institutional elements, through insights arising from their interpretations of external (and internal) constraints. An archetype, as Greenwood and Hinings (1993,

p. 1055) define it, is '(…) an interpretative scheme, or a set of beliefs and values, that is embodied in an organisation's structures and systems'.

The way an interpretative scheme becomes dominant in an organisation depends on power structures developed by different groups of actors in a specific field (Fligstein, 1999). Changes in archetypes are not harmonious and do not follow a linear process, consequently resulting in ambiguous outcomes, as the hybridisation thesis demonstrates (Carvalho & Santiago, 2010). In this sense, an in-depth comprehension of archetype formation can be improved through the conceptual insights brought by other institutionalism approaches. This is the case, for example, of those theories emphasising the cognitive processes at work in the enactment of the organisational actors' preferences and choices (Greenwood & Hinings, 1993; Oliver, 1991; Simon, 1996). Following this line of thought, it can be hypothesised that there is no clear causal links in the selection and/or construction of archetypes. Choices, preferences and interpretative schemes can be imposed by dominant coalitions which emerge from negotiations, bargaining and political internal actions resulting from different power structures where actors and groups operate (Fligstein, 1999).

Following this line of thought, organisations (hospitals and HEIs included), can thus be analysed as political *arenas*, or at least as political *spaces* where professional groups try to manipulate the decision-making agenda. Through this manipulation these groups gain a sufficient amount of power to define the regulation and control rules that ensure them a hegemonic role in the organisation's structuring and functioning. The substance of this hegemony is as important as the processes that give rise to it. Actually, the social and ideological background shaping the dominant group's actions delimit the type of interests and values which they try to impose on the organisation at a given moment, such as those linked to changes in its power architecture and decision-making process (Carvalho, 2012).

In sum, one can consider that the theories on the cognitive processes involved in preferences and choice are relevant to grasping the dynamics that lead to the selection and/or the (re)construction of archetypes. In fact, in each organisation the generation and negotiation of meanings, symbolic codes, cultural categories (Zucker, 1991), norms, power (Fligstein, 1999) and organisational knowledge act as the basis for informing actors about organisational practices. And, in this way, they are also the main elements in the (re)production of the organisational archetypes and, subsequently, their organisations' *modus operandi* (Simon, 1996). The structures, processes and cultures of organisations are shaped by interpretative schemes which are supposed to be shared by all or a substantive part of organisational members, at least in their main traces. Changes in organisations involve the questioning of pre-existent dominant archetypes and eventually their replacement by new ones. But, this happens only if the new archetypes are legitimised by a different set of values, beliefs, norms, rules and ideologies which have to be shared by a large number of organisational actors. One of the aims of this study is thus to analyse the extent to which the bureaucratic professional institutionalised archetypes of hospitals and HEIs are giving way to new archetypes sustained in NPM principles. Before we consider this, one should reflect briefly on the peculiarities of the Portuguese context.

PUBLIC SECTOR TRANSFORMATIONS IN PORTUGAL

When analysing public sector transformations in Portugal, the country's singularities have to be taken into consideration. Two of them are especially relevant, namely the particular characteristics of its welfare state model and the way the country has responded to the recent global financial crisis initiated in 2008. Following the 1974 democratic revolution, both health and HE reforms were undertaken (Torgal, 2012). In 1976, the National Health Service (NHS) was institutionalised and new universities that had been created in 1972 were strengthened. After this first period, four other key moments or phases can be identified in public policies: (i) the progressive withdrawal from welfare state; (ii) the approach towards a market-based ideology; (iii) corporatisation and approach towards neoliberalism and (iv) the austerity's narratives and practices. Below we provide a succinct analysis of each one of these key phases.

The first period occurred between 1980 and 1994 and can be defined as 'the progressive withdrawal from traditional welfare state values'. In the realm of health, a new legal Act (1990) acknowledged private providers as a structural component of the NHS. At the institutional level, hospitals were ruled as professional bureaucracies, although under a more pronounced direct state control when compared to HEIs. Within this framework, doctors and nurses (particularly the former) held dominant positions either at the top (Administrative Council) or at the level of the clinical units. In the realm of HE, this first period is defined by 'normalisation', even though new public universities and polytechnics (following the institutionalisation of a HE binary system) were created, and private institutions (both universities and polytechnics) were emerging. Simultaneously, an autonomy law was approved (University Law 108/88; Polytechnic Law 5/90) allowing HEIs greater autonomy to establish their internal statutes. Both in hospitals and HEIs the alliance between bureaucracy and professionalism allowed their categorisation as bureaucratic-collegial or professional bureaucracies (Mintzberg, 1994).

From 1995 to 2001 a second momentum emerged in the health and HE systems that can be characterised as 'the approach to market-based ideology'. The rhetoric of the welfare state crisis echoed both in political narratives and in society at large. Attempts to provide hospitals with more autonomy and managers with the right to manage resulted in a first experience of private management in a public hospital in 1993, extended later to other hospitals. In HE, in this same period, market and managerial pressures over HEIs become more explicit as well (Carvalho & Santiago, 2010).

A third momentum of 'corporatisation and approach to neo-liberalism principles' erupted between 2002 and 2010. This was the time when public policy formation and implementation were informed by NPM/managerialism (Carvalho & Bruckmann, 2014). In health, a growing wave of NPM initiatives found its way into hospitals when 31 public hospitals were transformed into corporate organisations, that is state enterprise hospitals (Law 27/2002, 8 November). As a consequence of these changes, hospitals' annual budgets started to be based on performance contracts negotiated with the Ministry of Health. This was followed by attempts to formalise an accountability culture and to institutionalise human resource management policies focused on individual contracts. Inspired by NPM, hospitals' organisational chains of command were redesigned. Power was then concentrated at the top, and line management was deployed, supported by a recomposition of the previous bureaucratic hierarchic chains of command and control. In HE, a new legal Act (Law, 62/2007), known as the RJIES (*Juridical Regime for Higher Education Institutions*), was passed, imposing a new internal governance and management model. In 2008 the new legal framework expanded NPM/managerialism principles to professionals. Law 12A-2008 changed all public servants statutes, transforming them into workers in public duties (the new professionals established a contractual relation with public organisations based on individual contracts). The Decree-Laws 205/2009 (for universities) and 207/2009 (for polytechnics) changed the academic career paths that had remained unchanged since the end of the 1970s. Even if this new statute maintained the bureaucratic, hierarchical logic it nonetheless altered the access to the academic career that started to be based on possessing a PhD degree. Temporary and part-time contracts were also introduced, turning the attainment of a tenured position more difficult.

The fourth and last moment can be defined as 'the austerity narratives and practices' which emerged in 2010 and are still present today. In Portugal political initiatives to decrease the public expenses (especially human resources) started to be developed as a consequence of the financial and sovereign debt crisis. In Portugal, since that time, there has been a decrease in public employment and impressive cuts in workers' salaries. The reduction in public expenses was mainly exercised in the form of wage cuts and staff reductions. Attempts were made to approach public and private Human Resource Management (HRM), namely with individual contracts and by increasing insecurity and flexibility.

METHODS

The study is based on a mixed-method case study design (Bryman, 2006), with desktop analysis of major policy documents and face-to-face interviews as the main data gathering devices. On the desktop front, the main legal acts intending to promote transformations in HEIs (Law 62/2007) and hospitals (Law 27/2002 and Decree-Law 93/2005) were analysed in detail. A total of 55 semi-structured interviews were carried out with 17 academics, 18 physicians and 20 nurses between July 2012 and July 2013. All the interviews were voluntary. The qualitative study was preceded by a quantitative one, based on an online survey, in which respondents could state their availability to be interviewed. The majority of academics were from universities, with only four interviewees working in polytechnics. Physicians and nurses were working in central hospitals located all over the country. Taking professional groups' internal heterogeneity into consideration, only those with management responsibilities were selected. The reason for this is because these professionals assume a *mediating* role between organisational policies and the professionals groups. Interviews were based on a guideline developed around three main sets of questions: one based on professionals' perceptions of the recent reforms in HE and health; another based on professionals' perceptions of their own profession and their specific roles and a third group about socio-demographic variables. Content analysis was used to interpret the data (Miles & Huberman, 1994). Categories were first created from the interviewees' discourses, contrasted and compared with the theoretical framework. These processes generated a set of themes based on which analysis was developed, namely changes imposed by state policies, the impact of changes on the institutions' (re) organisation, influence of the new organisational environment in professional behaviour and the concentration of power and constrains to collegiality.

CHANGES IN THE REGULATORY PILLAR AND ITS IMPACT ON ORGANISATIONS

Based on the content analysis of policy documents, three categories were identified as relevant, namely the legal status, the organisational structure and the professionals' regulation. Furthermore, the organisational structure was subdivided into three additional themes, namely strategic top, organisation of units and rhetoric.

The Legal Status

The proposed transformations in the legal status of public institutions include one of the main differences in state proposals for steering health and HE. It was in the hospitals' governance and management structures that changes were imposed in a more coercive way. In contrast, a more flexible space of action was allowed to HEIs to operationalise their organisational structures. In this context, both transformations translated to, in practice, a retreat from the traditional, bureaucratic-collegial framework and an approach towards a more enterprising/entrepreneurial model. These changes are also related to the attempts to cut public expenses. In fact, hospitals were coercively transformed into public enterprises with the main objective of leaving health costs out of the public expenditure. With this new statute hospitals are still in the state public sphere but are ruled by private law. In HE, the possibility for HEIs to be transformed into public foundations (ruled by private law) was exercised on a voluntary basis. Actually, in HE, political initiatives seemed to be more cautious of the temptation to impose coercive changes from the outside, revealing the historical levels of autonomy enjoyed by HEIs (academic oligarchy). As opposed to hospitals where the top administrators have always (and still are) been appointed by the Ministry, the election principle was maintained in HEIs, as a legal-rational principle of power legitimacy. And, although expectations for line management were visible in the 2007 HE Act, an internal space of negotiation was allowed with regards to the definition of the size of general councils, the type of basic units (Faculty, School or Department) and the models of academic management. Attempts to de-institutionalise the traditional archetype on governance and management were only partially achieved. It is thus possible to argue that with the 2007 HE Act, the bottom-up collegial model, strongly institutionalised in the HE system, was replaced by a sort of limited top-down collegial model (Lazega & Wattebled, 2011).

Two main factors can be identified to justify these different strategies of reform or, more specifically, of change in the legal statutes of hospitals and HEIs. The first is linked to the distinct historical transformations that occurred in the two systems and institutions following the 1974 Portuguese democratic revolution. In HEIs, collegial structures were deployed at all universities' organisational levels, from the bottom to the top, mainly as a reaction against the strong elitist and repressive character of the 'political university' of the previous dictatorship regime (Torgal, 2012). The fragmentation and dispersion of power and of the *locus* of decision-making were seen as a way to improve representative democracy at the institutional level. At the same time, this power fragmentation was interpreted as a mechanism to support the institutionalisation of the Humboldtian and welfare-state principles, that is the articulation between teaching, research and services to society (Carvalho, 2012). In organisational terms, this configured a way of structuring and functioning that was closer to the metaphor of 'organisational anarchy' (Cohen et al., 1972) or to the idea of loosely coupled organisations (Weick, 1976) similar to what was common in other western HE fields (Clark, 1983). In spite of the attempts of the reform initiated in 2007 to promote a rupture with these organisational structures, the legislation left a great space for HEIs to choose their organisational structures, especially at the middle level. Most probably this was because the key political actors involved in these reforms (the ministry and consultants) were academics and did not want to confront their peers with an imposition that would turn the reform unacceptable as institutions and academics had been achieving greater levels of autonomy since 1974.

In hospitals on the other hand, the 1974 democratic revolution did not promote transformational changes in administrative and management models. This was to be expected since HE was used as the 'ideological arm' of the dictatorship (Carvalho, 2012) while hospitals were less instrumentally used by the regime and so the need for change was not so pressing after 1974. The vertical integration of their administrative functions was maintained, configuring a multi-divisional structure model, typical of the traditional liberal corporate capitalism (Larson, 2013). In this model there was the recognition of the professional authority (doctors and nurses were members of the hospitals administrative councils with executive functions) but in a more subordinate way when compared with HEIs. Furthermore, as opposed to HE, the 2002 reform in the hospital system was mainly designed by a minister coming from the industry. The second factor is connected to the technological complexity involved in the operations of hospitals and HEIs. This complexity is higher in health than in HE, which induces an increasing need for specialised administrative roles. Health operations and practices imply the well-being and even the life of patients, being a 'vital and universal need for individuals and communities' (Larson, 2013, p. 24), which is not the case in HE, although it has a key cultural, social and economic relevance in modern societies. Thus, management of hospitals by hierarchy was, eventually, considered as more effective to politically achieve the objective of controlling health costs while maintaining the hospital services and professionals under the control of the state, meaning assuring that health provision remained mainly a public responsibility.

Changes in Organisational Structures

Governance and Management Bodies

When analysing the proposed changes in the organisational structure, it becomes evident that state policies intended to transform the governance and management models of traditional hospitals and HEIs. The organisational system imposed on HEIs included as bodies at the top: the General Council (in charge of approving the planning, budgets, creation and extinction of basic units and for the rectors/president election); the Rector (for universities) or President (for the polytechnics), who became executives supported by a Management Council (in charge of decisions regarding operational matters); the Chief Financial Officer (*Fiscal Unico*) and in the Foundation case the board of trustees (*Conselho de Curadores*). Within this new organisational system the General Council has the prominent role. The law stipulates that this body can be constituted by 15–35 members including representatives of teachers and researchers (>50%), students and administrative staff (≥20%) and invited individuals of recognised merit external to the HEIs (≥30%). So, within this new governance structure, academics, particularly at the organisational heartland level, have fewer opportunities to participate in institutional policies and strategies formulation. In the previous bureaucratic-collegial governance and management model, this role was accomplished by a great number of elected academics in the Senate (in some institutions academic Senates still exist but only with a consultant role). For hospital institutions the law imposes the existence of three governance and management bodies, namely the Administrative Council (in charge of administration, planning and operations), Chief Financial Officer (*Fiscal Unico*) and Consultative Council (integrating professionals designated to advise the Administrative Council). The Administrative Council or Management Board is composed of one president (CEO) and two executives (that can be extended to four taking into consideration the size of the hospital). All are general managers having the designation of public managers and are directly appointed by the Health Ministry. The president or CEO can be a doctor but usually is someone with a first degree in law or economics and a post-graduate in health or hospital management. He/she has overall responsibility of the hospital and is supported by an executive committee of two to four other general managers. This Administration Council also includes a technical direction with two non-executive elements: the clinical director and the nurse director appointed by the president of the Management Board. However these professionals are not full equals in the running of the hospital. Medical or clinical directors only have consultant roles, and their influence on strategic decision is dependent on their negotiation of the hierarchy, at least informally, with the president or CEO. The CEO figure and the reference to external audits are common to both hospitals and HEIs which translates to attempts to institutionalise an accountability culture, based on quality assessment and performance evaluation exercises. The analysis of the proposals for changes in organisations' leadership structures makes it evident that in both institutions the community principle is giving way to hierarchical forms with a strong concentration of power in the top and in committees with a low participation of professionals. So, even if using different configurations and, once again, with HEIs having more freedom to decide on their structures than hospitals, it is clear that the main intent of the recent reforms is to restrict professionals' participation in institutional policies and strategic decisions formation and to focus on fewer and more managerial-oriented bodies.

Changes in the Middle Organisational Level

In analysing changes proposed at the middle level – in the organisation of the unit – it is again evident that changes are more coercively imposed in hospitals. For HEIs, it was provided that the governance and management bodies at the middle level would be defined by internal legal norms and rules. This means that it is possible to find different structures in the basic units between HEIs, and even that institutions can create middle level structures which are not exactly aligned with the expectations and general regulatory principles stemming from the top. Contrary to what would be expected given the adapted model, in hospitals the operational decentralisation is delegated to basic units, which are incentivised to work as Responsibility Centres (*Centros de responsabilidade integrada*). The main intent of this decentralisation is to allow service directors (doctors) to be more in charge of management duties and be accountable for the units' management. Similar to what has happened in France (Neogy & Kirkpatrick, 2009) clinical directors are now committed to an executive role encompassing a strong concentration of operational matters such as budget responsibility for staff, small equipment and pharmaceuticals, issues of quality, practice protocols and budgets.

Another reason for giving HEIs more freedom to decide on their internal structures may be related to the fact that HEIs, more than hospitals, are conceived as knowledge intensive organisations (Deem et al., 2007). This is in the sense that knowledge production and dissemination, in its different epistemological (the what, why and how of knowledge is produced) and ontological (for what purposes and for whom) forms are mediators of all HEIs' operations (teaching, research, consulting, cooperation with and services to society). It is expected that to produce and disseminate knowledge, and to promote scientific advancement, academics should enjoy a relatively high level of autonomy and independence in their work. In fact, the prototypical characteristics of HEIs as knowledge intensive organisations were still acknowledged in the law that maintained all different structural elements of autonomy (academic, cultural, scientific, pedagogical, disciplinary, administrative and financial).

Rhetoric on Strategic Change

The use of language is one important tool to allow organisational cultural-cognitive change aligned with organisational structures. As argued by Greenwood and Hinings (1993), to change an organisational archetype presupposes change in the structure and also in the interpretative scheme used by local actors. Hence, if structures are changing – to be more competitive and enterprise-like – so does language, as a fundamental tool to institutionalise new norms, beliefs, scripts and values. Using this general context, one could expect that the rhetorical arguments used would be the same in both the health and the HE regulatory frameworks. However, important differences were found. The principles of economic rationality are more prevalent in health when compared to HE. Throughout the text (legal documents) one can find several references to efficiency and efficacy in the use of resources. An example of this is Article 5 of Law 27/2002 when it refers to the management principles that must be accomplished: '*b) To guarantee to users the delivery of care with quality and a rigorous control of the resources used*' or '*d) To finance the activities in accordance with the valorisation of the acts and services that are effectively accomplished, based on a predefined price by common accord with the NHS*' (authors' own translation). These management principles translate into a new conceptualisation and legitimation for public health services. The references to the traditional service public ethos or to the patients' welfare are almost absent without a clear reference to the rational use of available resources.

In the case of HE, the existing legislation seems to be on the opposite side as there is an emphasis on the traditional mission and the public service ethos of HEIs. An example is Article 106 of Law 62/2007 defining independence and role conflict: '*1. Members of HEIs' governing and management bodies are exclusively in service of the public interest of their institutions and are independent in exercising their roles*' (authors' own translation). Nevertheless, there are also references to the possibility for creating economic value from research, resulting in a tendency to approach HEIs along a market orientation already mentioned in earlier studies (Santiago, Carvalho, & Relva, 2008). The same ambiguity is also visible for students. On the one hand, HE is defined as an important instrument to promote equal opportunities, meaning that there is legitimacy to support public provision of social services for students (like scholarships for students with economic difficulties). On the other hand, enhancing students' employability is identified as one of HEIs' core responsibilities, inducing the idea that students should be trained for the labour market or for a specific profession. In this sense students simultaneously assume the roles of citizens and consumers or clients. In fact, even if there are no explicit references to students as consumers or clients, there is a general sense that the trust relations between students and teachers have been broken since the figure of Student Ombudsman (*Provedor do Estudante*) was created in 2007. That said, one cannot ignore the fact that the creation of this figure can also be the result of attempts to prevent professors from behaving unethically towards their students, contributing to balancing a previously unequal power relation between the two.

Professionals' Regulation

One important dimension in the way professional bureaucracies can transform their dominant archetype is related to professionals' regulation. Both in health and in HE, changes in the legal framework have allowed the respective institutions to employ staff directly and to determine the terms and conditions of employment. As a consequence, health and HE professionals no longer have the traditional standardised employment practices which have characterised public bureaucracies (Ferlie et al., 1996). Coexisting in each type of institution there are now, at least, two different groups with distinct employment status: public employees, with a collective contract, and public employees, with individual contracts. The first group's career prospects maintain the traditional bureaucratic-like terms of work based on full-time employment, job security and standard salary levels. The others do not have a job-for-life expectation, seeing their salary and career prospects mainly dependent on line managers' perceptions of their performance and, in this regard, are much closer to private professionals' working conditions. This is usually classified as one of the most dramatic changes in the public sector. Even if this is a common feature in the two sectors, once again there is an important difference in the case of HE, as there has been an increasing tendency for externally regulating the deregulated professionals. For instance, Law 62/2007 presents norms for the balance that all institutions must find between tenured and non-tenured staff. At the same time, this Law assumed the employment stability principle, which is an important device to stabilise the teaching programmes and research activities, and for stipulating the existence of similar working conditions for academics at public and private institutions alike.

To sum up, one can say that changes coercively imposed by the regulatory framework are not similar in both sectors and public institutions. When analysing the cases of Portuguese health and HE it is possible to find common tendencies for turning organisations into hierarchical forms, through managerialism and in contrast to the traditional bureaucracies (Weber, 1995), and for concentrating power at the top. This does not necessarily mean those professionals (like doctors or academics) are not taking part in institutional decisions, nor that in previous organisational models professionals' groups were not internally diverse and hierarchical. What it means is that alternative organisational forms emerged as a result of a structural downsizing with the middle level collegial bodies being almost suppressed. The centralisation process at the top is also seen in the middle level. There is a decentralisation of the management operations at this level, with a high concentration of executive power in middle managers. These changes, which can be interpreted as an attempt to substitute professional bureaucracies by more vertically integrated and corporate-like organisational models, are supported by an economic and managerial rhetoric, especially within health care. Adding to this, in both sectors, professionals have experienced a decline in their work and employment conditions. However there are important differences between the two sectors. Changes are imposed more coercively in hospitals. HEIs have more freedom to decide on their intermediated model of governance, since state policies endorsed some of the traditional bureaucratic-professional archetypes and have imposed limits on professionals' de-regulation. The previous cultural-cognitive environment in the two sectors may influence these differences. However, a relevant hypothesis is that these can be the result of the specific struggles that different actors develop in the field (Fligstein, 1999).

Professionals' Perceptions

As a result of social transformations in modernity, with organisations assuming an increasing importance within society, it has been widely accepted that it is not possible to analyse professionals' archetypes without considering the organisational structures within which these professionals operate (Faulconbridge & Muzio, 2008; Ferlie et al., 1996; Neogy & Kirkpatrick, 2009). Knowing that the bureaucratic-collegial frameworks of hospitals and HEIs have changed in different ways (as mentioned above), it is therefore relevant to analyse how professionals within these institutions are interpreting these changes. As shown earlier, changes in the organisational structures of hospitals and HEIs can be conceived as enablers for transforming the roles of dominant or more traditional professional groups (like academics in HE and doctors and nurses in health) by allocating more power to managers and to external stakeholders. In a certain sense the external constraints imposed by coercive isomorphism favour managers (general managers, academic managers and health professional managers) since their beliefs, values and norms are supposed to be better aligned with the new interpretative schemes proposed by NPM/managerialism. In fact, being the mediators between external constraints and professionals, the translation by managers of the NPM/managerialism assumptions and instruments to the inner fabric of organisations enables the *de-institutionalisation* of the previous bureaucratic-collegial interpretative schemes. This can be also enacted by copying successful practices attained by some organisations in either sector.

However, the picture is a bit more complex. There are also local conflicts, bargains, coalitions, negotiations and compromises which can contribute to shaping the reconfiguration and/or replacement of the conflicting interpretive schemes in each individual organisation (Fligstein, 1999). These processes occur not only in vertical terms, for instance in the conflicts and negotiation of the hierarchy jurisdictions, but also in horizontal ones, between groups who try to turn their preferences and choices hegemonic. The work of Oliver (1991), which categorises the organisations' strategic responses to external impositions – acquiescence, compromise, avoidance, defiance and manipulation – is not only a pertinent illustration of the limitation of the organisational homogenisation thesis but also a mirror of the complexity of the internal processes in negotiating archetypes. Mahoney and Thelen (2010) also argue that institutions contain within them the possibility of change which is driven by the potential effects this change may have in institutions' power distribution.

Interviews conducted with academics, nurses and doctors reveal that all of them recognise the existence of deep changes in their organisational structures and interpretative schemes. These changes streaming from NPM/managerialism informed interpretative schemes – budget constraints, regulatory devices, efficiency and output-driven forms of control, value for money and the like – encompassing rhetoric devices or tangible aspects. In this sense, it can be detected that some actors perceived externally imposed homogeneity in top governance and management. But, when talking about the felt impact on their work and practices, the statements are less homogeneous. The three professional groups (especially academics) recognise that changes imposed by state policies interfere with hospitals and HEIs' autonomy and, in this way, also impact on their own professional autonomy.

> I think that the most painful is the loss of autonomy of the university. Each time this is more regulated by the Directives and by outside pressures, many are indirect, are by budgetary and regulatory constraints, and other things. Each time there is less space for the institutions, their departments, their groups, seeking their space, their own partnerships. (Interview 14A; Male Academic)

However there are relevant differences in the professionals' narratives in health and HE. For instance, both professionals in health and HE recognise the existence of a more managerial culture in the institution's environment. However academics tend to interpret this phenomenon mainly as a consequence of external constraints over HEIs' strategies:

> (...) The university's strategy, which is more managerial, is more oriented to financial issues. The pedagogic and training issues, which should be the aim of the university, are not taken into account in the same way (...). These issues have to be more present in the university policies and strategies. (...) the management issues have been limiting our action. (Interview 7E; Female Academic)

Nurses and doctors tend to emphasise that changes are not only rhetorical but also translate into transformation of the institutions' mission and purposes.

> People with management responsibilities, anyone (being a, b or c) always think: 'I'm here to manage the hospital in an efficient way' .... (Interview 7I; Female Nurse)

> For me the main differences in the hospital is that before we had already some concerns with the results but the main concern was to do the best for the patient; today the first and most important concern/value is the hospital's profit. (Interview 9A; Male Doctor)

These changes are having some impacts on professionals' subjectivity and professionalism, or at least on the previous archetypes based on the alliance and co-determination between bureaucracy and professional logics. However, the avoidance, non-consent or resistance attitudes against the institutions' new NPM/managerialism scripts, belief and values are not shared by all professionals. It was possible to find in a few nurses an almost integral incorporation of some of the managerialist assumptions in their discourse – value for money, efficiency and the alignment of professional work by customer satisfaction:

> One of our main goals is to combat the waste of money, manage resources in an efficient way and, most of all, to satisfy our customer. (Interview 27C; Female Nurse)

However, this new discourse does not seem dominant since there is also another relevant group who is resisting the 'intrusion' of a managerial discourse in health:

> I think that now people are more concerned with profitability than with care and I don't agree with it. People talk a lot about resources and economy and less about caring. I think we are concentrating in efficiency, because 'it has to be' ... and the other side is also made but with a minor emphasis. (Interview 82J; Female Nurse)

Taking the previous analysis of legal changes in the organisational structures one would also expect differences in the perceptions among the three professional groups over their participation in decision-making that, in turn, relates to their professional autonomy.

Actually, interviewees refer to a feeling of threat to professional autonomy, particularly at the organisational decision-making governance level. Following the professional views, the organisational archetypes of 'bottom-up' power, translating the deliberative power professionals have into decision-making, institutionalised under professional bureaucracy hegemony (Mintzberg, 1994) seem to be questioned by a new top-down rationality and line management. This is particularly highlighted in academics' discourses that recognise a decrease in their presence in collegial bodies configuring what can be called as a loss of professional organisational autonomy.

> I would say we lost voice. Lost our voice (…). We do not always have this ability as directors because we do not always have access to the right bodies. We do not have a presence in the scientific board where everything is decided. (Interview 11A; Male Academic)

The recognition of a decreased presence in collegial bodies is also accompanied by references to the loss of control over professional regulation which was transferred to external evaluation apparatuses, formalised by the state and implemented by regulatory agencies. Academics and medical professionals recognise that they lost control over organisational initiatives which are seen as crucial for regulating the profession, including work practices. Decisions over recruitment and performance evaluation are among the areas of professional action which were acknowledged as being out of the professionals' self-control.

> Now it is clear that evaluation systems that exist and are being implemented are systems that regulate, control … we had an evaluation system very independent, very autonomous … this new one, from my point of view, will be more restrictive and imposing some values. We know that those norms which are presented for the evaluation can't be modified in any way by us. I know … I know that even if my team has 50% of very good professionals, I can't make that assessment, it is something that is imposed on me, this is an external control of the profession. (…) the legislation imposes on me and this is a way to control the profession. (Interview 5E; Male Nurse)

Alongside the decline of participation in collegial decisions, there is also recognition by professionals that information and power have been increasingly concentrated at the top governance and management levels. This is particularly evidenced by health professionals – both doctors and nurses.

> When we speak of a public corporation, in any area, one thing everyone should know is organisation strategy. It must be shared with employees and this is not happening … we live in obscurity, no one has the faintest idea … the information is simply not shared. What do I mean by this? Nobody has the faintest idea of what you're doing. (Interview 7E; Male Nurse)

The absence of deliberative participation in decision-making processes at the central administration level leads to the perception of professionals in both sectors of a rather unclear definition of management objectives and strategies for the organisation, partly since professionals and managers work on opposite sides. It seems that organisational initiatives are distributed by managers (management of institutions) and professional groups (professional objectives) in a distinct way. As such, there are no causal links, or no interconnections between the two. In this sense, professionalism and managerialism emerged embedded in different archetypes, being also identified as opposite and conflicting, which is typical from loosely coupled organisations (Weick & Westley, 1999). This phenomenon can persist in the professional organisations functioning, despite the aims of NPM inspired reforms to make organisational structures more vertical.

> To me what is more painful and takes more time is the huge number of documents we need to have to respond to management and administration, sometimes things are a bit repetitive because it gives me the idea that managers who are in health still do not know much about health. Often when a document is requested is the repetition of another and they end up not realizing where is the problem of the patient in the middle of those squares where there are only numbers. Therefore, the relationship with directors and top management is sometimes a bit tricky. (Interview 4M; Male Doctor)

However there is not a single discourse or tendency in this domain. Some discourses focus on the negative impact of organisational changes in professional autonomy, whereas others refer to the maintenance or even an increase in professional autonomy given the present institutional context. At the organisational level, this process can enact conflicting interpretations of changes and political confrontations to gain power and hegemony over the definition of the regulated rules in respect to organisations' internal functioning and the management of professionals and professional work. There is clear evidence in some academics' narratives that they are called to take decisions that affect them or their professional group. At the same time, a collegial way of working is said to be still in place and is highly appreciated by health professionals, especially doctors.

> We are called too, and I am also called to participate in decisions related with management, with reallocation and reorganisation of resources, especially the economic and financial resources which then has implications in terms of hiring people, the reorganisation of the distribution of the teaching service, and all this at the moment, this is the problem that is affecting us more. (Interview 1A; Male Academic, Polytechnic)

This evidence confirms previous studies sustaining that NPM/managerialism and professionalism are interrelated in a complex manner and that autonomy cannot simply be defined in a 'loss' or 'gain' perspective (Carvalho & Santiago, 2010; Noordegraaf, 2013). As contended by Carvalho and Santiago (2015), one cannot analyse professional autonomy without taking into consideration the institutional level. The authors identify three levels of autonomy, namely: structural autonomy that highlights collective professional power, organisational autonomy representing the space professionals have to make decisions concerning their own group in the interplay between professionals and bureaucracies and autonomy of practice, which refers to the discretionary power professionals have in their daily activities (Carvalho & Santiago, 2015). Our data suggest that there are conflicting interpretative schemes on the ground, but also intersections and hybridisation (Berg & Pinheiro, forthcoming). The way these archetypes are anchored in practice may also present some specific features that can be re-institutionalised; for instance, in the form of profound changes in professionals' subjectivities towards the alignment of their organisational and professional practices with NPM/managerialism assumptions and technologies; or, alternatively, as symbolic compliance or even via resistance, avoidance and defiance (Oliver, 1991).

In sum, there are differences in the discourses over organisational and professional autonomy not only from an *inter-professional* perspective (academics referred more to the loss in organisational autonomy while doctors and nurses alluded to the decline in professionals' self-regulation) but also from an *intra-professional* one, with different actors belonging to the same professional group having different normative and cognitive positions when it comes to the changes being enacted and experienced. This may result, as Fligstein (1999) argues, from the way actors use their cognitive capacities to read the organisational reality on the one hand, and the ways in which they can influence change in matters that are perceived as best for them (i.e. aligned to their professional roles, identities and strategic aspirations).

CONCLUSION

This paper analysed to what extent professional bureaucracies in hospitals and HEIs were affected by changes in state policies as well as on how professionals are interpreting and responding to those changes. One of the main conclusions is that one cannot analyse changes in the organisational context without taking into account the institutional field in which these are embedded. Political reforms in different fields follow different tactics and strategies, taking into account the way the different institutional contexts – national and each specific field missions, principles of organisation and professional values and practices – emerged in Portuguese society after the 1974 democratic revolution. The analysis of legal documents reveals significant differences in the way the State changed the regulatory framework and the professional archetypes in hospitals and HEIs. In hospitals, structural changes in their governance and management systems were imposed in a more coercive fashion. Probably, the reasons behind this political behaviour, if compared with HE, are linked to the fact that the key actors in designing these reforms were 'outsiders' to the health world. Moreover, the centrality of health to the welfare policies, its operational complexity, inducing increased specialised management, and, last but not least, the 'tradition' of health administrative integration, also seems to have played an important role in the rather authoritarian mode in which hospital reforms were enacted.

In HE, changes in the *locus* of decision-making were more evidenced, putting into question the importance of professionals as the main actors of the 'operational centre'. Because the key actors in political initiatives towards changes were academic peers, the principles of collegial organisation institutionalised in the HE field were only partially put into question. However, although academics are still the majority of the members in the new HEIs' governance and management bodies, the reconfiguration of power structures, based on the concentration of power in a small number of bodies at the top level, seem to have distanced academics from the bottom-up dynamics in institutional decision-making. A sort of top-down model of collegiality, with heterogeneous traces (the presence of external stakeholders in HE governance bodies), has gradually but steadily replaced the previous endogenous bottom-up model of collegiality, shifting decision-making from the 'heartland' to HEIs' central vertex (see Lazega & Wattebled, 2011).

Nevertheless, when analysing professionals' perceptions on these changes, these were found to be heterogeneous. Academics refer more to a decline in the participation in collegial bodies, reproducing mostly archetypes of their professional power exercise connected to the previous hegemonic bureaucratic-collegial model. Health professionals seem to be more concerned with the preservation of professional groups' autonomy (with the 'voice' of their professional group expertise in decision-making) being also more receptive (more nurses than doctors) to the new managerial assumptions and values in practice in their organisations. This does not mean that these two professional groups perceived restrictions on their technical autonomy (Freidson, 2001) in the narrow sphere of their working process. But, it enables their consent on changes and favours the reproduction, at least partially, of the health principles of organisation which are institutionalised at the macro, meso and micro levels.

The above findings appeal to further analysis to better understand who the main actors involved in the definition of this new regulatory frameworks were and how negotiations and bargaining between the different groups have led to these observed outcomes.

ACKNOWLEDGEMENT

This research was supported by the Portuguese Foundation for Science and Technology (FCT) [Grant PTDC/CPE-PEC/104759/2008 and EXCL/IVC-PEC/0789/2012] funded by the Program COMPETE.

REFERENCES

Amaral, A., Magalhães, A., & Santiago, R. (2003). The rise of academic managerialism in Portugal. In A. Amaral, V. Meek, & I. Larsen (Eds.), *The higher education managerial revolution?* Dordrecht: Kluwer.

Berg, L., & Pinheiro, R. (forthcoming). Handling different institutional logics in the public sector: Comparing management in Norwegian universities and hospitals. In R. Pinheiro, F. Ramirez, K. Vrabæk, & L. Geschwind (Eds.), *Towards a comparative institutionalism? Forms, dynamics and logics across health and higher education fields*. Bingley, UK: Emerald Group Publishing Limited.

Bryman, A. (2006). *Mixed methods*. London: Sage.

Carvalho, T. (2009). *Nova Gestão Pública e Reformas da Saúde. O profissionalismo numa encruzilhada*. Lisboa: Edições Sílabo.

Carvalho, T. (2012). Managerialism and professional strategies – A case from nurses in Portugal. *Journal of Health Organization and Management*, *26*(4), 524–541.

Carvalho, T., & Bruckmann, S. (2014). Reforming Portuguese public sector: A route from health to higher education. In *Reforming higher education* (pp. 83–102). Dordrecht: Springer.

Carvalho, T., & Santiago, R. (2010). New public management and 'middle-management': How do deans influence institutional policies? In L. Meek, L. Goedegebuure, R. Santiago, & T. Carvalho (Eds.), *The changing dynamics of higher education middle management* (pp. 165–196). London: Springer.

Carvalho, T., & Santiago, R. (2015). Organizational autonomy in a comparative perspective: Academics, doctors and nurses. In T. Carvalho & R. Santiago (Eds.), *Professionalism, managerialism and reform in higher education and the health services: The European welfare state and rise of the knowledge society*. London: Palgrave Macmillan.

Clarke, J., & Newman, J. (1997). *The managerial state: Power, politics and ideology in the remaking of social welfare*. London: Sage.

Cohen, M., March, J., & Olsen, J. (1972). A garbage can model of organizational choice. *Administrative Science Quarterly*, *17*, 1–25.

Deem, R., Hillyard, S., & Reed, M. (2007). *Knowledge, higher education, and the new managerialism: The changing management of UK universities*. Oxford: Oxford University Press.

DiMaggio, P. J., & Powell, W. W. (1983). The iron cage revisited: Institutional isomorphism and collective rationality in organizational fields. *American Sociological Review*, *48*, 147–160.

DiMaggio, P. J., & Powell, W. W. (Eds.). (1991). *The new institutionalism in organizational analysis* (Vol. 17). Chicago, IL: The University of Chicago Press.

Enders, J., De Boer, H., & Leisyte, L. (2008). On striking the right notes: Shifts in governance and the organisational transformation of universities. In A. Amaral, I. Bleiklie, & C. Musselin (Eds.), *From governance to identity: A Festschrift for Mary Henkel* (pp. 113–130). London: Springer.

Faulconbridge, J., & Muzio, D. (2008). Organizational professionalism in globalizing law firms. *Work, Employment & Society*, *22*(1), 7–25.

Ferlie, E., Ashburner, L., Fitzgerald, L., & Pettigrew, A. (1996). *The new public management in action*. Oxford: Oxford University Press.

Fligstein, N. (1999). *Fields, power and social skill: A critical analysis of the New Institutionalisms*. Berkeley, CA: Center for Culture, Organizations and Politics.

Freidson, E. (2001). *Professionalism, the third logic: On the practice of knowledge*. Chicago, IL: The University of Chicago Press.

Greenwood, R., & Hinings, C. R. (1993). Understanding strategic change: The contribution of archetypes. *Academy of Management Journal*, *36*(5), 1052–1081.

Hayek, F. A. (2014). *The road to serfdom: Text and documents: The definitive edition*. London: Routledge.

Hood, C. (1991). A public management for all seasons? *Public Administration*, *69*(Spring), 3–19.

Larson, M. (2013). *The rise of professionalism. Monopolies of competence and sheltered markets*. New Brunswick: Transaction Publishers.

Lazega, E., & Wattebled, O. (2011). Two definitions of collegiality and their inter-relation: The case of a Roman Catholic diocese. *Sociologie du Travail*, *53*, e57–e77.

Lounsbury, M., & Ventresca, M. (2003). The new structuralism in organization theory. *Organization*, *10*(3), 457–480.

Magalhães, A. M., & Santiago, R. (2012). Governance, public management and administration of higher education in Portugal. In *Higher education in Portugal 1974–2009* (pp. 227–247). Dordrecht: Springer.

Mahoney, J., & Thelen, K. (2010). *Explaining institutional change: Ambiguity, agency, and power*. Cambridge: Cambridge University Press.

Miles, M., & Huberman, M. (1994). *Qualitative data analysis: An expanded sourcebook*. London: Sage.

Mintzberg, H. (1994). *Le management, voyage au centre des organisations*. Paris: Les Editions de L'Organisation.

Neogy, I., & Kirkpatrick, I. (2009). *Medicine in management: Lessons across Europe*. Leeds: Centre for Innovation in Health.

Noordegraaf, M. (2013). Reconfiguring professional work: Changing forms of professionalism in public services. *Administration & Society*. doi:10.1177/0095399713509242

Oliver, C. (1991). Strategic responses to institutional processes. *Academy of Management Review*, *16*, 145–179.

Olsen, J. (2007, January). *Organization theory, public administration, democratic governance*. Working Paper No. 1. ARENA – Centre for European Studies, University of Oslo.

Pollitt, C., & Boukaert, G. (2000). *Public management reform: A comparative analysis*. Oxford: Oxford University Press.

Reed, M. (1999). Organizational theorizing: A historically contested terrain. In S. R. Clegg & C. Hardy (Eds.), *Studying organization theory and method* (pp. 25–50). London: Sage.

Santiago, R., Carvalho, T., & Relva, R. (2008). Research and the universities' image. *European Journal of Education*, *43*(4), 495–512.

Santiago, R., Magalhães, A., & Carvalho, T. (2005). *O surgimento do managerialismo no sistema de Ensino Superior Português*. Coimbra: FUP.

Scott, W. R. (2001). *Institutions and organizations*. Thousand Oaks, CA: Sage.

Selznick, P. (1996). Institutionalism "Old" and "New". *Administrative Science Quarterly*, *41*(2), 270–277.

Simon, H. A. (1996). Bounded rationality and organizational learning. In D. Cohen & L. Sproull (Eds.), *Organizational learning* (pp. 175–188). Thousand Oaks, CA: Sage.

Torgal, L. (2012). University, society and politics. In G. Neave & A. Amaral (Eds.), *Higher education in Portugal 1974–2009. A nation, a generation* (pp. 67–88). Dordrecht: Springer.

Weber, M. (1989). *Sobre a Universidade*. São Paulo: Cortez Editora.

Weber, M. (1995). *Economie et société. 1, Les catégories de la sociologie*. Paris: Plon/Pocket.

Weick, K. (1976). Educational organizations as loosely coupled systems. *Administrative Science Quarterly*, *21*, 1–19.

Weick, K., & Westley, F. (1999). Affirming an oxymoron. In S. Clegg, C. Hardy, & W. Nord (Eds.), *Managing organizations: Current issues* (pp. 190–208). London: Sage.

Zucker, L. (1991). The role of institutionalization in cultural persistence. In W. Powell & P. DiMaggio (Eds.), *The new institutionalism in organizational analysis* (pp. 83–107). Chicago, IL: The University of Chicago Press.

MANAGERIALISM IN COMPLEX SYSTEMS: EXPERIENCES OF STRATEGIC PLANNING IN NON-PROFIT HOSPITALS

Victor Meyer, Jr., Lucilaine Pascuci and Diórgenes Falcão Mamédio

ABSTRACT

The aim of this study was to analyse strategic planning practices in complex systems by investigating the experiences of Brazilian non-profit hospitals. Growing pressures have been imposed upon hospitals to improve the quality of their services, to increase access to them by reducing costs and to improve their reliability. In order to respond to these demands, managerial approaches such as strategic planning based on business-sector practices have been adopted by non-profit hospitals. The purpose of this study was to identify the most significant results of the experience with strategic planning in two non-profit hospitals. The study is a qualitative one, and the research was based on the concepts of organizational complexity, strategic planning and managerialism in non-profit hospitals. Data were collected by non-participant observation, from documents

Towards a Comparative Institutionalism: Forms, Dynamics and Logics Across the Organizational Fields of Health Care and Higher Education
Research in the Sociology of Organizations, Volume 45, 271–295

ISSN: 0733-558X/doi:10.1108/S0733-558X20150000045024

and in interviews and were analysed using narrative analysis and document-analysis techniques. Three main factors related to strategic planning in non-profit hospitals were identified: firstly, the unsuitability of strategic planning for hospitals given that they are complex, professional organizations, something that was disregarded by managers; secondly, the significant role played by core operating professionals in strategy making; and thirdly, the representation of strategic planning as fancy management in the eyes of internal and external stakeholders, conferring legitimacy on and generating trust in the hospital. The findings indicate that strategic planning as a traditional managerialist approach applied in a hospital context was dysfunctional and failed to produce a significant contribution to organizational performance.

Keywords: Managerialism; strategic planning; non-profit hospitals; complex systems

INTRODUCTION

Hospitals are complex, pluralistic, paradoxical, professional organizations (Etzioni, 1961; Mintzberg, 1994). The hybrid nature of non-profit hospitals in particular poses an additional challenge to managers, who have to juggle economic and financial sustainability with the inherent social dimensions of these organizations. These characteristics, as pointed out by scholars of organizations such as Etzioni (1961), Perrow (1986), Bolman and Deal (2003), Stacey (2010) and Locke and Spender (2011), have been neglected by managers when developing models and implementing management practices. Organizations are not governed by natural laws. Therefore, in applied social sciences, there is no 'real truth' or right answer to a problem. Hence, any managerial approaches available to managers have their own potentialities as well as pitfalls.

To respond to the challenges imposed by a dynamic environment, managers are impelled to search for managerial models and approaches. The models adopted in hospitals are often imported from other sectors and follow managerialist guidelines with dubious benefits and results. Strategic planning (SP), for example, has spread into different types of organizations, such as companies, government, social organizations, museums, universities and hospitals. However, its effectiveness has been questioned because it incorporates a different form of management based on rational assumptions that do not exist in most organizations. Unlike the 'machine organization' (McDaniel, 2007; Mintzberg, 1994), in which management is based on essentially rational premises, hospitals are organizations whose concerns extend beyond economic sustainability and focus on social commitment.

In this paper, we analyse SP practices by investigating the impact of a managerial approach with roots in the business world, the benefits of such an approach and the results of its application in two non-profit hospitals. More specifically, we seek to answer the following question: what were the most significant results of the experience with SP in Brazilian non-profit hospitals that incorporated the SP concept in their management practices?

This paper discusses two important aspects of the strategic approach in organizations: the first concerns the practice of managerialism rooted in the axiom that management is a science and that managerial approaches and tools can be transferred to any and every organization, irrespective of its specific context and characteristics. This approach has been encouraged by business schools (Mintzberg, 2004) and gained further support from the work of consultancy firms (Stacey, 2010). The second has to do with hospitals as organizations and complex systems, whose ambiguity, unpredictability and uncertainty greatly influence the way SP is managed in these organizations (Meyer, Pascucci, & Murphy, 2012; Pascucci & Meyer, 2013). Excessive rationality in managerialist practices has usually proved to be inappropriate, not very effective and sometimes dysfunctional, especially in complex systems like hospitals. As Ghoshal (2005) warns, bad management theories may sometimes destroy good practices.

Following the reasoning of some scholars, certain organizations should be viewed as complex systems and this complexity should be taken into consideration when changes in managerial practices occur, especially when practices influenced by the machine view of organizations are introduced as the guiding reference for actions and forecasts. We criticize these practices, which pose a challenge for managers, who have to integrate the essential rational elements of the strategic approach with the unique characteristics of hospitals as complex, professional organizations. The consequences of these practices are analysed from a theoretical and practical perspective.

MANAGERIALISM, SP AND STRATEGY

Managerialism is a phenomenon that has spread throughout the capitalist world as companies develop managerial approaches based on rationality and control by seeking efficiency in operations and maximum profitability (Parker, 2002; Quiggin, 2003).

On the one hand, we have the hegemony of the private organization as an efficient organizational model and the misunderstanding that management practices deemed appropriate for a particular organizational context will have the same results in all types of organizations (McDaniel, 2007). However, organizations have specific characteristics that influence the effectiveness of the results achieved by rational practices. This is the case of public organizations, hospitals, universities and other organizations that can be considered *complex* (Etzioni, 1964; Perrow, 1986; Zimmerman, 2011) and *pluralistic* (Jarzabkowski & Fenton, 2006; Meyer et al., 2012). The unsuccessful application of managerial practices is therefore not always a result of the incorrect application of the principles associated with such practices but a consequence of underestimating the varied nature of organizations (McDaniel, 2007; McDaniel & Driebe, 2004; Stacey, 1996, 2010; Stacey, Griffin, & Shaw, 2000).

Furthermore, a competitive scenario exists where organizations compete not just for resources and customers but also for political power and institutional legitimacy (Dimaggio & Powell, 1983). Legitimacy, in turn, is related to the widespread perception that certain actions are desirable or appropriate within a socially constituted context (Suchman, 1995). In this setting, the spread of managerialism in all kinds of organizations would appear to reinforce the understanding that organizational changes are guided more by isomorphic pressures than by the need for efficiency (Dimaggio & Powell, 1983).

SP is one of the most common manifestations of managerialism and is widely disseminated among a diversified range of organizations including businesses, governments and non-profit organizations (Bryson, 2004; Carter, Clegg, & Kornberger, 2008). The essence of SP can be summarized as an externally oriented *managerial approach* based on stakeholder's interests, a process of strategy making that combines rational and economic analysis, political manoeuvring and psychological interplay (Keller, 1983). According to Steiner (1979, p. 3), 'strategic planning is inextricably interwoven into the entire fabric of management'. As a process, SP includes a statement of organizational intentions, and what is achieved is a result of intended (Ansoff, 1965) and emergent (Mintzberg & Waters, 1985) strategies. While the former are planned, the latter bubble up along the way based on the dynamic relation between the organization and its environment (Mintzberg, 1994).

For some authors, such as Ansoff (1965) and Steiner (1979), SP is a means of producing plans in terms of competitiveness, profitability and sustainability in the long term, while for others, including Cohen and March (1974), SP in organizations is important for other reasons, including its use as symbols, advertisement, games and an excuse for interaction. For Birnbaum (2000), SP is a fad, fashion or buzzword. Weick (1979, p. 11) stresses that plans in organizations are usually '[...] a pretext under which several valuable activities take place', and he supports his statement by quoting Ambrose Bierce, according to whom to plan is to 'bother about the best method of accomplishing an accidental result' (1946, p. 327). According to Bryson (2004), SP is a smart practice involving a rational process that integrates internal and environmental analysis and value identification and focuses on key issues such as decision-making procedures, implementation and evaluation.

More recently there has been a trend in the literature on organizational strategy to move the focus from SP to strategy as this managerial approach encompasses distinct processes, practices and people (Cummings, 2008). More and more the focus of analysis is moving away from long-term plans and rational analysis to approaches that combine intention and emergent and fluid activities involving different organizational levels in an attempt to come up with a strategy that actually contributes to the performance of organizations (Cummings, 2008; Cummings & Wilson, 2003).

The main function of strategy is to lead an organization towards future growth and sustainable success (Carter et al., 2008). Traditionally, it has been understood to be the responsibility of the top management team, which sets the goals and makes the necessary decisions for the lower organizational ranks. However, the reality is that most strategic actions are not actually conducted by top managers themselves but are a result of the collective effort of various agents operating at all levels within the organization (Carter et al., 2008; Chakravarthy & White, 2002). This is particularly true in the case of hospitals, which are complex, professional, pluralistic organizations where power is unevenly distributed and internal political interaction takes place (Bolman & Deal, 2008; Mintzberg, 1989), influencing the way strategic thinking and acting take place.

SP in Hospitals as Complex Organizations

The complexity of hospitals derives from a variety of elements that affect their structure and operations (Meyer et al., 2012). Multiple authority and multiple subordination (Perrow, 1965), multiple purposes (Etzioni, 1964), ambiguity of goals (March & Olsen, 1976) and pluralistic interests (Jarzabkowski & Fenton, 2006) all make this kind of organization a *complex adaptive system* (McDaniel, 2007; Stacey, 1996, 2010; Stacey et al., 2000). Complex organizations of this kind can be better understood not only as systems made up of many parts interconnected in a nonlinear way but also primarily as systems with nonlinear feedback loops that allow for emergence, self-organization, adaptation and learning among other concepts linked to complexity thinking (Richardson, 2011). All these elements constitute serious obstacles to be overcome by managers, especially when SP is practiced in hospitals.

In such institutions, the existence of a significant number of divisional units where a variety of health professionals enjoy autonomy to carry out their activities leads to a kind of loosely coupled (Orton & Weick, 1990) yet interdependent system. Furthermore, ambiguous goals and vested interests triggering conflicts and political disputes for resources and power hinder any new initiatives. In such a setting, managerial practices must take into account specific internal characteristics so that they can achieve (or not) tangible results in terms of effectiveness.

Unlike the dominant concept in the literature on organizational strategy, SP in hospitals, as *complex* organizations, is not the result of rational intentions previously established in a formally planned process. Rather, strategy in these organizations occurs interdependently as a result of cooperation between internal groups and dynamic interrelations with the environment, which is neither inert nor stable – let alone predictable – and where factors such as the interpretation of reality, improvization and creativity on the part of an organization's members are much more important (McDaniel, 2007; Cummings, 2008; Stacey, 2010; Stacey et al., 2000).

One of the critical aspects of the strategic approach in hospitals is the multiple interests involved. Strategies always imply goals, policies, priorities and resource allocation, generating conflict and negotiations between interest groups. The fine line between *administrative authority* and *professional authority* in hospitals highlights the various conflicts and diverging interests that influence management (Bolman & Deal, 2008; Pfeffer, 1994). The convergence of goals and stakeholders' expectations therefore proves to be both a strategic factor and a permanent obstacle because of organizational complexity (Correia, 2011; Jarzabkowski & Fenton, 2006; Mintzberg, 1994; Pascucci & Meyer, 2013). In this setting, power, influence and prestige play a major if not dominant role in strategic actions.

For these reasons, decisions and actions in hospitals are interdependent and stem from sensemaking (Weick, 1995, 1998), creativity (Stacey, 1996), learning (McDaniel, 2007), interactions (Ritter, Wilkinson, & Johnston, 2004), negotiations (Bolman & Deal, 2008; Clegg, 1989; Clegg, Carter, Kornberger, & Schweitzer, 2011; Mintzberg, 1985) and cooperation among agents (Stacey et al., 2000), compromising the effectiveness of methodologies that require rules, control and restrictions on the autonomy of specialists.

While management of *machine organizations* seeks to maximize financial returns to stakeholders, in social organizations such as hospitals management pursues social values (Moore, 2000). These different organizational purposes mean that adopting managerial practices that earned their legitimacy in the market leads to questionable results when such practices are applied in a hospital context, whether the institution is for-profit or non-profit. Reconciliation of the modern managerial style – guided solely by economic and financial performance – with the social dimension poses considerable challenges for managers of these organizations (Meyer et al., 2012; Porter & Teisberg, 2006; Schlesinger & Gray, 2006).

As critical organizations in society, hospitals are social institutions whose management and performance cannot be neglected. Managerial practices in these organizations should ensure added value in terms of the quality and reliability of the health services provided and performance improvements. Following this line of thought, Moore (2000) points out that strategies in non-profit organizations should focus on the creation of public value, sources of legitimacy and operational capacity to deliver value. Thus, in non-profit hospitals strategic actions should also contribute to the pursuit of the social mission, adding value and generating legitimacy and trust among stakeholders and society.

METHODOLOGY

We adopt a comparative, qualitative case study design (Stake, 1994) based on two Brazilian non-profit hospitals, referred to here as Beta and Gamma. The hospitals provide health services, teaching and research and were chosen because of their similar size, social characteristics, performance and core functions (teaching and research) as well as their recent efforts towards professionalization and the adoption of strategic management.

Hospital data were analysed for the 10-year period from 2003 to 2013. This period was chosen so that more than one SP cycle could be investigated in the two hospitals. Although Gamma has not yet formally adopted SP cycles, we identified two changes in the SP model adopted during the study period that were treated as being in different cycles. In Beta, three SP cycles were considered during the study period. The aim was to identify the changes made to the adopted methodologies and the learning generated by each experience. Data were collected by non-participant observation, from documents and in interviews with middle- and upper-level administrators and specialists at the two hospitals. Thirty-eight professionals (18 from Beta and 20 from Gamma) were interviewed in two stages: the first between May and October 2011, and the second between October and December 2013. We used *guided interviews* to collect technical data as this method 'questions *what, how and why* something happens' (Richardson, 2008, italics added).

The interviewees were selected using non-probability or purposive sampling in view of our interest in people directly involved in the strategic management of hospitals. The purpose of the interviews was to identify the characteristics and most important results of the hospitals' experiences with SP, as well as the changes required during the process and the reasons for them. The interviews lasted one hour on average and were recorded and transcribed. Notes were also taken by the researchers as non-participant observers and recorded in field diaries for use in the analysis stage. The transcriptions (interviews and field diaries) covered 550 pages. Archival materials were also used and included reports of activities, strategic plans, publications and information available on the hospitals' websites.

The data analysis was conducted using narrative analysis – with 'meaning' as the analysis technique, as presented by Eriksson and Kovalainen (2008) – and document-analysis techniques (Tsoukas & Hatch, 2001). Cognitive maps were drawn up using IHMC Cmap Tools software (Novak & Cañas, 2008) as a complementary method to analyse the interviews in order to gain a better understanding of how situations and events were interpreted by the organizational agents, causing the process to be conducted the way that it was.

THE BRAZILIAN HEALTH CARE SECTOR

In Brazil, universal access to health care is the responsibility of the State and is provided through the Unified Federal Health System (*Sistema Único de Saúde*, or SUS, in Portuguese). The SUS offers a wide range of services free of charge, mainly to individuals in low-income brackets. The services offered range from a standard appointment with a physician to more sophisticated medical care, such as transplants. Implementation of the goal of universal access to health care has made the SUS the largest purchaser of health services in Brazil (Ribeiro, 2009), as the provision of health care services to the whole population requires that, in addition to providing its own services, the SUS contract the services of private providers. Of the 6,633 hospitals in Brazil, fewer than 30% are public, and more than half of the private hospitals (i.e., approximately 2,600) are non-profit (CNEs, 2015).

However, universal access to health care through a public system financed by taxes has given rise to considerable discontent among health care providers and members of society (Ribeiro, 2009). On the one hand, the slowness and inefficiency of some services have encouraged ever-greater migration (approximately 30% of the population) to private health insurance. On the other, hospitals contracted by the SUS have lived with growing deficits because of the government's outdated pricing policy, as a result of which investments in essential areas, such as labour, technology and innovation have been limited. The situation is compounded by the fact that health care providers are paid by the public system (SUS) for the services they provide only after the services have in fact been provided. As public financing of services to hospitals is limited to 60% of the real cost of health care procedures, hospitals are faced with a deficit. Consequently, the great challenge for non-profit hospitals is to fulfil their social mission to provide quality health services with scant resources. Like any non-profit Brazilian hospital, Beta and Gamma are required to assign between 60% and 70% of their services to SUS patients. The many challenges facing non-profit hospital managers thus include striking a balance between limited revenue and rising operational costs, dealing with a competitive environment and constantly having to raise funds.

Because of internal and external pressures and their poor relations with the public sector, Brazilian non-profit hospitals have sought to change their image from that of *welfare organizations* to *professional* ones to allow them to compete with private hospitals in order to attract private patients. Notable among measures that reflect the professionalization of non-profit hospitals in Brazil are the appointment of management specialists to the staff, the reviewing of internal processes with a view to improving the quality and effectiveness of the services provided and, most importantly, the emphasis on financial performance in order to ensure sustainability and reduce dependence on public funding (Meyer et al., 2012). As part of this

Table 1. Profile of the Two Hospitals Studied. *Source*: Beta and Gamma Hospitals. Data from December 2013.

Characteristics	Beta Hospital	Gamma Hospital
Founded	1972	1919
Position in health market	Renowned for oncology in the South of Brazil	The largest children's hospital in the country
Beds	152	229
Clinical staff	120	239
Staff/bed	5.68/bed	4.36/bed
Average attendance	12,300 per month	14,200 per month

initiative, some non-profit hospitals have imported market-based business management models, such as SP, quality programs, strict controls and systems of targets, whose essentially rational premises have very often failed to produce satisfactory results. This is the case of the two hospitals in this study, whose profiles are presented in Table 1.

SP AT BETA

SP was adopted at Beta in 2003 (first SP cycle) as an initiative by a group of medical managers to minimize a serious financial crisis. The roots of the crisis were the political conflicts and managerial business approach adopted by the senior management team, which had implications for the financial sustainability of the hospital. At the same time, a process was initiated to professionalize management by hiring professionals from the market to adopt modern managerial practices such as SP, total quality management and risk and budget management. This was done to improve the image of the hospital and change its culture, which had until then been a welfare culture, and improve conditions for organizational sustainability. As a large number of the top managers are elected, many decisions tend to become political in nature. SP at Beta involves top administration, middle management and employees at an operational level to varying degrees. In the middle of 2005 (second SP cycle), a department was set up and a specialist was hired to coordinate the breakdown of SP into targets and actions systematically defined for each unit and aligned with strategic institutional goals. The resulting document was known as the Annual Work Plans (AWP). Based on the changes introduced by the new department, objectives, strategies and targets started to be monitored in regular meetings at different organizational levels in what was a predominantly rational process. The strong internal resistance resulted in changes being incorporated in the SP model adopted in 2009 (third SP cycle), particularly to the types of criteria used to define organizational targets. Despite the constant changes made to it, the SP model used has a strong rational bias.

SP AT GAMMA

Gamma is known as a traditional, family-run business. It first incorporated elements of formal SP such as goals and performance indicators in 2006 (second SP cycle), although strategic management had been in place informally since 2000 (first SP cycle). The hospital now uses management practices such as SP, total quality management and budgets. However, the dynamic nature of the decision-making process means that SP and other managerial practices are treated more like guidelines, with decision making being more informal and relying heavily on the sensemaking abilities of top management. Strategic management at the hospital is restricted to guidelines and strategic directives, with no details of actions and operational goals. This helps make strategies essentially emergent in nature. Formally, the strategy-formation process involves the top administration and middle management, with the latter enjoying 'assisted autonomy', that is, some middle managers – those closest to the top administration – have the autonomy to take urgent operational decisions thanks to the informal communication channels with top administration and the trust that top administration has placed in them.

ANALYSIS

SP Characteristics and Strategies

The development of a strategic plan at each of the hospitals studied – from formulation to implementation – showed that managerial adaptability and willingness to negotiate, especially among middle managers, were essential to achieve results regardless of what had previously been established as part of the strategic plan. Therefore, while the actions taken in the hospitals may have been strategic in terms of what they achieved, they did not represent the *original* SP any of the cycles analysed.

We identified that the existence of a plurality of agents with different expectations (Jarzabkowski & Fenton, 2006) greatly limited the realization of deliberate plans. This was particularly the case with the preliminary results of the first SP cycle at Beta, which resulted in changes being made to the SP method and content so that the SP was more suited to a hospital environment. The existence of diversified and politically active interest groups also increases the demands on hospital managers involved with SP. The solution found by the hospitals' top managers to enable them to conduct SP was to direct strategic actions towards issues that generated less conflict, such as defining general directions (Gamma) or more operational actions (Beta), and empowering lower-level managers. The initiatives at Gamma were justified by one of its directors in the following terms: '*We know perfectly well what we want when we make a plan, but there is always some leeway and room to move, and you work with the team to ensure this*' (interview extract). For this reason, it is a practice in both hospitals to interact informally with and listen to the people involved before making a decision. As a clinical director at Gamma stressed (considering both SP cycles), it is important to gain their support and minimize conflict: '*I quite often do that. I say, 'Come on, help me, I would like to have your support on this one' or 'I would like to hear what your opinion is on ...'. I don't always get the person's support, but the most important thing is to keep him, as an enemy, at a distance*' (interview extract). This happens because people find a way to be flexible and creative and indulge in political interaction (Bolman & Deal, 2008; Mintzberg, 1989).

In both hospitals, the strategies adopted were often the result of individual initiatives or micro-actions that emerged from the search for workarounds for actions previously drawn up (Johnson, Melin, & Whittington, 2003). For some strategies to be executed they had to undergo adaptations and adjustments in the light of the original plan, as a Beta assessor highlighted: '*It is a process of continuous learning [...] You state what needs to be done, then you adjust the desired context based on the answers. As time passes it starts to work, with ups and downs, but it already represents an improvement*' (interview extract). These efforts by Beta led to adaptive actions (Stacey, 2006) as a result of the attempt to make SP (in pluralistic and complex organizations like hospitals) more effective, especially from the third cycle (started in 2009) onwards.

One major practice in the traditional model, namely, the systematization of meetings between sectors as mechanisms for monitoring, interaction and feedback, was only found at Beta. In contrast, at Gamma a practice was adopted that encourages *informal interactions* among the agents involved in certain decisions – between the top management team and middle managers or between the former and specialist professionals, for example. At this hospital, although formal meetings at the top management level were rather sporadic and held only to handle major (long-term) corporate decisions, the communication process required for the development of strategies seemed to flow better.

Because of its functionalist bias, the schedule for systematized meetings used at Beta from 2005 until 2008 had to be changed to ensure the participation and cooperation of specialist professionals (Ritter et al., 2004), whose activities and autonomous profiles do not easily fit the formal rules. Another reason for this change was the perception that the dynamic nature of the hospital context meant that most decisions could not wait until the 'day of the meeting'. In connection with this, an advisor emphasized that '*it took some time for us to realize that the meetings model initially adopted hindered, rather than helped*' (interview extract). After this practice was adapted at Beta in 2008, few formal meetings were defined (on guidelines and financial reports) and interactions concerning everyday tasks and decisions took on a very informal character. This change resulted from the sensemaking (Weick, 1979, 1995) of the hospital managers, who felt that systematizing natural interaction processes would destroy the flow of more effective creativity and organizational learning on the part of the agents themselves (McDaniel, 2007; Mintzberg, 1994; Ritter et al., 2004). However, as Weick (1987) indicates, it is the action that is responsible for providing meaning although formal planning and symbols mistakenly get the credit.

Based on the experiences in the hospitals studied, it is clear that managerialist practices – such as SP in a hospital context – can only be maintained if adaptive or innovative adjustments that cater for the specificities of the complex nature of this kind of organization are made (McDaniel, 2007; Stacey, 2010). In both the hospitals studied, there was an organizational learning process (Argyris, 1999; Crossan & Berdrow, 2003; March, 1991) – already observed after the first SP cycle – that was responsible for identifying flaws and making any necessary adjustments to improve continuously the managerial actions of such complex systems.

Power, Politics and SP

Another significant aspect of the strategic process in hospitals concerns the implications of the political dimension for SP. Pfeffer and Salancik (1974) and Mintzberg (1985) point out that the strategic decision-making process is essentially political since it becomes an arena for bargaining and negotiating where different groups fight for their own interests (Mintzberg, 1985). On the one hand, there is the prestige and authority of those who design the strategic plan, that is, top managers (but who require implementation support) and, on the other, the power given by professional competence (expertise) to perform the tasks at hand (by those who want to obtain advantages from supporting the plan), in terms of Clegg (1989). This was the case with a set of indicators developed at Beta that became the subject of much debate among specialist staff as in their view the indicators implied a degree of rationality that could not be applied to all the decisions in a hospital context. The indicators had been developed by a planning manager – recently hired by the hospital after working in industry – in the belief that internal controls would help optimize decisions. As another Beta assessor pointed out: '*We created all sorts of indicators. [...] none of them were ever considered in decision-making*' (interview extract).

Thus, the strategic process concerns a relationship involving power and a dispute as to when and how much to give in (yield) on both sides (March & Olsen, 1976). As a Beta middle manager highlighted: '*It looks to me like a power struggle*' (interview extract). This was reflected in our finding of different negotiations between dominant coalitions (Cyert & March, 1963) in the hospitals, which led to conflicts, especially between *managers* and *specialist professionals*. As pointed out by another Beta manager: '*The order to carry out a task is one of the big problems. When somebody from the top administration 'orders' somebody to do something, that in itself is an obstacle to adhesion. It's important to discuss things a lot – always.*' (interview extract). This was one of the reasons why the SP methodology adopted was changed three times at Beta during the study period: *an attempt to do things differently* to garner more support.

The old problem of scarcity of resources and the wide range of intentions and interests of the many internal groups were the main reasons for most conflicts. The structuring of strategic actions through projects – implemented after 2006 – was the solution found by Gamma in 2006 to prioritise actions and justify negative responses. Each proposal was required to be both beneficial and financially viable. As a top manager at Gamma revealed: '*I ask whether the project will have a return in terms of quality. How will it be paid for? How are we going to make money out of it?*' (interview extract). Although project management is based on rational premises, shared understanding (Weick, 1979) facilitated its acceptance by the internal public, including the specialist professionals. The adoption of shared understanding came to demand, especially of doctors, that when a project was presented it should include details of where the resources would come from, the advantages and disadvantages, a schedule and the name of a person in charge of its development.

As in any other kind of organization, resources are critical to enable strategic actions to be carried out (Pfeffer & Salancik, 2003). Thus, objective analysis of the viability of a project complements planning, making it easier for Gamma managers to approve or reject proposals. Despite these incongruities, having an SP was seen by hospital managers as a very important symbol as it conveyed the idea that modern management was being practiced within each organization and thus conferred social credibility and legitimacy (Suchman, 1995).

LEGITIMACY

Regarding the goals set as part of the SP process, we observed that in both non-profit hospitals these proved to be linked more to legitimacy (Suchman, 1995) than to the hospitals' performance. The experience of SP in both hospitals revealed a limited attempt to reconcile a modern rational managerialist approach with a social dimension, the *raison d'être* of a hospital. In connection with this, a director at Beta stated, '*If you begin a transformational process geared toward a capitalist business model, let's just say that you destroy the hospital as an institution. With a serious mission, we have managed to balance the situation*' (interview extract).

Aware of this need, Gamma began to adopt strategic projects, which also proved to be an essential mechanism for obtaining resources from public funds, such as funds from the Ministry of Health, parliamentary amendments or even the state government. In addition to solving the problem of constant conflicts about investment decisions and turning intentions into actions, some projects, such as the expansion of the hospital's facilities, the acquisition of new equipment and social awareness campaigns, also helped significantly to legitimize the image of Gamma as a socially responsible institution.

The decision to use a project-based methodology also reflects a learning process by managers, who introduced successful fund-raising initiatives targeting governmental sources, exploiting the institution's image of a non-profit hospital that despite its financial difficulties is concerned with prevention and the provision of guidance and care for society in its specific areas – oncology and child care. An example of a successful strategy was when Gamma managers decided to strengthen the hospital's image (Scott, 1995) as a friend of children and adolescents in the community. To do this Gamma interacted politically with its various stakeholders (government, society, child protection agencies, etc.) and, following a 'small-wins' strategy (Weick, 1985), managed to change a specific piece of legislation about donations in 2005. The change in the legislation allowed funds from the Childhood and Adolescent Fund – which was distributed politically by the state government – to be targeted at non-profit organizations chosen by the donors themselves. Although simple, this change encouraged non-profit hospitals to be even more concerned about their institutional images and to be more competitive in their attempts to raise funds.

After this 'small-wins' approach, Gamma developed an internal methodology with strong roots in organizational learning and a culture of projects and from 2007 spread these to non-profit hospitals throughout the South of Brazil (Argyris, 1999; March, 1991). As pointed out by one top Gamma manager, '*Everybody tries to invent a way to do things. There was no magic formula; we just made it up as we went along*' (interview extract). This example shows that sensemaking, feeling and creativity (Stacey, 2010; Weick, 1979, 1985) are essential factors in SP for non-profit organizations

Added to this internal necessity (resources) is the importance given by the market to management practices of a managerialist origin, such as SP. Referring to new management methodologies, a Gamma top manager complained that '*Modernization tends to make managers want everything. 'We have to have some software that automates everything' or 'We have to buy and adopt such and such a model from consultancy X.'. These things are developed to serve people and be controlled by them. I see the opposite happening: you buy a piece of software and then people have to adapt to it*' (interview extract). This market orientation – associated with acceptability and credibility – has led to the indiscriminate use of functionalist methodologies and a disregard for complex organizational specificities (Stacey, 2010). As highlighted by Powell and Dimaggio (1991), organizations change to become *more equal* without necessarily becoming *more efficient*. A possible external influence via consultants that led to isomorphic practices could be identified in both cases studied here (Powell & Dimaggio, 1991).

In both hospitals, the need to balance economic and financial issues with the institution's social mission constituted a challenge for managers. In connection with this conflict between mission and sustainability (Meyer et al., 2012; Moore, 2000), a Gamma clinic director observed, '*I respect any doctor who comes to argue with me to defend a child, to show that the values involved are not just monetary. The second main value is the institution. The third is the doctors*' (interview extract). Tensions and conflicts increased whenever hospital managers were required to balance these two elements in an attempt to make continuous improvements to the organization based on financial sustainability while at the same time fulfilling the social mission (Meyer et al., 2012) and conferring legitimacy (Dart, 2004; Suchman, 1995) on the institution and its actions in the eyes of their stakeholders.

It can be inferred from the cases studied here that SP came to be seen much more as a *drive for legitimacy* for organizational actions and performed a symbolic role (Bolman & Deal, 2008; Cummings & Wilson, 2003; March & Olsen, 1976) rather than serving as a *rational guide* or even a map to guide and motivate strategic activities. In this sense, a Gamma director stressed, '*Sometimes they are one-off projects, but from the point of view of marketing they are very attractive, even if they do not generate a profit. They emphasize our concern with quality and strengthen our image as a respectable institution that strives to do things better*' (interview extract). The adoption of SP by this type of organization is also the result of isomorphic pressures (Powell & Dimaggio, 1991; Scott, 1995; Suchman, 1995). These pressures impose a challenge for Brazilian hospitals: to reverse the image of inefficiency associated with traditional managerial models imported from the private and public spheres, which exert a strong influence in the health sector.

DISCUSSION

As described in the business literature, SP involves a set of essentially functional and logical assumptions that bear little relationship to the dynamic reality of organizations, regardless of their nature, size and complexity (Mintzberg, 1994; Stacey, 2010). In the case of SP in the two non-profit hospitals studied here, we found huge gaps between theory (as described in the literature) and practice (how it is adopted) in complex organizations such as hospitals, as shown in Table 2.

The main differences between the characteristics of the SP process in the two hospitals and the traditional planning model highlight (1) the specificities of hospitals as complex organizations and the implications for the preponderance of emergent – rather than deliberate – strategies; (2) the

Table 2. Comparison of the Characteristics of SP as Described in the Literature and as Practiced at the Two Hospitals Studied.

Aspect	Characteristics of Strategic Planning		
	Traditional Model[a]	SP at Beta[b]	SP at Gamma[b]
Rationale	Fixed, formal rules	Formal rules	Few rules, informal
Decision process	Centralized	Vertical	Dispersed
Participation	Select groups	All stakeholders	Select people
Emphasis	Logic	Flexibility	Creativity
Process	Analytical and deductive	Analytical and adaptive	Adaptive and creative
Changes	Imposed	Negotiated	Negotiated
Phases of the process	Formulation + implementation	Formulation + Implementation	Formation
Nature of strategy	Deliberate	Emergent over deliberate	Emergent over deliberate
Nature of action	Integrated	Dispersed and non-linear	Dispersed and non-linear
Interactions	Formal	Formal + informal	Informal
Execution	Achievement of goals	Flexible goals	Practices with learning
Measurement/ control	Systematized, with indicators and goals	Systematized, with indicators and goals	Informal with little systematisation

[a]*Sources*: Adapted from Ansoff (1965), Steiner (1979), Keller (1983), Mintzberg (1994) and Bryson (2004).
[b]Empirical findings of this study.

interpretative, informal, adaptive social – rather than purely analytical and systematic – nature of the SP practiced in both hospitals and (3) the use of SP as a source of legitimacy for non-profit hospitals rather than just as a rational approach to planning. All these factors had a significant influence on the way that SP was conducted in both hospital settings.

The existence of pluralistic goals, multiple actors and a nonlinear, loosely coupled system in hospitals leads to gaps and conflicts in terms of intentions, decisions, sensemaking and strategic actions in these organizations (Mintzberg, 1994; McDaniel, 2007; McDaniel & Driebe, 2004; Perrow, 1986; Weick, 1979, 1987). The non-linearity and plurality of interests in the daily life of a hospital, together with the autonomy of its health professionals, render traditional rational models and machine-like management forms less effective (McDaniel, 2007; Pascucci & Meyer, 2013; Perrow, 1986; Zimmerman, 2011).

We would argue that, although businesses and non-profit organizations have a similar need for an organizational strategy – to remain purposeful and effective (Moore, 2000) – non-profit hospitals, as social institutions, are value-oriented entities and that their main value lies in fulfilling social objectives by meeting the expectations of their stakeholders (Oster, 1995), including trustees, donors, managers, volunteers and users of their services. Any attempt to link decisions, actions and outcomes tends to be particularly difficult in hospitals – labour-intensive service organizations whose core work is loosely coupled and intangible by nature.

In the context of non-profit hospitals, where the relevance of strategies is related to the value they add to the hospital's services and the extent to which they help it achieve its mission, resources are not an end in themselves but a critical means for achieving social purposes. However, as noted by Moore (2000), in non-profit organizations resources come from different sources and the quality of the services the organization provides and the relevance of its mission depend on public perception. It is clear in both the cases studied here that key strategies in the health area were an initiative of, and developed by, health professionals acting as amateur managers in their units rather than deliberate actions aligned with the central administration's decisions as expressed in the strategic plan. While some strategies were informally negotiated beforehand with the administration, others were stamped *ex post facto* by the top administration.

Studies on organizational performance and effectiveness are the subject of considerable controversy in the literature. In the case of SP and outcomes, there is weak alignment between strategic decisions, actions and outcomes, considerable inconsistency and a lack of common ground (Forbes, 1998; Hodgkinson & Starbuck, 2008; Snow & Hambrick, 1980). Hospitals typically use performance indicators such as cost-recovery, mortality, morbidity and occupancy rates (March & Sutton, 1997). However, these indicators measure only certain quantifiable elements rather than the essence of the productive effort of such organizations, namely, the value that health services add for individual users, something that is difficult or even impossible to measure. This has long been one of the key conundrums of hospital management.

Legitimacy and trust are key elements in any social organization. This is particularly true in the case of non-profit hospitals because of the social importance of the added value of the health services they provide. The findings of the two cases studied here indicate that some initiatives, such as fund-raising campaigns to finance particular health services, were seen by the stakeholders as initiatives linked *ex post facto* to SP that helped to reinforce the institutional image and create trust and legitimacy among stakeholders. Initiated by the top administration and conducted by operating core professionals, these strategies also play a public–relations role, strengthening the hospital's image and creating trust and prestige in the eyes of the community at large.

The discrepancies between the findings reported in the literature and our empirical results highlight a key aspect of hospital management. This has to do with the failure, mainly by top managers, to take into account the complexity of hospitals as organizations, for example, when managers insist on treating them as 'machine-like organizations', revealing a misunderstanding or an unwillingness to understand how a non-machine-like organization works (McDaniel, 2007; Mintzberg, 1994). Mintzberg (1994, p. 405) makes the following criticism in connection with this: 'Universities, hospitals, engineering firms, and the like fit better a configuration called professional driven by operating work that is highly complex if rather stable in execution'.

Finally, the empirical case studies described here serve to illustrate that SP in hospitals not only is unique but also offers certain practical and theoretical lessons. Among the latter is the fact that we must recognize that the time is ripe, not for developing strategic plans, but for investigating why hospital managers adopt managerial approaches and what their expectancies are in terms of outcomes and benefits. Indeed, research into the experiences of other hospitals may produce information and knowledge that could be of use to hospital managers. Another area that could be investigated is the concept of hospitals as complex, pluralistic, non-linear systems that produce distinct responses to changes as a result of the introduction of managerial fads like SP.

In practical terms, managerial approaches such as SP may be potentially disruptive when applied to hospital management. Firstly, it is quite evident that SP does not fit in the complex, unique context of hospitals as professional organizations. Secondly, hospital managers are usually amateurs and, lacking experience, are sometimes not fully aware, let alone critical, of the strengths and weaknesses of the new *managerialist* approaches sold in the market. They should be more concerned not about SP as a representation of managerial status but about how it can contribute to the success of a hospital, the fulfilment of a hospital's mission and the long-term survival of such a complex organization.

CONCLUDING REMARKS

The adoption of SP in complex systems brings with it the risk of ignoring the complex nature of hospitals and adopting a logical but artificial and simplistic approach. The findings of this study indicate that SP as a rational, *managerialist* approach in non-profit hospitals acts much more as a handicap than as a useful tool for managers in their efforts to cope with the pace of change resulting from the dynamic forces in the environment.

The case studies reported here revealed that *managerialist* practices face insurmountable problems because of the incompatibility between the Cartesian foundations and rationalist tools of SP and the unique organizational features of hospitals as complex systems. Cognitive, interpretive, social and political factors undermine any *managerialist* effort in such systems, leading to wasted resources and frustration among managers and stakeholders. Instead, SP efforts should provide guidance, integrate intentions and actions and motivate people so that benefits are generated for an organization. In the context of hospitals, SP takes on less importance and the benefits it confers are essentially symbolic. It allows the institution to project an image of sophisticated management, trust and legitimacy to its stakeholders and society but has little, if any, impact on organizational performance.

Even though there is a vast and growing body of research on SP and management, there is a major need for further studies on the management of strategies in complex systems such as hospitals. Progress in this field may emerge from areas such as daily managerial practices, in which routines and new initiatives are based on linear and non-linear interactions. Similarly, there is a need for research studies that seek to gain a better understanding of how organizational complexity affects the management of systems like hospitals.

However, hospital managers need to learn from their mistakes and improve the management of SP so that the necessary outcomes can be achieved. Furthermore, they should not neglect the contribution made by new research focused on hospital management, particularly new approaches that are better suited to the complex reality of such organizations. Effective hospital managers should use their knowledge and intuition to adapt theories and approaches to their own organization's culture. Otherwise, as Quinn (1980) reminds us, they will be continuously dancing the rain dance like the Indians, improving the ritual but not the weather.

REFERENCES

Ansoff, I. (1965). *Corporate strategy: An analytical approach to business policy for growth and expansion*. New York, NY: McGraw-Hill.

Argyris, C. (1999). *On organization learning*. Oxford: Blackwell.

Birnbaum, R. (2000). *Management fads in higher education*. San Francisco, CA: Jossey-Bass.

Bolman, L., & Deal, T. E. (2003). *Reframing organizations*. San Francisco, CA: Jossey-Bass.

Bolman, L., & Deal, T. E. (2008). *Reframing organizations* (4th ed.). San Francisco, CA: Jossey-Bass.

Bryson, J. M. (2004). *Strategic planning for public and nonprofit organizations* (3rd ed.). San Francisco, CA: Jossey-Bass.

Cadastro Nacional de Estabelecimentos de Saúde [CNEs]. (2015). Retrieved from http://cnes.datasus.gov.br/Index.asp?home=1. Accessed on March 06.

Carter, C., Clegg, C., & Kornberger, M. (2008). *A very short, fairly interesting and reasonably cheap book about studying strategy*. London: Sage.

Chakravarthy, B. S., & White, R. (2002). Strategy process: Forming, implementing and changing strategies. In A. Pettigrew, H. Thomas, & R. Whittington (Eds.), *Handbook of strategy and management* (pp. 183–205). London: Sage.

Clegg, S., Carter, C., Kornberger, M., & Schweitzer, J. (2011). *Strategy: Theory and practice* (Pt. 1–3). London: Sage.

Clegg, S. R. (1989). *Frameworks of power*. London: Sage.

Cohen, M. D., & March, J. G. (1974). *Leadership and ambiguity: The American college president*. Boston, MA: Harvard Business Press.

Correia, T. (2011). New public management in the Portuguese health sector: A comprehensive reading. *Sociologia Online*, *2*, 573–598.

Crossan, M., & Berdrow, I. (2003). Organizational learning and strategic renewal. *Strategic Management Journal*, *24*(11), 1087–1105.

Cummings, S. (2008). Strategy: Past, present and future. In D. Barry & H. Hansen (Eds.), *The Sage handbook of new approaches in management and organization* (pp. 184–194). London: Sage.

Cummings, S., & Wilson, D. (2003). *Images of strategy*. Oxford: Blackwell.

Cyert, R. M., & March, J. G. (1963). *A behavioral theory of the firm*. Englewood Cliffs, NJ: Prentice-Hall.

Dart, R. (2004). The legitimacy of social enterprise. *Nonprofit Management and Leadership*, *14*(4), 411–424.

Dimaggio, P. J., & Powell, W. W. (1983). The iron cage revisited: Institutional isomorphism and collective rationality in organizational fields. *American Sociological Review*, *48*(2), 147–169.

Eriksson, P., & Kovalainen, A. (2008). *Qualitative methods in business research*. London: Sage.

Etzioni, A. A. (1961). *Comparative analysis of complex organizations*. New York, NY: Free Press.

Etzioni, A. A. (1964). *Modern organizations*. Upper Saddle River, NJ: Prentice-Hall.

Forbes, D. P. (1998). Measuring the unmeasurable: Empirical studies of nonprofit organization effectiveness from 1977 to 1997. *Nonprofit and Voluntary Sector Quarterly*, *27*, 183–202.

Ghoshal. (2005). Bad management theories destroy good management practices. *Academy of Management Learning*, *1*, 75–91.

Hodgkinson, G., & Starbuck, W. H. (2008). Organizational decision making: Mapping terrains on different planets. In G. Hodgkinson & W. H. Starbuck (Eds.), *The Oxford handbook of organizational decision making* (pp. 1–29). Oxford: Oxford University Press.

Jarzabkowski, P., & Fenton, E. (2006). Strategizing and organizing in pluralistic contexts. *Long Range Planning*, *39*(6), 631–648.

Johnson, G., Melin, L., & Whittington, R. (2003). Micro strategy and strategizing: Towards an activity – Based view. *Journal of Management Studies*, *40*(1), 03–22.

Keller, G. (1983). *Academic strategy: The management revolution in higher education.* Baltimore, MD: Johns Hopkins.

Locke, R. R., & Spender, J. C. (2011). *Confronting managerialism: How business elite and their schools threw our lives out of balance*. London: Zed Books.

March, J. D. (1991). Exploration and exploitation in organizational learning. *Organization Science*, *2*(1), Special Issue, 71–87.

March, J. D., & Olsen, J. P. (Eds.), (1976). *Ambiguity and choice in organizations.* Bergen: Universitesforlaget.

March, J. G., & Sutton, R. I. (1997). Organizational performance as a dependent variable. *Organization Science*, *8*, 698–706.

McDaniel, R. R. Jr. (2007). Management strategies for complex adaptive systems: Sensemaking, learning, and improvisation. *Performance Improvement Quarterly*, *20*(2), 21–42.

McDaniel, R. R. Jr., & Driebe, D. J. (2004). *Uncertainty and surprise in complex systems.* Berlin: Springer.

Meyer, V. Jr., Pascucci, L., & Murphy, J. P. (2012). Implementing strategies in complex systems: Lessons from Brazilian hospitals. *Brazilian Administration Review – BAR*, *9*(Special Issue), 19–37.

Mintzberg, H. (1985). The organization as a political arena. *Journal of Management Studies*, *22*, 133–154.

Mintzberg, H. (1989). *Mintzberg on management: Inside our strange world of organizations.* New York, NY: Free Press.

Mintzberg, H. (1994). *The rise and fall of strategic planning*. New York, NY: Free Press.

Mintzberg, H. (2004). *Managers not MBAs: A hard look at the soft practice of managing and management development*. San Francisco, CA: Berret-Koehler.

Mintzberg, H., & Waters, J. A. (1985). Of strategies: Deliberate and emergent. *Strategic Management Journal*, *6*(3), 257–272.

Moore, M. H. (2000). Managing for value: Organizational strategy in for-profit, nonprofit, and governmental organizations. *Nonprofit and Voluntary Sector Quarterly*, *29*, 183–204.

Novak, J. D., & Cañas, A. A. (2008). *The theory underlying concept maps and how to construct and use them: technical report IHMC Cmap tools.* Ocala, FL: Institute for Human and Machine Cognition.

Orton, J. D., & Weick, K. E. (1990). Loosely coupled systems: A reconceptualization. *The Academy of Management Review*, *15*(2), 203–223.

Oster, S. (1995). *Strategic management for nonprofit organizations.* New York, NY: Oxford University Press. Chap. 4.

Parker, M. (2002). *Against management*. Cambridge: Polity Press.

Pascucci, L., & Meyer, V. Jr. (2013). Estratégia em Contextos Complexos e Pluralísticos. *Revista de Administração Contemporânea*, *17*(5), 536–555.

Perrow, C. (1965). Hospitals: Technology, structure and goals. In J. G. March (Ed.), *Handbook of organizations* (pp. 910–971). Chicago, IL: Rand McNally.

Perrow, C. (1986). *Complex Organizations: A critical essay* (3rd ed.). New York, NY: McGraw-Hill.

Pfeffer, J. (1994). *Competitive advantage through people: Unleashing the power of the workforce.* Boston, MA: Harvard Business School Press.

Pfeffer, J., & Salancik, G. (1974). Organizational decision making as a political process: The case of a university budget. *Administrative Science Quarterly*, *19*, 139–151.

Pfeffer, J., & Salancik, G. (2003). *The external control of organizations: A resource dependence perspective.* Stanford, CA: Stanford University Press.

Porter, M., & Teisberg, E. O. (2006). *Redefining healthcare: Creating value-based competition on results.* Boston, MA: Harvard Business School Press.

Powell, W. W., & Dimaggio, P. J. (1991). *The new institutionalism in organizational analysis* (pp. 41–62). Chicago, IL: The University of Chicago Press.

Quiggin, J. (2003). Word for wednesday: "managerialism" (definition). In R. R. Locke & J. C. Spender (Eds.), (2011), *Confronting managerialism: How the business elite and their schools threw our lives out of balance* (p. 5). New York, NY: Zed Books.

Quinn, J. B. (1980). *Strategies for change: Logical incrementalism.* Homewood, IL: Irwin.

Ribeiro, J. M. (2009). UHS development and hospital services rationing. *Ciência e Saúde Coletiva*, *14*(3), 771–782.

Richardson, K. A. (2008). Managing complex organizations: Complexity thinking and the art and science of management. *Emergence*, *10*(2), 13–26.

Richardson, K. A. (2011). Complexity and management: A pluralistic view. In P. Allen, S. Maguire, & B. McKelvey (Eds.), *The Sage handbook of complexity and management* (pp. 366–381). London: Sage.

Ritter, T., Wilkinson, I. F., & Johnston, W. J. (2004). Managing in complex business networks. *Industrial Marketing Management*, *33*(3), 175–183.

Schlesinger, M., & Gray, B. H. (2006). Nonprofit organizations and health care: Some paradoxes of persistent scrutiny. In W. W. Powell & R. Steinberg (Eds.), *The nonprofit sector: A research handbook* (2nd ed., pp. 378–414). New Haven, CT: Yale University Press.

Scott. (1995). *Institutions and organizations* (1st ed.). Thousand Oaks, CA: Sage.

Snow, C. C., & Hambrick, D. C. (1980). Measuring organisational strategies: Some theoretical and methodological problems. *Academy of Management Review*, *5*, 527–538.

Stacey, R. D. (1996). *Complexity and creativity in organizations.* San Francisco, CA: Berret-Koehler.

Stacey, R. D. (2006). *Complexity and creativity in organizations.* San Francisco, CA: Berret-Koeheler.

Stacey, R. D. (2010). *Complexity and organizational reality* (2nd ed.). New York, NY: Routledge.

Stacey, R. D., Griffin, D., & Shaw, P. (2000). *Complexity and management: Fad or radical challenge to systems thinking?* New York, NY: Routledge.

Stake, R. E. (1994). Case studies. In N. K. Denzin & Y. S. Lincoln (Eds.), *Handbook of qualitative research* (pp. 236–247). London: Sage.

Steiner, G. (1979). *Strategic planning.* New York, NY: The Free Press.

Suchman, M. C. (1995). Managing legitimacy: Strategic and institutional approaches. *Academy of Management Review*, *20*, 571–610.

Tsoukas, H., & Hatch, M. J. (2001). Complex thinking, complex practice: The case for a narrative approach to organizational complexity. *Human Relations*, *54*(8), 979–1013.
Weick, K. E. (1979). *The social psychology of organizing* (2nd ed.). New York, NY: Tandom House.
Weick, K. E. (1985). Cosmos vs. chaos: Sense and nonsense in electronic contexts. *Organizational Dynamics*, *14*(2), 51–64.
Weick, K. E. (1987). Substitutes for strategy. In D. J. Teece (Ed.), *The competitive challenge*. Cambridge, MA: Ballinger.
Weick, K. E. (1995). *Sensemaking in organizations* (Vol. 3). Thousand Oaks, CA: Sage.
Weick, K. E. (1998). Improvisation as a mindset for organizational analysis. *Organizational Science*, *9*(5), 543–555.
Zimmerman, B. (2011). How complexity science is transforming healthcare. In P. Allen, S. Maguire, & McKelvey (Eds.), *The SAGE handbook of complexity and management* (pp. 617–635). London: Sage.

VIVA SOLIDARITY!: FRAMING REPERTOIRE OF EMERGING SOCIAL MOVEMENTS AGAINST INSTITUTIONAL CHANGE IN TWO TURKISH UNIVERSITIES

Kutay Güneştepe and Deniz Tunçalp

ABSTRACT

Purpose of this paper is to explore how resistance of individual and collective actors play role in maintenance and change of institutions. Framing tactics of two emerging social movements in Istanbul Technical University and Middle East Technical University, which emerged against institutional changes in Turkish higher education, were examined by hybrid ethnography, using both online and offline data sources. Findings show that framing tactics of institutional entrepreneurs comprise different discourses and different forms of power, which also vary during different life stages of these movements. This paper contributes to existing literature in three ways. First power dynamics in institutional change, which is mostly disregarded in institutional theory, is taken into consideration. Second, with a longitudinal comparative study, it is shown that

Towards a Comparative Institutionalism: Forms, Dynamics and Logics Across the Organizational Fields of Health Care and Higher Education
Research in the Sociology of Organizations, Volume 45, 297–326

ISSN: 0733-558X/doi:10.1108/S0733-558X20150000045022

outcomes of social movements with similar demands may diverge according to different framing tactics based on power mechanisms that appealed at different stages of their life cycle. Third, this paper, as one of the few examples of a hybrid ethnographic approach, underlines the key role of considering both offline–online data sources, as an important part of actors' life that take place in the online world.

Keywords: Institutional change; social movements; resistance; power; online ethnography

INTRODUCTION

How does individual and collective resistance participate in the maintenance and change of macro institutions and micro routines of everyday life? Institutional theory has been traditionally considered as an actor-free explanation of social stability and was relatively silent on institutional change until the introduction of the concept of institutional entrepreneur (DiMaggio, 1988). Institutional entrepreneurs are actors who leverage their resources to construct or transform institutions (Maguire, Hardy, & Lawrence, 2004). For instance, Battilana, Leca, and Boxenbaum (2009) have reviewed the literature on institutional entrepreneurship and proposed a process model, describing different phases from the emergence of institutional entrepreneurs to their implementation of change. Later, institutional work perspective has been put forward as a key concept to describe the purposive action of institutional entrepreneurs "aimed at creating, maintaining and disrupting institutions" (Lawrence & Suddaby, 2006, p. 215).

Extant literature has conceptualized institutional entrepreneurs mostly as collectives, such as professional bodies, associations, business elites, networks, and social movements (Hardy & Maguire, 2008; Scott, 2008). On the other hand, social movements, as a distinct perspective of social inquiry, represent an important opportunity to extend institutional entrepreneurship, as both perspectives share views on embedded agency and how new institutions are created (Schneiberg & Lounsbury, 2008). However, while institutional entrepreneurship focuses on specific actors, social movements literature places greater emphasis on collectives and macro level struggles (Battilana et al., 2009).

Institutional entrepreneurs, both individuals and collectives, do their work mostly through discursive actions in micro-political struggles by framing their vision, description and purposes to build social support among people to change and reconstruct their respective fields (e.g., Fligstein & McAdam, 2012; Lounsbury, Ventresca, & Hirsch, 2003; Rao, Monin, & Durand, 2003). For example, a movement of chefs reframed their role and crafted an institutional change toward nouvelle cuisine (Rao et al., 2003). Similarly, art houses focusing on contemporary Indian paintings purposefully reframed Indian art as "modern" to institutionalize a new market category (Khaire & Wadhwani, 2010). During such struggles, groups dynamically create their collective action frames and challenge each other's framing until one particular group wins the framing contest and a shared understanding of reality is generally diffused (Benford & Snow, 2000; Rao & Kenney, 2008).

Political contest and debates between prevailing and emerging actors involve extensive power struggles, possibly resulting in the victory of one of the competing sides, thereby giving the winner an opportunity to extend its logic in the specific field. Such actors purposefully use discourses that attempt to shape the relevant institutions to gain legitimacy for their actions. These attempts also have a potential to realize those actors' interests. Discourses, enmeshed with the practice of power (Foucault, 1977), are key to understand practices of these institutional entrepreneurs (Clegg, Courpasson, & Phillips, 2006).

Discursive tactics and action framing are studied extensively in the extant literature (e.g., Misangyi, Weaver, & Elms, 2008; Rao, Morrill, & Zald, 2000; Snow & Benford, 1992). Action frames are frequently classified as diagnostic, prognostic, and motivational (Marullo, Pagnucco, & Smith, 1996; Snow & Benford, 1988). Discursive framing by various actors has also been studied extensively. For example, in a remarkable review of framing processes and social movements, Benford and Snow (2000) studied framing processes and social movements. They argued that framing is central to "understanding the character and course of social movements" (p. 611), and linked framing processes to other processes and outcomes of these movements. Whereas Fligstein and McAdam (2011) argue that individual and collective actors in "strategic action fields" use framing to interpret the actions of others. According to their perspective, frames of incumbent actors comprise their view of the field but challengers are expected to have oppositional perspectives. More recently, Werner and Cornelissen (2014) focus on the discursive tactics that are used to mobilize and align actors in an institutional field to support some institutional change and argued that, embedded actors make use of "frame shifting" and "frame blending" tactics to change the status quo, linking the micro and macro levels of analysis. However, how social movements, as institutional entrepreneurs, employ different types of framing in their discursive repertoire for political contestation and power struggles still needs further analysis.

In this paper, we study framing types used by social movements participating in the maintenance and change of institutional order in the field of Turkish higher education. We employed both different framing types in our analysis and have also theorized additional categories of framing based on their enmeshing with the micro-processes of institutionalization and power (Lawrence, Winn, & Jennings, 2001). Considering also the temporality of contestation, we have explored what types of frames have been employed at which stage of the struggle. Specifically, we have analyzed the framing of research assistants' solidarity movements at two leading Turkish universities, namely Istanbul Technical University (ITU) and Middle East Technical University (METU).

By analyzing different contexts and with different outcomes of the same struggle, we aim to understand how framing repertoires may impact development of a resistive identity and how enduring social movements enmesh their framing with power differently. Analyzing these mechanisms in a university, as a professional organization makes it more interesting, because professional organizations provide a more complex environment for institutional change, as professional roles and identities actively participate or impede such attempts. To make the story even more interesting, both movements emerged shortly before the time of the Gezi revolt in Turkey, where masses have taken the streets all around the country as the largest and the longest anti-government protest in Turkish history. We also describe how the wider social context relates to the life of these social movements.

Our contribution, in this paper, is threefold. First, we develop a novel framework for power dynamics and temporality in framing. Second, we explain how social movements employ different framing tactics with different power processes as institutional entrepreneurs. Third, we have implemented a hybrid ethnographic method in developing our case studies, working with both online and offline data sources.

The paper is organized in six sections. After this introduction, in the second section we review the social movements and framing actions literature in relation to institutional change. The methodology of our study is described next, while the fourth section describes our case studies in the organizational and social context of those movements together with the history of Turkish Higher Education. Finally, in the last two sections, we discuss our results and conclude our argument by suggesting avenues for future research inquiries.

SOCIAL MOVEMENTS AND THE FRAMING OF INSTITUTIONAL CHANGE

A social movement is "a network of informal interactions between a plurality of individuals, groups and/or organizations, engaged in political or cultural conflict on the basis of a shared collective identity" (Diani, 1992, p. 13). It is different than other "forms of collective action which are more structured and which take in the form of parties, interest groups or religious sects, as well as single protest events or ad hoc political coalitions" (della Porta & Diani, 1999, p. 16). Therefore, social movements are different than other voluntary organizations or collectivities and have been key agents in criticizing institutional assumptions (Offe, 1985), as they have an inclusive, open and fluid organization (Diani, 1992) striving for material and symbolic resources to achieve some greater good.

With symbolic and material objectives, analyzing the framing activities of social movements became a dominant approach after the early 1990s (Benford, 1997; Goodwin & Jasper, 1999). Frames are interpretative schemas that simply explain and codify the world, thereby mobilizing potential participants, guiding their action toward what is meaningful, legitimating their activities, and organizing people's experiences (Benford & Snow, 2000; Snow & Benford, 1992), especially when these resonate well with target audiences (Benford & Snow, 2000; Marullo et al., 1996). The frame concept originated in the psychology of communication studies (Goffman, 1974) to analyze how culture is implicated in social interactions. Frame analysis has further evolved into an empirical and analytical approach to understand how political and social problems are understood by different groups of people (Gamson, 1992). However, frames are not simple aggregate or average representations of collectivities but integrate the results of multilateral negotiation processes and shared meanings (Benford & Snow, 2000; Snow & Benford, 1988; Snow, Rochford, Worden, & Benford, 1986).

A framing process has three general forms: diagnostic, prognostic, and motivational framing (Marullo et al., 1996; Snow & Benford, 1988). *Diagnostic framing* identifies a condition as problematic and requiring improvement. It is employed to discredit the conventional order, to establish the authority of the speaker, to vilify the adversary and to establish responsibility. *Prognostic framing* prescribes solutions to the problem. It proposes a new order, forms of punishment, and primacy of objectives, specifying a set of targets regarding the issue under focus. *Motivational framing* mobilizes the members toward implementing the solution and advances identity claims. Such frames, generating urgency, call their audience to action. There are also other types and classifications of framing in the literature. For example, there are hegemonic frames (Blum-Kulka & Liebes, 1993), injustice frames (Gamson, Fireman, & Rytina, 1982), master frames (McAdam, 1994), or non-violence frames (Marullo et al., 1996). However, we have decided to classify frames as diagnostic, prognostic and motivational not only because it is the most frequently employed classification but also since it correlates directly with the different stages of institutional change: first creating the need for change; then maintaining an alternative argument; and therefore disrupting the existing institutional order. Thus, we think this classification follows our intention of uncovering framing tactics of institutional entrepreneurs well, at different temporal stages of institutional change.

In addition to this classification, we have also devised an additional frame classification based on frames enmeshing with the micro-processes of institutionalization and power, as we are interested in understanding how framing contests enacted by different social movements participate at different stages of power struggles. Based on Lawrence et al. (2001), we have defined four frame categories as influencing frames, forcing frames, disciplining frames and dominating frames. *Influencing frames* involve specific forms of language that promote a certain vision or action for others. These frames assume an episodic/agential power base and aim the decision-making or non-decision making of others, making them its subjects. This mechanism might be voluntary or manipulative in nature. *Forcing frames*, on one hand, have an episodic/agential power base but involve a language that treats its audience as objects, trying to leave no legitimate decision-making capacity to behave otherwise. On the other hand, *disciplining frames* have a systemic/social power base, such as law or social norms, and justify their claims from some external interpersonal reference, still leaving a range of alternative behaviors of others under surveillance and potential examination of that specific external reference. *Dominating frames* are also empowered from a systemic/social power base, claiming that there are no legitimate options of behaving other than the suggested practice. In terms of temporality of the behavioral change, influencing and disciplining frames need more time to create the desired change (Lawrence et al., 2001). On the other hand, for stability of outcomes, disciplining and dominating frames are expected to create more enduring results (Lawrence et al., 2001) and therefore a more persistent social movement.

To sum up, we are in agreement with Benford and Snow (2000) and Snow (2004) about the existence of a research gap that considers framing not only as a strategic, but also as an ongoing, emergent, interactive. and dynamic process. Hence, we contend that there is value in examining the micro-processes of institutionalization by which social movements construct their framing at different stages of their life cycle. We address this knowledge gap by exploring how frames are constructed and reconstructed in relation to the power and temporality of social movements. We have employed the two types of frame classifications described above simultaneously to collectively analyze the frame types observed, with respect to their substantive content and power substance. In the next section, we explain our methodology on how we engaged with the research field to explore the framing of these social movements.

METHODOLOGY

In this study, we have developed two qualitatively interrelated case studies (Yin, 1994), based on online and conventional ethnographic fieldwork on the assistants' solidarity movements in two different universities, to develop an understanding of the meso-level dynamics (McAdam, 2003) with their contextual richness and complexity (Dyer & Wilkins, 1991). One of the authors employed participant observation (Jorgensen, 1989) to study the assistants' solidarity movements at both universities for 8 months between October 2013 and May 2014. The other author kept his empirical distance, playing an anchor role and addressing possible reflexivity shortcomings in "going native" (O'Reilly, 2009) and potential problems of participant observation due to becoming too involved with the target community.

Studying these movements by hybridizing both online and offline ethnographic methods is a recommended research practice, as online media increase their importance in our daily life (Tunçalp & Lê, 2014). Online secondary data, such as announcements, e-mail bulletins, blog sites, and textual data generated in the social media has been the main source of our empirical material. Textual field data from online sources, such as blog and social media posts and e-mail bulletins, were manually content analyzed against the categories of framing described or developed in the previous section. For the content analysis, one author, who had immersed himself in these movements during the ethnographic study, did the content analysis by reading and classifying the written material. The other author controlled the classification and coding generated, comparing the coded texts against the definitions of the framing categories.

We also supplemented our field data with offline ethnographic material, in-depth interviews and focus groups to gain better understanding of the foundational histories, internal dynamics and external links of these movements. One of the authors has interviewed participating and non-participating assistants at both universities, members of the university administration and faculty members. We did snowball sampling and asked our informants to introduce us to other informants. In order to ensure reliability, we started snowball sampling of multiple members in every informant group. While this does not create a fully representative random sample, we consider our sampling as sufficient, as we reached a comprehensive level of understanding, as we continued this process until a satisfactory level of empirical saturation was reached. We consider this an appropriate sampling strategy, as the movements in both groups are very fluid and dynamic and so it was impossible to create a fully random sampling frame. In total we undertook 24 interviews as part of the ethnographic process. All interviews were digitally recorded by permission and transcribed verbatim. Detailed notes that also contained short quotes from informants were taken during interviews directly after the interview. The same author has also kept an ethnographic diary of extensive handwritten field notes during the study, covering events, interactions, observations, and discussions.

During the data collection, the emergence and the early stages of these movements had also been questioned retrospectively (see Appendix A for our interview guide). All of our questions were collected from multiple informants. Answers were validated using other interviews and secondary data to triangulate interview accounts for construct validity (Yin, 1994). Since both movements have attempted to gain the support of public opinion, we were able to assemble a large archive of multimedia data, including blog posts, newsletters, letters to members of the respective universities, flyers, forum discussions, and online videos of protests.

One of our authors' participation in these movements was not covert. All informants were openly informed about the identity of the researchers and the objectives of this research prior to gaining access to these groups and at the beginning of every interview or group meeting. Participant observations in meetings, protests, and forums of these movements were done both online and offline, and longitudinal data collection strategy helped us to develop insights into dialectic mechanisms of power and resistance.

One of the authors, who actively collected data, is a graduate student but has not been employed as an assistant at either of these universities. He participated in meetings, forums, and protests by these movements and collected data. Our primary data sources were the member interviews, Internet sites, and social media profiles of these movements; however, the mentioned author did not become fully embedded into these movements, in order to keep one's distance and thus be able to objectively analyze the collected data both from an insider and outsider perspective. While we have taken an interpretive perspective of inquiry from the inside, we have also tried to maintain an outside view of the phenomena, thus keeping ourselves at the boundary of the research field.

Our experiences of these movements and our social positions have necessarily influenced our analysis of the data. While we have carefully crafted our methods to meet methodological reflexivity up to certain extent, trying to establish reliability, validity and repeatability, our formative social locations, relations and dispositions as graduate student and faculty member at one of these universities, has influenced our accounts and understanding of these movements. In order to compensate for this and develop epistemic reflexivity (Johnson & Duberley, 2003), we have constantly discussed the assumptions, values and preferences inherent in our social positions throughout the project, to discover the underlying social reality. As the meanings of events, stories, and practices can only be understood in relation to "frame of meaning" (Giddens, 1976, p. 142), through the double hermeneutics process, we tried to involve our self-understanding of science through science. As theoretically reflexive individuals (Giddens, 1991), our accounts also construct the self-image of our social worlds and ourselves.

Our participant observation of the focal phenomena necessarily created reflexive situations for our research subjects and affected the subjects' own perceptions of the phenomena and their own role in it. This necessarily helps them question their own pre-assumptions of the movements themselves, unavoidably influencing movements and challenging our own assumptions about movements and our subjectivity. While our methodology cannot be considered as action research, this circularity creates a "participatory action research" situation in our research (McIntyre, 2008). Through the research process, we have taken both subject and object roles, bringing the discussion of self-reflexivity (Johnson & Duberley, 2003) to our agenda, leading us to question who "we" are and who "they" are in our accounts and to understand where our researcher selves and research subjects became joined. With inherently circular knowledge claims (Giddens, 1976), we do not assert perfect objectivity or seek for entirely subjective evaluations, but rather we have tried to be "critically intersubjective" (Fay, 1996), taking a fallibilist, perspectivist epistemology in trying to develop an understanding of our focal phenomena "both within and across traditions of inquiry" (Martin & Sugarman, 1999, p. 63).

CASE STUDIES: A TALE OF TWO SOCIAL MOVEMENTS

Two Leading Turkish Universities: ITU and METU

Assistants' solidarity movements have emerged in different universities in Turkey as separate and independent movements within a short time frame, as the government changed the employment scheme of assistants at universities. In our study, we focus on two of those movements taking place at two leading Turkish universities, namely Istanbul Technical University (ITU) and Middle East Technical University (METU). The movements at these universities are by far the largest and the most active compared to other similar movements. Both ITU and METU are state universities that identify mostly with engineering and architectural education. While both are also technical universities, they have very different histories, representing diverse social settings for our analysis.

ITU's history goes back more than 240 years. It was established in 1773 as the Imperial School of Naval Engineering of the Ottoman Empire. On 1928, it evolved into a modern university under the influence of early German technical universities. Currently, ITU has both graduate and postgraduate programs on diverse fields of engineering and architecture. It enrolls more than 30,000 students, and employs 1,130 faculty members and 1,300 research assistants across five campuses (in 13 faculties and 6 research institutes) located in the country's largest urban area, Istanbul. METU, on the other hand, was founded in 1956 with strong direct and indirect support of the American government. It has one central campus, located in Ankara (the country's capital), and it currently holds a student population of nearly 23,000. METU currently employs 750 faculty members and 1,400 research assistants (in five faculties and five graduate schools).

Traditionally, ITU graduates have assumed top-level public administrative and political positions. For instance, since 1980, three prime ministers of Turkey, who identified themselves with the right wing of the political spectrum, have been graduates and/or faculty members of ITU. However, there have also been strong leftist movements at ITU. METU, on the other hand, is well known for its pro-revolutionary identity and a strong on-campus presence of leftist political movements. Similar to ITU, METU has also had several graduates who became prominent politicians and government officials. However, with its remarkable political symbol, "Revolution" Stadium, (see Fig. 1) and with frequent protests and boycotts

Fig. 1. The REVOLUTION Stadium of Middle East Technical University.

against the ruling elite, METU's single campus is much more politicized when compared to all five ITU campuses.

Wider Social Context and the Gezi Revolt

To have a comprehensive understanding of the institutional change and the resistance to it, it is important to grasp the contemporary political environment of Turkey. At the time this paper was written, the Justice and Development Party (AKP), which had defined itself as a conservative democratic party (Öncü, 2013), has shaped the country's political environment for nearly 15 years. Various AKP governments have undertaken neoliberal and partly conservative ("Islamic") changes, mostly guided by the World Bank's economic recommendations. These have been strongly endorsed by local political circles across the world (Öncü, 2013). Despite the implied reformism in the main political discourse, some of the institutional changes under the AKP government have been causing tensions, mostly amongst the secular part of the population. However, up to the Gezi Revolt in 2013, the AKP's political transformation never faced major popular opposition (Öncü, 2013).

At the end of May 2013, a group of protestors resisting the construction of a shopping mall in the small, "Gezi" park, located in central Istanbul, occupied the former to block the removal of trees by construction workers. Sudden and harsh Police intervention against the protesters set off the Gezi Park revolt which, while it began in Istanbul, quickly spread across the 79 districts of Turkey. While the whole unrest had arisen over the protection of a small park, it evolved into an uprising against the current political regime. Protests lasted for nearly one month, especially in the big cities of Turkey such as Istanbul, Ankara, and Izmir. However, even much smaller cities of Turkey, with no history of political unrest, experienced major political protests. Diverse political identities, social groups, and movements, such as socialists, revolutionary Marxists, Kurdish parties, gay, and lesbians, as well as anti-capitalist Muslims (Öncü, 2013), all took part in these protests.

The assistants' solidarity movement emerged and grew in this socio-political context. Moreover, the movement at ITU not only established relations with the Gezi resistance but also became one of the central groups of the revolt. For example, at one of the ITU campuses, namely the Taşkışla campus close to the Gezi Park, one of the members of the movement, Ceyda Sungur, an assistant at the ITU Architecture Faculty, became a central icon of the Gezi resistance (see Fig. 2). Furthermore, the ITU central administration's decision to close the Taşkışla campus to Gezi protesters and ITU students trying to escape the police intervention became one of the main issues of the ITU Assistants' Solidarity movement.

Turkish Higher Education and the Emergence of the Assistants Solidarity Movements

Turkish higher education underwent a major change in the early 1980s with the military coup that introduced large-scale changes in the field, imposing a highly centralized regime with a strong regulatory body called the Council of Higher Education (Yüksek Öğretim Kurumu – YÖK), "imposing a range of strict requirements that would force sameness, and introducing aspirations for greater marketization" (Üsdiken, Topaler, & Koçak, 2013, p. 191). Since 1980, YÖK regime has introduced a system

Fig. 2. Woman in Red Dress: An ITU Assistant, Who is a Member of the Solidarity Group, Became One of the Icons of the Gezi Resistance.

that is mostly inspired by an American university model and the structure of METU, to become a reference for all Turkish universities. First of all, it removed the historically dual structure in Turkish Higher education by converting all academies into universities. Following a continental European Model, departments in Turkish universities have been historically organized in separate faculties with variety of different types of naming. After the YÖK regime, different departments are collected together as large faculties; for example, the Department of Management and the Department of Economics became parts of a larger *Faculty of Economics and Administrative Sciences*. Similarly, the separate departments of Mechanical Engineering and Civil Engineering were joined together as the *Faculty of Engineering*. Also, nation-wide, all department and faculty names have been standardized, except ITUs. Due to its historical significance, traditional department names and faculty structures have remained intact only at ITU (Üsdiken, 2004).

Over time, METU became a de facto organizational form, functioning as an ideal model for other universities. While other universities began changing their organizational model and nomenclature to one based on that of METU, ITU remained distinct by keeping its strong department-centered faculties tradition (Üsdiken et al., 2013). For example, as opposed to the situation at other Turkish universities, management is not just a faculty department but also rather a stand-alone faculty. Similarly, engineering education is not organized under different departments within a single faculty. There are independent faculties such as the Faculty of Civil Engineering, the Faculty of Mechanical Engineering, etc. (Üsdiken et al., 2013). However, ITU has also undergone its own evolution toward a more managerialized university (Erden Bayazıt, 2005).

One of the more recent changes toward marketization has manifested itself in the way assistants are employed in universities, moving from permanent employment to temporary contracts. Regardless of their contract type, all assistants are responsible for assisting in teaching, research, and experiments, and "additionally perform other related tasks that are ordered by authorized other units" (Higher Education Law, 1981). The permanent staff contract is called "33a," named after the clause of the respective law that designates this type of contract. Similarly, "50d" corresponds to a temporary employment contract for graduate students with the same set of responsibilities that needs to be reviewed and renewed annually. While "33a" assistants have some sort of employment guarantee at the same university after completing their Ph.Ds, "50d"s do not have such rights and universities are actually being discouraged from hiring their own "50d"s, to avoid "academic inbreeding" (Horta, Veloso, & Grediaga, 2010).

In June 2012, drawing on earlier legislation passed by the Turkish parliament in February 2011 defining the maximum graduation period for masters as three years and for PhDs as six years, YÖK ordered all universities to dismiss all those "50d" assistants unable to complete their graduate degrees within the defined period, since they no longer had the right to their student status. The Education and Science Workers' Union (Eğitim-Sen) took this decree to the higher administrative court and received a court interpretation that may help university administrations avoid implementing the YÖK decree. However, ITU and METU administration had already dismissed a large number of research assistants following the initial receipt of the decree. Since the average duration of masters and Ph.D. degrees is claimed to take longer for assistants due to workload, this policy has created significant resistance and strong rejection among research assistants and the Assistants' Solidarity movement flourished first at ITU, and then at METU in 2012.

While both ITU and METU groups were aware of, and sometimes even communicate with, each other, they operated as independent entities with their own decision-making procedures and agenda setting. Both showed a network type of organizing (Juris, 2004) with no defined hierarchical position or division of responsibility. A willing member took each task and there was no central apparatus to make decisions or assign roles and responsibilities to different members. Issues were discussed and decisions were made by consensus in regular meetings with the agreement of whoever was present at a particular meeting. The preference was to avoid voting, but rather they discussed and tried to convince others regarding planned actions. However, this strategy also made decision-making a lengthy process and sometimes caused some members to avoid showing disagreement or speaking-up for their arguments in order to avoid long discussions. In some cases, it had also caused some members to leave the movement, as it was hard to disagree, or when there was an internal debate, it took too long to solve an open issue. While their name, main focus, and governance/decision-making structure was the same, both movements had a different path with different framing tactics, contextual relations, and their resulting evolution.

Milestones of Emergence, Growth, Maturity, and Decay

The ITU movement issued a press release on September 2012 and stated its demands. Their main one was to remove all time limitations regarding student status for all assistants. They also officially sent their request to the Rectorate and this marked the beginning of the movement. Following this, the protests began at the various ITU campuses. The movement started organizing forum meetings in front of the main cafeteria and organized marches to the Rectorate building. As members pointed out, the initial events were designed to grab the attention of the university community, popularize the movement, and to make people take notice of the assistants' employment-related problems.

At the emergence stage, the ITU movement mostly used forcing and disciplining frames to point out problematic situations arising from the new YÖK order and practices of the university administration. For example, in one of their posts they try to coerce the university administration regarding the solution of the problem:

> … to declare that we are pursuing our demands which are supported by hundreds of signatures and intend to provide support to our friends and until they return to their jobs, we will not leave our university. (Asistan Dayanışması, 2012b)

They also refer to disciplining frames to provide their actions with greater legitimacy than that of the higher order institutions. Especially they blame university administration because of its "unlawful" practices:

> We are calling on the ITU Rectorate to give up the illegal practices which are a trial of the new YÖK decree that will be on the agenda of the Turkish parliament on the following days .... (Asistan Dayanışması, 2012c)

The METU movement emerged after that of ITUs. At METU, academics have an NGO called Instructors' Association (Öğretim Elemanları Dernegi – OED). OED holds regular meetings with a working agenda with its active members every month. The assistants' employment security became a part of the meeting agenda of OED at the October 2012 meeting. Assistants at that meeting acknowledged their solidarity with the ITU movement and suggested establishing a similar group at METU to "come together to defend assistants' rights." While there are different organizations active in METU campus that are supporting assistants' rights, such as OED and Eğitim-Sen, they are not fully focusing on these issues, as they do not directly represent assistants. Thus, a large group of METU assistants held a number of face-to-face meetings and e-mail discussions and decided to start resistance at METU in December 2012.

While both movements mainly demanded the removal of the employment time limits and advocate the protection of assistants' rights, the problems of the METU movement are somewhat different from those at ITU. Without any resistance for several years, the METU administration had already been enforcing shorter time limits to master and Ph.D. education that imposed heavier requirements than those of ITU and YÖK. While ITU assistants were asking for the revoking of the YÖK decree, the METU movement was asking the university administration to relax the special rules imposed by the university itself. As one interviewee explained:

> The Assistants' Solidarity movement at ITU reminded us that practices that we had become used to at METU are not normal ... our tenure of office is not finished, we are fired by the university but most of the people perceive this as end of a duty and considered it to be normal.

Members of the METU movement made use of influencing frames while diagnosing the problems. They tried to get involved in negotiations at the emergence stage of their movement. A blog post of the movement, for instance, reads as follows:

> We are inviting the university administration to hear our demands, ... and together find solutions to our common problems .... (Anonymous, 2013a)

While offering solutions, both movements used forcing frames and mostly preferred dictating their demands by objectifying the other side. For example:

> ... The University Senate's decisions defining assistants' working period at METU should be repealed immediately .... (Anonymous, 2013a)

The ITU movement has also supported their arguments with dominating frames by mentioning previous court decisions regarding the dismissed assistants.

> We are demanding [the ITU administration] not to violate legal rights of assistants regarding the 33a designation. (Asistan Dayanışması, 2012a)

On the other hand, the METU movement used another episodic mechanism, influencing frames, to develop prognoses.

> We demand all assistants, who complete their PhDs successfully and have departmental approvals, to have job security (according to the 33a clause of the current regulation) and all related criteria to be set in the form of objective and transparent processes. (Anonymous, 2013a)

After their emergence, both movements started disseminating their messages to promote their diagnosis of the problem and their suggested solution, while also trying to mobilize potential and existing members. Influencing frames are prevailing mechanisms to motivate these members regardless of the life cycle stage. Both movements have tried to call and convince people to support their movement with similar announcements:

> We are expecting everyone who is worried about ITU's current position to our activities .... (Asistan Dayanışması, 2013)

> ... as METU assistants we do not accept conditions worse than those YÖK has decreed and expect your support for the struggle against these decisions .... (Anonymous, 2013b)

Both movements had demanded to be considered seriously, and to deal directly with the university administration. When the ITU movement managed to sit down at the table with the Rector, it also enhanced its legitimacy on campus and started its growth period, where more assistants began participating regularly in their meetings. In contrast, the METU movement never entered such a growth period and only achieved recognition of the university administration shortly before their complete termination in June 2013. At that time, the university had arranged a fair for high school graduates to convince them to choose METU. The movement requested permission from the organizers to hold a forum during the festival. However they were not allowed to do so. Despite this rejection, they set up their tent and had their posters. This was the last known protest of the movement at METU and they have not held any activities since then. The regular meetings stopped, as increasingly fewer assistants were attending them. Currently, the METU movement is no longer active, as one informant described:

> We established the assistant's movement as an umbrella group to cover all assistants who are not members of Eğitim-Sen or ÖED. However we were not successful. A few members of the movement are now part of ÖED, which is at least recognized by the METU Rectorate. (Anonymous, 2014)

Thus, while the ITU movement gained some status and acknowledgment that fueled its growth, the METU movement remained marginal and became extinct. Therefore, we have taken the Rector meeting at ITU as a milestone indicating the first meaningful achievement of the movement and the starting of its growth stage. In the growth stage the ITU movement continued to employ forcing frames while diagnosing problems.

> Until this injustice comes to an end, the resistance of the assistants will continue at the tent that is placed in front of the Rectorate building in the ITU Maslak campus. (Asistan Dayanışması, 2012d)

The movement also preferred forcing frames while offering solutions at this stage. Until the end of this period, one of the movements' main demands was canceling the dismissal of "overdue" assistants and letting them return to their jobs again. They mostly applied forcing frames to get results before any more assistants were dismissed.

> We will not allow future of ITU to be pillaged and will protect the rights of assistants. (Asistan Dayanışması, 2012d)

The ITU movement reached its maturity stage when all "overdue" assistants were dismissed but the movement has survived nonetheless. While the termination of existing contracts and dismissed assistants represent an ultimate failure, the Assistants' Solidarity movement at ITU is still living and very active. They are still organizing protests, marches and regular meetings, and updating their blog and Facebook pages.

At the maturity stage, the ITU movement referred to problems by using influencing frames. For example, during those days some assistants returned to work in accordance with a court decision, however, as the movement argued, other assistants under the same circumstances were not reinstated. The movement tried to influence the university administration as follows:

> We are expecting that members of the university administration will not remain quiet and will become a part of the offence. (Asistan Dayanışması, 2014b)

They also offered solutions by employing influencing frames:

> ... as the ITU Assistant Solidarity Movement, we are saluting the resistance of students and inviting the ITU Rectorate to satisfy the demands mentioned .... (Asistan Dayanışması, 2014a)

As the employment terminations for "overdue" assistants have been completed, the movement shifted its interest to the legal process where dismissed assistants took the university administration to court to obtain a legal order for their reinstatement. The ITU movement is still trying to attract new members from the newcomer and "50d" assistants and maintain itself as an active group at ITU today, discussing issues about the university, academics, assistants and students. It is also more concerned with broader national political issues – aiming to participate in, and bring those debates to, the ITU campus.

DISCUSSION: FRAMING REPERTOIRE OF TWO MOVEMENTS

We have analyzed the framing of textual material with two framing typologies: General Framing and Power-Based Framing. Table 1 describes the predominant power types identified as diagnostic, prognostic and motivational frames in emergence, growth, and maturity stages of the ITU movement, whereas Table 2 describes the same for the emergence stage of the METU movement.

Table 1. Framing Repertoire of the ITU Movement.

	Diagnostic Frames	Prognostic Frames	Motivational Frames
Emergence	Forcing frames (32%) Disciplining frames (11%)	Forcing frames (25%) Dominating frames (13%)	Influencing frames (%19) –
Growth	Forcing frames (33%) –	Forcing frames (33%) –	Influencing frames (33%) –
Maturity	Influencing frames (26%) –	Influencing frames (10%) –	Influencing frames (29%) Disciplining frames (15%)

Note: Frequency% values higher than 9% are reported to locate predominant types.

Table 2. Framing Repertoire of the METU Movement.

	Diagnostic Framing	Prognostic Framing	Motivational Framing
Emergence	Influencing frames (%35)	Forcing frames (%26)	Influencing frames (%18)
	–	Influencing frames (%17)	–

The data show that, in both of the movements, episodic framings (Clegg, 1989; Lawrence et al., 2001) prevail at every stage of their life cycle. Powerful actors are able to exercise systemic power and maintain it over others through the control of information, mass media, and process of socialization (Lukes, 1974). In this case, the power balance is against solidarity movements since university administrations and YÖK have greater access to such hegemonic sources of power (Levy & Scully, 2007). Accordingly, movements may need to refer to more episodic framings during their struggle to gain legitimacy (Suchman, 1995).

During the initial stages of the ITU movement, problem and solution descriptions were more forceful, possibly creating faster results in terms of establishing the movement, compared to a scenario with more influencing frames. As the movement gained legitimacy and recognition over time, the influencing frames increasingly replaced forcing frames. During the emergence and growth stages, the movement objectified its targets in its rhetoric and discourses. This objectification was employed to gather results within a short time. According to Lawrence et al. (2001, p. 635) "... the way in which acts of force objectify their targets will have a significant effect on the pace of institutionalization processes. Unlike influence, where the target's choice processes cause delay, the use of force acts immediately and directly on the practices themselves ...." For example, during its emergence, the ITU movement occupied the Mechanical Engineering Faculty after a protest march that began from Taksim Square and ended at the ITU Gümüşsuyu campus.

On the other hand, at all stages of the ITU movement and during the emergence of the METU movement, motivational frames were employed for the mobilization of members and for establishing identities. According to our analysis, these frames were primarily influencing frames. A number of papers consider "influence" as a form of manipulation, as a component of framing (Clegg, 1975; Lawrence et al., 2001; Lukes, 1974). According to the literature, social movements use framing to align their ideologies, understandings and identities with their supporters and members (Snow et al., 1986). As Davis, McAdam, Richard, Mayer, and Zald (2005, p. 49) argues "... framing involves the strategic creation and manipulation of shared understandings and interpretations of the world, its problems, and viable courses of action." In our analysis, we understood that both movements use influencing frames primarily to exercise power over others, thus making them subjects, to provide support, gain more members and establish their identities. Although this type of framing requires time and causes delay in the institutionalization process, the actors need time for decision-making and to evaluate the costs and benefits of engaging in social movements (Hendry, 2000).

While influence and force had been the primary mechanisms, the ITU movement has anchored its problem diagnosis and suggested solution with social and external references at the emergence stage, and with disciplining and dominating frames toward its central opponent, the university's administration. This may have helped the movement in acquiring further legitimacy for its claims. According to the literature, actors, as institutional entrepreneurs, refer to higher order logic prevailing in the field and "embed their project more firmly in one of the possible institutional foundations" (Clemens & Cook, 1999, p. 459). The movement at ITU especially acquired such legitimization in the early stages of its life cycle. Their claims are made against decisions of YÖK and the ITU administration, both more powerful than the ITU Assistants' Solidarity Movement. Therefore, they grounded their basic message on higher-level institutional references, such as "autonomy of universities," "job security," and "law and justice."

Another interesting observation is that, once the ITU movement matured, it started employing more disciplining frames. At the same time, it also employed influencing frames, as a secondary mechanism, to create a faster and more enduring alignment among its members and potential supporters. Lawrence et al. (2001) argue that, as influence and discipline slowly diffuse among members, their combination will affect the situation faster. It also provides institutional support for the influence mechanisms, leading to enhanced stability. Consequently, members of the movement begin participating in a movement's actions without external motivators (Lawrence et al., 2001).

Comparing the framing repertoire of the METU movement (see Table 2) also reveals interesting results. The terminal failure of the movement at METU may have multiple explanations. It took a milder attitude in explaining its diagnosed problems by using influencing frames, and did not appeal using forcing frames. This movement also did not provide additional support to its claims with systemic/social powers, or with disciplining and dominating frames. We argue that this is mostly because of the assistants were already acquainted with METU's routinized practices on assistantship such as hiring and firing criteria, job descriptions etc., and thus considered this as taken for granted (Zucker, 1977) and appropriate (March & Olsen, 1989), until the emergence of protests and the movement against similar practices at ITU was initiated. So, they had never tried to relate their claims with prevailing institutions (Friedland & Alford, 1991) to gain higher legitimacy and acceptance.

CONCLUSION

How does the framing of issues change during the emergence, growth and maturity of social movements targeting institutional change? What is the role of power while framing and legitimizing the demands of social movements? In this paper, we have focused on the framing tactics of two emerging social movements at two different universities in Turkey that aim to de-institutionalize an enforced employment practice in higher education. We have synthesized two framing classifications from the literature, one of which is used as a general approach while analyzing the framings of social movements (Marullo et al., 1996; Snow & Benford, 1988) and the other one was devised by us to understand power-related dynamics during institutionalization processes (Lawrence et al., 2001). With the help of these lenses, we have analyzed the online textual material that has been enriched with in-depth interviews and focus groups. Accordingly, we assessed the framing repertoire of the Assistant's Solidarity Movement at two universities, over different stages of the movements' life cycle.

This paper contributes to the existing literature in three ways. First of all, it takes into consideration power dynamics, which has been mostly neglected in neo-institutional theory (Mizruchi & Fein, 1999) and in framing research (Carragee & Roefs, 2004). We devised a novel approach to understand covert or overt power relationships in discourses and framings of social movements toward institutional change. Clegg et al. (2006, p. 17) mentioned the link between power and discourse as: "Power and discourses are equally intermingled in so far as they constitute the political structure of organizations through diverse circuits of power. Discourses shape structures and provide the means for ordering the political structure. Thus, organizations and individuals use discourses purposefully to shape the political situations in and through which they can act and perform." The enmeshed relationships between the discourses and power relations are central to understand institutional entrepreneurship and change (Mahoney & Thelen, 2010).

Secondly, we developed an understanding of how social movements, as institutional entrepreneurs, appeal to different framing tactics with different power processes. Institutional entrepreneurs deploy different strategic actions to reconfigure power relations and distribute resources according to their own interests (Levy & Scully, 2007). We explored power mechanisms that had been exercised by two different movements for different life cycle stages and found that tactics diverged between the movements and also varied for different time frames. We conclude that, even if social movements start out with very similar demands and in the same organizational field, their outcomes may diverge according to the differences and changes in their framing strategies during their life cycle. We argue that these tactics are mostly based on different power mechanisms that influence the legitimization of the movements' demands and actions, leading toward the establishment of a more enduring movement.

Thirdly, we have worked both with online and offline empirical data to understand these social movements. Using online sources of data for ethnography is a relatively novel methodology and needs to be considered as vital when an important part of the informants' life takes place online. Hence, this paper is one of the few examples of a hybrid, offline – online ethnographic approach (Tunçalp & Lê, 2014).

Finally, in this study we have examined social movements in two different organizations within the Turkish higher education field. Considering them as "institutional entrepreneurs" offers the potential to enrich our understanding of social movements and institutional change regarding their framing tactics. We believe that more studies are needed to further analyze these interrelationships and the dynamic, contested, dialectical nature of framing processes. In the future, frames of university administrations and media frames surrounding these debates can be further analyzed to better understand the multi-sided and multi-faceted nature of framing contests. For example, future studies could cast light on whether framing tactics differ between different professions and organizations with strong professionalization, such as attorneys, healthcare professionals, or journalists. Alternatively, how power mechanisms are exercised for institutional change in different institutional fields also needs further investigation. While we are constrained to generalize from our cases, we suggest that the framing repertoire of social movements may further enrich our understanding of institutional entrepreneurship and change using different framing tactics exercising power over time.

REFERENCES

Anonymous. (2013a). *ODTÜ Yönetimine Taleplerimizi ilettik [We sent our requests to METU administration]*. March 29, 2013. Retrieved from http://odtuasistandayanismasi.blogspot.com.tr/2013/03/taleplerimiz.html?view=sidebar#!/2013/03/taleplerimiz.html. Accessed on October 25, 2014.

Anonymous. (2013b). *ODTÜ Yönetimine Çağrımızdır! [Our call to METU administration!]*. March 30, 2013. Retrieved from http://odtuasistandayanismasi.blogspot.com.tr/2013/03/odtu-yonetimine-cagrmzdr.html?view=sidebar#!/2013/03/odtu-yonetimine-cagrmzdr.html. Accessed on October 25, 2014.

Anonymous. (2014). Personal interview. Performed: January 16, 2014.

Asistan Dayanışması. (2012a). *İmza Kampanyası [Petition]*. October 7, 2012. Retrieved from http://ituasistandayanismasi.blogspot.com.tr/2012/10/imza-kampanyasi.html#!/2012/10/imza-kampanyasi.html. Accessed on October 25, 2014.

Asistan Dayanışması. (2012b). *Üniversitemizi Terketmiyoruz Çağrısı [We don't leave our university call]*. October 10, 2012. Retrieved from http://ituasistandayanismasi.blogspot.com.tr/2012/10/universitemizi-terketmiyoruz-cagrs.html#!/2012/10/universitemizi-terketmiyoruz-cagrs.html. Accessed on October 25, 2014.

Asistan Dayanışması. (2012c). *Sanatçılar İTÜ'lü Asistanlara Sahip Çıkıyor [Artists take side with ITU assistants]*. October 15, 2012. Retrieved from http://ituasistandayanismasi.blogspot.com.tr/2012/10/sanatclar-itulu-asistanlara-sahip-ckyor.html#!/2012/10/sanatclar-itulu-asistanlara-sahip-ckyor.html. Accessed on October 25, 2014.

Asistan Dayanışması. (2012d). *İTÜ'deki 50D tiyatrosunda son perde: '81 Araştırma Görevlisi için yapılabilecek hiçbir şey yok' [The last scene in 50D theather at ITU: Nothing can be done for 81 research assistants]*. October 21, 2012. Retrieved from http://ituasistandayanismasi.blogspot.com.tr/2012/10/itudeki-50d-tiyatrosunda-son-perde-81.html#!/2012/10/itudeki-50d-tiyatrosunda-son-perde-81.html. Accessed on October 25, 2014.

Asistan Dayanışması. (2013). *Başka bir ITÜ Mümkün! [An alternative ITU is possible]*. December 1, 2013. Retrieved from http://ituasistandayanismasi.blogspot.com.tr/2014/01/baska-bir-itu-mumkun.html#!/2014/01/baska-bir-itu-mumkun.html. Accessed on October 25, 2014.

Asistan Dayanışması. (2014a). *Soma için Maden Fakültesi'ni İşgal Eden İTÜ Öğrencilerinin yanındayız! [We support ITU students occupying mining faculty for the Soma accident]*. May 19, 2014. Retrieved from http://ituasistandayanismasi.blogspot.com.tr/2014/08/itu-ogrencilerinin-yanndayz.html#!/2014/08/itu-ogrencilerinin-yanndayz.html. Accessed on October 25, 2014.

Asistan Dayanışması. (2014b). *Suç duyurusunda bulunduk [We made a criminal complaint]*. September 30, 2014. Retrieved from http://ituasistandayanismasi.blogspot.com.tr/2013/06/polis-siddetine-kars-imza-kampanyas.html#!/2014/09/suc-duyurusunda-bulunduk.html. Accessed on October 25, 2014.

Battilana, J., Leca, B., & Boxenbaum, E. (2009). How actors change institutions: Toward a theory of institutional entrepreneurship. *Academy of Management Annals*, *3*(1), 65–107.

Benford, R. (1997). An insider's critique of the social movement framing perspective. *Sociological Inquiry*, *67*, 409–430.

Benford, R. D., & Snow, D. A. (2000). Framing processes and social movements: An overview and assessment. *Annual Review of Sociology*, *26*, 611–639.

Blum-Kulka, S., & Liebes, T. (1993). Frame ambiguities: Narrativization of the intifada experience by Israeli soldiers. In A. Cohen & G. Wolfsfeld (Eds.), *Framing the intifada: People and media* (pp. 27–52). New York, NY: Ablex.

Carragee, K. M., & Roefs, W. (2004). The neglect of power in recent framing research. *Journal of Communication, 54*, 214–233.

Clegg, S. R. (1975). *Power, rule and domination*. London: Routledge.

Clegg, S. R. (1989). *Frameworks of power*. London: Sage.

Clegg, S. R., Courpasson, D., & Phillips, N. (2006). *Power and organizations*. London: Sage.

Clemens, E. S., & Cooks, J. M. (1999). Politics and institutionalism: Explaining durability and change. *Annual Review of Sociology, 25*(1), 441–466.

Davis, G. F., McAdam, D., Richard, W., Mayer, S., & Zald, N. (2005). *Social movements and organization theory*. Cambridge: Cambridge University Press.

della Porta, D., & Diani, M. (1999). *Social movements: An introduction*. Oxford: Blackwell.

Diani, M. (1992). The concept of social movement. *The Sociological Review, 40*, 1–25.

DiMaggio, P. J. (1988). Interest and agency in institutional theory. In L. Zucker (Ed.), *Institutional patterns and organizations* (pp. 3–22). Cambridge: Ballinger.

Dyer, W. G. Jr., & Wilkins, A. L. (1991). Better stories, not better constructs to generate better theory: A rejoinder to Eisenhardt. *Academy of Management Review, 16*(3), 613–619.

Erden Bayazıt, Z. (2005). *Histories, institutional regimes and educational organizations: The case of Turkish higher education*. Unpublished doctoral dissertation, Sabancı University, Istanbul, Turkey.

Fay, B. (1996). *Contemporary philosophy of social science: A multicultural approach*. Oxford: Blackwell.

Fligstein, N., & McAdam, D. (2011). Toward a general theory of strategic action fields. *Sociological Theory, 29*, 1–26.

Fligstein, N., & McAdam, D. (2012). *A theory of fields*. Oxford: Oxford University Press.

Foucault, M. (1977). *Discipline and punish: The birth of the prison* (A. Sheridan, Trans.). London: Allen Lane, Penguin. First published in French as *Surveiller et punir*, Gallimard, Paris, 1975.

Friedland, R., & Alford, R. R. (1991). Bringing society back in: Symbols, practices, and institutional contradictions. In W. W. Powell & P. J. DiMaggio (Eds.), *The new institutionalism in organizational analysis* (pp. 232–263). Chicago, IL: University of Chicago Press.

Gamson, W. (1992). *Talking politics*. New York, NY: Cambridge University Press.

Gamson, W., Fireman, B., & Rytina, S. (1982). *Encounters with unjust authority*. Chicago, IL: Dorsey.

Giddens, A. (1976). *New rules of sociological method*. London: Hutchinson.

Giddens, A. (1991). *Modernity and self-identity: Self and society in the late modern age*. Cambridge: Polity Press.

Goffman, E. (1974). *Frame analysis: An essay on the organization of experience*. New York, NY: Harper and Row.

Goodwin, J., & Jasper, J. (1999). Caught in a winding, snarling vine: The structural bias of political process theory. *Sociological Forum, 14*, 27–54.

Hardy, C., & Maguire, S. (2008). Institutional entrepreneurship. In R. Greenwood, C. Oliver, R. Suddaby, & K. Shalin-Anderson (Eds.), *Handbook of organizational institutionalism* (pp. 198–217). Thousand Oaks, CA: Sage.

Hendry, J. (2000). Strategic decision making, discourse, and strategy as social practice. *Journal of Management Studies*, *37*(7), 955–977.

Higher Education Law. (1981). No. 2547, Article No. 33, Ministry of Education, Ankara.

Horta, H., Veloso, F. M., & Grediaga, R. (2010). Navel gazing: Academic inbreeding and scientific productivity. *Management Science*, *56*(3), 414–429.

Johnson, P., & Duberley, J. (2003). Reflexivity in management research. *Journal of Management Studies*, *40*, 1279–1303.

Jorgensen, D. L. (1989). *Participant observation: A methodology for human studies*. Newbury Park, CA: Sage.

Juris, J. S. (2004). Networked social movements: Global movements for global justice. In M. Castells (Ed.), *The network society: A cross-cultural perspective* (pp. 341–362). Northampton: Edward Elgar.

Khaire, M., & Wadhwani, D. (2010). Changing landscapes: The construction of meaning and value in a new market category: Modern Indian art. *Academy of Management Journal*, *53*, 1281–1304.

Lawrence, T. B., & Suddaby, R. (2006). Institutions and institutional work. In S. R. Clegg, C. Hardy, T. B. Lawrence, & W. R. Nord (Eds.), *Handbook of organization studies* (pp. 215–254). London: Sage.

Lawrence, T. B., Winn, M. I., & Jennings, P. D. (2001). The temporal dynamics of institutionalization. *Academy of Management Review*, *26*(2), 7–28.

Levy, D. L., & Scully, M. (2007). The institutional entrepreneur as modern prince: The strategic face of power in contested fields. *Organization Studies*, *28*, 971–991.

Lounsbury, M., Ventresca, M., & Hirsch, P. M. (2003). Social movements, field frames and industry emergence: A cultural-political perspective on US recycling. *Social Economic Review*, *1*, 71–104.

Lukes, S. (1974). *Power: A radical view*. Houndsmill: Macmillan.

Maguire, S., Hardy, C., & Lawrence, T. (2004). Institutional entrepreneurship in emerging fields: HIV/AIDS treatment advocacy in Canada. *Academy of Management Journal*, *47*(5), 657–679.

Mahoney, J., & Thelen, K. (2010). *Explaining institutional change: Ambiguity, agency and power*. Cambridge: Cambridge University Press.

March, J. G., & Olsen, J. P. (1989). *Rediscovering institutions: The organizational basis of politics*. New York, NY: The Free Press.

Martin, J., & Sugarman, J. (1999). *The psychology of human possibility and constraint*. Albany, NY: SUNY Press.

Marullo, S., Pagnucco, R., & Smith, J. (1996). Frame changes and social movement contraction: U.S. peace movement framing after the cold war. *Sociological Inquiry*, *66*(1), 1–28.

McAdam, D. (1994). Culture and social movements. In E. Larana, H. Johnston, & J. R. Gusfield (Eds.), *New social movements: From ideology to identity* (pp. 36–57). Philadelphia, PA: Temple University Press.

McAdam, D. (2003). Beyond structural analysis: Toward a more dynamic understanding of social movements. In M. Diani & D. McAdam (Eds.), *Social movements and networks: Relational approaches to collective action* (pp. 281–298). Oxford: Oxford University Press.

McIntyre, A. (2008). *Participatory action research: Qualitative research methods series 52*. Thousand Oaks, CA: Sage.

Misangyi, V. F., Weaver, G. R., & Elms, H. (2008). Ending corruption: The interplay among institutional logics, resources and institutional entrepreneurs. *Academy of Management Review*, *33*(3), 750–770.

Mizruchi, M. S., & Fein, C. (1999). The social construction of organizational knowledge: A study of the uses of coercive, mimetic, and normative isomorphism. *Administrative Science Quarterly*, *44*, 653–683.

Offe, C. (1985). New social movements: Changing boundaries of the political. *Social Research*, *52*, 817–868.

Öncü, A. (2013). Turkish capitalist modernity and the Gezi Revolt. *Journal of Historical Sociology*, *27*(2), 151–176.

O'Reilly, K. (2009). *Key concepts in ethnography*. London: Sage.

Rao, H., & Kenney, M. (2008). New forms as settlements. In R. Greenwood, C. Oliver, K. Sahlin, & R. Suddaby (Eds.), *The Sage handbook of organizational institutionalism* (pp. 352–370). London: Sage.

Rao, H., Monin, P., & Durand, R. (2003). Institutional change in de Toqueville: Nouvelle cuisine as an identity movement in French gastronomy. *American Journal of Sociology*, *108*(4), 795–843.

Rao, H., Morrill, C., & Zald, N. (2000). Power plays: How social movements and collective action create new organizational forms. *Research in Organizational Behaviour*, *22*, 239–282.

Schneiberg, M., & Lounsbury, M. (2008). Social movements and institutional analysis. In R. Greenwood, C. Oliver, R. Suddaby, & K. Sahlin (Eds.), *Handbook of organizational institutionalism* (pp. 648–670). Thousand Oaks, CA: Sage.

Scott, W. R. (2008). *Institutions and organizations: Ideas and interests* (3rd ed.). Thousand Oaks, CA: Sage.

Snow, D. A. (2004). Social movements as challenges to authority: Resistance to an emerging conceptual hegemony. In D. J. Myers & D. M. Cress (Eds.), *Authority in contention* (Vol. 25, pp. 3–25). Research in Social Movements, Conflicts and Change. Bingley, UK: Emerald Group Publishing Limited.

Snow, D. A., & Benford, R. D. (1988). Ideology, frame resonance, and participant mobilization. *International Social Movement Research*, *1*(1), 197–217.

Snow, D. A., & Benford, R. D. (1992). Master frames and cycles of protest. In A. D. Morris & C. M. Mueller (Eds.), *Frontiers in social movement theory* (pp. 133–155). Binghamton, NY: Vail Ballou Press.

Snow, D. A., Rochford, E. B., Worden, S. K., & Benford, R. D. (1986). Frame alignment processes, micromobilization and movement participation. *American Sociological Review*, *51*, 464–481.

Suchman, M. C. (1995). Managing legitimacy: Strategic and institutional approaches. *Academy of Management Journal*, *20*(3), 571–610.

Tunçalp, D., & Lê, P. L. (2014). (Re)Locating boundaries: A systematic review of online ethnography. *Journal of Organizational Ethnography*, *3*(1), 59–79.

Üsdiken, B. (2004). The French, the German and the American: Higher education for business in Turkey, 1883–2003. *New Perspectives on Turkey*, *31*, 5–38.

Üsdiken, B., Topaler, B., & Koçak, Ö. (2013). Law, market and organizational diversity: Turkish universities in the post-1981 period (in Turkish). *Ankara Üniversitesi SBF Dergisi*, *68*(3), 191–227.

Werner, M. D., & Cornelissen, J. P. (2014). Framing the change: Switching and blending frames and their role in instigating institutional change. *Organization Studies*, *35*(10), 1449–1472.

Yin, R. K. (1994). *Case study research: Design and methods* (2nd ed.). Newbury Park, CA: Sage.

Zucker, L. G. (1977). The role of institutionalization in cultural persistence. *American Sociological Review*, *42*, 726–743.

APPENDIX

Interview Guide for the Members – Translated Version

Warm-Up Questions

1. When did you start working at this university?
2. How would you define your job here?
3. What differences do you recognize between being an assistant and a research specialist?
4. How are you coping with being an assistant and a graduate student at the same time?
5. Assume I am a new assistant who has just started working here. How would you describe "the assistant solidarity movement" to me?
   History – Think about the beginning of the movement
6. How did the movement emerge?
7. Do you know or remember how the movement first started?
8. Do you remember/know about the first meeting of the movement? What was the main agenda of the meeting?
9. Who were the founders of the movement?
10. How did you decide on what actions to take in the early days of the movement?
11. What was the first protest? First action?
12. Who attended the first actions and protests?
13. How has the movement evolved since the beginning?
14. What things have changed in the movement since the beginning?
15. What things have remained the same?
   Protests and Activities – Think about the protests and activities of the movement from the beginning
16. What were the main topics focused on by the movement at the beginning? How has this changed over time?
17. What types of protests took place? Could you tell us about a few of them?
18. How did you decide on the protest, and choose its location and agenda?
19. Do you remember a very unusual protest?
20. Do you remember a very successful protest?
21. Do you remember any protest that was unsuccessful?
22. What was your most often used protest location? What has been a regular and recurring protest?

23. Where did you meet before and after the protests?

Responses and Relationship

24. How do you think the movement has impacted on your work life?
25. How did the school or your department respond to your participation in the movement?
26. How did the students respond?
27. How did the movement establish or attempt relationships with other groups inside and outside the university?
28. How did the movement establish or attempt relationships with other social groups and movements in the country?

Online Behavior

29. How did the movement use the Internet? Which online venues are most utilized?
30. For which purposes did your movement use the Internet?
31. How did the movement select which social media site to use? How are you using them today?
32. Who was active on the Internet? How were these actions decided on? How were the messages decided?

Organization of the Movement

33. How do you organize within the movement? How has the division of labor been decided? How do you coordinate activities?
34. How do you make decisions? Who leads the group?
35. (If they say – no hierarchy): What do you mean by hierarchy? How would you define hierarchy?
36. How many meetings have you attended since the beginning?
37. How has the meeting agenda/decision-making/duration changed since the beginning?
38. Where do you meet? How often do you meet? Inside/outside campus?
39. How have the meeting places, time, and agenda been decided?
40. Do you remember a very important/long meeting? Why? What? Who? Decision?
41. Do you remember a very short meeting? Why? What? Who? Decision?